The Reflexivity of Pain and Privilege

The Reflexivity of Pain and Privilege

Auto-Ethnographic Collections of Mixed Identity

Edited by

Ellis Hurd

BRILL

SENSE

LEIDEN | BOSTON

Cover illustration: *De Indio, y Mestisa. Coyote (From Indian and Mestiza, Coyote)*.
Gift of the nieces and nephews of Wright S. Ludington in his honor, 1980
[1980-139-1]. Courtesy: Philadelphia Museum of Art.

All chapters in this book have undergone peer review.

The Library of Congress Cataloging-in-Publication Data is available online at
http://catalog.loc.gov

ISBN 978-90-04-39379-0 (paperback)
ISBN 978-90-04-39380-6 (hardback)
ISBN 978-90-04-39381-3 (e-book)

This book is printed on acid-free paper and produced in a sustainable manner.

To the greatest *Mestizo* I ever knew, my dad:
Franklin Thomas Hurd, Jr 1931 to 2018

My Mestizo *father, Franklin Thomas Hurd, Jr., adorned with Indian headdress
and bone shell breast plate*

CONTENTS

ACKNOWLEDGEMENTS

I would like to thank Peter de Liefde, from Brill | Sense, for giving me the platform and opportunity to elucidate the beautiful voices of those who are of mixed race, heritage, ability, language, ethnicity, and culture. These are their stories. This is their great work. And I am truly blessed to be part of such a momentous experience and effort to raise awareness, to create a cause for crusading on behalf of those who did not have a voice, could not share their stories, who were (and still are) largely misunderstood with being in two or more races and cultures at once, and yet in neither one at the same time.

I also wish to thank the Philadelphia Museum of Art for their willingness to allow me to use and credit their collection of paintings on this sensitive topic. In addition, I am in debt to Quality Leadership University, its President, Oscar de Leon, and its faculty members, Mariana León and Guillermina-Itzel de Gracia, in Panama City, Republic of Panama, for their interest and generosity in partnering with me for this project.

Many of the poems, stories, research, and artifacts contained in this volume have been on the minds and in the hearts of its contributors. For years they have fought, suffered, and endured the pains and privileges of being of more than one, of belonging to more than a singularly constructed race, ethnoculture, ability, language, or background. They have carried with them the secret awkwardness and peculiarity of being able to (and not) cross borders, transcend cultures and time, and to transgress the entities of social constructions placed on them and others. May this volume collectively offer them a sense of peace, of liberation, in belonging to an idea and to a people they can call their own, and to offer its readers a greater sense of knowledge, compassion, and engagement for those who surround them daily that are of the great homily of pain and privilege.

FIGURES

NOTES ON CONTRIBUTORS

EDITOR

Ellis Hurd is professor of middle level and bilingual education in the School of Teaching and Learning at Illinois State University. He has 20 years of teaching experience in diverse settings across Illinois and Iowa. He has published on teacher, middle grades and bilingual, and urban education, equity and cultural responsiveness, and mixed identities. He is co-editor of *Equity and Cultural Responsiveness in the Middle Grades*. Ellis serves as former chair and a member of the Collaborating Sites Network (CSN) Advisory Committee for the International Congress for Qualitative Inquiry (ICQI) and the International Association of Qualitative Inquiry (IAQI). He is also co-editor of *Middle School Journal* and a member of the AMLE Program Review Board for the Council for the Accreditation of Educator Preparation (CAEP). E-mail: ehurd@ilstu.edu

Ellis is also a man of mixed identity. He has lived in the throes of pain and privilege in being a mixed man. As W. Somerset Maugham said:

> For men and women are not only themselves; they are also the region in which they were born, the city apartment or the farm in which they learnt to walk, the games they played as children, the old wives' tales they overheard, the food they ate, the schools they attended, the sports they followed, the poets they read, and the God they believed in. It is all these things that have made them what they are and these are things that you can't come to know by hearsay, you can only know them if you have lived them. You can only know them if you *are* them. (Maugham, W. S., 1954, *The razor's edge*, p. 2. Garden City, New York: Double Day. [Original work published in 1944])

AUTHORS

Raymond Adams is assistant professor of social work in the College of Liberal and Performing Arts at Southern Arkansas University. He has 12 years of social work experience in diverse settings across four states. He has a publication (in press) entitled, "Louisiana Black Men at risk for prostate cancer: An Untold Autoethnography" in the *Journal of Social Work & Christianity*. Raymond is a member of the National Association of Black Social Workers, National Association of Christian Social Workers and the Council of Social Work Education. E-mail: raymondadams@saumag.edu

Lisa A. Boskovich is a doctoral candidate in the Donna Ford Attallah College of Educational Studies at Chapman University in Orange, CA with an emphasis

in Disability Studies. Her research interests include, fathers who have a child on the Autism Spectrum, and the phenomenological master narratives of individuals with learning disabilities. Lisa currently is working as a Research Assistant at The Thompson Policy Institute on Disability and Autism.
E-mail: bosko103@mail.chapman.edu

Iman Fagan is an undergraduate student at the University of Nevada Las Vegas, pursuing a Bachelor of Science degree in Elementary Education. Iman is a member of the Multicultural Educational Services Alliance at UNLV which works to recruit and provide resources for students of color to college and into teaching as a profession. Following her graduation, she will pursue a career in teaching at the elementary level.
E-mail: fagani@unlv.nevada.edu

Guillermina-Itzel de Gracia is a specialist in Anthropology, Heritage Education, and Museum Studies. She is a doctoral candidate in History of America at University of Barcelona in Spain. Guillermina has worked as an anthropologist and Deputy Director for Panama's National Department for Historical Heritage. She was also co-editor of the magazine "Canto Rodado" of the Panama Viejo Patronage. Guillermina is currently an independent consultant in anthropology museum studies, and history, and is a college professor at Quality Leadership University.
E-mail: itzelopez@gmail.com

David I. Hernández-Saca is assistant professor of Disability Studies in Education within the Department of Special Education at University of Northern Iowa (UNI). Dr. Hernández-Saca' responsibilities at UNI include undergraduate teacher preparation courses in the areas of post-school transition programming and issues and applications in special education. The nucleus of his research agenda is problematizing the common-sense assumptions of what learning disabilities are.
E-mail: david.hernandez-saca@uni.edu

Mariana León is a doctoral candidate of Education (Ed.D.) at Johns Hopkins University and serves as Academic Vice President and member of the Board of Directors at Quality Leadership University. She is a member of Global Shapers, a youth leadership initiative of the World Economic Forum, and a member of the Asociación Panameña de Ejecutivos de Empresa (APEDE).
E-mail: mariana.leon@qlu.pa

Susan Y. Leonard is a doctoral student in the Educational Theory and Practice with emphasis in Middle Grades Education PhD program at the University of Georgia. She has eleven years of teaching experience with young adolescents. In 2015, she was chosen as Teacher of the Year at the middle school where she taught. Her research interests include professional development and critical pedagogies. Susan is

a teacher and teacher educator who also serves as Graduate Student Representative for the AERA Middle Level Education Research Special Interest Group.
E-mail: susan.leonard@uga.edu

Lynnette Mawhinney is associate professor and chair of the Department of Curriculum and Instruction at the University of Illinois at Chicago. Her work focuses on the lives of teacher of color and teacher diversification. She is author of *We Got Next: Urban Education and the Next Generation of Black Teachers, There Has to be a Better Way: Lessons from Former Urban Teachers*, and co-editor of *Teacher Education Across Minority-Serving Institutions: Programs, Policies, and Social Justice.*
E-mail: Lynnette@uic.edu

Dian Mitrayani is a doctoral candidate at University of Wisconsin-Milwaukee's Social Foundations of Education program focused on youth leadership and civic engagement. She is an alumnus of the Asian Development Bank scholars and has conducted research & evaluation in the area of youth development and leadership for over 10 years in both US and international settings. She is also a certified Play for Peace trainer and a peace education research evaluator.
E-mail: mitrayani@gmail.com

Anne Ryen is professor of sociology at University of Agder, Norway, and has been doing research in Tanzania for 25 years on gender issues and fringe benefits in international businesses, and ethnography on Asian business in East-Africa. Her teaching across three continents and publications focus on qualitative methods and research ethics, particularly in cross-cultural contexts. She is former Chair of the European Sociology Association Research Network on Qualitative Research (ESA RN20 QR) and member of the ESA Executive board. She is leader of a research group on cultural sociology.
E-mail: Anne.Ryen@uia.no

Jessica Samuels is an Academic Success Counselor at the University of Idaho and is the Associate Editor in Chief of the Journal for the Study of Postsecondary and Tertiary Education. She holds a BA in Sociology with a Minor in American Indian Studies, a Diversity and Stratification Certificate, and a Master's of Public Administration. Jessica is a McNair/TRIO Alumni whose research was entitled Changing Directions for Youth and Families: An Interdisciplinary Look at Cultural Advocacy. She is currently a Political Science PhD Candidate and a member of Zeta Phi Beta Sorority Incorporated.
E-mail: jsamuels@alumni.uidaho.edu

Cristina Santamaría Graff is assistant professor of special education, teacher education in the School of Education at Indiana University in Indianapolis (IUPUI).

She has been both a bilingual elementary school teacher and a bilingual special educator in school districts with large Latino populations. Though her expertise is in bilingual special education her research focuses on 'family as faculty' approaches that position families' expertise as central to pedagogy in teacher preparation programs. As a self-identified biracial Mexicana, Cristina's publications center on mixed identities as well as teacher education.
E-mail: santamac@iupui.edu

Hannah R. Stohry is a doctoral student in Educational Leadership (leadership, culture, and curriculum) at Miami University in Oxford, Ohio. Her research interests include: contemplative practices, multiculturalism, third culture kids, intersectionality, humanizing pedagogy, cultural humility, vulnerability, whiteness studies, autoethnography, and mixed identities. She is a member of the National Association of Social Workers (NASW) and holds her license in social work with experience working as a home-based family therapist prior to beginning her graduate degree.
E-mail: strohrhr@miamioh.edu

Francisco J. Villegas is assistant professor of Sociology in the Department of Anthropology and Sociology at Kalamazoo College. He received his PhD from the Ontario Institute for Studies in Education of the University of Toronto. His research focuses on race and migration, particularly the ways boundaries of belonging are defined, maintained, and navigated. His work has ranged from access to schooling for undocumented migrants in Toronto, Canada to the development of a County ID in Kalamazoo, Michigan.
E-mail: francisco.villegas@kzoo.edu

Paloma E. Villegas is an assistant professor in the Department of Sociology at California State University San Bernardino. As an interdisciplinary researcher and artist, her work centers the intersection between migrant illegalization, borders, race and gender in North and Latin America. She teaches courses on migration, transnationalism, race, gender, and community engagement.
E-mail: paloma.villegas@csusb.edu

Hwa Pyung Yoo is a student at Villanova University, pursuing majors in Political Science and Neuroscience with minors in Education Policy and Peace and Justice. He has a wide range of volunteer teaching experiences often working with students in under-resourced areas, and has presented independent and collaborative research projects on international mindedness and contemporary youth activism under Dr. Jerusha Osberg Conner. He comes from an international background as a third culture kid from South Korea and the U.S., and seeks to continue fostering this international identity along with his passion for education pursuing international education development going forward.
E-mail: Yoo.hwapyung@gmail.com

ELLIS HURD

THE HOMILY OF PAIN AND PRIVILEGE

Understanding the Need for a Discourse on Mixed Identity

INTRODUCTION

Limited research exists on the *intricacies of identity* (Rodriguez, 2011). Clearly absent in the literature is an exposition or homily of the recursive, reflexive, and seemingly dichotomous identity experiences of those who are of mixed racial, socio-economic, linguistic, and/or ethno-cultural backgrounds and/or experiences. Because many people of mixed heritage and/or identity continuously find themselves marginalized (Foley, 2005), it makes sense to elaborate on their pain distinctively from their privilege. This critical yet vital stance helps to elucidate mixed identity journeys, those characterized by both pain and privilege.

Auto-ethnographical works on mixed Native American, African, and Mestiza/ Feminist experience (Anzaldúa, 2007; O'Connor, 1983; Simmons-Bonnin, 1899) show the complex dichotomy between what a person wants to be and what a person is forced to be. These stories vividly illustrate the plight of those who find themselves torn between one race or culture and another. These historical Mestizx[1] never completely fit into the White or Native American/African/Latina cultures, caught in the middle between binary oppositions.

Yet these storied individuals remain disconnected from each other and from the interrelated discourse of pain and privilege. There is little to no mention of the discourse and its interrelated nature (Hurd, 2010). In fact, while some researchers have published works on the mixed identity of adults and youth (Hurd, 2012a, 2012b) and the intersection of marginalized identities among youth (Harrison, 2015), there have been no volumes such as this one focused exclusively on the exposition or homily of the recursive, reflexive, and seemingly dichotomous identity experiences of those who are of mixed backgrounds. Thus, this volume is a small and yet important step toward closing the significant gap that still exists within the research field and literature concerning this discourse, especially that of an international perspective, and step toward responding to the ignorance and ill-treatment of those of mixed backgrounds. People of mixed identity need to be empowered so that we can resist against racism and oppression of any kind (Harding, 1993; Hurd, 2012a).

This volume seeks to elucidate the mixed identity journeys of adults and youth, those characterized by both pain and privilege. Moreover, it aims to offer a fresh and critical perspective to people of indigenous and/or marginalized descent and identifications, a voice as we continue clearing a path for ourselves and others that may soon follow.

Accordingly, this volume highlights the research, shared experiences and personal stories, and the artistic collections of those of us who are of mixed heritage and/or identity. This volume also shares on the perspectives of young adolescents (ages 10 to 15 years) who identify as being of mixed racial, socio-economic, linguistic, and ethno-cultural backgrounds and experiences.

On a broader scale, it is my hope that this volume elucidates the historically silenced-voices of those who identify as of mixed heritage, of those who have a story to tell about their identity past, present, and futures, of those who negotiate between the pains and privileges of not belonging and yet of belonging to each unique identity. The reflexivity of pain and privilege and these auto-ethnographic collections of mixed identity within this volume serve as an impetus for the untold stories, the homilies of millions of marginalized and mixed people who may find solace here and in the stories of others who are of mixed identity.

THE BACKGROUND

Historical Renderings of Being Mixed

Investigating how and why those of mixed background(s) might arrive at their identity is important. It empowers educators, researchers, and those of mixed identity to critically understand what factors historically influenced (and continue to affect) mixed identity. This background might also offer insight into why dominant societies may perceive those of us with mixed identity in certain ways. These factors are both ethnographical and phenomenological, equally impacting identity (Amundsen-Meyer, 2011; Hurd, 2008, 2012a, 2012b; Probert, 2006).

It is also important to understand how and why adolescents of mixed heritage construct their personal identities. Considering the United States, Gollnick and Chinn (2017) report that more than half of all students in P-12 schools currently are *students of color*; by 2023 it is anticipated they will comprise nearly 55% of all elementary and secondary students. "However, the race and sex of their teachers match neither the student population nor the general population" (p. 2). In fact, 80% of all teachers are White and 76% are female (National Center for Education Statistics, 2014).

Even more telling than those facts are the ones specific to mixed identity, or as the NCES titles it, those of *Two or more races*. Prior to 2008, no statistics were available for school-aged students of mixed identity due to the low percentage of reporting states with elementary and secondary students with two or more races. However, the percentage of states reporting students with two or more races has increased exponentially. From 2008 to 2011 alone, representing the entire United States, the number of students having reported being of mixed races increased from approximately 247 students to 1,272. The numbers during that short 3-year period represent a 414.98% increase. The projections for 2023 include 1,838 students, or a total combined increase of 644.13% (NCES, 2014). The rate of increase is rapid for states reporting having students of two or more races. Similar trends can be seen in other countries. Therefore, it empowers researchers, educators, and even adolescents to critically understand what factors historically influenced (and continue to affect) mixed identities and why educators might perceive minority adolescents in certain ways (Hurd, 2012a).

The history and review of those of us who identify as mixed is complex and controversial. While some researchers have exclusively studied our genetics or racial identities statistically (see Bowman, 1974; Brookover, LePere, Hamachek, Thomas, & Erikson, 1965; Capelli et al., 2001; Crawford, 1979; Healey, 1969; Wang et al., 2008), many others argue that we of mixed identity must be studied from a socio-cultural context, as constructions or designations of power and culture (Bruhl, Henderson, Marvin, & Morgan, n.d.; Forbes, 2005; Rodriguez, 1999). Either methodological approach shows that the descriptor and idea of being of mixed identity or background is derived from Spanish Colonialism, a racial construction that has since had enormous influence on humanity.

The Spanish conquest.   The word Mestizo is a term of Spanish origin, created to designate the peoples of mixed European and Native American ancestry. Typically, a Spanish father and an Indian mother had children referred to as Mestizos (Anzaldúa, 2007; Kicza, 1997). They occupied the areas of the Americas from Canada in the north to Argentina and Chile in the south during the sixteenth century, when European Spaniards sought to colonize what they believed were newly discovered territories. Under establishment of the European "policy of divide and conquer" (Forbes, 2005, p. 3), elite Spanish rulers sought superior status by constructing what is now known as a Mestizo race, with all its arbitrary divisions placed between different groups of the population (see also Weismantel & Eisenman, 1998). This left Mestizos in "isolation from Spanish and Indian society along with the lack of their own [control and] culture...often [feeling] pushed and pulled by different segments of society" (Burns, 1994, p. 6). As such, these mixed-race individuals never became fully accepted into Spanish society. It was too advantageous for the Spaniards to maintain their status and distance from Mestizos (Burns, 1994). This social stratification led to at least three socially constructed races by the Spaniards: the Indian inhabitants, the Mexican inhabitants, and the Mestizos, or mixed Spanish-Indian and/or Mexican inhabitants.

The minor caste system and mestizo variations.   With these new descriptors, the Spaniards maintained their power needed for controlling native inhabitants. They also infused privileges upon them "in order that the native leadership would prevent their people from rebelling" (Forbes, 2005, p. 3). This allowed the Spaniards to further exert superiority over inhabitants, namely the mixed-race peoples who had trouble settling into any singular group. The Spaniards and these various native groups did eventually intermarry. Over time, those groups adopted terms indicative of their particular dialects and geographical areas (see table below). However, these terms were pejoratively used for those of mixed identity and their progeny (see Forbes, 2005; Pilgrim, 2000). Such mixed identity formations represent socio-political and cultural-ecological descriptors of position and power; these are not just ones of race or ancestry. Historically, the (non) acceptance of minorities, especially those of mixed heritage, has been rather hegemonic (Hurd, 2008, 2012b).[2]

Of Pain and Privilege

The reflexivity of pain.   As a collective group, we of mixed identity may sometimes assimilate well against societal oppressions. The benefits that counteract those oppressions offer hope during a rather difficult transition in a monolingual or phobic society closed off to change. However, the oppressions that we indeed face cannot be overlooked. These are our pains.

We of mixed identity experience the discourse of pain in various ways. Referring to the layered relationship between pain and privilege, Johnson (2005) states:

> Living in a particular society can make people feel miserable, but we can't call that misery "oppression" unless it arises from being on the losing end in a system of privilege. That can't happen in relation to society as a whole, because a society isn't something that can be the recipient of privilege. Only people can do this by belonging to privileged categories in relation to other categories that aren't. (pp. 106–107)

This description explains how we of mixed identity experience pain as we identify with/in at least two groups while also being part of a privileged system. But those privileges only extend as far as other groups allow. We are also part of a losing system by being mixed, unable to fully identity (e.g., experience no tension) within a singular racial, social, or cultural group. According to Johnson, this is possible because "like privilege, oppression results from the social relationship between privilege and oppressed categories, which makes it possible for individuals to vary in their personal experience of being oppressed" (p. 106).

Identifying with more than one identity may also be a source of pain based on the treatment of one's skin color. Sadly, this oppressive act still exists, and it strongly impacts one's beliefs and identity constructions. One way that this causes suffering is through racial profiling. Foley (2005) explains that the "wages of whiteness" exist from a convoluted system of privileges that many of us of mixed identity seem to enjoy (pp. 62–63). Yet all too often, we see certain groups with darker skin tones treated differently, indeed worse, than others with lighter skin tones. Those with lighter skin tones are more easily accepted into higher status and privileged groups, whereas others are shunned and berated. We of mixed identity then become relegated to inferior positions simply because of our darker skin-color. This treatment can be traced to ill-conceived perceptions rooted in hegemony, existing for any minoritized and ethnoculturally mixed group.

Critical Mestizo variations used historically and pejoratively throughout locales and nations. Illustrates several nations' responses to indigenous people of mixed heritage or identity, with respects to African, Spanish, and Indian groups

Nation	African	⇕	Spaniard	⇕	Spaniard	⇕	Indian	⇕	African
U.S. North	Negro	Mulatto; Mixed; Buck	Criollo			Mestizo; Cholo	No-caste; Out-caste; Outcast	Zambo	
U.S. South	Quad-roon; Nigger	Mulatto; Mustee; Tom; Coon; Buck	Criollo			Half-breed; Half-blood; Quarter-blood	Injun; Squaw; Brownie; Redskin; Timber nigger		High-yellow
Mexico	Negro; Mayate	Mulato; Mulo	Criollo			Mestizo; Mexicano; Cholo	Coyote; Pardo	Lobo	
Guatemala	Negro	Mulatto	Criollo			Ladino	Cholero		
Canada	Negro	Mulatto				Métis	Eskimo; Aboriginal		African-Canadian
Brazil	Negro	Mulatto				Caboclo; Mameluco; Pardo		Cafuzo	Black
Peru	Negro bozale or ladino	Mulatto	Criollo			Amazonian Chola/o; Campesino	Incan	Zambo	Black

Another pain in the mixed identity construct concerns how dominant U.S. cultures "still know little about how the family ideology shapes the consciousness and expectations of those growing up in the margins of the mainstream" (Pyke, 2004, p. 438). We can see this phenomenon with how we of mixed identity cannot always find authentic foods reflective of our native cultures, how we live with environmental racism (Bullard, 2006, p. 189; Lipsitz, 2005, p. 73), and how we must reconcile against a climate and economic structure very different from our own. Instead, we must consciously swallow the dominant cultural norms at the sacrifice of our own family beliefs. These situations are painful, can lead to a "numbness" and "dislocation between two cultures" (Baker, 2000, p. 69). I have comprehensively explored these ideas in my earlier works on mixed identity (see Hurd, 2008, 2010, 2012a, 2012b).

The reflexivity of privilege. Contemporaneously, we of mixed identity experience privilege. There is a general increased acceptance simply from being mixed (Burns, 1994, p. 224). Even though "much still remains to be done", it seems the overall treatment of people and groups with mixed identity has "changed considerably" and has improved (p. 224). Consider former President Barack Hussein Obama who claims to be of mixed identity and historically marginalized based on having a White mother from Kansas and Kenyan father from Africa. Like others, President Obama is able to thwart the advances of the "raceless economic" movement, or those without any ancestral roots, by simply identifying with exploited or marginalized groups, even though he may not have personally suffered their pains. This is a privileged act seen as a "resistance" against "Western racism" (Harding, 1993, p. 13).

Likewise, different social situations compel those with mixed identity to attach ourselves to different self-identities which then allow some of us to travel between and negotiate within different groups and self-identifications. These different selves lead to constructed and deconstructed images, dichotomized between what we want to be (the ideal self) and how others may see us (the limited self). Our educational backgrounds and occupational stati significantly influence identity formation in this regard (Hurd, 2010; Ogbu, 2004).

This ability to travel between identities can be clearly seen with those of us who are bilingual or multilingual; we are able to travel between two or more languages simultaneously through what is called "language juxtaposition" (Wildman & Davis, 2005, p. 97). This position allows us to think and proceed in more than one language yet speak in only one when needed, or vice versa. The advantages of growing up bilingual or biliterate include: communication, cultural, cognitive, character, curriculum, and cash aspects (Baker, 2000, p. 2). Ultimately, bilingualism will "affect the rest of [our] lives" (p. 1). This privilege may also translate into societal advancement.

Another way those of mixed identity may be privileged is through cultural inversion (Ogbu, 1992). A similar concept known as cultural opposition (Ainsworth-Darnell &

Downey, 1998) is more recently discussed in the literature. Yet Ogbu (2004) himself indicated that this idea neglects what he originally called "oppositional collective identity and cultural frame of reference" (p. 3). Just before his unfortunate death in 2003, Ogbu further developed the ideas of collective identity as a response to others who were misusing and/or misrepresenting it as oppositional culture.

Oppositional collective identity, as represented in cultural inversion (or cultural-ecological theory), demonstrates how we of mixed identity create alternative subcultures and identities against dominant cultural belief systems (Ogbu, 1992, 2004). "The persistence of a group's collective identity depends on the continuity of the external (historical and structural) forces that contributed to its formation" (Ogbu, 2004, p. 3). Ogbu also explained that the collective identities of oppressed minorities (voluntary and/or involuntary) are "created and maintained by two sets of factors: status problems and minority response to status problems" (p. 4). Their response to the status problem (or cultural frame of reference) is then seen in their privilege of having and travelling to other self-appropriated belief systems and oppositional identities (Ogbu, 1992, p. 8). These different subcultures/identities act as privileges to which we of mixed identity can collectively identify.

Thus, we of mixed identity can at times escape the injustices surrounding us. As Wildman and Davis (2005) claim, "members of privileged groups can opt out of struggles against oppression if they choose" (p. 99). This choice is available to us because we are of mixed ancestry and identity. We can either veil ourselves in the dominant identity, temporarily free from the oppressions of those that cannot, or we may choose to endure pain.

This framework implies that researchers must employ a holistic lens for gaining insights into affective histories. They must examine different identities from within the reflexive discourse of pain and privilege. Researchers must also consider power and stati as they relate to oppositional collective identities. That is, researchers must investigate socio-political and cultural-ecological identities, not just genetics or race. Some researchers may even find the study of their own affective identities provide counter-point interests and interrelated connection into the understanding of the mixed identity construct.

The reflexivity of pain and privilege supports Ogbu's (1991) oppressed minority theory as well as Ogbu's (1992, 2004) and Ogbu and Simons' (1998) theory of cultural inversion. Yet unlike these past theories, the reflexive discourse of pain and privilege actually elucidates how we of mixed identity suffer from yet simultaneously benefit as a result of the economic system. How we advance within this inequitable system is not a matter of *either, or* so much as it is a matter of *when* and *by what means*. The discourse also provides evidence for the influencing belief systems that amass and further develop to influence our identity construct which remains fluid and flexible, not necessarily culminating to an end belief or identity. Again, I have explored these ideas in depth in earlier research (see Hurd, 2008, 2010, 2012a, 2012b).

Considering Others of Mixed Identity

I recently had the opportunity to travel to three separate, transnational locations: Panama City, Republic of Panama; Ontario, Canada; and Lower Manhattan, New York. Each of these areas represents a multiethnic/national flavor and are home to millions of people of different and rich cultures. While at each of these places, I was immensely curious as to how people of indigenous and/or mixed identity might have been or currently are treated. *Are these intercontinental areas inclusive of the internationalization and (in some cases) the Americanization (in the non-liberatory sense) of immigrants and others of mixed identities?* This question was the focus of my visits. Having done a considerable amount of work in the Midwestern United States already, I was hoping a more international lens might inform my own knowledge, especially as the focus and scope of this volume surround those of mixed identity from an international perspective.

I arrived in Panama City, Panama in March during their country's winter and less humid season. The weather was certainly hot (32.2°C) but at the same time very pleasant. I was able to travel within the city and outer city-limits while interacting with Panameños,[3] friends, and business partners at the local university. I made a few school visits and took time for some site-seeing. The main thing that I wish to share here, for time and space limit me from divulging into more detail about such a rich environment, is that Panama boasts a wide and vast history of those who are of mixed identity. In fact, because of the Panama Canal and industrial-age, canal workers brought slaves from Africa, the Caribbean, and surrounding areas, and visitors from France and Central, North, and South America to make Panama their home. Some could even argue that Panama and its canal was much like the United States during the late 19th century with the transcontinental railroad. The canal brought many immigrants to the work of making Panama stronger, faster, and better. Panama also sought to Americanize its inhabitants by offering (sometimes by no real-choice or by force) a different life by means of intermarrying, by racially mixing with either indigenous peoples or with natural-born citizens. Today, one can easily see the effects of the interrelatedness and mixed identities of its inhabitants by looking at the language-richness of Panama. Every day, I heard people using Castilian Spanish, Central American Spanish, and dialects of Spanish from Venezuela and Colombia. This was in addition to hearing Hindi, English, Arabic, and other various languages. In terms of phenotype differences, I was able to observe every color, tone, and variation once could expect to see in a transnational location. And for ethnocultural and religious aspects and variations, fast food restaurants, little shops, and shopping malls adorn most street corners, as do Jewish temples, Catholic and Christian churches, universalist places of worship, and Muslim mosques. Despite these things and Panama's rich history, I did not witness, nor did I engage in much dialogue about the mixed identities of Panama's inhabitants. In fact, most people (outside of a few immigrant Uber drivers) seemed reluctant to identify as anything other than pure Panamanian or of one of Panama's indigenous tribes.[4] Few Panamanians identified as of mixed identity. And others with whom I spoke mentioned that those of mixed identity might be at first seen as an immigrant or treated with less respect due to the current and large influx of Venezuelan immigrants coming into Panama. These instances suggest much more dialogue and work is yet to be done in Panama and other areas like it.

In Canada, I was able to travel around the Ontario Province. I travelled from upstate New York into Niagara and continued into Sturgeon Falls, eventually making my way over to Salt (Soo) Ste. Maria and down into the Upper Peninsula of Michigan. I touched each of the five Great Lakes.[5] While travelling, I was able to witness the handiwork of the Canadian Artic and Inuit People. We can see their mark on the territory and into the hearts of its Canadian inhabitants in the *Inukshuk* (pronounced in-ook-shook), or stone figures created "in the image of man". The Inuit and others place these stone figures, some very small and other rather large, near almost every road or highway, a visual reminder of the struggle of humans and the fight to live and be remembered. The Inuit People use these as communication markers to signify survival for the safest passageway across dangerous and desolate areas. Much in the same way, people of mixed identity seem to fight for survival and acceptance wherever they may live. In Canada, the rich history of First Peoples, French-Canadians, and other early settlers reminds us that being of mixed identity does not automatically occur. That is, it not something that happens to us because of where we are born or where may live or to into which family we may be born. One does not grow up speaking French in Canada, for example, unless that person works to maintain that language and identity. In the same way, one must fight to keep his or her identity(ies) alive and recognized.

My third transnational visit was to Manhattan, New York. Upon my travels there, I visited both Liberty and Ellis Islands. These national monuments are a testament of the liberty and justice so many immigrants had come to expect and find in the United States, namely in New York. In fact, according to the National Park Foundation (2017), early observers once proclaimed the Statue of Liberty as the eighth wonder of the world. Even though French nationalists originally sought to bring attention to their own country, the ideals of liberty for all humankind began to change the image of the Statue of Liberty around the world. "Amid massive immigration in the late 1800s, the notion of Liberty as the 'Mother of Exiles' touched the minds and hearts of the public despite a growing number of restrictive immigration laws" (sec. 4, p. 1). It is now declared a world heritage site. This is not surprising as Emma Lazarus in 1883 scribed what is known as *The New Colossus* which reads:

Not like the brazen giant of Greek fame,
With conquering limbs astride from land to land;
Here at our sea-washed, sunset gates shall stand
A mighty woman with a torch, whose flame
Is the imprisoned lightning, and her name

Mother of Exiles. From her beacon-hand
Glows world-wide welcome; her mild eyes command
The air-bridged harbor that twin cities frame.
"Keep, ancient lands, your storied pomp!" cries she
With silent lips. "Give me your tired, you poor,
Your huddled masses yearning to breathe free,
The wretched refuse of your teeming shore.
Send these, the homeless, tempest-tost to me,
I lift my lamp beside the golden door!" (NPF, 2017, sec. 2, p. 1)

What inspirational and powerful words to those who struggled in their lands, with their own unrealized dreams, with their own forlorn identities. Sadly, even the word *refuse* from the poem itself was a cryptic foreshadow for how authorities received many immigrants into the New York harbor and later processed them at Ellis Island. I saw firsthand just how the U.S. handled the internationalization and Americanization of immigrants and others with mixed identities from the late 1800s. These immigrants were forced to adopt identities not their own, especially if they were of mixed identity. Authorities even detained and later interned a small number of immigrants who were of enemy countries, nationalities, or if they could not claim a single country or ethnicity (NPF, 2017, sec. 1, p. 2). One would think that such unique places as the Statue of Liberty and Ellis Island (beacons of hope for the larger United States) would offer much more than just the hope of dreams unrealized. Ideally these places offered liberty to those who visited U.S. shores. If any place in the modern world could offer stories on how others of mixed identity were treated and eventually were (hopefully) accepted into the "land of the free", it would be these two places. In fact, as compared to San Francisco, New York processed more incoming immigrants during the influx of the 19th Century than any other port in the world. Ellis Island alone processed more than 12 million immigrants during its peek years, only slowed by immigration quotas and laws, World War I and II, and its own closing in 1954 (NPF, 2017, sec. 1, p. 2). Sadly, I was filled with awe and shock at the fact that out of hundreds of placards located across both monument exhibits/museums within the many rooms and halls offered, only three mentioned information about the existence of people of mixed identity. And of these three, only one-half of one placard (approximately 100 words) discussed the idea of being of mixed identity and the pain and privilege resulting. It was in reference to the Chinese-American "paper sons" who after the Chinese Exclusion Act of 1882 by the U.S. Congress forced many incoming Chinese immigrants who were of mixed identity to claim having American Citizen fathers (NPF, 2018). Again, the inspiration and magnitude of what these places of liberty in New York stand for are sadly and rapidly lost on the massive misuse of misrecognition of those of mixed identity.

Even with these recent travels, and others I have made in the past to Hawaii, Hong Kong, Japan, the Philippines, Thailand, the Netherlands, Belgium, Germany,

Switzerland, and France, I was bound by time and ability to fully engage and conduct the necessary research to gain a strong sense for how other people of mixed identity might thrive in other areas. And yet this unique volume does just that, as it offers the perspectives of those who have in fact lived with mixed identities in Africa, Asia, Europe, the Middle East, and in North, Central, and South America. It highlights those who have lived with more than one race, class, language, dis/ability, faith, and ethnoculture. More importantly than world regions, geographical areas, or identifying aspects, this volume explores the inner landscape of a person's life and soul as being of mixed identity.

STRUCTURE OF THE VOLUME

Guiding Questions and Framework

This volume offers collections of various research essays and artifacts (poems, letters, narratives, questions, etc.) on the mixed identity experiences of indigenous and marginalized peoples, including adults and middle school youth. These works utilize a strength- or asset-based perspective, as opposed to one that draws from a deficit approach where others (such as schools) expect or require the individual to change versus the system of oppression. These works also consider the middle grades philosophy in their discussions of youth and educational systems. Contributors have done this because middle grades education has proven to be one of the best educational structures that can be offered to youth between the ages of 10 and 15. The Association for Middle Level Education (formerly National Middle School Association) (NMSA, 2010) developed *This We Believe: Keys Educating Young Adolescents* which is an innovative document discussing the essential attributes of both educating youth and for the preparation of teachers of young adolescents, as seen in their 16 characteristics (NMSA, 2010).

This volume features the following five parts:

1. Exploring the Reflexivity of Pain and Privilege
2. Supporting Youth with Marginalized Identities
3. Exploring the Convergences of Identity and Cultural Responsiveness
4. Interrelated Homilies (movements) of Mixed Identity: An International Lens
5. On Being Mixed and Moving Forward

I developed these parts after having spent considerable time and years in research around those of marginalized and mixed identities. Those data and works demonstrated the need for a volume that would consider the past, present, and future, one that would also provide a context for mixed identity and dialogue around the needs to both respond to and support youth of marginalized identity and the international scope of mixed identity and how to move forward.

The guiding questions which frame this volume and were used by the contributors include the following:

- How do you see yourself? How do others (i.e., family and friends) see you? Why? How has your mixed identity been received (or not) by those closest to you and by others?
- What personal experiences have made you who you are today?
- Do you feel your living, working, and/or schooling experiences have helped or hurt your mixed identity formation?
- How has/will your mixed identity affect the town or locale and/or those round you, now and in the future?
- How might we elucidate the voice of people of mixed identity, as they live and work and attend schools?

I gleaned the guiding questions from earlier years of research (Hurd, 2008, 2010, 2012) where I had considered the seminal protocols of what it means to be mixed and experience the pains and privileges of being more than one race, language, ethnocultural background and yet neither and none of those at the same time. These are questions I have used in my years of research investigating myself and others of mixed identity.

Contributions from authors address this pain-privilege framework, recollections, personal reflections, and advice for professionals working alongside those of mixed identity.

This volume also uses the context of the pain and privilege framework (Hurd, 2008, 2012a, 2012b) as its guide. This context includes the following elements:

- Those of mixed identity construct/deconstruct their identities resulting from social systems.
- These identities are socio-political and cultural-ecological descriptors of position and power, constantly developing who people may be and/or become.
- Those of mixed identity may find they cannot fully identify (e.g., feel no tensions) within a singular race, culture, or social class due to societal fragmentations (change).
- Those of mixed identity bear the insinuations of the past, for how their particular identity descriptors have come to exist.
- Those of mixed identity experience pain and privilege by travelling between and negotiating within racial, cultural, or social groups and oppositional collective identities.

As with the guiding questions, the pain and privilege framework above emerges from my work with myself and other individuals who hold to a mixed identity.

Parts of the Book

As mentioned, this volume presents five parts with works spanning Africa, Asia, Europe, the Middle East, and North, Central, and South America. The first of these parts, *Exploring the Reflexivity of Pain and Privilege*, offers works by authors who

THE HOMILY OF PAIN AND PRIVILEGE

explain what is to be of mixed identity. Dian Mitrayani writes about her pain and privilege in being of Chinese-Indonesian identity. Cristina Santamaría Graff provides her experiences in being of mixed White-Mexican identity, with Italian and Irish heritages included. Lisa A. Boskovich and David I. Hernández-Saca vividly share via dual auto-ethnographic combinations and intersectionalities on their schooling experiences while being of learning disability (LD), ethnicity, language, and mixed class and gender identities.

The second part, *Supporting Youth with Marginalized Identities*, investigates youth with marginalized identities from Canada, Korea, Mexico, and the United States. It also offers a transnational poem and a comprehensive list of questions which middle school students themselves, educators, and researchers would do well to consider in their navigation of and work with those of mixed identity. Hwa Pyung Yoo writes about his middle school experiences as a third culture kid while being of mixed Korean and American identities. Paloma E. Villegas offers a poignant poem on the journeys from Mexico to Canada to the United States. Susan Y. Leonard uses her own experiences and reflections to frame mixed identities as funds of identity that can inform and enrich interactions between and among adults and youth with her transracialism. This part concludes with transformative consciousness raising questions provided by Hannah R. Stohry.

The next part is titled, *Exploring the Convergences of Identity and Cultural Responsiveness*. This section highlights works from African, the rural south, and territories of First Peoples of the United States. Raymond Adams writes on his African Louisianan Creole experiences while considering race, ethnicity, and belonging. Jessica L. Samuels follows with her personal experiences of being of mixed ethnic and racial identities of Black, Native American, and White backgrounds.

The fourth part, *Interrelated Homilies (movements) of Mixed Identity: An International Lens*, is specific to works from other countries while its writers were abroad and/or from those countries. These areas include Canada, South Africa, Egypt, Kenya, Norway, Panama, and the United States. Lynnette Mawhinney constructs an auto-ethnography in three acts which explores her South African, Egyptian, and Kenyan experiences and identity. Mariana León and Guillermina-Itzel de Gracia investigate the rich and mixed identities of middle school youth in Panama. Francisco J. Villegas and Paloma E. Villegas as siblings explore their past and current journeys from Mexico, Canada, and the U.S. with mixed and transnational citizenry. Anne Ryen revisits memories as a Norwegian privileged woman navigating the academy while living in conflicting spaces within African contexts.

The final part of this volume is no less important than the rest. It offers the powerful and collective voices from its authors *On Being Mixed and Moving Forward*. These who have identified as mixed while moving toward the future provide hope in a time of trouble, a light in the darkness, a sign to this age of what is to come, if we hold on to more than antiquated ideals of being singular, of being just one thing and not accepting of all of one's identities. Areas visited in this part include Korea, the United States, and, arguably, the deep recesses of the mind. It also offers four emotion-laden talk-poems. Hannah R. Stohry writes on raising consciousness for multi-racial third culture kids in being of mixed Korean and American identity. David I. Hernández-Saca shares his poems of resisting learning disability oppression through healing through dis/ability voice. Similarly, Lisa A. Boskovich explores being mixed and moving forward in her mixed identity. And Iman Fagan offers a concluding perspective on walking the line of being of African and White mixed identity.

NOTES

[1] Mestizx is a more sensitive word including Mestizo (male), Mestiza (female), and individuals who might identify as gender-neutral. Historically, Mestizos were those of native American and European or Spaniard blood or ancestry.
[2] For a comprehensive review of the historical concept of being of mixed identity, race, or of being Mestizo, please see Hurd (2008, 2012a).
[3] Panameños are the inhabitants or citizens of Panama. The word is a more accurate and inclusive term signifying the many immigrant inhabitants of Panama.
[4] Panama is home to at least seven indigenous groups: Ngäbe (western mountains near Costa Rica), Kuna (Guna; coastal Caribbean regions), Emberá (rain forest and mainland regions), Buglé (west island provinces), Wounaan (Darién Province), Naso Tjerdi (Teribe; west mainland near Costa Rica), and Bri (Costa Rican territories).
[5] The five great lakes of Canada and the United States include: Lake Superior, Lake Michigan, Lake Huron, Lake Erie, and Lake Ontario. History records the impact and importance these lakes have had on First Peoples and early settlers in their ways of life.

REFERENCES

Ainsworth-Darnell, J. W., & Downey, D. B. (1998). Assessing the oppositional culture explanation for racial/ethnic differences in school performance. *American Sociological Review, 63*, 536–553.
Amundsen-Meyer, L. M. (2011). Introduction. In L. M. Amundsen-Meyer, N. Engel, & S. Pickering (Eds.), *Identity crisis: Archaeological perspectives on social identity. Proceedings of the 42nd annual chacmool conference* (pp. 1–10). Calgary: University of Calgary.
Anzaldúa, G. (2007). *Borderlands/La Frontera: The new Mestiza* (3rd ed.). San Francisco, CA: Aunt Lute Books.
Baker, C. (2000). *A parents' and teachers' guide to bilingualism* (2nd ed.). New York, NY: Multilingual Matters.
Bowman, D. O. (1974, September). *A longitudinal study of selected facets of children's self concepts as related to achievement and intelligence* (The Citadel: Monograph Series No. XII). Charleston, SC: The Military College of South Carolina.
Brookover, W. B., LePere, J. M., Hamachek, D. E., Thomas, S., & Erikson, E. L. (1965). *Self-concept of ability and school achievement, II: Second report on the continuing study of the relationships of self-concept and achievement* (Educational Research Series, No. 31, Cooperative Research Project, No. 1636). East Lansing, MI: Michigan State University, College of Education, Bureau of Educational Research Services.
Bruhl, J., Henderson, S., Marvin, J., & Morgan, C. (n.d.). The construction and function of race: Creating the Mestizo. *In Spanish conquest: Conquistadors – Mestizo Culture – Social Changes (Women) – Disease* (Section 2). Retrieved July 7, 2008, from http://www2.truman.edu/~marc/webpages/andean2k/conquest/mestizo.html
Bullard, R. D. (2006). Introductory essay: Assuring environmental justice for all. In T. Smiley (Ed.), *The covenant with Black America* (pp. 187–211). Chicago, IL: Third World Press.

Burns, E. B. (1994). *Latin America: A concise interpretive history* (6th ed.). Englewood Cliffs, NJ: Prentice Hall.

Capelli, C., Wilson, J. F., Richards, M., Stumpf, M. P. H., Gratrix, F., Oppenheimer, S., Underhill, P. A., Pascali, V. L., Ko, T.-M., & Goldstein, D. B. (2001). A predominantly indigenous paternal heritage for the Austronesian-speaking peoples of insular Southeast Asia and Oceania. *American Journal of Human Genetics, 68,* 432–443. Retrieved July 7, 2008, from http://hpgl.stanford.edu/publications/AJHG_2001_v68_p432.pdf

Crawford, Z. (1979). *Skin color, race, and self image: An exploratory study of a group of high school youths.* Palo Alto, CA: R & E Research Associates.

Foley, N. (2005). Becoming Hispanic: Mexican Americans and Whiteness. In P. S. Rothenberg (Ed.), *White privilege: Essential readings on the other side of racism* (2nd ed., pp. 55–65). New York, NY: Worth Publishers.

Forbes, J. D. (2005). *The Mestizo concept: A product of European imperialism* (Unpublished manuscript). University of California, Davis, CA. Retrieved July 7, 2008, from http://www.quechuanetwork.org/news_template.cfm?news_id=3583&lang=

Gollnick, D. M., & Chinn, P. C. (2017). *Multicultural education in a pluralistic society* (10th ed.). Upper Saddle River, NJ: Pearson.

Harding, S. (1993). Introduction: Eurocentric scientific illiteracy—a challenge for the world community. In S. Harding (Ed.), *The racial economy of science: Towards a democratic future* (pp. 1–22). Bloomington, IN: Indiana University Press.

Harrison, L. M. (2015). Redefining intersectionality theory through the lens of African American young adolescent girls' racialized experiences. *Journal of Youth and Society, 49*(8), 1023–1039. doi:10.1177/0044118x15569216

Healey, G. W. (1969). *Self-concept: A comparison of nego-, anglo-, and Spanish-American students across ethnic, sex, and socioeconomic variables* (Doctoral dissertation, New Mexico State University, 1969). R & E Research Associates, San Francisco, CA.

Hurd, E. (2008). *The reflexivity of pain and privilege: An autoethnography of (Mestizo) identity and other Mestizo voices* (Doctoral dissertation). Retrieved August 13, 2009, from ProQuest Dissertations and Theses database. (UMI No. 3343925)

Hurd, E. (2010). Confessions of belonging: My emotional journey as a medical translator. *Qualitative Inquiry, 16*(10), 783–791. doi:10.1177/ 1077800410383117

Hurd, E. (2012a). A framework for understanding multicultural identities: An investigation of a middle level student's French-Canadian Honduran-American (Mestizo) identity. *Middle Grades Research Journal, 7*(2), 111–127.

Hurd, E. (2012b). The reflexivity of pain and privilege. *International Journal of Critical Pedagogy, 4*(1), 36–46. Retrieved from http://libjournal.uncg.edu/ojs/index. php/ijcp/article/view/151

Johnson, A. G. (2005). Privilege as paradox. In P. S. Rothenberg (Ed.), *White privilege: Essential readings on the other side of racism* (2nd ed., pp. 103–107). New York, NY: Worth Publishers.

Kicza, J. (1997). Native American, African, and Hispanic communities during the middle period in the colonial America. *Historical Archeology, 31,* 9–17.

Lipsitz, G. (2005). The possessive investment in Whiteness. In P. S. Rothenberg (Ed.), *White privilege: Essential readings on the other side of racism* (2nd ed., pp. 67–90). New York, NY: Worth Publishers.

National Center for Education Statistics. (2014). *Digest of education statistic: Enrollment and percentage distribution of enrollment in public elementary and secondary schools, by race, ethnicity and region: Selected years, fall 1995 through fall 2023.* Retrieved July 27, 2018, from http://nces.ed.gov/programs/digest/d13/tables/dt13_203.50.asp

National Middle School Association. (2010). *This we believe: Keys to educating young adolescents.* Westerville, OH: Author.

National Park Foundation. (2017). *Statue of Liberty and Ellis Island: Liberty enlightening the world* [Brochure]. Washington, DC: U.S. Department of the Interior.

O'Connor, F. (1983). *A good man is hard to find and other stories* (Rev. ed.). Orlando, FL: Harcourt Brace and Company.

Ogbu, J. U. (1992). Understanding cultural diversity and learning. *Educational Researcher, 21*(8), 5–14.

Ogbu, J. U. (2004). Collective identity and the burden of "acting White" in Black history, community, and education. *The Urban Review, 36*(1), 1–35.

Ogbu, J. U., & Simons, H. D. (1998). Voluntary and involuntary minorities: A cultural-ecological theory of school performance with some implications for education. *Anthropology & Education Quarterly, 29*, 155–188.

Pilgrim, D. (2000). *The tragic mulatto myth.* Retrieved July 17, 2008, from http://www.ferris.edu/news/ jimcrow/mulatto/

Probert, A. (2006). Searching for an appropriate research design: A personal journey. *Journal of Research Practice, 2*(1), D3. Retrieved August 14, 2011, from http://jrp.icaap.org/index.php/jrp/article/view/24/44

Pyke, K. (2004). "The normal American family" as an interpretive structure of family life among grown children of Korean and Vietnamese immigrants. In S. Coltrane (Ed.), *Families and society: Classic and contemporary readings* (Rev. ed., pp. 438–450). Belmont, CA: Wadsworth.

Rodriguez, D. (2011). Silence as speech: Meanings of silence for students of color in predominantly White classrooms. *International Review of Qualitative Research, 4*(1), 111–144.

Rodriguez, L. V. (1999). *The Mestizo-Mexicano-Indian history.* Retrieved July 7, 2008, from http://sonic.net/~doretk/Archive ARCHIVE/NATIVE%20 AMERICAN/TheMestizo-Mexicano-Indi.html

Simmons-Bonnin, G. (1899). Impressions of an Indian childhood, 1899. In C. Glynis (Ed.), *The online archive of nineteenth-century U.S. women's writings.* Retrieved May 25, 2008, from http://www.facstaff.bucknell.edu/gcarr/19cUSWW/ZS /IIC.html

Wang, S., Ray, N., Rojas, W., Parra, M. V., Bedoya, G., Gallo, C., et al. (2008). Geographic Patterns of genome admixture in Latin American Mestizos. *PLoS Genet, 4*(3). Retrieved July 7, 2008, from http://www.plosgenetics.org

Weismantel, M., & Eisenman, S. (1998). Race in the Andes: Global movements and popular ontologies. *Bulletin Latin American Research, 18*, 121–142.

Wildman, S. M., & Davis, A. D. (2005). Making systems of privilege visible. In P. S. Rothenberg (Ed.), *White privilege: Essential readings on the other side of racism* (2nd ed., pp. 95–101). New York, NY: Worth Publishers.

PART 1

EXPLORING THE REFLEXIVITY
OF PAIN AND PRIVILEGE

DIAN MITRAYANI

1. NAVIGATING THE AMBIGUITY OF MIXED IDENTITY AS CHINESE-INDONESIAN

BEING *PERANAKAN*: THE FORGETTING OF PAST IDENTITY

I will begin my narrative by describing my own identity. I am a millennial woman of Chinese descent, born in Indonesia. I am the oldest among three siblings. I grew up in Surabaya, the second largest city in Indonesia. Indonesia consists of 236.7 million people and more than 600 ethnic groups, with Chinese comprising 1.2% of the population (Arifin, Hasbullah, & Pramono, 2016). Despite the small percentage, the Chinese are the 15th largest ethnic group in Indonesia. The Chinese Indonesian position has been seen as ambiguous and uncertain (Ang, 2001). Since colonial times, the Chinese have been subjected to "othering" in Indonesia because of their cultural and religious differences, their perceived dominance in the economy, and their purported complicity with Communism (Allen, 2003). The legacy of Suharto's New Order regime,[1] which unofficially continues to the present day, divided Indonesian citizens into *pribumi* (native) and *non-pribumi* (non-native). This division is an artificial national construct because there is no single *pribumi* identity in context of ethnic origin (Heryanto, 1999). Yet, this internal diversity of ethnic is ignored, placing the Chinese Indonesian in a single category as *non-pribumi*, or foreign, "other" (Hoon, 2008).

The diversity of Chinese Indonesians also appears nationwide. Ethnic groups of Chinese Indonesian mostly originate from the Hokkien, Teochiu, Hakka, and Cantonese, where each has their own language, dialect, culture, and place of residency (Allen, 2003; Arifin et al., 2016). In broader categories, some Chinese Indonesians identified themselves as *totok,* somebody who still can trace back their family ancestry into China and usually are first or a more recent generation (Aguilar, 2001; Freedman, 2003). *Totok* Chinese also speak the Chinese language or Chinese ethnic dialect and practice various Chinese traditions. My parents identify themselves as *peranakan*, a descendant of Chinese born in Indonesia who speak Indonesian or the regional language as their first language (Pausacker, 2005). Another definition of *peranakan* also highlights the possibility of some mixed Indonesian blood in their lineage (Coppel, 2002). *Peranakan* do not adhere to the traditional Chinese culture yet adopt some Chinese customs such as marrying with another Chinese descent (Pitt, 2005). The status of *peranakan* also described as a person in the state of in-between, where someone is not considered as a 100% Chinese or 100% Indonesian. *Peranakan* is defined as "*Cina wurung, Londa durung, Jawa tanggung*

© KONINKLIJKE BRILL NV, LEIDEN, 2019 | DOI:10.1163/9789004393813_001

("no longer a Chinese, not yet a Dutchman, a half-baked Javanese") (Blussé, 1991). The manifestation of peranakan identity in my family appears through the limited collective memory and oral history of our ancestry. My parents can only trace back their family tree a few generations back without an understanding their original Chinese ethnic group. However, I consider myself not lacking in family oral history. We built a *peranakan* oral history for our own immediate family. We understood that our oral history would consist of a mix between our life experience in Indonesia, as Indonesian citizens, as Chinese descendants, and as a Dutch influenced family.

My family's main *peranakan* identity is always Indonesian first. My father shared his love of Indonesia stemming from his father (my grandfather). He shared how his dad was an engineer with the Dutch *Marine* during the Dutch colonization, which then became the Indonesian Navy. My grandfather joined the *Marine* because of his Dutch friend, who offered him the job. This same friend asked my grandfather to move to the Netherlands when the Dutch left Indonesia. My grandfather rejected the offer and chose to stay in Indonesia. His rejection to leave Indonesia stemmed from his love of Indonesia as a new nation. He saw his role was to help Indonesia and continued to work in the Indonesian Navy for 42 years. My grandfather's position in the Indonesian Navy served my family very well. The government of Indonesia automatically gave all of my father's family members, Indonesian citizenship because of my grandfather's service. My grandfather's nationalism to Indonesia also served as the foundation of my family's *peranakan* identity. For my grandfather, there was no other home outside Indonesia. My mother's family, on the other hand, was different. My grandparents from my mother's side worked as grocery merchants in Surabaya, a "typical" occupation for Chinese Indonesian since the Dutch colonization (Soebagjo, 2008). My mother's father (my other grandfather) was a trader who bought and sold tobacco from Hong Kong and Indonesia. My mother's mother (my grandmother) opened and maintained a small grocery store in their house. My grandmother went to a Dutch speaking school when she was a child. This resulted in a Dutch-speaking household, mixed with both Indonesian and Javanese languages (local language). They were blue-collar people who did not have the knowledge and connection with Indonesian nationalism like my father's family. Their perception of being an Indonesian meant following the rules, making enough money to support family, and going with the flow of the majority. The identity of being Indonesian for my mother's family is fluid, which aligns closely to their role as merchants. As a merchant, they observe how the market behaves and follow the market demands. Being an Indonesian means not rocking the boat and supporting the status quo. In 1955, all Chinese Indonesians had to choose whether they wanted to become an Indonesian or a People's Republic of China citizen (Winarta, 2008). My mother's family chose to stay in Indonesia because they felt they had established a home and business in this new republic. My parent's marriage was a unification where both families gained an understanding from each other about their new role as Indonesian citizens. My father's family brought the nationalistic and hopeful perspective of

Indonesia, while my mother's family highlighted the more pragmatic point of view of becoming Indonesian citizens.

My first inquiry of my own identity started when I was in the first grade of elementary school. I recall some of my classmates shared their Chinese name, in addition their official Indonesian name. I felt confused of the singularity of my Indonesian name and the lack of a Chinese name. Both of my parents have Chinese names when they were born but they had to change theirs to Indonesian in 1966. As part of the fear of communism, the Suharto regime created the Cabinet Presidium Decree no. 127/U/Kep/12/1966 that mandated converting their Chinese names to that having an Indonesian context. In addition, the 1967 Presidential Instruction no. 14/67 on Religion, Beliefs, and Chinese Culture in Indonesia eliminated public Chinese religious, cultural, and linguistic expression as well as Chinese media, organizations, and schools (Allen, 2003; Hoon, 2006; Suryadinata, 2005; Winarta, 2008). The discriminatory policies definitely affected the Chinese psyche because it stripped Chinese Indonesians from their identity, both as people and an ethnic group. It combined the diverse Chinese population into one ethnic group and ignored its many sociocultural aspects. Without knowing the historical aspect of these discrimination policies, I asked my mom of my Chinese name. According to Myra Sidharta (as cited in Allen, 2003) this was a phenomenon many young Chinese Indonesians experienced, who were given only an Indonesian name at birth, and began asking their parents for a Chinese name. My mom explained that I did not have one because we are a *peranakan* family. She also stated that I do not need one because I am not a Chinese citizen, but I am an Indonesian. This moment highlighted my in-between identity. On one hand, my physical appearance put me into the Chinese Indonesian category, while my family taught me to see myself as an Indonesian.

I felt a bit sad and left behind because of the lack of a Chinese name. I was satisfied as an Indonesian, but in comparison to my friends, I felt that I was not Chinese enough because I have a missing identity in comparison to them. My identity without the Chinese name continued until 1999 when I was in high school. In 1999, there was a repeal on the 1967 Decree that banned Chinese language material. I wanted to learn Mandarin and joined a tutoring group. My Mandarin teacher asked us to write our Chinese name. I mentioned to her that I did not have one. She provided a verbatim translation of my name, Dian, to Li An (丽安). The teacher asked me about my father's Chinese family name, which then she used as my Chinese family name. I was very happy to finally have a Chinese name. I shared this excitement and new name with my parents. After seeing my happiness on the new name, my father explained the real reasoning behind my parent's decision on not giving any of their children Chinese names. He described the difficulty and bureaucracy in Indonesia as the main reason. All Chinese Indonesians with a Chinese name, who changed their name into an Indonesian name, had to apply for a Declaration of Name Changes at a government office. This declaration would have complicated aspects of civic life as an Indonesian. For example, if my parents needed to apply or extend their ID card or passport, they had to attach this Declaration with their application. The

Declaration would then become a proof of their Indonesian identity. That regulation had been eliminated in early 2000. However, its application still exists in some part of Indonesia (Freedman, 2003). My parents did not want their children to experience the same hassle and difficulty in any of their civic life. This reasoning helped me to come to terms of my singular, Indonesian name.

My contentment with my family's *peranakan* and nationalist oral history family gave me a sense of happiness yet at the same time separated me from other Chinese Indonesian collective memories. The core meaning of group identity is sustained by remembering the assumed identities. Both identities and memories change over time and are revised repeatedly to suit our current identities. Yet the collective memories can be traced through various forms of both public and private commemoration (Gillis, 1994). My parents rarely talked about the collective memory of Chinese Indonesians in general. I also did not learn about Chinese Indonesian experiences from any of my schooling experience. I barely understood the previous traumatic past and memory, such as prosecution and discrimination. One example was the G30P/PKI or the violent failed coup of October 1965. The official history I learned was the Indonesian Communist Party (PKI) masterminded the coup with support from Beijing's communist regime. In class, I learned about the cruelty of communist party members, their danger to Indonesians, which then justified the need to eliminate communist sympathizers by any means necessary. However, this official story masked the reality of mass killing and prosecution of perceived communist sympathizers, such as any labor union members and Chinese Indonesians (Coppel, 1983; Oppenheimer, 2014). My parents also did not publicly share their opinion about G30S/PKI. I only recall both grandparents' decision to join one of six official organized religions (Catholic and Christian Protestant) to avoid the perception of being a Communist. My grandparents chose to abandon their Chinese religious belief (*sembayangan*) and embraced Christianity to protect their families from being perceived as Communist. I recall the impact of this forced religion conversion on my grandparents, parents, and myself. My grandparents from father's side, my father, and my grandmother from mother side became devout Christians who happily join every aspect of their new religion. My grandfather from mother's side and my mother took the nonchalant approach. Their new "religion" did not alter their practice other than attending a Catholic church to take on an image of a non-communist Indonesian.

The 1965 prosecution against Chinese Indonesians reoccurred in 1998. This time I was old enough to be impacted by the experience. I was a high school student in a Catholic school in Indonesia. I recall I never paid specific attention to politics or critical events in the news. I enjoyed my schooling as a teen and focused on being a good student. May 1998 served as a pivotal era in Indonesian history. The 1997 Asian economic crisis and distrust towards the Suharto regime led to mass protests by university students. The mass protest resulted in the killing of three students by the Indonesian army. Public anger led to three days of mass riots and angry mobs in many large cities in Indonesia. Many Chinese owned businesses were looted, burned down, and many Chinese women were raped and killed. I vividly remember the quiet streets of Surabaya during and after the riot period. Surabaya itself was fortunately safe without any rioting. This largely contributed to the strong relationship with the leaders of *Nahdlatul Ulama*, a Muslim organization with strong base in East Java, the *guyub* or friendship culture, and strong collaboration between Chinese business community, Chinese youth activists, local government, and the security agency (Panggabean & Smith, 2011). Despite the safety of Surabaya, I could not escape the fear of being raped and killed. My parents still sent me to school despite how many of my classmates were skipping school or even leaving Indonesia. I recall the eerie quietness of many major roads to my school. When I arrived at school, less than half of the students were there. We only watched movies in the language lab and then the teachers sent us home early. I asked my parents why we didn't leave Java to seek safety in Bali (where it was perceived safer for Chinese Indonesian) or even relocate to Singapore. They kept reassuring me that Surabaya is safe and escaping from Indonesia was not an option at that time. Indonesia will always be home for my parents. They kept reminding me of my grandparents who stayed in Surabaya for safety. I recall my confusion in seeing many business places in Surabaya boarded up with plywood and sprayed paint with sign "*milik pribumi*" (not-Chinese owned business). I asked myself why it mattered if Chinese owned this business. Does it justify the looting or burning? I never questioned or perceived my Chinese-ness as a taint mark but at that time, my Chinese identity separated me from the non-Chinese and branded me as a potential victim. My new painful understanding became my new identity. My feeling of bliss diminished in 1998. I realized that my identity in Indonesia would always be Chinese or non-*pribumi* first, despite being born in the country. I felt lost and not sure, what my future would be with this newly formed understanding of my identity.

THE PRIVILEGE OF EDUCATION

Educational institutions and the learning process became my sanctuary after my painful realization of 1998. I saw education attainment as a pathway to safety. If I could be successful enough in my work, then I would be able to find the safest solution for any future riots in Indonesia. This new, naïve motivation pushed me to study harder and get into the best university. Educational opportunities have been always held as a privilege of my family. Both of my parents were able to pursue higher education. Both sets of my grandparents instilled the notion that education is the key of success and encouraged us to advance our education as a strategy to better ourselves. My mother was an example of their philosophy as she constantly attained the first or second grade ranking while attending school. My father, on the other hand, had to repeat one of his high school grade levels. It was my mother that worked as tutor to help my father to graduate from high school. Both of my parents applied for Math and Science programs in a public university in Surabaya, at the standard tuition fee (some of my Chinese Indonesian friends' parents were accepted by paying a higher tuition rate). Unfortunately, both of them received rejection letters. The Suharto regime had put a cap on the number of non-native Indonesian students in public university, which pushed most Chinese-Indonesian students into private, often faith-based universities. My parents could not afford the extra tuition rate targeted specifically at Chinese Indonesian, which led them to enter a private, Christian university to pursue bachelor degrees in Civil Engineering. Both my parents graduated from the university. My mother was able to secure a job as a civil engineering professor in the same university, while my dad went on as a contractor in a private company.

I spent most of my elementary and middle school years without much fanfare. I went to a private, Christian K-9 school. This school is a part of the same Christian educational institute at which my mother teaches. My mother's employee position helped us with a school tuition reduction. I considered myself an average student. I worked hard in school, but I was not what people considered a smart student. My grades in mathematics and science were average, but I did very well in languages such as English, Javanese, and Indonesian. I did not hate school, but I also did not like it. For me, my schooling experience was my duty that I had to fulfill as a young person. I graduated from a Catholic high school. The motivation to use education as sanctuary started from my third year of high school. Students must choose their specialization in the third year of high school. There are specializations in science and math, social sciences, and language. Specialization in science and math is considered most prestigious. I chose to specialize in science and math in my last year of high school despite my average ability in these subjects. I was interested in getting into architecture or interior design, both requiring the science-math specialization. Higher education in Indonesia required students to choose a major from day one of their college program, as switching a major along the way meant starting over from the beginning again. Having the science-math specialization is an entry to all university majors whereas the other specializations limit the option of university majors. I worked extremely hard to overcome my limited skills in both Mathematics and Science. Upon high school graduation, I chose to pursue a degree in Interior Design at the same university where my mother teaches. My reasoning to choose this university was also affected by monetary scholarship. As a faculty's dependent, I was able to have some scholarship to support my undergraduate tuition. My mother suggested to be a translator or English teacher and to pursue a degree in English literature. She suggested it because of my good grades in English and she saw this as a good career for travel and work with many different people. My lack of interest in English made me continue to pursue my original plan of an in Interior Design degree.

Enrolling in a Christian university put me back in the same Chinese Indonesian bubble that I experienced throughout my schooling years. Majority of the students were Chinese Indonesian. This strengthened my understanding on the existence of ethnic and cultural bubbles in Indonesia. The separation of Indonesian citizen based on ethnicity itself was a legacy of the Dutch colony (Kemasang, 1985). In the context of my university, I felt this separation created by a tendency for students to develop friendships based on ethnic and cultural similarities. Despite my painful memory of the 1998 riots, I felt my college life should help me build more opportunity in building friendships that are more diverse. Luckily, the structure of the Interior Design classroom diminished this tendency, as the students were split into several design groups randomly. This random grouping provided the students a chance to work and meet people who were non-Chinese Indonesian. The structure of design work itself also forced everyone to help each other. This gave me a new sense of excitement in building new diverse friendships. Friends I gained in Interior Design were diverse in terms of ethnicity and place of origin. The new friendships expanded my understanding of different ethnic and religion narratives that my peers experienced. One peer shared her reservation of being a non-Chinese student among the majority of Chinese students. The minority experience was new for her. This new friendship opened a dialogue between as we shared our experiences expanding our understanding of one another's perspective. Another peer shared her desire to work as faculty member in the same Christian university. But she was worried that being a Catholic may affect her career trajectory in a Christian university. I confirmed her concern with the discriminatory policy when I shared my mother's story of her career limitation as a Catholic faculty in a Christian university.

I graduated college with a Bachelor Degree in Art and then pursued a career in design. My first interior designer job with a small ceramic company was a stepping-stone to a ceramic designer position for one of the largest ceramic companies in Indonesia. During this career, I also noticed the privilege I had as a college graduate. I was one of four designers in the company; two of us were millennial, college graduates, while the other two were a Gen X and a baby boomer, vocational design school graduates. My college experience helped me gain more modern and contemporary design knowledge in comparison to my older, vocational school co-workers. I considered my older co-workers were better in doing design work. However, they always received criticism on their ability to create higher end, more modern style ceramic designs. My supervisor always gave my millennial coworker and me the modern and higher end design projects. I felt this was a form of discrimination based on age and educational background connected to the perception of limited ability to design higher end, modern ceramic tile. The privilege of my higher education and my exposure to modern arts put me in a higher status in comparison to my more able senior co-workers. This discrimination led to a sense of discontent because I considered my older co-workers as mentors. I learned the most from them in developing my ceramic design skills. I tried to mitigate the workplace discrimination by building collaboration in design work and friendships. Design collaboration helped both my co-workers and I in learning from each other and building an intergenerational relationship.

THE SEARCH OF MY CALLING

I enjoyed my budding career as a ceramic designer. I understood if I continued, I would excel in my career trajectory. I felt I could reach my high school goal of being monetarily successful. However, I always felt a strong calling to pursue my passion for youth related work. I became interested in youth because of my involvement in a Catholic youth organization. I joined the organization because I wanted to develop more friendships and have fun. The membership involved me with various social activities. One of the most memorable ones was traveling to local village to work on fundraiser for their village. I travelled with other youth and we all stayed in the local's houses. My stay with the local family helped me to connect and understand the life in the community from the native perspective. The family members shared their stories of what they do and what the children learn in the school. The next day, all the youth groups hosted a fundraising market of clothing and groceries we brought from Surabaya. All the money we raised we donated to the village. This experience helped me to heal my own race and religious based fear. The family I stayed with in the village was Javanese and Muslim. They welcomed us warmly despite our ethnic and religion differences. This experience helped me heal myself and understand the larger context of my fear. I felt I grew from generalizing my own stereotype perception and fear. The process of knowing others and building social bonding helped me to enhance tolerance, acceptance, and start healing my own fears (Janzen, 2016; Sliep, 2014).

Looking at this experience now, I also see the problematic and general perception of social related work in Indonesia. In Indonesia social work, including youth work, receives little support, making them undesirable career options leading to be handled through volunteer work (Chen, 2009; Santoso, 2016; Shin, Rachmatullah, Roshayanti, Ha, & Lee, 2018). My goal at that time, along with the youth, was to help the village. I felt good because I did a good deed, then I came back to my career as a designer. The separation of feeling satisfied through voluntary work while supporting myself through a career disturbed me at that time. I felt that the act of being good was not related to a good money career in Indonesia. My father ingrained a sense of helping others, but he could only fully pursue this aspect once he retired. Therefore, I concluded my desire to work with youth and community should lead to a career, whether it was in Indonesia or not.

These conditions led me to explore alternative career options, triggering the need to apply for a graduate studies scholarship. I was inspired to pursue a graduate degree because of my mother. She finished her master's degree at the age of 51 by joining the ranks of my own generation to graduate with excellence in Civil Engineering. Two pathways I considered were focused on scholarships for a master's degree outside Indonesia or pursue a graduate school in Indonesia. I was heavily focused on the outside path, but I understood the difficulty that I faced. As a private sector worker, I was not an ideal candidate as a scholarship recipient. The majority of scholarship recipients were university professors, public sector workers, or non-profit workers. I was none of those. I kept a list of various scholarship opportunities to visit and apply. I filled up many forms, writing personal statements, took both TOEFL and GRE as part of the scholarship requirements. Yet rejection after rejection letters came.

The feeling of disappointment surged in. My mom tried to ease the pain by saying that this might happen because I was not a professor. I sent a few more applications and decided to pursue the Indonesian graduate school option. I started looking at a MBA degree in Jakarta. Deep inside, I hated this decision. I did not have any interest in learning business administration, yet I felt this degree would work the best for my career. I felt this would move me farther away from my calling. I also did not feel any interest to move to Jakarta because of the memory of riots and lack of sense of security in Jakarta. I felt hopeless and lost. In 2006, I received an acceptance email from Asian Development Bank (ADB) about a scholarship for master degree in University of Hawai'i Mānoa with a residency at the East West Center. My disbelief prompted me to think this email as a fraud. Fortunately, it was reality. I was accepted into Urban and Regional Planning Master Degree program. I chose this program because I felt this line of study provided ample career opportunities to work within communities, while opening access to young people.

SCHOLAR IN TRAINING

Arriving in Hawai'i was an exhilarating and empowering experience for me. I came with pure excitement for the new adventure. My parents' and family excitement for my opportunity was displayed during their send off at the Surabaya airport. In Hawai'i I found many international students from different countries and some from Indonesia. I also met with many Indonesians from different ethnicities in Hawai'i. I noticed that my Chinese Indonesian identity morphed into a diaspora identity in the U.S. Vertovec (2005) described that belonging to a diaspora entails both consciousness and emotional attachment to commonly purported origins and cultural attributes such as language, regional, religious, national, or other features. Sheffer (2006) clarifies that a diasporic community has a coherent narrative of the "original" homeland. I felt the Indonesian diaspora status united many Indonesian from various religious and ethnicities. In the U.S., we are all minorities, immigrants, and united by our Indonesian language, our origins, and even our cultural attributes such as our love for Indonesian foods. As international students in U.S., the focus of Indonesian diaspora is to bring comfort and help newcomers adjust to the new life. The sentiment was we only had each other in Hawai'i. We were each other's family in Hawai'i.

However, I experienced one observation of my identity as Chinese Indonesian and scholarship recipient. An Indonesian friend in Hawai'i expressed his observation that usually scholarship recipients do not look like me. I asked him what he meant by that. He elaborated that usually a scholarship recipient is non-Chinese Indonesian and Muslim. This was the first time he saw a Chinese Indonesian and Catholic scholarship recipient. I pondered on this observation and reflected back on my scholarship application process. The stereotypical Indonesian students in the U.S. come from rich families. This matched the stereotypical association of wealth with Chinese Indonesians. My Chinese Indonesian identity and scholarship recipient identity challenged my friend's perspective. I felt proud, guilty, and sad on this perceived anomaly of my scholarship. On one hand, I was proud of my persistence and effort to look for a scholarship and receive it. I felt both ADB and East West Center acknowledged my skill and merit of research in relationship to youth and community. On the other hand, I felt a sense of guilt. I wondered whether I took this scholarship from the hands of a non-Chinese, "native" Indonesian. Lastly, I felt sad because of the generalization of being a Chinese Indonesian international student. The perceived rarity of diverse ethnic and religious scholarship recipients brought into light the need of giving everybody an equal opportunity and chance. In 2017, Lembaga Pengelola Dana Pendidikan or the Indonesia Endowment Fund for Education received criticism from the scholarship applicants over the interview questions that probed more on the issues of the applicants' race, religion, ethnicity, and sex, while ignoring their study plan or research agenda. This current example showed the need to push for more equal and skill-based opportunities for scholarship seekers in Indonesia. The status of ethnicity, religion, and sex should not be the main determinant of providing scholarship to any Indonesian (Ariyanti, 2017, November 9; Utama, 2017, November 7).

My arrival in the U.S. helped me to reconstruct my identity as a young Indonesian woman. I felt the freedom to be independent and live in ways that did not follow the traditional expectation of Indonesian young women. This sense of freedom was also shared by many other women who came as international students in U.S. (Swaminathan, 2004). In the U.S., I had the ability to live alone, travel with my male peers, and enjoy nightlife activities (i.e. going to a bar, dancing in a club, etc.). This freedom and opportunity rarely appeared in Indonesia. Most Indonesian women will live with their parents before they are married. Traveling alone with any male friend or staying out late for nightlife activities is frowned upon and can damage my reputation as a "good girl". My parents never forced me to follow the traditional expectation of Indonesian young women. But they always reminded me of "what will people say" scenario. My "good girl" image is not so much important for my parents, but it is very important for the surrounding community. If I strayed from this expectation, the consequences would fall on both my parents and myself. My new independence in the U.S. helped me understanding myself in similar manner with Wardhana's, Call me, Peng Hwa (*Panggil aku, Peng Hwa*) novel where he describe that he "no longer felt like a stranger to myself, a feeling which had always been present within me ... I felt as if I'd been born again" (Wardhana, 2002, p. 8). I was free to be myself, away from the judgment and expectation of the larger Indonesian society.

The most important aspect of my graduate school experience was I absorbed the identity from Hawai'i as my learning environment. One of the new understandings I learned in Hawai'i was the experience of oppression that native Hawaiians experienced through American colonization, illegal annexation, and the suppression of indigenous language and culture (Goodyear-Ka'opua, Hussey, & Wright, 2014; Sai, 2011; Vogeler, 2009). I saw similar methods of discrimination that happened in Indonesia towards Chinese Indonesians also happened in the U.S. The removal and banning of language and cultural identity of Native Hawaiians hit especially close to home. Native Hawaiians were punished for speaking Hawaiian and had to converted into English after the overthrow of the Hawaiian Kingdom in 1893 (Hawaii State Department of Education, 2017). The removal of the sociocultural aspect of Native Hawaiians intersected with the experience Chinese Indonesian had before early 2000s. However, I also saw the impact of both government policy and public allies in relationship to healing. The policy to promote Hawaiian culture, history, and language in school appeared in 1979 through the State Constitutional Convention. There was also a surge of desire from younger generations to tap into their identity as Native Hawaiian. I saw the similarity of government policy strategy in Indonesia. Abdurrahman Wahid or Gus Dur, the president of Indonesia between 1999–2001, established law that allowed the revival of Chinese cultural tradition such as Chinese New Year, Chinese characters, and Chinese political and social groups (Chua, 2004). The revival of Chinese cultural tradition has now become a mainstream aspect in Indonesia. Many schools offer Mandarin language as part of their curriculum. Chinese New Year is a national holiday, celebrated in many public places in Indonesia. However, I felt there was a need to create deeper changes that truly empowered the Chinese Indonesian community. One aspect of that could create this deeper change was initiating the type of support I witnessed in Hawai'i. There, many non-Hawaiians who speak out for Native Hawaiians recognize the oppression of Native Hawaiians. The surge of acknowledgement and removal of discrimination policy against Chinese Indonesian is very positive. But policy without action at a community level, as it is evident in Hawai'i, will not lead to change.

The most recent scandal against Jakarta's former Governor, Basuki Kusuma or Ahok highlighted the center role of both ethnicity and religion in Indonesia civic life. Ahok, a Chinese Indonesian and Christian governor, is currently in prison for blasphemy accusations (Cochrane, 2017, May 9). Before his imprisonment, Ahok was in competition against Agus Yudhoyono and Anies Baswedan. Both were non-Chinese and Muslim governor candidates, despite Anies as an ethnically an Arab-Indonesian. Yet, both candidates put the issue of Ahok's ethnicity and religion on the center to push people to vote against him. As an incumbent, Ahok has many records of accomplishment yet is often criticized for being blunt in his way of talking. A majority of Jakarta people voted Ahok out and chose Anies Baswedan as the new governor. Despite Ahok's loss, there was much support from both Chinese and non-Chinese Indonesian, including popular performer artists (Mustaqim, 2017, February 3). The alliance showed me the growth of understanding and tolerance between Chinese Indonesian and Christians, but at the same time there was still a huge sector of the Indonesian community who perceives ethnic and racial differences as the number one element for governing Indonesia (Lamb, 2017, April 19). This highlights the question of the role of Chinese Indonesians. Do we have a role in Indonesian civic society or will we always be boxed into an economic/trader/merchant role, in similar manner to the Dutch colony period?

SCHOLAR IN PRACTICE

When I reflect back to my journey as a graduate student in Hawai'i, I always conducted my research on the topic of youth focusing on the Native Hawaiian and continental American youth. My choice to select these youths came through/from practicality reasoning. Travelling between Indonesia and the U.S. is expensive. In order to save money, I chose to conduct research practices (i.e. data collection) targeting accessible U.S. youth. This led me to become an Indonesian scholar with an outsider's perspective of American youth. From this perspective I felt I had much to objectively offer in this field of study.

As an outsider researcher, I found I needed to excerpt a higher conscious effort to be actively engaged with a thoughtful behavior and build cultural knowledge when researching people who are from different races and cultures (Milner, 2007; Tillman, 2002). As an outsider, I focused in a co-researching process where I worked closely with the youth and adult participants to build the narrative of my research. I relied heavily on my participants to guide and introduce me to their own culture.

One aspect that I believe I can share is my minority identity. All my research with U.S. youth have been with minority youth. They can be minority based either on race, ethnic, or immigrant status. My own minority status in the U.S. and in Indonesia helps me share experiences in a larger context with my research participants. I can empathize on some aspects that they experience, such as the discrimination and the ongoing search for identity, but at the same time, I also must be conscious to understand their own unique strength and challenges as minority in the U.S. Their unique voices, which often are stifled out in the U.S., must be the center of the research. On a positive note, there is a growing acknowledgement in putting student's voices in the center of educational experiences and research (Fox, 2016; Kennedy, Brinegar, Hurd, & Harrison, 2016; National Middle School Association, 2010; Robinson, 2015). The next challenge that I have is presenting the research to the U.S. audience. I attempt to share my voice and participants' voices equally. The youth's narratives serve as an opening, while my voice serves as footnotes that help audiences understand deeper and broader in context.

Currently I am in the process of finishing my doctorate in Social Foundations of Education in the University of Wisconsin-Milwaukee. As a Ph.D. candidate, I still continue to pursue my passion in researching about youth but this time, I chose to do my research with Surabaya youth. My choice to work with Surabayan youth came from my interest to switch the direction of my research lens to my own community. I observed that most research about Indonesian youth in higher education comes from Australian education institutions. I felt a compelling need to introduce the Indonesian youth to the U.S. My decision to connect with Surabayan youth was both exciting and worrisome. It was exciting to come back to Indonesian and learn from the youth in my hometown, but I was also worried of rejection and discrimination. Luckily, I was introduced to a children's forum organization in Surabaya. My initial meeting with the youth was promising. I felt extremely welcomed with both curiosity and eagerness. My research in Surabaya also helps me to burst the Chinese Indonesian bubble. The youth I collaborated with consists of 99% non-Chinese youth and 1% Chinese Indonesian. I spent much time in the forum, talking, observing, and hanging out with the youth. They sometimes shared their curiosity on why a U.S. based scholar is interested to work with them. I explained the important work that they do in the world of youth leadership and civic participation. My dissertation also gives me opportunities of mentoring for the youth. Some of them are interested in finding scholarships or learning English. I shared my knowledge on scholarship selection and helped with the application process. I also help any youth who is interested in English learning through conversation. In this research, I am both an outsider and insider researcher. I am an insider because I know the cultural aspect of Surabaya, which helps me interpret the context of my research process. I am also an insider because I am familiar with the general context of global youth culture, which helps me connect and build relationship with the Surabayan youth. I am an outsider because I have never worked together with Indonesian youth for such a prolonged term. I am aware of my experience working with American youth but now I must consciously avoid categorizing Indonesian youth in an American context.

My Indonesian dissertation experience also taught me to share an "othering" and harassment experience (Fabian, 1991; Hall, 2001; Holliday, 2011; Holliday, Hyde, & Kullman, 2004). The children's forum was located in the middle of housing complex. There was always a group of adult males who gathered in a nearby *warung* or street eatery stall. The adult males were relentless in catcalling me every time I walked to the forum. They also called me *Cina* or Chinese in addition to the catcalling. I shared this experience with the youth, who surprisingly also shared similar negative experiences. The young women shared the ongoing catcalling they experienced; despite there was any specific ethnic slur. The young women shared their frustration and hoped for a place where they can be young Indonesian women freely and safely. This experience brought me back to the freedom I have as a young woman in the U.S., where there is less public pressure to conform to the "good girl" behavior. In Indonesia, both the young women and I were constantly reminded that the eyes of public are always observing women's behavior. My positionality as a researcher and as a Chinese Indonesian must shift fluidly when I am inside the safety of the forum and when I am outside in public. Inside the forum, I can freely express both my ethnicity and status as a woman scholar. But, outside the forum itself, I must camouflage my identity to maintain the "good girl" image.

CONCLUSION

By reflecting on my life experiences as a Chinese Indonesian scholar in practice, I have become more aware of the fluidity and complexity of my individual and scholar identities. I started as a young person who was interested in knowing more about my Chinese Indonesian identity. My curiosity led me to learn the history of oppression, discrimination, and also privilege. I used both my college education and career to build my family and myself a good and safe life in Indonesia. I equated a good job and monetary achievement to the ability to "buy" safety in Indonesia. I wanted to build a wall to protect myself from the possibility of violence against Chinese Indonesians.

However, my academic experiences in Hawai'i and the U.S. continent shifted my focus in life towards appreciating freedom of exploration and freedom to be my own self. I expanded my identity in the U.S. as both a minority and a young woman scholar. My minority status is no longer my number one identifier, but it becomes a common denominator that allows me to see the commonalities and differences that I share with other minorities. I gain allies, mentors, and friends who help me navigate my minority status. I learn about minority struggles along with the victories and achievements that bring hope to my life.

This identity-negotiation process gave me courage to explore my Indonesian roots and put aside my fear of discrimination based on my ethnicity and religious belief. When I conduct my research in Indonesia, my main identity is a scholar first. The non-profit organization I worked with, focused on my credential as a scholar in approving my research. The youth in the children's forum also saw me as scholar first, who came to do research with them. Their curiosities focused on my studies and my learning experiences in the U.S.

However, I also understand I must still negotiate my identity outside this educational sphere. I recognize I still use education as my sanctuary but this time, I want to blur my civic life sphere with my education sphere. My research took place in the children's forum itself, where I spent approximately four days a week every night. When I blur my civic and educational life, people in the civic life sphere still see my Chinese Indonesian as my first identity. My Chinese identity can help open dialogue or can be a target for ethnic harassment. I must constantly negotiate both my identity and space in order to push myself out of my fear. I can't afford to run away and build a wall. Through the journey I have gained an understanding of the deepness of oppression that has and continues to influence my identity, in addition to its global scope of influence. It is my duty to keep negotiating my identity and challenge others, both Chinese and non-Chinese, to see the fluidity of a Chinese Indonesian female scholar in context with their own identity.

NOTE

[1] The Suharto's New Order regime is described as "one of the most effective and enduring of the world's Cold War military-based authoritarian regimes" (Aspinall & Fealy, 2010, p. 1). The regime lasted for 32 years (1966–1998) and successfully created economic development. Yet at the same time, the regime demanded obedience and passivity from Indonesian society through state bureaucracy, military, and strict control of the media. See Chua (2004) to understand the implementation of New Order/Suharto's regime strategies in tackling "Chinese problem" through marginalization, discrimination, and stigmatisation; See Suryadinata (1976) to understand the Chinese Indonesian assimilationist strategies through New Order policies.

REFERENCES

Aguilar, F. V. (2001). Citizenship, inheritance, and the indigenizing of "Orang Chinese" in Indonesia. *positions: East asia Cultures Critique, 9*(3), 501–533.

Allen, P. (2003). Literature and the media contemporary literature from the Chinese 'Diaspora' in Indonesia. *Asian Ethnicity, 4*(3), 383–389.

Ang, I. (2001). Trapped in ambivalence: Chinese Indonesians, victimhood, and the debris of history. In M. Morris & B. de Bary (Eds.), *"Race" panic and the memory of migration* (pp. 21–48). Hong Kong: Hong Kong University Press.

Arifin, E. N., Hasbullah, M. S., & Pramono, A. (2016). Chinese Indonesians: How many, who and where? *Asian Ethnicity, 18*(3), 1–20.

Ariyanti, F. (2017, November 9). Penjelasan LPDP soal Seleksi Beasiswa Langgar Kode Etik. *Liputan 6.* Retrieved from https://www.liputan6.com/bisnis/read/3156708/penjelasan-lpdp-soal-seleksi-beasiswa-langgar-kode-etik

Aspinall, E., & Fealy, G. (2010). Introduction: Soeharto's new order and its legacy. In E. Aspinall & G. Fealy (Eds.), *Soeharto's new order and its legacy: Essays in honor of Harold Crouch* (Vol. 2, pp. 1–14). Canberra: ANU E Press.

Blussé, L. (1991). The Role of Indonesian Chinese in shaping modern Indonesian life: A conference in retrospect. *Indonesia, 51*, 1–11.

Chen, D. (2009). *Vocational schooling, labor market outcomes, and college entry.* Retrieved from http://documents.worldbank.org/curated/en/771881468049456978/Vocational-schooling-labor-market-outcomes-and-college-entry

Chua, C. (2004). Defining Indonesian Chineseness under the new order. *Journal of Contemporary Asia, 34*(4), 465–479.

Cochrane, J. (2017, May 9). Christian governor in Indonesia found guilty of blasphemy against Islam. *New York Times.* Retrieved from https://www.nytimes.com/2017/05/09/world/asia/indonesia-governor-ahok-basuki-tjahaja-purnama-blasphemy-islam.html

Coppel, C. A. (1983). *Indonesian Chinese in crisis.* Kuala Lumpur & New York, NY: Oxford University Press.

Coppel, C. A. (2002). Mapping the Peranakan Chinese in Indonesia. In C. Coppel (Ed.), *Studying ethnic Chinese in Indonesia* (pp. 106–123). Singapore: Singapore Society of Asian Studies.

Fabian, J. (1991). *Time and the work of anthropology: Critical essays 1971–1991.* Chur, Reading, Paris, & Philadelphia, PA: Harwood Academic Publishers.

Fox, K. (2016). *Young voice, big impact: Teach young children essential skills, such as asking questions and making decisions.* Retrieved from https://www.naesp.org/sites/default/files/Fox_ND16.pdf

Freedman, A. (2003). Political institutions and ethnic Chinese identity in Indonesia. *Asian Ethnicity, 4*(3), 439–452.

Gillis, J. R. (1994). *Commemorations: The politics of national identity.* Princeton, NJ: Princeton University Press.

Goodyear-Ka'opua, N., Hussey, I., & Wright, E. K. (2014). *A nation rising : Hawaiian movements for life, land, and sovereignty.* Durham: Duke University Press.

Hall, S. (2001). The spectacle of the 'other'. In M. Wetherell, S. Taylor, & S. Yates (Eds.), *Discourse theory and practice: A reader* (pp. 324–344). London, Thousand Oaks, CA & New Dehli: Sage Publications.

Hawaii State Department of Education. (2017). *History of Hawaiian education.* Retrieved from http://www.hawaiipublicschools.org/TeachingAndLearning/StudentLearning/HawaiianEducation/Pages/History-of-the-Hawaiian-Education-program.aspx

Heryanto, A. (1999). Nonpribumi: Dibiarkan, dibaurkan, atau dibubarkan? In Sindhunata (Ed.), *Pergulatan Intelektual Dalam Era Kegelisahan: Mengenang Y.B. Mangunwijaya* (pp. 185–200). Yogyakarta: Kanisius.

Holliday, A. (2011). *Intercultural communication and ideology.* Los Angeles, CA: Sage Publications.

Holliday, A., Hyde, M., & Kullman, J. (2004). *Intercultural communication: An advanced resource book.* London & New York, NY: Routledge.

Hoon, C.-Y. (2006). Assimilation, multiculturalism, hybridity: The dilemmas of the ethnic chinese in post-Suharto Indonesia. *Asian Ethnicity, 7*(2), 149–166.

Hoon, C.-Y. (2008). *Chinese identity in post-Suharto Indonesia: Culture, politics and media.* Brighton & Portland, OR: Sussex Academic Press.

Janzen, J. M. (2016). The anthropology of violence: Context, consequences, conflict resolution, healing, and peace-building in Central and Southern Africa. *Journal of Public Health Policy, 37*(1), 122–132.

Kemasang, A. R. T. (1985). How Dutch colonialism foreclosed a domestic bourgeoisie in Java: The 1740 Chinese massacres reappraised. *Review (Fernand Braudel Center), 9*(1), 57–80.

Kennedy, B. L., Brinegar, K., Hurd, E., & Harrison, L. (2016). Synthesizing middle grades research on cultural responsiveness: The importance of a shared conceptual framework. *Middle Grades Review, 2*(3), 1–20. Retrieved from http://scholarworks.uvm.edu/mgreview/vol2/iss3/2/

Lamb, K. (2017, April 19). Muslim candidate beats Christian in divisive Jakarta governor vote. *The Guardian.* Retrieved from https://www.theguardian.com/world/2017/apr/19/divisive-campaign-for-jakarta-governor-sees-muslim-candidate-elected

Milner, H. R. I. V. (2007). Race, culture, and researcher positionality: Working through dangers seen, unseen, and unforeseen. *Educational Researcher, 36*(7), 388–400.

Mustaqim, A. (2017, February 3). Dukung Ahok, Slank hingga Project Pop akan gelar konser besok. *Detik.* Retrieved from https://news.detik.com/berita/d-3413065/dukung-ahok-slank-hingga-project-pop-akan-gelar-konser-besok

National Middle School Association. (2010). *Position paper executive summary of "This we believe: Keys educating young adolescents essential attributes".* Retrieved from https://www.uww.edu/Documents/colleges/coeps/academics/This_We_Believe_Exec_Summary.pdf

Oppenheimer, J. (Writer). (2014). *The act of killing* (S. B. Sørensen, Producer). Littleton, CO & New York, NY: Drafthouse Films; Cinedigm Entertainment Corp.

Panggabean, S. R., & Smith, B. (2011). Explaining anti-Chinese riots in late 20th century Indonesia. *World Development, 39*(2), 231–242.

Pausacker, H. (2005). Peranakan Chinese and wayang in Java. In T. Lindsey & H. Pausacker (Eds.), *Chinese Indonesians: Remembering, distorting, forgetting* (pp. 185–208). Singapore: Institute of Southeast Asian Studies.

Robinson, K. (2015). *Creative schools: The grassroots revolution that's transforming education/Ken Robinson and Lou Aronica*: New York, NY: Viking.

Sai, D. K. (2011). *Ua mau ke ea = Sovereignty endures : An overview of the political and legal history of the Hawaiian Islands.* Honolulu: Pūʻā Foundation.

Santoso, W. M. (2016). *Ilmu sosial di Indonesia: Perkembangan dan tantangan.* Jakarta: Yayasan Pustaka Obor Indonesia.

Sheffer, G. (2006). Transnationalism and ethnonational diasporism. *Diaspora: A Journal of Transnational Studies, 15*(1), 121–145.

Shin, S., Rachmatullah, A., Roshayanti, F., Ha, M., & Lee, J.-K. (2018). Career motivation of secondary students in STEM: A cross-cultural study between Korea and Indonesia. *International Journal for Educational and Vocational Guidance, 18*(2), 203–231.

Sliep, Y. (2014). Healing and integrated development as part of peacebuilding in post-conflict areas: A social capital lens. In A. Keasley, L. DeLuca, & S. B. Maphosa (Eds.), *Building peace from within* (pp. 53–73). Pretoria: Africa Institute of South Africa.

Soebagjo, N. (2008). Ethnic Chinese and ethnic Indonesians: A love-hate relationship. In L. Suryadinata (Ed.), *Ethnic Chinese in contemporary Indonesia* (pp. 137–153). Singapore: Institute of Southeast Asian Studies.

Suryadinata, L. (1976). Indonesian policies toward the Chinese Minority under the new order. *Asian Survey, 16*(8), 770–787.

Suryadinata, L. (2005). Buddhism and Confucianism in contemporary Indonesia: Recent developments. In T. Lindsey & H. Pausacker (Eds.), *Chinese Indonesians: Remembering, distorting, forgetting* (pp. 77–94). Singapore: Institute of Southeast Asian Studies.

Swaminathan, R. (2004). Relational worlds: South Asian immigrant women talk about home/work. In M. V. Alfred & R. Swaminathan (Eds.), *Immigrant women of the academy: Negotiating boundaries, crossing borders in higher education* (pp. 89–104). New York, NY: Nova Science Publishers.

Tillman, L. C. (2002). Culturally sensitive research approaches: An African-American perspective. *Educational Researcher, 31*(9), 3–12.

Utama, A. (2017, November 7). Program beasiswa LPDP dikritik soal tanya-jawab tentang agama, suku, dan gender. *BBC*. Retrieved from http://www.bbc.com/indonesia/indonesia-41895626

Vertovec, S. (2005). *The Political importance of diasporas*. Retrieved from https://www.compas.ox.ac.uk/media/WP-2005-013-Vertovec_Political_Importance_Diasporas.pdf

Vogeler, S. (2009). *"For your freedom and ours"*. *The prolonged occupations of Hawai'i and the Baltic States* (Unpublished doctoral dissertation). University of Hawai'i at Manoa, Honolulu.

Wardhana, V. S. (2002). *Panggil aku, Pheng Hwa*. Jakarta: Kepustakaan Populer Gramedia.

Winarta, F. H. (2008). No more discrimination agains the Chinese. In L. Suryadinata (Ed.), *Ethnic Chinese in contemporary Indonesia* (pp. 57–74). Singapore: Institute of Southeast Asian Studies.

CRISTINA SANTAMARÍA GRAFF

2. THE UNBEARABLE WHITENESS OF BEING

THE UNBEARABLE WHITENESS OF BEING

In this chapter I borrow from Milan Kundera's (1984) title, "Unbearable Lightness of Being", and adapt it to reflect the *unbearable* quality of and tension between being both Mexican and White.[1] It is important to state that I am, in no manner, equating Kundera's understanding of *lightness,* as an inner force and awareness, to *whiteness*, as a racialized understanding of domination over others. I intentionally situate unbearable whiteness as an exploration of the complex and multifaceted ways in which *whiteness*, in my own lived experience, has afforded privilege and inflicted pain.

As a phenotypically white biracial Mexicana of Irish/Italian-American and Mexican heritages, there is a dichotomy between how I self-identify and how others tend to perceive me. Though I am at ease in my own skin and in who I am as a person– a mother, wife, educator, cancer thriver – I have, in specific contexts, felt dissonance with my own light-skinned body suit. I recognize my phenotypical appearance automatically privileges me in a dominant white society and prevents me, to some degree, from getting closer to some of my colleagues and friends of Color.[2]

Pain and privilege as conceptualized by Ellis Hurd (2011, 2012) is the "discourse and homily of one's plight and affordance concerning mixed identity(ies)" (Hurd, 2018, personal communication). The simultaneous and dichotomous interplay of experiencing both the benefits and the marginalization of identifying with more than one race or ethnicity is a common phenomenon for those with mixed identities. The *pain and privilege* of being mixed[3] is tied not only to my individual recognition of carrying the oppressor/oppressed paradox in my DNA, but also knowing that on a subconscious level I represent to others – depending from which lens they view me – the worst or best of society. This paradox is further complicated by others' categorizations and understandings of people with multiracial[4] identities. As explored later in this chapter, multiracial people are used to frame neoliberal arguments that race is no longer an issue, that somehow by being products of interracial or multiracial unions, we are representations of a post-racial panacea (Johnson-Guerrero & Chaudhari, 2016; Lee, 2008). At the same time, to monoracial[5] minoritized[6] groups, we are a threat to the ongoing struggle for civil rights "when mixture itself becomes a racial category" (Bost, 2005, p. 201). Our existence and its acknowledgement have the potential to reify race and reproduce continued white oppression if our multiraciality[7] is seen as an antidote to racism (Osei-Kofi, 2012, 2013).

© KONINKLIJKE BRILL NV, LEIDEN, 2019 | DOI:10.1163/9789004393813_002

With these initial statements of multiracial identity on an individual and collective level, I now move us into understandings of being a biracial Mexicana in educational settings.

***

An educator for over twenty years, I find irony in the fact that the majority of experiences in which I have had my identity questioned is not in the world at-large but in my own profession. This sense of irony is connected to my belief that those who teach in schools and in higher education institutions and who consider themselves to be socially progressive often make assumptions (many times with good intentions) about where multiracial people belong or fit along a racialized colorline[8] (Gatztambide, 2014). They may view us through simplistic biological understandings that focus on phenotypical characteristics or stereotypical behaviors reinforcing immutable racial categorizations which, oftentimes, focus purely on appearance and physicality (Dalmage, 2003). Conversely, they may challenge the social constructions of race and connect multiply marginalized[9] oppression of multiracial individuals with systemic racism (Kali, 2017). But frequently, they are reticent to expand upon traditional racial classifications *if* their recognition and acceptance of us somehow means compromising power and ownership over their perceived sense of who they are in relation to the group to whom they have invested membership (Chen & Hamilton, 2012). More directly stated, multiracial individuals, become "a source of discomfort and momentarily a crisis in racial meaning" (Omi & Winant, 1994, p. 59) particularly for monoracial group members who, upon encountering these individuals, must decide *how, when,* and *if* this person fits into specified schema of who should belong and who should not (Johnston & Nadal, 2010).

Another layer to my positionality as a biracial Mexicana (my preferred self-identity) educator is my leadership role as faculty member and instructor in a general and special education teacher preparation program. I cannot separate my biracial[10] lived experience from the conscious pedagogical choices I make in the classroom. From the course readings I choose to the reflective activities I create in which my students engage, I am constantly cognizant of my own positionality as a Mexican and White individual who has experienced both oppression and privilege throughout my schooling. In particular, I am critically aware of the responsibility I have to historically minoritized students of Color in pre-K-12 classrooms who will, one day, be taught by the pre-service teachers I am currently preparing. Since the majority of these teachers are white, monolingual English-speaking, middle-class, female teachers, I feel the significance of being multiracial is that, although I look and am white, I can provide a critical lens grounded in my Brownness.[11] Through this orientation, I can engage my students in challenging conversations in which White hegemony is rejected for its oppression and historical violence against people of Color and other marginalized groups. The end goal, for me, is to develop critically conscious teachers who disrupt systemic oppression in school settings, who advocate fiercely for equitable opportunities for minoritized and multiply marginalized students, and who create inclusive, responsive learning environments that intentionally support the needs of *all* students.

With these basic understandings of who I am in relation to my biracial identity, I ask several questions in this chapter, the first two of which are presented through autoethnographic accounts and the third in the discussion section:

a. What does it mean to self-identify as a biracial Mexicana? How does this self-identity impact me and others as an educator and leader in higher education?

b. How are pain and privilege embodied and enacted in the choices I have made or circumstances I have confronted in higher educational settings? In what ways is whiteness 'unbearable'?

c. How, as teacher educators, can we integrate multiraciality into our pedagogy to prepare future teachers to work with minoritized monoracial[12] and multiracial students?

To answer these questions, I draw heavily from critical multiracial theory (MultiCrit) which is rooted in and has expanded upon critical race theory (CRT) to include "a critique of the role that white supremacist structures play in the (re)construction of multiraciality, thus uncovering far more profound effects of racism for multiracial *and* monoracial people of color …" (Harris, 2016, p. 797). As a self-described, biracial Mexicana, Multi-Crit does not explicitly account for imperialism and colonization of indigenous peoples in Latin American countries, specifically Mexico, nor the manner in which *mestizaje* (Spanish and indigenous mixing) complicates multiraciality. For this reason, I integrate conceptualizations of colonization to flesh out their impact on the Latinx[13] multiracial identity. Additionally, I discuss the complexities of whiteness in my own self-identification. This positioning of whiteness is critical in unpacking my biracial identity as I interrogate my privilege of being able to easily "pass for" white, if I so choose. This ability to choose is heavily critiqued through the narratives I present, particularly as I examine my role as educational leader in school and higher educational environments.

I use autoethnography as methodological tool to position myself as a person who exists in a liminal space navigating the tensions between Brownness and whiteness. Through autoethnography, I focus on specific incidents in my schooling and career that highlight my choice – my privilege – to side with my *Brownness* while, at the same time, acknowledging my White heritage (Chávez, 2012). I explicitly make the distinction between my White racial identity and whiteness to recognize the honor I feel toward my Irish and Italian heritages and the distain I have for dominant white hegemony and supremacy. These distinctions are multi-layered. Inherent within them is the unbearable pain of how whiteness, both ancestral and personal, contributes directly to the dichotomous oppressor/oppressed identities that reside within me.

Finally, I consider multiraciality from the indigenous understanding of *Nepantla,* an in-between space where conflict and harmony are valued simultaneously

(Delgado Bernal & Alemán, 2017). I intentionally situate Nepantla in this story to evoke hope and a higher level of meaning-making from multiraciality as *unity* rather than division.

MULTICRIT AS A LAUNCHING PAD

Critical multiracial theory (MultiCrit) provides a firm grounding for understanding the lived experiences of multiracial individuals while intentionally connecting these to societal, institutional, and systemic racism. Racism exists when race is essentialized for the purpose of creating hierarchies of domination (Omi & Winant, 1994). It comes in many forms – biological, intentional, unconscious, institutional, nativist, sexist, etc. – and is created and sustained to benefit dominant white groups while, simultaneously and intentionally, disadvantaging non-whites (Bell, 2007). MultiCrit, like Critical Race Theory (CRT) directly challenges racism. It utilizes CRT tenets – *challenge to ahistoricism, interest convergence, experiential knowledge* and *challenge to dominant ideology* – as a foundation from which to build (Delgado & Stefancic, 2017). It expands upon CRT by asking questions about race and racism that go beyond monoracial categorizations (e.g., Black, White, Asian, Native American) and deliberately considers multiraciality in relation to the tenets listed above. For example, under the category of *challenge to ahistoricism,* a MultiCrit scholar may ask about the historical context of hypodescent (i.e., one drop rule) and how the understanding of it has impacted multiracial students on college campuses when they are asked to check only one box to self-identify.

Where MultiCrit distinguishes itself from CRT is in four tenets that build off of CRT and are renamed to reflect specific experiences unique to multiracial individuals. These include: *a monoracial paradigm of race; racism, monoracism, and colorism; differential micro-racialization;* and *intersections of multiple racial identities* (Harris, 2016). In this chapter, I recognize or address all eight MultiCrit tenets, directly or indirectly, but focus mainly on three 'renamed' tenets unique to MultiCrit as these three provide solid ground in which to root my own lived experiences. These include: monoracial paradigm of race; racism, monoracism, and colorism; and differential microracialization. Though I define these in this section, it is important to state that additional understandings of multiraciality, colonization, and whiteness will be discussed within or apart from these tenets to situate the framework more firmly into a foundation from which to launch and examine my experiences of *pain and privilege* as a biracial Mexicana in educational settings.

A Monoracial Paradigm of Race

This MultiCrit tenet emerges directly from CRT's *structural determinism* defined as a "concept that a mode of thought or widely shared practice determines significant social outcomes, usually without our conscious knowledge" (Delgado & Stefancic, 2017, p. 185). One example of structural determinism in the US is the black/white binary to which non-Black races and other minoritized populations situate their own grievances in comparison. To center the racialized experiences of multiracial individuals, MultiCrit attempts to expand beyond the black/white binary and focus on the subtler forms of racism that are "unconscious, psychological, intersectional, and internalized" (Harris, 2016, p. 804) and that directly affect multiracial individuals. Harris explains that multiracial students often are subjected to being reduced to monoracial categorizations by institutions or individuals who, many times, force the multiracial individual to identify as one race.

To complicate matters, even when institutions or individuals recognize multiraciality, whether on demographic data forms (e.g., check 'more than' one box) or through personal awareness (e.g., "I know he's mixed"), there has been a tendency to use the 'multiracial' category to group individuals into a singular category (Howard, 2018). This means that multiracial individuals who identify as Asian-White, Afro-Latina, Filapeno-Black can be perceived as a monolithic group even if their experiences with race, ethnicity, and culture are completely distinctive. Multiracial categorization, when used for sampling convenience or data analyses used to un-problematize a very complex sociohistorical reality, must be critically interrogated. In other words, if the purpose of creating a multiracial category is to simplify how we sort and classify human beings that are not easily categorized (Bowker & Star, 1999), then we are reproducing structures that perpetuate continued oppression.

Oppression is also present in the ways in which legal and social systems are established to "force individuals to assign themselves, or be assigned to, a category that may not be their primary identity" (Harris, p. 805). Harris (2016) makes an important distinction between the *external* or *internal* imposition of *forced identity choice* on multiracial people by institutions or individuals. Externally, institutions can create structures or tools, such as campus surveys that only allow for one racial category to be checked. This is what Renn (2012) describes as *identification* or the external process by which a multiracial individual is classified monoracially. Internal forced identity choice is connected to the meaning a multiracial person subscribes to her/his *identity* when s/he feels forced to self-identify monoracially at the expense of another lived identity (Renn, 2012).

This concept of *external* and *internal* forced identity choice can further be expanded upon to include the tensions between how a multiracial person internally identifies or prefers to identify (the ideal self) and the way others 'force' that person into monoracial categories that restrict that individual's identity (the limited self) (Hurd, 2011). This concept, though situated under 'a monoracial category of race' is also represented through other forms of racism and microaggressions described in subsequent MultiCrit tenets. Specifically, the external and internal ways in which multiracial individuals are forced to choose a monoracial identity, oftentimes, occur in contexts where little to no negotiation or discussion about a person's lived identities are considered. Multiracial individuals often have the experience of being erased, invisible, or silenced when they are not supported by institutional structures or by individuals who exert power over or have influence in the multiracial person's life (Cuyjet, 2008). Forced identity choice is important to elaborate upon because it "poses a severe stress to positive identity development" (Root, 1990, p. 188). Externally this stress manifests when a person's identity is not valued or recognized. Internally, stress can occur when an individual denies a part of her/himself to conform to others' expectations.

Racism, Monoracism, and Colorism

This tenet addresses the social construction of race as permanent and endemic to living in and being a part of United States society. Harris (2016, 2017), as well as CRT scholars (Gildersleeve, Croom, & Vasquez, 2011; Yosso, Smith, Ceja, & Solórzano, 2009) provide context for and examples of ways in which racism impacts higher education students who are either monoracial or multiracial. Racism and all its complex manifestations also impact faculty of Color who experience overt and covert forms of micro-aggressions working in dominant, white hegemonic institutions (Flores Niemann, 2012a, 2012b). Harris (2016) posits that MultiCrit accounts for these 'encounters', particularly as multiracial individuals confront racism through monoracism and colorism.

Monoracism is based on the assumption that race is a taxonomy of fixed monoracial classifications and, endemic to this sorting system, are implicit exclusionary criteria for those who do not fit into these singular, discrete racial categories (Johnston & Nadal, 2010). Monoracism as a form of racism can simultaneously erase the multiple racial or ethnic identities a multiracial person identifies with and, reify – through this erasure – monolithic and static notions of racial classification. Moreover, in higher educational institutions that have not moved beyond a monoracial paradigm of race, monoracism "may be horizontally perpetuated by communities of color, vertically perpetuated by white communities, and may also be internalized and maintained by multiracial individuals" (Harris, 2016, p. 806). Because monoracism can be consciously or subconsciously enacted by both monoracial Whites and people of Color, for multiracial faculty members who choose to disrupt white supremacy in daily practice, being "tokenized, objectified, exoticized, [or] assumed to be monoracial" (p. 806) can have deleterious effects, internalized and psychological, on one's sense of belonging among colleagues and in higher education institutions.

Colorism, unlike monoracism, also impacts monoracial individuals. It "perpetuates a system of white over color dominance and maintains a racial/skin color hierarchy" (Harris, 2016, p. 806). This hierarchy or skin color stratification is what Gaztambide (2014) and Moss (2006) refer to as "the color line". It is when we color-check one another based on external physical and phenotypical characteristics. Sadly, color-checking – at its most base level – has influenced and created legal precedents that detrimentally impact people of Color (Chávez, 2008). From the 'one-drop rule' classifying mixed race people as 'colored' to immigrant cases in which 'half-breeds', regardless of their white ancestry, have been denied naturalization for being 'free white persons' multiracial classifications have advantaged white individuals (Rousseau Anderson, 2015). In the United States, we have historically positioned lighter-skin as a desired commodity and, more recently under the Trump administration, as a signifier of being "more American" (Santamaría Graff, 2017).

In my personal experience, monoracism and colorism are deeply interconnected, particularly around exclusionary criteria based in underlying understandings of what is 'not enough'. In higher educational contexts, there are multiple ways a multiracial individual may feel excluded. Multiracial individuals – whether they are students or faculty members– report *not enough* being a common experience (Grier, 2014). *Not enough* means having one's multiraciality discounted. It is generally what a multiracial individual undergoes when s/he is policed by monoracial groups who act as gatekeepers and determine the authenticity and relevance of that individual as a racial being worthy or not of group membership (Root & Kelly, 2003).

Colorism is particularly problematic in educational settings where 'socially progressive' monoracial students, educators, or faculty members espouse inclusive, culturally responsive, and equitable practices and, at the same time, are challenged – on psychological, ideological, or emotional levels – by the choice of fully accepting multiracial individuals for their multiraciality or not. Multiracial individuals (with White identities) are seen as both a *problem* contributing to and a *solution* toward our country's racism (Goffman, 1963; Grier et al., 2014). For monoracial individuals, how and when multiracial persons are counted as either white or as Black or Brown becomes a highly charged political act. Additionally, how and when multiracial individuals choose to side with their whiteness or Black- and Brownness is also a conscious political action. The act of choosing one's identity or having it chosen for you is considered in the discussion and conclusion sections in relation to identity development among adolescents and young adults who are discovering who they are in relation to their multiracial heritages (Burke & Kao, 2013).

Differential Micro-Racialization

In CRT, differential racialization recognizes the multiple ways through which racial classification systems construct, position, and manipulate racially minoritized or 'disfavored' groups for the purpose of serving dominant white group agendas (Delgado & Stefanic, 2017). Along these same lines, MultiCrit's differential micro-racialization accounts for *how, when, why,* and *for whose purpose* multiracial individuals are racialized differently (Harris, 2016). The main difference between CRT's and MultiCrit's interpretation of this tenet is that in MultiCrit, the multiracial individual is presented, packaged, or commodified as *more white* or *more Black or Brown* to meet the needs of white dominant institutions. For example, a multiracial person may serve as a "buffer", or a whiter, more palatable, person of Color for a white dominant or majority group (Derrick Horton, 2006). This intentional positioning of a multiracial person's 'whiteness' or 'blackness/brownness' for exploitative purposes is also, as described earlier, a form of objectification or tokenism. It is also similar to MultiCrit's tenet, *interest convergence,* which, addresses the ways in which multiracial individuals "are positioned as objects ... [and] are acknowledged only when it benefits the needs of the white institution" (Harris, 2016, p. 800). Regardless if this positioning is done with the 'best intentions' in mind for the multiracial individual (e.g., to give her/him more experience) or for the institution as a whole (e.g., this person will help recruit more diverse students), differential micro-racialization leverages the individual's skin color and multiracial background for specific capital gains.

AUTOETHNOGRAPHY – A PERSONAL METHODOLOGY

As a biracial Mexicana whose father was born in Coahuila, México and who came to the United States as a youth, I first became aware of the interplay between racism, monoracism and colorism playing out through macro- and micro-aggressions in my observations of others' responses and depictions of my father and his family (Chávez, 2008; Pérez Huber & Solórzano, 2015). For example, as a child, some of my peers would refer to my father as a "wetback" and "gardener" and tell me to "go back from where we came from". Though this chapter does not extend to my lived, childhood experiences with racism in relation to my father, it is important to provide context for my deliberate positioning as 'biracial Mexicana' as I unpack what it means to be on both sides of a Brown/white color line "not knowing what side to turn to, run from" (Anzaldúa, 1987, p. 194).

I choose autoethnography as an entry point to explore the multiple identities I inhabit and how these identities are interrogated in higher educational settings. Autoethnography as a personal methodology is an important tool to use in uncovering micro-aggressions that often leave multiracial individuals scratching their heads and asking, "Is it just me or did *that* really happen?" (Gilderseeve, Croom, & Vásquez, 2011). By sharing lived experiences with monoracism, colorism, and differential micro-racialization, I have the opportunity to problematize interactions with monoracial peers and colleagues in ways that shed light on the complexities inherent in biracial or multiracial categorizations of identification and identity. Moreover, these complexities unearth how monolithic racial classifications are reified in higher education institutions when multiracial faculty members or students are forced to assign themselves or to be assigned to a category, group, or organization not reflective of their primary identity.

Autoethnography, according to Ellis (2004), is an inward journey that, simultaneously, considers the sociocultural aspects of an individual's personal experience. Autoethnography "refers to writing about the personal and its relationships to culture" (p. 38) to uncover the individual's vulnerability in relation to the external context in which s/he finds her/himself. By making sense of the macro- and micro-worlds the person inhabits, we, as an audience, have opportunities for connecting more subjectively to an individual whose personal choices within specific contexts may jar us emotionally and make us question our perceptions. These opportunities, particularly when making meaning of multiraciality, create a "dialectical space where new understanding might emerge through the integration of polarity" (Rendón, 2009, p. 68). In this case, stories by a biracial individual may cause dissonance that disrupts monoracial paradigms and challenges higher education institutions that privilege whiteness.

Methodologically, I used story to center my biracial identity within higher educational contexts. I agreed with Ellis (2004) that stories should be both "a subject and a method" (p. 32) of social science as well as educational research. The process of autoethnography, for me, began with reading reflective writing I composed over the last twenty years. The majority of these pieces have been saved digitally, but some of my writing during my undergraduate years, including a poem titled, *"Not Mexican Enough"*, was found in old composition notebooks. I read original papers and journal reflections that centered around making sense of my biracial identity and chose several examples that reflected specific MultiCrit Tenets. After determining how to frame this experiential writing through a MultiCrit lens, I reflected upon other ways these lived moments also captured complexities of being a biracial Mexicana that were not explicitly unpacked through MultiCrit. Specifically, two additional understandings emerged through the (re)telling of my stories. One included specific nuances around the *mestizo identity* which complicated my initial perceptions of why I was not accepted by a specific Latino group. The other was the realization that the mestizo identity was, in many ways, distinctive from multiraciality in the United States. Examinations of both are described below in the 'reflection and analysis' section under the heading: *Racism, Monoracism, and Colorism.*

PAIN AND PRIVILEGE

In this section, I use personal stories to (re)live, (re)conceptualize, and (re)tell specific incidents in which I had to negotiate my identity as biracial Mexicana in educational settings. The purpose is to examine my identity, through a MultiCrit framework, to better understand the pain and privilege of being bi/multiracial and acknowledging the unbearable whiteness I embody and acknowledge by owning oppressor/oppressed identities. Moreover, I reflect on my role as a biracial Mexicana educator, leader, and scholar in higher education and what these roles mean to mono- and multiracial students with whom I interact and the pre-service teachers I instruct. The stories I narrate span over 20 years and focus on higher educational institutions where I have been a student, an instructor, an administrator, and a professor. I intentionally do not name specific institutions or individuals because the purpose in this writing is not to confess, lash out, or expose. Instead, their anonymity elicits my honest and transparent reflections of being biracial in a racialized and racist society.

A Monoracial Paradigm of Race

I am on a Diversity and Equity (D & E) committee as a faculty member and representative of teacher education at a university. There are several people on this committee including men and women of Color. We are preparing for a conference in which a prominent scholar of Color is visiting our campus to speak about culturally responsive pedagogy. This conference also includes members from the local community who are engaged in projects that position equity at the center of their work. All of us are excited to host this event so we meet several times to make strategic decisions about planning and organization.

During the time of this conference, there are two committee co-chairs who are charged with running the meetings and co-sharing leadership responsibilities. One is a Jewish male the other is an African American female. About two weeks before the conference, the intensity of planning heightens. To meet all the deadlines, we decide to form an ad hoc committee which consists of two White males, and four women of Color (I include myself). Both co-chairs of the D & E committee are on the ad hoc committee as well. One major detail we commit to is ensuring diverse faculty and student turnout as well as large numbers. One committee member, a woman of Color, who I will call Tai, has a personal and direct connection with the main scholar/presenter. Tai has a vested interest in the event, for she is the one who has secured this prominent, well-respected speaker.

About one week before the event, the ad hoc committee gathers to decide whether or not we should have concurrent sessions. We have only three hours for the conference. Of the two committee co-chairs, only the male is present. The question arises: Should we structure the conference format in such a way that audience members would have to choose between two sessions or should we instead shorten sessions so that one session would follow immediately after the other? The issue with the latter scenario for Tai is that, if we shorten the sessions to allow audience members to hear from both the main presenter and the community members, then the main presenter's time would be lessened. This option does not sit well with Tai, for she perceives this shortened time for the scholar/presenter of Color to be a disrespectful gesture.

With such little time left before the conference, we, the ad hoc committee have to vote on whether we want concurrent sessions or shortened, back-to-back sessions. With the African American co-committee chair not present at this meeting, I am not comfortable with voting because I want to hear her perspective and weigh out the two options based on her assessment of the situation. I am also concerned that a prominent scholar's knowledge may be perceived as privileged over community members' if we have concurrent sessions. Forcing audience members to choose between sessions, of which there are only two, rather than positioning the community members' experiences as equally important is problematic to me. When pressed, I vote to have shortened sessions in order to be more inclusive of *all* presenters. I vote in opposition to the concurrent sessions to which Tai and another woman of Color support. And, with my vote, I happen to side with two White men.

Subsequently, Tai marks me as a White woman who did not side with the "minority" (women and people of Color). When pressed in an email by a colleague who argued that I was not 'White', Tai, responded, "I do consider [her] as white actually, no matter how she herself identifies".

Reflection and analysis. As a biracial Mexicana who is light-skinned with freckles and has medium-brown, wavy hair, I often am perceived by others as White. In the US, people say I am "White" or "American;" in Spain I have been called "German" and "Italian;" in Mexico I have been mistaken for "Argentinian;" and in Guatemala, I have been referred to as a 'güera' (fair-skinned) Mexican. Whiteness, however, is not defined alone by phenotype or by "having origins in any of the original peoples of Europe, the Middle East, or North Africa" (US Census, 2010). Whiteness is also defined through power and domination. To choose to *side with* whiteness means defining myself as a White racial being within a larger hierarchical structure that positions whiteness at the top and other racialized and minoritized identities as lower and less valued (Spanierman, Todd, & Neville, 2006). It also means that I embrace White racial attitudes and use my privilege to reap all the benefits to which I am entitled without giving thought to how my actions impact others, particular those who are non-White (Hayes & Júarez, 2009).

Choosing to examine the interpersonal exchange between my colleague, Tai, and me forces me to consider how my actions and words may have perpetuated whiteness or may have been perceived by her as oppressive. This critical reflection, in itself, feels raw. For even though I am clear about where I was coming from, the fact that another person of Color would see and experience me as *only* white raises questions about whether or not I am truly stepping into my Brownness and fighting white supremacy.

This particular example also reveals the challenges many monoracial individuals experience when interacting with multiracial people, like myself. Their discomfort with racial meaning-making when confronted with people of Color who are ambiguous and appear white can be jarring (Omi & Winant, 2015). Their initial reaction may be to reject the person's multiraciality and then impose 'identification' upon the multiracial person to regain a sense of racial order (Renn, 2012). In my case, Tai identifies me as "White" even though she knows I self-identify as Mexican, too. Her identification of me can be interpreted as an example of external forced identity choice, whereby she classifies me, a multiracial person, monoracially (Harris, 2016).

What is particularly difficult for me, painful even, is that I do not know for certain *why* Tai, a self-identified 'minority-minority' who is also an Asian immigrant, identifies me as white in this context. Is it because of my actions in a single moment, 'siding with' my White male colleagues on one vote? Or is it because of something much deeper, a perception of me as *only* white that has already taken root and is sprouting branches?

Though I cannot represent her inner thoughts, nor do I pretend to fully understand her identification of me as white, I surmise that she is intentionally making a choice to invalidate my self-identification as a Latina, as a person of Color. In an email she wrote to a colleague, who after weeks of deliberation decided I should read her words about me, she considers me white "regardless of how [I] self-identity". From her statement, I assume she had made up her mind about my identity, even before the incident I describe occurred. Johnson and Nadal (2010) provide insight to help me understand where Tai may be coming from: "… individuals who do not fit monoracial categories may be oppressed on systemic and interpersonal levels because of underlying assumptions and beliefs in singular, discrete racial categories" (p. 125).

From her view, how can I possibly be considered a person of Color when I look or behave white? To her, my identity as a Mexican woman is a ruse, a smokescreen, to privilege my whiteness while packaging myself as 'Brown'. To her, my motives of self-identifying as biracial Mexicana *when convenient* to me is most likely reified, in her mind, when I choose to side with White men and not 'minority – minority' women of Color. To her, I am the oppressor who has invalidated her through my choices.

Racism, Monoracism, and Colorism

I am an undergraduate student, age 18, attending a prominent university in northern California known for its liberalism and diversity. I am excited. I'm about 300 miles away from home and I'm thrilled to explore my *Mexicanidad,* my Mexican ancestry, in ways I never could at an all-girls Catholic high school in Southern California. I have just attended the Summer Bridge program for minoritized students and am dating a Chicano student who I met through that program. I suggest we 'check out' a La Raza meeting thinking that, together, we can explore our own identities through community-engaged activism.

We approach the student center carrying heavy backpacks and holding hands. We enter into a room where all colors of Brown surround us. Different Spanish accents fill the room. Several La Raza members are code-switching weaving colloquial Spanish phrases and words with English. I am overwhelmed by emotion. I immediately hear a voice in my head say, "This is where you *belong.* Here are *your* people". My boyfriend is unfazed. He doesn't speak much Spanish, but he follows the conversations as he helps himself to a plate of chilaquiles. Several people speak. One indigenous Mexicana from Oaxaca talks about her precarious journey crossing the U.S. – Tijuana border at age five. Another Mexicana who self-identifies as Xicana, "with an X", speaks to logistics around organizing events to bring awareness to the Chicano movement. I listen to every story, every word. Never before have I been around so many Mexican people my age. It's incredible.

As the meeting comes to an end, the president of La Raza, who is a light-skinned Mexican male student from Jalisco, approaches my boyfriend and me. He offers my boyfriend a friendly handshake, smiles, and says, "Bienvenido, bro". We talk about where we are from, our families' heritages, our favorite Mexican food, and why we are interested in joining La Raza. After a few minutes of conversation, my boyfriend thanks him and walks over to the refreshments leaving me in private conversation with La Raza's leader. Looking behind him to make sure my boyfriend is out of earshot, the president leans in closer to me and says in a soft, but stern voice, "*Why are you here?*" I am caught off-guard. I smile thinking he is joking, then realize he is completely serious. I answer, "What do you mean?" Both his eyebrows raise in incredulity, as if saying, "Really?" Then he replies more purposefully, "You don't belong here. You're not Mexican enough". He then turns his body from me and walks away. He has just met me, but he has already make up his mind. I am *not enough.*

Reflection and analysis. There are multiple forms of microaggressions and microinvalidations occurring in this example that touch on both monoracism and colorism. Monoracism, in this experience, is "horizontally perpetuated" (Harris, 2016, p. 806) by a Mexican male, person of Color, who acts as gatekeeper in deciding who is and who is not "Mexican enough". From a monoracism lens, my authenticity as a Mexican is questioned because I only have one parent who is of Mexican origin. In his eyes, my white identity automatically disqualifies me as a La Raza member even though I speak Spanish proficiently, am deeply connected to my Mexican roots, and self-identify to him as *Mexican American.*

Colorism is a system that maintains a racial/skin color hierarchy, generally favoring "white over color dominance" (Harris, 2016, p. 806). However, in this case, among my Mexican and Chicano/a peers, I am color-checked for presenting as white in a dominant Brown space (Gatzambide, 2014). Here my multiraciality – as part white – automatically negates my membership in this group. But my white phenotype is not the entire story.

Even though La Raza's president is light-skinned, in this context, his Mexican nationality positions him with greater status than mine. My identity markers – light-skinned, English-speaker (without an accent), U.S.-born person whose mother is White – affords me certain privileges in the United States that, perhaps, he has not experienced. This form of colorism – the determination of me not being Mexican enough – intersects with national origin, primary language, and other factors that lead to within-group sorting (Aranda & Rebollo-Gil, 2004; Osei-Kofi, 2012, 2013). In this case, Mexican origin students use exclusionary criteria, not fully defined, to validate their status in La Raza.

To add another layer of complexity to this experience, this La Raza meeting is taking place on a campus known for its prominent role in the Free Speech Movement and in historic protests against the oppression of people of Color. There is a palpable energy resonating in the room as young Mexicans reclaim Brown power and proclaim Aztlán[14] as their true home. It is in this politically-charged environment that the president heavily scrutinizes me. 'What *are you*?', is most likely the question boring into his head.

If I am *mestizo*[15] then he has to accept me. I would be like almost everyone else in the room, a Spanish-indigenous mixture representing hundreds of years of colonization through forced intermixing. If I am *only* mestiza then I can claim Chicana or Mexicana identity with the knowledge that *this* multiracial identity is valued among La Raza members. Mestiza acknowledges the colonizer/colonized identity *and,* when invoked as a political stance, means rejecting whiteness while reclaiming the power of my indigenous roots.

But I am not *only* mestiza. I am a *double*-oppressor. My whiteness not only represents the Spaniards in Mexico, but also the White dominant race in the United States. It is the White American oppressor I represent that the La Raza president rejects. As gatekeeper, he must decide who to 'claim' and who to discard (Johnston & Nadal, 2010, p. 133). My ambiguity when seen through a "deviant", "tainted and discounted", or "problematic" lens (Goffman, 1963) complicates his decision. If he accepts me, then he will be responsible for me. He will need to defend me and convince others that this white oppressor is one of them.

Differential Micro-Racialization

At a university, on my first day of teaching, one of my White colleagues runs up to me excitedly and says, "I'm so happy you're here!" We begin talking about all the possibilities I have in front of me and she says, "You're just what we need! A Mexican, female! That's two boxes checked!"

On another day at the same university, at a teacher education meeting, there is a broad discussion about culture that ranges from what we, as faculty, are doing to situate culture at the forefront of our teaching as well as reflecting upon our belief systems about explicitly acknowledging culture in our teacher education programs and in K-12 schools. A reputed white, male colleague of mine who has been asked, along with the rest of us, to recognize in his class discussions the importance of culture among historically minoritized students says in an exasperated tone, "Listen. Culture does not matter and *should not* matter if you are implementing evidence-based practices with fidelity".

A white female colleague chimes in a few minutes later about our Latinx teacher education candidates, "We shouldn't have to go out of our way if they haven't learned English yet. If they can't pass the state exams, that's their issue". I sit there. I listen. Have they forgotten my Mexican heritage? I retort, "Culture *does* matter". They look sideways at one another, but not at me. Up until this moment, they have considered me an "insider" most likely because my white phenotypical features put them at ease. But my words remind them – I'm one of *them*. Now another White female colleague deliberately catches my gaze. She rounds on me, "Well, don't take offense! We don't mean that culture doesn't matter. We just mean that all students should perform well if the instruction is good. Good teaching is just good teaching". I am stunned; I don't say more. I feel outnumbered. At the time, I am only in my second year as an assistant professor. I retreat into the back of my mind looking for a safe place, a space, to hide.

Reflection and analysis: Example 1. Differential racialization accounts for the timing and context of how, when, and why and for what purpose a multiracial individual is racialized differently (Harris, 2016). In the first example, a white female colleague who sat on the search committee who hired me makes it clear, once I've been hired, that being a double-minority helped me get the position.

What is fascinating to me in examining this moment is that, although she knew I was biracial, she completely disregarded my whiteness. Harris (2016) explains this erasure as *interest convergence*. To demonstrate our department supported a 'diverse' faculty, it was imperative that my colleague recognize *only* my Latina ethnicity. To problematize this situation more, over the years, this colleague turned out to be an enormous ally for me. Several times she stood up for me, her 'Latina colleague', against systemic oppression that manifested in the form of white, male dominance over specific faculty of Color.

Example 2.　To my white colleagues I am safe. I am racialized as white because I am the 'good Latina' who phenotypically presents as white in spite of my Spanish surname (Auerbach, 2006). If I agree with them or stay silent, they assume I am serving dominant group agendas (Delgado & Stefanic, 2017). But, as soon as I speak up and disagree with their thinking, I am no longer palatable (Derrick Horton, 2006). I am racialized differently. Now I am a person of Color, someone who needs to be put in her place or silenced (Onwuachi-Willig, 2012).

∗∗∗

"Culture *does* matter". The words are mine, but they represent a collective resistance against dominant ideologies that undermine historically minoritized groups' rich cultural legacies (Solórzano & Delgado Bernal, 2001; Solórzano & Yosso, 2001). Once I position myself as Latina, I deliberately cross the color line (Chang, 2014; Gatztambide, 2014). Although I do not feel fully qualified to position myself as a "leader" or representative of my Mexican heritage, I am compelled to speak up. I challenge my white colleagues' assumption that *culture*, when equated with *difference,* often places emphasis on deficit perspectives through which historically minoritized students are considered or evaluated (Tuck, 2009; Valencia, 2010). I question their notion that culture is separate from learning and does not need consideration if "good teaching" is present. Further, I indirectly confront what "good teaching" means in the context of instructing historically minoritized students. What is "good?" Whose knowledge is being reproduced through this "teaching" and whose knowledge is deemed "legitimate" (Delgado Bernal & Villalpando, 2002). In essence, I am challenging them to take responsibility for their assumptions and to own these viewpoints that perpetuate the continued marginalization of Latinx and other minoritized students.

I should feel safe. I am a faculty member among 'liberal-minded' colleagues. Instead, I feel anxiety. I respect their knowledge and experience, but I am intimidated by the manner in which they freely direct their frustrations at me about recognizing and valuing students' culture. I become aware of my relational status as assistant professor and my positionality as a Mexicana. I am cognizant that by exerting my position on culture I may be placing myself at risk professionally as some of these colleagues will, most likely, weigh in on whether or not I qualify for promotion and tenure (Machado-Casas, Cantú Ruiz, & Cantú, 2013). Like so many other women of Color in academia, I realize that by speaking up and challenging my colleagues' comfortable world views, I am also inviting direct rebukes and microaggressions (Martinez, Alsandor, Cortez, Welton, & Chang, 2015; Pérez Huber & Cueva, 2012; Sánchez & Ek, 2013). DiAngelo and Sensoy (2014) explain that when a non-dominant[16] "minority" person challenges dominant ideologies they are often positioned by White colleagues as "perpetrator[s] of violence" (p. 108). By speaking my truth as a person of Color, I destabilize my colleagues' fundamental belief that *every* person is valued and treated equally regardless of their culture or background (DiAngelo, 2011; DiAngelo & Sensoy, 2014). Their reaction is swift. In the end I back down; my silence deafening to me.

DISCUSSION: PREPARING FUTURE TEACHERS FOR WORKING WITH MULTIRACIAL YOUTH

This section is partly a response to how my positionality as a biracial Mexicana and as a teacher educator impacts youth, particularly young adolescents, whose self-identity as conscious multiracial beings is just beginning to form. I situate some of this discussion around preparing teachers to work with middle school-aged students in consideration of this chapter's relationship to the larger book, "*The Reflexivity of Pain and Privilege: Auto-Ethnographic Collections of Mixed Identity*" edited by Ellis Hurd. Though I do not work directly with youth at this point of my educational career, I do prepare future teachers who will. My clarion call, my underlying hope and message to these future teachers is: Open your eyes! See the oppression. Then ask, what am I doing to reproduce or dismantle it?

As a teacher educator, I am highly cognizant of the dispositional assumptions many of my pre-service teachers arrive with about students and families of Color that are laden with deficit-driven understandings (Santamaría Graff, & Vásquez, 2013). As a teacher educator and as an educational leader among those working with historically marginalized families of children with dis/abilities, I am deliberate about the ways in which I position students' and families' assets at the core of my pedagogy. Like other educators committed to anti-racist and liberatory pedagogical practices (Darder, 2012; Delgado Bernal & Alemán, 2017; Paris & Alim, 2017), I am committed to disrupting racism in all of its forms.

Writing this chapter, I feel an urgency to assist future teachers in deepening their sociocultural and historical knowledge around systemic racism in our country and how racist attitudes inform and perpetuate continued oppression for monoracial students of Color and multiracial students, alike. During these times of social and political divisiveness in our country, particularly with overt acts of racism against Black and Brown people being more visible in social and mass media, it is imperative that our preparation of future teachers intentionally connects historical events with current times (Nash et al., 2017).

One-way teacher educators can prepare future teachers is to unpack their own racialized beliefs and to deliberately teach race as a sociopolitical construction reinforced by federal and state legislation. For future teachers, to begin conceptualizing racism through a monoracial paradigm of race, they first need to understand the intentional establishment of racial categorization in the U.S. They need to know that categories such as White, Black, Asian, and Native American have not occurred in a vacuum. They also should recognize that these monoracial categories are a gatekeeping mechanism that serves the dominant White race.

We, as teacher educators, need to assist our future teachers in examining the arbitrary nature of racial categorization. For example, if white pre-service teachers knew that Italian and Irish immigrants were not considered a part of the White race until the mid-20th century because they were considered 'undesirable' (Ngai, 2003; Powell, 2006), then maybe their judgment of immigrant Latinos would change. Maybe they could begin seeing themselves through others' eyes.

Racial categorization, as specific to multiracial individuals, is not only capricious but also hazy, at best. Future teachers, need to understand not only the ways in which monoracial categories perpetuate systemic inequities for Black and Brown students, in particular, but also how they neglect the biological reality that we are, in fact, all genetically multiracial (Bodenhausen, 2010). In other words, there are no "pure" races. Even those who maintain their "monoracial" identity will have ancestors who, biologically, are members of different races (Graves, 2006).

Future teachers who will be teaching young adolescents, particularly middle school-aged students, must realize the tenuous nature of identity-forming multiracial students face. For many multiracial students, navigating their individual identities means finding their voice among peer groups with whom they want affiliation, belonging or group membership (Hurd, 2012). This navigation in school settings is complicated. For example, a thirteen-year-old Mexican/White mixed-race student may find herself code-switching – through language, gestures, or appearance – to appear 'cool' with different groups of peers and, within the same space of time, may switch or adjust her outward messaging to be considered seriously for her academic aspirations (Harrison, 2017). Though code-switching may appear to teachers as dichotomous, disingenuous, or problematic behavior, in essence, multiracial students are displaying a keen and nuanced skill of 'reading the scene' and adapting to complex social environments (Irizarry, 2007).

These fundamental understandings of race and the racialization of people, if explicitly taught to future teachers as the lens through which to look at and interrogate the world around them, could assist with their conscious interruption of essentialized beliefs of race. This means that they begin to question how and why institutions and individuals categorize students by race, class, ability, language, and other identifiers. Moreover, they would be more cognizant of what they say to students, particularly to those who are 'ambiguous'. For example, Howard (2018) discusses how her biracial (Black/White) second-grade son self-identified as African only to be told by a teacher that, because he "looked Hispanic, [...] he was probably Hispanic" (n.d.). She, along with Hamako (2014) not only call for anti-racist discourse in education but also for intentional conversations around multiraciality. Critical discussions about race, racism, and multiraciality are particularly important as the multiracial student population currently represents 3.1% of all school-age children in the U.S. (Office of Civil Rights) and has increased 32% between 2000 and 2010 (Ginsberg, 2017). Teachers who are intentional about minimizing bias can begin by unpacking their own assumptions about race and question why they or others force or impose identification of racial categories onto students (Harris, 2016, 2017).

CONCLUSIONS

Identifying as a biracial Mexicana has been an evolving journey. I recognize this self-identity as a choice. Biracial Mexicana is not a label or classification my parents gave to me. It is an identity label I gave to myself that represents a constellation of choices I have had the privilege to choose from (Wijeyesinghe, 2012). Being an ambiguous multiracial person who presents to many as white, but who speaks Spanish, keeps her Spanish surname, and chooses to call herself 'Latina' or 'Mexicana', is, for many, *too much* or *not enough* (Grier et al., 2014; Johnston & Nadal, 2010). In either case, the majority of monoracial individuals I encounter on a daily basis choose to see and understand me through their own racialized schemas, regardless of how I may self-identify. This is the quandary for many multiracial people. No matter who we say we are, there are very few who will take the time and make the effort to truly understand our self-branding.

It is not lost on me that perhaps the reason my choice of self-identity, *biracial Mexicana,* is controversial is because I *do* look white. Does a Black or Brown person with multiple racial and ethnic identifiers who presents as *a person of Color* have the choices to self-identify as I do? Or has it already been decided, through our arbitrary understandings of monoracism and colorism, that they are *only* Black or Brown, regardless of how they self-identify? *What makes my experience and their experience different?* The answer is I can self-identity as White in a white dominant society that privileges whiteness. This is the difference, conundrum, and controversy with being biracial Mexicana.

As an educator in a teacher preparation program, how I self-identify and unpack *biracial Mexicana* is essential. I intentionally introduce myself as Dr. Cristina Santamaría Graff being deliberate about using the Spanish pronunciation of vowel sounds so my first name is Cree-stee-na and my maiden name is Sahn-tah-ma-ree-a. Using correct Spanish pronunciation signals to my students the importance of recognizing my Mexican heritage. At the same time, I acknowledge my whiteness and speak to them about the privileges I have directly benefited from in this country by looking and being white. By positioning my own whiteness in relation to theirs (the majority of the future teachers I instruct are white), I call out our own complicity in perpetuating oppression when we don't speak up and for historically minoritized students. To me, this is an important way to role-model to them how they, in their own classrooms, can be transparent and honest about their privilege when working with Brown, Black and multiracial students.

For all future and current teachers, who work with multiracial students it is imperative to study the intersectionality of race, ethnicity, and identity. Youth, who are solidifying who they are, need to be validated and recognized not for who we think they are (the limited self), but rather for the person into whom they are developing and want to be (the ideal self) (Hurd, 2011). Further, it is imperative for all teachers to understand that when multiracial middle school-aged students transition from elementary to middle school they not only have to navigate their multiple identities (racial, social, cultural, etc.) but also school systems and structures that place greater emphasis on grades, advanced placement classes, and college preparatory tracks (Burke & Kao, 2012). Multiracial students who want to 'hang with' peers representative of their minoritized identities (i.e., Black or Brown) who are also resistant to dominant white pedagogy and practices (Ogbu, 2004) may also struggle with wanting to 'belong' versus doing well in school. Some of these students confront the hard choice of either being accepted by their Brown or Black peers or being academically successful (Ogbu, 2004; Ogbu & Simons, 1998). To them, in today's white dominant schools, there are two distinctive paths: belonging or selling out. There is no in-between or merging point. Our ability to support youth's evolving and growing sense of identity requires that we break down current 'fixed' notions of racial categorizations and, instead, accept the constructivist and fluid nature of identity formation (Chang, 2013). It also means that we unpack racialized systems that privilege whiteness to open more spaces for these students to explore their identities without feeling the need to 'sell out' or give up who they are and want to be in educational classrooms and settings.

IMPLICATIONS FOR OUR SOCIETY

The United States people, as a collective, are in their infancy in understanding the ways in which their lives have been determined and controlled by socially constructed mechanisms that, in reality, act like a large machine sorting and sifting individuals by phenotypical characteristics (Giroux, 2016). Though grossly oversimplified, the point I am making here is that so few people question *why* we continue to uphold and support the White race as the preferred one. What would our world *look, feel,* and *be* like with no racial classifications and hierarchies? What if, instead, what we valued was measured, not by our skin color or racial group membership, but in the amount of love we carried for one another or the generosity we showed to a stranger?

For some, the questions I am asking are dangerously close to me saying, "I don't believe in race" or "I don't see color". But I've taken too many punches related to my identity over the years to believe such nonsense. Of course, there is race. Of course, there is racism. It's in the air we breathe. What I am saying is that we, as a society, are just waking up. Like a toddler learning to walk, there are some baby steps we need to identify before we can flat out run. As a multiracial human being, I consider the acknowledgement and understanding of multiraciality as one of these first steps.

Even before recognizing multiraciality and the forms of monoracism and colorism that it can evoke, our society has to first recognize racism and the white dominant systems that perpetuate it. Multiraciality is another step toward unpacking how whiteness fractures relationships among, within, and between non-dominant monoracial and minoritized multiracial people and groups (Osei-Kofi, 2012, 2013). At this point on our collective journey of unearthing the oppressor and oppressed residing within us, it is not possible to imagine multiraciality as a panacea or anecdote to racism. Even though multiracial individuals are, in essence, a product of blending and mixing races, we cannot, *must not*, try to leap over the violence, dispossession, and horror inflicted through colonization and forced assimilation. We have not yet reckoned, reconciled, or healed from the deep collective wound suffered by our humanity, our souls.

THE HARD WORK AHEAD

How do we begin healing? One of the first steps to healing the oppressor/oppressed identity that we all hold within (to varying degrees) is to listen. This is a process of *active listening* where we bear witness to the lived testimony of another human being (Burciaga & Cruz Navarro, 2015; Cruz, 2012). Drawing from my Mexican ancestry is the nahuatl understanding of *Nepantla*. Nepantla means "the space between two bodies of water, the space between two worlds" (Ikas, 2002, p. 13). This is the space where active listening can occur. Nepantla is a place of transformation where conflict is accepted and resolution is encouraged. It is a co-constructed gathering of different minds whose purpose is to unify around a common goal, build coalitions, and use existing tensions as a catalyst for change (Delgado Bernal, & Alemán, 2017).

Nepantla inspires, within me, a higher understanding of my multiraciality and Brown/White identities. Through a symbolic lens, multiraciality is a manifestation of two juxtaposing forces coming together in union to create balance or harmony. When held in the highest light – far beyond colonization and forced relations, multiraciality is a product of *love* representing the union of two individuals who, by society's norms, are crossing racial boundaries to be with one another. Assuming love is at the core, these are two human beings who – in spite of their positionalities and differences – have found a way to bear witness to each other's histories, even if conflict is experienced. It is interesting to note, with a cosmic *wink,* that *love* between the Lovings, an interracial couple, in the *Loving v. Virginia case* (1967) is what probably led them to fight so fiercely against state miscegenation laws that banned interracial marriage (Pascoe, 2010).

On an abstract or more esoteric level, if we can conceive of multiraciality or mixed race as a bridge between oppressor/oppressed – colonizer/colonized, we can, perhaps, begin to imagine what it is like to love the *other*. We can, in our imaginings, find a way to forgive the oppressor *within* and in others; then, reconcile the devastation caused by this oppression. The hard work ahead lies in each of us committing to substantive and transformative change. This work means extracting, from within, our own racist, biased understandings of others and deeply contemplating the ways we perpetuate our own and others' oppression. We must first enact *love* and acceptance of Self[17] and those closest to us before we can imagine a world in which systemic racism does not exist. The dismantling of whiteness and colonization begins with individual choice. Like a pebble thrown into a pond, *each* act of consciously co-creating a reality where every person is valued for their individuality rather than disparaged for their racial affiliation, ripples outwardly and changes the entire composition and structure. This ripple is the clarion call: Open your eyes! See the oppression. Then ask, what am I doing to reproduce or dismantle it?

NOTES

[1] I borrow from C. E. Matias' (2016) work to describe why I capitalize *White* and use lowercase for *whiteness.* She writes: "... since 'whiteness' is a state of being that goes beyond an individual's racial identity – Blacks can express gestures of whiteness – I choose not to capitalize this word or its adjectival from 'white'. ... I capitalize the words, 'Black', 'White', to represent races ..." (p. xvii). Further when I refer to phenotype, I use lowercase *white* to refer to skin color and physical characteristics/features.

[2] Again, I borrow from C. E. Matias' (2016) work and capitalize "people of Color" to represent those of specific races who identify in this manner.

[3] Mixed Race, by definition, refers to individuals who are of two are more racial heritages as a result of their parents or grandparents being of different heritages from one another (Root & Kelly, 2003). In this chapter, the terms 'mixed race', 'multiracial', 'mixed-ness', 'biracial', and 'hybrid' are used interchangeably unless intentionally differentiated or otherwise noted. "Mixed race" as, Chang (2014) points out often implies White mixture.

[4] Multiracial and mixed race are used interchangeably (see note 3). However, multiracial, unlike most understandings of *mixed race,* is inclusive of non-dominant (see note 16), non-White racial or ethnic mixing (e.g., Afro-Latina).

[5] Monoracial refers to individuals who are categorized or who self-identify as being from one race (e.g., Native American), with no 'mixture'.

[6] Minoritized when used within the context of race or ethnicity refers to non-White, non-dominant populations. "Minority" is not used intentionally because it does not capture white power and dominance. Even if there are more Black and Brown people represented in a room (the majority by numbers), they are still *minoritized* because their power in relation to whites in a white-dominant society is minimized.

[7] Multiraciality is the "scholarly discourse pertaining to multiracial identity, groups, categorization or other phenomena" (Johnston-Guerrero & Chaudhari, 2016, p. 254) that encompasses evidence for both the biological reification and social construction of race.

[8] Color line here refers to MultiCrit's understanding of colorism, which is a form of racism, that impacts both monoracial and multiracial individuals. It is connected to "color-checking". To color-check means to "draw a clear and concise boundary between what is an ethnic minority – and hence worthy of all the legal and social protections that entails – and what is not" (Gatzambide, 2014, p. 93).

[9] Multiply marginalized and multiply minoritized can be different phenomena (Kali, 2017). People who are 'marginalized' are not considered to be within circles of power or influence. They exist on the periphery – whether because of race, ethnicity, language, citizenship status, religious affiliation, ability, gender, sex, or any other *difference* as defined by white dominant norms. The word, "multiply" implies that they have more than one identifier that positions them as 'less than' (e.g., an undocumented woman who is also deaf). In the context of this paper, multiply minoritized refers to non-White individuals who are also marginalized by at least one other identifier (as listed in the examples above) (e.g., a Black, Muslim man).

[10] In my own individual case, *biracial* is the term I used to self-describe my distinctive heritages – Latina of Mexican ancestry and White of Irish and Italian nationalities. I realize, however, that biracial is technically a misnomer as "Hispanic" or "Latino" is not considered a monoracial category such as Black, White, Native American and Asian per U.S. Census guidelines.

[11] "Brownness" and "Brown" are intentionally capitalized to refer to my Mexican heritage, rather than placing emphasis solely on skin color and phenotype.

[12] Refer to notes 5, 6, and 9.

[13] Latinx is the gender-neutral alternative to Latino, Latina, and Latin@ (an appellation used to include Latinos and Latinas). I intentionally use Latinx to be inclusive of people who are of Latino heritage while acknowledging the need to move beyond gender binaries (Ramirez & Blay, 2016).

[14] Aztlán derived from the Nahuatl language of ancient Mexico is the legendary ancestral home of the Aztec people.

[15] I define *mestizo* within the paper as Spanish (White colonizer)/indigenous mixing. I use mestiza to refer to myself in the feminine form.

[16] I use Gutierrez's (2008) term "non-dominant" to refer to traditional labels of "students/people of color" and "minority" to emphasize the role coercive power relations play in the identification and categorization of historically marginalized raced and classed populations.

[17] *Self* capitalized refers to our higher selves and the full-integration of mind/body/spirit. Lowercase *self* generally refers to our persona and the ways we identify who we are in a specific context (e.g., educator, teacher, mother, student, etc.). Lower case *self* also captures what Hurd (2011) describes as the dichotomy "between what Mestizos (Spanish/indigenous mixed-race individuals) want to be (the ideal self) and how others may see them (the limited self)" (p. 42). *Self* capitalized also encapsulates our humanity, our authentic human person who is not only aware of the individual persona, but also his/her/their connection and purpose to the collective humanity.

REFERENCES

Anzaldúa, G. E. (1987). *Borderlands la frontera: The new mestiza* (3rd ed.). San Francisco, CA: Aunt Lute Books.

Aranda, E., & Rebollo-Gil, G. (2004). Ethnoracism and the 'sandwiched' minorities. *American Behavioral Scientist, 47*, 910–927.

Auerbach, S. (2006). "If the student is good, let him fly": Moral support for college among Latino Immigrant parents. *Journal of Latinos & Education, 5*(4), 275–292.

Bell, L. A. (2007). Overview: Twenty-first century racism. In M. Adams, L. A. Bell, & P. Griffin (Eds.), *Teaching for diversity and social justice* (2nd ed., pp. 117–122). New York, NY: Routledge.

Bodenhausen, G. V. (2010). Diversity in the person, diversity in the group: Challenges of identity complexity for social perception and social interaction. *European Journal of Social Psychology, 40*, 1–16.

Bost, S. (2005). *Mulattas and Mestizas: Representing mixed identities in the Americas, 1850–2000*. Athens: University of Georgia Press.

Bowker, G. C., & Star, S. L. (1999). *Sorting things out: Classification and its consequences*. Cambridge, MA: MIT Press.

Burciaga, R., & Cruz Navarro, N. (2015). Education testimonio: Critical pedagogy as mentorship. *New Directions for Higher Education, 171*, 33–41.

Burke, R., & Kao, G. (2013). Bearing the burden of whiteness: The implications of racial self-identification for multiracial adolescents' school belong and academic achievement. *Ethnic and Racial Studies, 36*(5), 747–773.

Chang, A. (2014). Identity production in figured worlds: How some multiracial students become racial atravesados/as. *Urban Review, 46*(1), 25–46.

Chávez, L. (2008). *The Latino threat: Constructing immigrants, citizens, and the nation*. Sanford, CA: Stanford University Press.

Chávez, M. S. (2012). Autoethnography, a Chicana's methodological research tool: The role of storytelling for those who have no choice but to do critical race theory. *Equity & Excellence in Education, 45*(2), 334–348.

Chen, J. M., & Hamilton, D. L. (2012). Natural ambiguities: Racial categorization of multiracial individuals. *Journal of Experimental Social Psychology, 48*, 152–164.

Cruz, C. (2012). Making curriculum from scratch: Testimonio in an urban classroom. *Equity & Excellence in Education, 45*(3), 460–471.

Cuyjet, M. J. (2008). Bicultural faculty and their professional adaptation. *New Directions for Student Services, 2008*(123), 73–82. doi:10.1002/ss.288

Dalmage, H. (2003). Patrolling racial borders: Discrimination against mixed race people. In M. P. P. Root & M. Kelly (Eds.). *Multiracial Child Resource Book: Living Complex Identities* (pp. 18–25). Seattle, WA: Mavin Foundation.

Darder, A. (2012). Neoliberalism in the academic borderlands: An on-going struggle for equality and human rights. *Educational Studies, 48*, 412–426.

Delgado, R., & Stefanic, J. (2017). *Critical race theory: An introduction* (3rd ed.). New York, NY: New York University Press.

Delgado Bernal, D., & Alemán, E. (2017). *Transforming educational pathways for Chicana/o students: A critical race feminista praxis*. New York, NY: Teachers College Press.

Delgado Bernal, D., & Villalpando, O. (2002). An apartheid of knowledge in academia: The struggle over the 'legitimate' knowledge of faculty of color. *Equity and Excellence in Education, 35*(2), 169–180.

Derrick Horton, H. (2006). Racism, whitespace, and the rise of the neo-mulattoes. In D. L. Brunsma (Ed.), *Mixed messages multiracial identities in the 'color-blind' era* (pp. 117–121). Boulder, CO: Lynne Rienner.

DiAngelo, R. (2011). White fragility. *International Journal of Critical Pedagogy, 3*(3), 54–70.

DiAngelo, R., & Sensoy, O. (2014). Getting slammed: White depictions of race discussions in arenas of violence. *Race Ethnicity and Education, 17*(1), 103–128.

Flores Niemann, Y. (2012a). The making of a token: A case study of stereotype threat, stigma, racism, and tokenism in the academe. In G. Gutiérrez y Muhs, Y. Flores Niemann, C. G. González, & A. P. Harris (Eds.), *Presumed incompetent: The intersections of race and class for women in Academia* (pp. 336–355). Boulder, CO: University Press of Colorado.

Flores Niemann, Y. (2012b). Lessons from the experiences of women of color working in academia. In G. Gutiérrez y Muhs, Y. Flores Niemann, C. G. González, & A. P. Harris (Eds.), *Presumed incompetent: The intersections of race and class for women in Academia* (pp. 446–500). Boulder, CO: University Press of Colorado.

Gatztambide, D. J. (2014). I'm not black, I'm not white, what am I? The illusion of the color line. *Psychoanalysis, Culture, & Society, 19*(1), 89–97.

Gilderseeve, R. E., Croom, N. N., & Vásquez, P. L. (2011). 'Am I going crazy?!': A critical race analysis of doctoral education. *Equity & Excellence in Education, 44*(1), 93–114.

Ginsberg, R. (2017). Finding comfort in the discomfort of being multiracial: Lessons from my schooling. *Multicultural Perspectives, 19*(2), 103–108.

Giroux, H. A. (2016). *American at war with itself.* San Francisco, CA: City Lights Books.

Goffman, E. (1963). *Stigma*. London, England: Penguin.

Graves, J. L. (2006, June 7). What we know and what we don't know: Human genetic variation and the social construction of race. *Is Race "Real?": Social Science Research Council* (Web forum). Retrieved April 12, 2018, from http://raceandgenomics.ssrc.org/Graves/

Grier, T., Rambo, C., & Taylor, M. A. (2014). "What are you?": Racial ambiguity, stigma, and the racial formation project. *Deviant Behavior, 35*, 1006–1022.

Gutierrez, K. D. (2008). Developing a sociocritical literacy in the third space. *Reading Research Quarterly, 43*, 143–164.

Hamako, E. (2014). *Improving anti-racist education for multiracial students* (Doctoral dissertation). University of Massachusetts, Amherst.

Harris, J. C. (2016). Toward a critical multiracial theory in education. *International Journal of Qualitative Studies in Education, 29*(6), 795–813.

Harris, J. C. (2017). Multiracial college students' experience with multiracial microaggressions. *Race Ethnicity and Education, 20*(4), 429–445.

Harrison, L. (2017). Redefining intersectionality theory through the lens of African American young adolescent girls' racialized experiences. *Youth & Society, 49*(8), 1023–1039.

43

Hayes, C., & Júarez, B. (2009). You showed your Whiteness: You don't get a 'good' White people's medal. *International Journal of Qualitative Studies in Education, 22*(6), 729–744.

Howard, J. (2018). That's not something we have to discuss: Interrupting silences about multiracial students in teacher work. *Urban Review* (Published online). Retrieved from https://doi.org/10.1007/s11256-018-0462-0

Hurd, E. (2011). The reflexivity of pain and privilege. *International Journal of Critical Pedagogy, 4*(1), 36–46.

Hurd, E. (2012). A framework for understanding multicultural identities: An investigation of a middle level student's French-Canadian Honduran-American (Mestizo) identity. *Middle Grades Research Journal, 7*(2), 111–127.

Ikas, K. R. (2002). *Chicana ways: Conversations with ten Chicana writers.* Reno, NV: University of Nevada Press.

Irizarry, J. G. (2007). Ethnic and urban intersections in the classroom: Latino students, hybrid identities, and culturally responsive pedagogy. *Multicultural Perspectives, 9*(3), 21–28.

Johnston, M. P., & Nadal, K. L. (2010). Multiracial multiaggressions: Exposing monoracism in everyday life and clinical practice. In D. W. Sue (Eds.), *Microaggressions and marginality: Manifestation, dynamics, and impact* (pp. 123–144). New York, NY: Wiley & Sons.

Johnston-Guerrero, M. P., & Chaudhari, P. (2016). 'Everyone is just mixed to me': Exploring the role of multiraciality in college students' racial claims. *Equity & Excellence in Education, 49*(3), 254–266.

Kali, C. (2017). Multiple minorities as multiply marginalized: Applying the minority stress theory to LGBTZ people of color. *Journal of Gay & Lesbian Mental Health, 21*(3), 194–202. doi:10.1080/19359705.2017.1320739

Kundera, M. (1984). *The unbearable lightness of being.* New York, NY: Harper & Row Publishers.

Lee, J. (2008). A post-racial America? Multiracial identification and the color line in the 21st century. *Nanzan Review of American Studies, 30*, 13–31.

Machado-Casas, M., Cantú Ruiz, E., & Cantú, N. E. (2013). Laberintos y *testimonios:* Latina faculty in the academy. *Educational Foundations, 27*(1–2), 3–14.

Martinez, M. A., Alsandor, D. J., Cortez, L. J., Welton, A. D., & Chang, A. (2015). We are stronger together: Reflective *testimonios* of female scholars of color in a research and writing collective. *Reflective Practice, 16*(1), 85–95.

Matias, C. E. (2016). *Feeling White.* Boston, MA: Sense Publishers.

Moss, D. (2006). Mapping racism. *Psychoanalytic Quarterly, 75*(1), 271–294.

Nash, K., Howard, J., Miller, E., Boutte, G., Johnson, G., & Reid, L. (2017). Critical racial literacy in homes, schools, and communities: Propositions for early childhood contexts. *Contemporary Issues in Early Childhood, 19*(3), 256–273. doi:10.1177/1463949117717293

Ngai, M. M. (2003). The strange career of the illegal alien: Immigration restriction and deportation policy in the United States, 1921–1965. *Law and History Review, 21*, 69–107.

Office of Civil Rights. (2016). *2013–2014 Civil rights data collection: A first look.* Retrieved April 11, 2018, Retrieved from https://www2.ed.gov/about/offices/list/ocr/docs/2013-14-first-look.pdf

Ogbu, J. U. (2004). Collective identity and the burden of "acting White" in Black history, community, and education. *The Urban Review, 36*(1), 1–35.

Ogbu, J. U., & Simons, H. D. (1998). Voluntary and involuntary minorities: A cultural-ecological theory of school performance with some implications for education. *Anthropology & Education Quarterly, 29*, 155–188.

Omi, M., & Winant, H. (1994). *Racial formation in the United States: From the 1960s to the 1990s.* New York, NY: Routledge.

Omi, M., & Winant, H. (2015). *Racial formation in the United States* (3rd ed.). New York, NY: Routledge.

Onwuachi-Willig, A. (2012). Silence of the lambs. In G. Gutiérrez y Muhs, Y. Flores Niemann, C. G. González, & A. P. Harris (Eds.), *Presumed incompetent: The intersections of race and class for women in academia* (pp. 142–151). Boulder, CO: University Press of Colorado.

Osei-Kofi, N. (2012). Identity, fluidity, and groupism: The construction of multiraciality in education discourse. *Review of Education, Pedagogy, and Cultural Studies, 34*(5), 245–257.

Osei-Kofi, N. (2013). Mixed, blended nation and the politics of multiraciality in the United States. *Critical Discourse Studies, 10*(1), 32–46.

Paris, D., & Alim, H. A., (2017). *Culturally sustaining pedagogies: Teaching and learning for justice in a changing world.* New York, NY: Teachers College Press.

Pascoe, P. (2010). *What comes naturally: Miscegenation law and the making of race in America.* New York, NY: Oxford University Press.

Pérez Huber, L., & Cueva, B. M. (2012). Chicana/Latina *testimonios* on effects and responses to microaggressions. *Equity & Excellence in Education, 45*(3), 392–410.

Pérez Huber, L., & Solórzano, D. G. (2015). Visualizing everyday racism: Critical race theory, visual microaggressions, and the historical image of Mexican banditry. *Qualitative Inquiry, 21*, 223–238.

Powell, M. (2006, September 20). Old fears over new faces. *Seattle Times.* Retrieved April 12, 2018, from https://www.seattletimes.com/nation-world/old-fears-over-new-faces/

Prieto, L., & Villenas, S. (2012). Toward pedagogies from Nepantla: Testimonio, Chicana/Latina feminisms, and teacher education classrooms. *Equity and Excellence in Education, 45*(3), 411–429.

Ramirez, T. L., & Blay, Z. (2017, October 17). Why people are using the term Latinx. *The Huffington Post: Latino Voices.* Retrieved April 12, 2018, from http://www.huffingtonpost.com/entry/why-people-are-using-the-term-latinx_us_57753328e4b0cc0fa136a159

Rendón, L. I. (2009). *Sentipensante (sensing/thinking) pedagogy: Educating for wholeness: Social justice and liberation.* Sterling, VA: Stylus.

Renn, K. A. (2012). Creating and re-creating race: The emergence of racial identity as a critical element in psychological, sociological, and ecological perspectives on human development. In C. L. Wijeyesinghe & B. W. Jackson III (Eds.), *New perspectives on racial identity development: Integrating emerging frameworks* (2nd ed., pp. 11–32). New York, NY: New York University Press.

Root, M. P. P. (1990). Resolving 'other' status: Identity development of biracial individuals. *Women and Therapy, 9*(1–2), 185–205.

Root, M. P. P. (2003). Racial development and persons of mixed race heritage. In M. P. P. Root & M. Kelly (Eds.), *Multiracial child resource book: Living complex identities* (pp. 34–41). Seattle, WA: Mavin Foundation.

Root, M. P. P., & Kelly, M. (Eds.). (2003). *Multiracial child resource book: Living complex identities.* Seattle, WA: Mavin Foundation.

Rousseau Anderson, C. (2015). What are you? A CRT perspective on the experiences of mixed race persons in 'post-racial' America. *Race Ethnicity and Education, 18*(1), 1–19.

Sánchez, P., & Ek, L. D. (2013). Before the tenure track: Graduate school *testimonios* and their importance in our profesorship today. *Educational Foundations, 27*(1–2), 15–30.

Santamaría Graff, C. C. (2017). "Build That Wall!": Manufacturing the enemy, yet again. *International Journal of Qualitative Studies in Education, 30*(10), 999–1005.

Santamaría Graff, C. C., & Vazquez, S. L. (2014). Family resistance as a tool in urban school reform. In E. B. Kozleski & K. King Thorius (Eds.), *Ability, equity, and culture: Sustaining inclusive urban education reform.* New York, NY: Teachers College Press.

Solórzano, D. G., & Delgado Bernal, D. (2001). Examining transformational resistance through a critical race and LatCrit theory framework: Chicana and Chicano students in an urban context. *Urban Education, 36*(3), 308–342.

Solórzano, D. G., & Yosso, T. J. (2001). Critical race theory and LatCrit theory and method: Counter-storytelling. *International Journal of Qualitative Studies in Education, 14*(4), 471–495.

Spanierman, L. B., Todd, N. R., & Neville, H. A. (2006). Psychology. In T. Engles (Ed.), *Towards a bibliography of critical whiteness studies.* Chicago, IL: University of Illinois at Urbana-Champaign. Retrieved April 13, 2018, from http://nathanrtodd.netfirms.com/documents/Spanierman_Todd_Neville(2006)Whiteness_Bib.pdf

Tuck, E. (2009). Suspending damage: A letter to communities. *Harvard Educational Review, 79*, 409–427.

U.S. Census (2010). *Race.* Retrieved April 13, 2018, from https://www.census.gov/topics/population/race/about.html

Valencia, R. (2010). *Dismantling contemporary deficit thinking: Educational thought and practice.* New York, NY: Routledge.

Wijeyesinghe, C. L. (2012). The intersectional model of multiracial identity: Integrating multiracial identity theories and intersectional perspectives on social identity. In C. L. Wijeyesinghe & B. W. Jackson III (Eds.), *New perspectives on racial identity development: Integrating emerging frameworks* (2nd ed., pp. 81–107). New York, NY: New York University Press.

Yosso, T. J., Smith, W. A., Ceja, M., & Solórzano, D. G. (2009). Critical race theory, racial microaggressions, and campus racial climate for Latina/o undergraduates. *Harvard Educational Review, 79(*4), 659–690.

LISA A. BOSKOVICH AND DAVID I. HERNÁNDEZ-SACA

3. STEPPING TOWARDS HEALING ABOUT LEARNING DISABILITY AT OUR INTERSECTIONALITY

How Learning Disability Pain and Privilege
Structured Our Schooling Experiences

INTRODUCTION

What is considered acceptable knowledge about learning disabilities?
Who decides? What are the origins of this knowledge?
Who uses it, and toward what ends?
Who, in the end, benefits?
(Ferri, Gallagher, & Connor, 2011, p. 229)

We created our chapter for the part *Exploring the Reflexivity of Pain and Privilege* to foreground dis/ability[1] experiences at our intersections from a Disability Studies in Education and Interdisciplinary approach. Our centering of dis/ability, that is, the attention to the social construction of our experiences of disability and ability and the pain that resulted, contributes a unique dimension of intersectionality that professionals oftentimes ignore in conversations of educational inequity. When taken up, disability is defined as a singular medical-psychological entity belonging to the individual, rather than a social construction and formation of an identity based on socio-political, spatial, historical, and emotional-psychological and spiritual phenomena. Educational systems, such as special education, however, continue to foreground a medical-psychological model that is based on hegemonic norms. This construction marginalizes the intersectionality of disability among diverse individuals given the hegemony of American society and schooling and its erasure of difference.

According to the 2004 Individuals with Disabilities Education Act (IDEA) an LD is a "disorder" in the "basic psychological processes involved in understanding or in using language, spoken, or written, which disorder may manifest itself in the imperfect ability to listen, think, speak, read, write, spell, or do mathematical calculations" (IDEA, 2004). The definition of LD includes an exclusionary clause that states: "C) DISORDERS NOT INCLUDED – Such term does not include a learning problem that is primarily the result of visual, hearing, or motor disabilities, of mental retardation, of emotional disturbance, or of environmental, cultural, or economic disadvantage" (IDEA, 2004). Our collaborative study contributes to the

© KONINKLIJKE BRILL NV, LEIDEN, 2019 | DOI:10.1163/9789004393813_003

much-needed reframing of policy master narratives of LD (Hernández-Saca, 2016), which situate LD only within the minds and neurology of people as opposed to the social construction of LD emotions and accounting for social and emotional contexts from an intersectional lens. By master narratives of LD, we mean the "pre-existent sociocultural forms of interpretation of [LD] that delineate and confine the local interpretation strategies and agency constellations [for individuals labeled LD]" (Bamberg, 2004, p. 287). The traditional canon of special education and the field of LD has constructed the meaning of LD within the body and mind only, and therefore, perpetuates dominant ideologies such as meritocracy and individualism – institutionalized Western epistemologies – and the coupling of racism and psycho-emotional disablism regarding dis/ability (Dudley-Marling, 2004; Hernández-Saca & Cannon, 2016; Valle, Connor, & Reid, 2006). Our experiences of LD at our intersections of pain and privilege then are not so much a reflection of us, as they are artifacts of hegemony structured within our primary school experiences, expressed at the nexus of LD, ethnicity, language, and the classification and sorting systems of special and general education within K-16. Given our past and continuous oppression – our LD pain and privileges at our intersections – we ask:

1. What are the experiences of being labeled with a learning disability at the intersections of other marginalized identities?
2. What implications do our felt-experiences have for critically reflecting on pain and privilege for educational contexts and equity?

Below we first provide the reader with a literature review about our topic. The review helped us develop our conceptual framework to create new knowledge about ourselves and each other as we navigate pain and privilege. Overall, our approach to our experiences with dis/ability, race, gender, ethnicity, and language was one of critical theory and pedagogy to voice and reflect on our pain and privilege at the intersections. We captured our emotions, feelings and experiences through narrative and emotion-laden talk. We assert that theory is critical to the healing process and letting go of dominant master narratives about our experiences that have been constructed by non-disabled and from non-critical lenses about what counts as learning, disability, social identities, and emotionality. After we present our narratives, poems, emotion-laden talk, we end with our discussion and conclusions before we make implications for the field of the social and emotional dimensions of LD and for others who may also experience the pain and privilege of being labeled with a special education category such as LD at their intersections.

LITERATURE REVIEW

Countering the Dominance of Master Narratives of LD at the Intersections

Historically, learning disability (LD) theory, research, policy and practice is dominated by "LD experts" that undertheorize the role of culture, emotionality, affect, and student voice as it relates to what we know about the meaning and phenomena of LD at its intersections (Artiles, King-Thorius, Bal, Waitoller, Neal, & Hernández-Saca, 2011; Gallagher, 2010; Hernández-Saca, 2016; Hernández-Saca & Cannon, in press). The cultural-historical master narratives of LD (Hernández-Saca, 2016) suggest students and adults with LD are "only boys and men" who struggle with reading and writing tasks and are "feebleminded" and are "a dangerous class prone to chronic unemployment, dependency on charitable institutions, and criminal behavior" (Danforth, 2009, p. 9). However, a growing movement within critical special education and disability studies in education scholarly communities emphasizes the role of intersectionality as it relates to not only LD but other high-incidence special education disability categories such as LD, intellectual disabilities (ID), emotional behavior disorder (EBD), and speech and language impairment (SLI) (Annamma, Connor, & Ferri, 2013; Artiles, 2011, 2013; Connor, 2008).

A handful of studies focus on the intersection of special education disability categories such as LD and gender (Annamma, 2014; Ferri & Connor, 2010; Ferri & Gregg, 1998; Madigan, 2005; Petersen, 2009). Woman and girls with learning disabilities have long faced oppression, stigma, and marginalization in schools and U.S. society (Horn & Moss, 2015). In their systematic literature review on the experiences of youth and young adults with dis/abilities, Hernández-Saca, Kahn, and Cannon (2018) found K-16 youth and young adults: (1) navigated intersectional disability discourses, (2) presented their dis/ability oppression as intersectional, and (3) engaged in their identity meaning making as a form of intersectional discourse. Hernández-Saca et al. (2018) defined navigating *intersectional disability discourses* as those tropes and representations about the socially constructed means of social identity markers such as race, gender, sexual orientation, class, language, among others such as disability.

In this duo autoethnographic study, the meanings of what counts as LD and who people with LD are touch on our ethnic and language identities, and each presents a structure in which our agency, individually and intersectionally, is either afforded or constrained given the dominant dehumanizing discourses. These *intersectional disability discourses* were at the structural level of intersectionality; while the theme of *dis/ability oppression as intersectionality* occurred between the structural and personal levels of the hegemonic system of society and schooling. Youth and young adults were exposed to oppression rooted in the social construction of the crossing of their identities as they experienced, witnessed, and made feeling-meaning (Lemke, 2013) of them. Youth and young adults' *dis/ability oppression as intersectional* illuminated how their intersectional lives affected their spiritual, social, and emotional personhood. Lastly, Hernández-Saca et al. (2018) found that across their 10 studies, participants described their identity formation of dis/ability as mutually constitutive of intersectional identities. Across the three key findings in education research focusing on K-16 youth and young adults with disabilities who are multiply situated in terms of race, gender, social class, sexual orientation, or other social markers, *discourses* (e.g., special education symbolism that included deficit thinking and assumptions about students with disabilities and their race or ethnicities and gender, etc.) *and material realities* (e.g., the special education resource room, the short bus, etc.) were found to be salient within U.S. society and schooling as the sources of oppression and injustice at the intersections of dis/ability.

CONCEPTUAL FRAMEWORK

Our conceptual framework for this collective duo autoethnography was a from a Disability Studies in Education (DSE) and Interdisciplinary frame that foregrounds a sociohistorical approach to dis/ability at its intersections (Artiles, Dorn, & Bal, 2016; Artiles et al., 2011; Hernández-Saca et al., 2018). All the elements in the research process are part and parcel of this conceptual frame to answer the research question of our study (Ravitch & Riggan, 2012). Our research elements included our research question, methods, literature, and our interests, histories, and positionalities. DSE provides us with a more humane understanding of dis/ability, even though we were subjected to the dominant medical-psychological model of disability within special education in K-16. The hegemony of the medical model has been the source of our oppression. We find healing within the framework of DSE and other disciplines that provide understanding, knowledge and therefore, re-appropriation of our dis/ability intersectional lives. In other words, who we are within society and educational contexts, given the structural, personal and political ways in which our positionalities, in particular our social identities and our emotionalities, affectives, and spiritualities as it relates to who we are becoming and doing matter for equity and justice (Goodley, Liddiard, & Runswick-Cole, 2018; Hernández-Saca & Cannon, in press). Given our unique life histories, we also weave throughout our narratives, poems, emotion-laden talk at our intersections of LD, ethnicity, and language our unique conceptual frames pulled from DSE and interdisciplinary literatures and traditions.

METHODOLOGY

Design

Understanding self and our intersectional identities within larger hegemonic structures is a life-long journey that is emotion-laden. We make sense of our lived-experiences within these sociocultural and historical contexts through the domain of autoethnography, to inform theory, research and practice regarding the questions we care about. This work is personal and political (Burdell & Swadener, 1999). Dual autoethnography is the combination of lived experiences, connected ideologies, and interrelated individual experiences (Anderson, 2006; Chang, Hernandez, & Ngunjir, 2012; Denzin & Lincoln, 2000; Hughes, Pennington, & Makris, 2012; McIlveen, 2008). Our collaborative dual autoethnography centered a critical continuous dialogue and friendship about our first-person experiences with the special education label of LD at our intersections of historically marginalized identities (Adams & Ellis, 2013; Ellis, Adams, & Bochner, 2011).

Participants

Two friends as colleagues and scholars have spent the past year dialoguing through messages, phone conversations, and written journal entries on what it is like to reflect upon our years in education dealing with an LD. The facing of the pain of our past was a collective challenge. We approached this with open hearts and open minds. To connect with another through pain and walk into victory has shaped both our lives as individuals, educators, and scholars. While we cannot truly measure pain in inches, feet, or yards, we reflect our inner growth by continuing the process of becoming more fully human. We did as Freire (2008) stated: "the oppressed unveil the world of oppression and through the praxis commit themselves to its transformation" (p. 54). The oppression we experienced as individuals was brought together as a collective whole into our individual and collective healing.

Data Collection and Analysis

Lisa and David collected data through written correspondence, messages, phone calls, journal entries, and Skype meetings throughout the course of a year. We met on a weekly basis for several months utilizing my (Lisa's) master thesis as a tool, *A Narrative and Poetic Exploration into Self-Defining Asperger's: Ceasing to be X-1.* This thesis was memoed and our dialogue increased as time progressed. Our data was comprised of narratives, poems, and emotion-laden talk, recollections were engaged in written thoughts, and combined questions and answer sessions.

Each author individually analyzed the data prior to coming together to share thoughts, feelings, and inner realizations. Journal entries, past and new poems created for this study, and our individual correspondence provided a road map for us to wrestle with our own journey of reconciliation.

Narrative Methodology

It is through the use of narrative conceptualization we restored our life events and made meaning and stepped towards becoming more whole individuals (Polkinghorne, 1991). "Narrative inquirers strive to attend to the ways in which a story is constructed; for whom and why, as well as the cultural discourse that it draws upon" (Trahar, 2009, p. 2). Narrative writing declines the instinct to summarize and justify, instead emphasizing the individual's journey over the destination (Trahar, 2012). This practice of narrative offered the authors opportunities to be honest in a way no other methodology can. Narrative methodology offers opportunities to assign meaning to the events in our lives (Andrews, Squire, & Tambokou, 2008). Our narrative writing broke down our false self–perceptions and shed light, offering opportunities for inner revelation. The use of narrative methodology answers the questions raised through an in-depth examination of self (Andrews et al., 2008; Polkinghorne, 1991; Trahar, 2009). Narrative research design offers an opportunity to tell and share our stories and answer the questions that drive our research.

1. What are the experiences of being labeled with a learning disability at the intersections of other marginalized identities?
2. What implications do our felt-experiences have for critically reflecting on pain and privilege for educational contexts and equity?

It is through our memories and our collective sharing that we formed our narrative, this tapestry of thoughts, feelings, and the reconciling of our LD experiences at our intersections. We carried out this process, between the two of us, through careful examination and connected inner levels of trust. The essence of narrative methodology is trust when doubt enters acknowledging that freedom is the other side of fear. Narrative methodology combines the construct of Freire's praxis, "which, as the reflection and action which truly transforms reality, the source of knowledge and creation" (Freire, 2008, p. 100).

Emotion-Laden Talk

Emotion-laden talk is comprised of reflections, meta-talk, meta-affective-talk, commentary, and personal narratives about a specific topic (e.g., LD, language, race, etc.) that include emotionality (Edwards, 1999; Prior, 2016). These constitute an emotion discourse (Moir, 2015). Emotion discourse constitutes the reactions, responses, opinions, etc. of the topic at hand and these occur within social practices (Moir, 2005). In our case, it would be within the discursive social and emotional practices of LD at the intersections within educational contexts (e.g., Reid & Valle, 2005). Critically reflecting on, talking about, and feeling our pain and privilege experiences to create new knowledge about what it means and feel to be labeled LD at our intersections of marginalized identities is critical to not only inform theory, research, and practice, but to heal from the vortex of dehumanizing messages within society and educational spaces that stigmatized us (Hurd, 2012). In other words, this dual autoethnographic piece allowed us to conceptualize our voices as both emotion-laden talk and narrative given that ours and others' like us who have been labeled perspectives are hardly given power within the hegemonic structures in the canon of special education and the academy. My (David's) dialogue with myself and society's master narratives about what counts as LD through my construction of emotion-laden talk is epistemological and serves as my critical analysis of my life experiences at the intersections of LD, ethnicity, and language within educational contexts (Freire, 2000).

LISA'S NARRATIVE

The Role of Resiliency

What is the role of resiliency in the narrative of an individual diagnosed with a learning disability? How does resiliency impact the individual's journey of identity? How does resiliency impact an individual's journey from "self"-perceiving victim to non-victim? Through resiliency I was able to adapt, manage, and mobilize my inner resources in the face of challenges, adversity, while overcoming negative outcomes (American Psychological Association, 2016; Morrison & Cosden, 1997; Rutter, 2012). The diagnosis of a learning disability brings each one of those words into the mirror of self, the mirror of identity formation, and the trauma of diagnosis.

Resiliency and Trauma

Inside the framework of recovery, I conceptualized theoretical approaches (Liu, Reed, & Girard, 2017; Rutter, 1987). Prior to my learning disability (LD) diagnosis as a child the othering I experienced was traumatic. My experiences of trauma renewed during my LD diagnosis process. While moments of resiliency occurred, my rise from victim to victor took years.

However, its ramifications shaped my internal and external foundations of self my entire childhood and adulthood. This self I had so desperately hoped I hide from the world. The critical reflexivity of pain and privilege. I had privilege because of my access to higher education and all it can offer. This privilege was masked in the shadows of hurt and pain.

FROM VICTIM TO VICTOR: TRANSFORMATION

Questions

There is power in the asking of questions. They open pathways of deeper understanding and inner revelations that helped me transform my LD diagnosis now 13 years ago. My breadth of knowledge on LD was limited to my experience and framed in the office of my community college's Disability Studies and Services building. I formed a construction of identity under the umbrella of deficit thinking and believing as feelings of marginalization, and victim hood connected into feelings of shame. Every child knows which of their peers are "smarter" and which kids are in "the other group" (Hatt, 2016; Leonard & Broderick, 2011). It is this often silent knowing that grips at the very core of an individual's feelings and construction of self-identity. Children are not aware of the word victim, but children are aware of feelings of marginalization and victimhood (Heshusius & Ballard, 1996). My adult self knew what the word victim meant. It would take a journey to reclaim the self and identity I had created before the shift to victor. I formed my identity and a deeper experience of self, when I heard the words, "Lisa you have an Learning Disability in perceptual organization", from the LD "specialist" and "expert". In that moment something inside of me began to shift, an overwhelming feeling of *less than* flooded my whole being. This was the moment my identity became marginalized, the moment of deep pain. Therefore, how did I define the word victim? Who is a victim? How does a definition shape the foundations of identity? Victim comes from the Latin *victim* Webster's dictionary. Later modern etymology of the word includes descriptions of a crime (Nansh, 2008). While working through my LD experiences as an undergraduate and master's student, having an *LD felt like a crime*. The crime was my inner adaption of my false beliefs of self and the identity I formed. I placed my own vulnerability like a curtain around my soul and mind. It would take years before the curtain would fall back and cease to hold me hostage.

The Curtain Pulls Back

Through the entranceway, truth continues to tumble out taking a journey I never knew was possible. While I graduated with my associate's degree and then my Bachelor of Science degree, I still held my inner feelings of marginalization combined with an inner feeling I was a victim, not a victor, in the acceptance of my LD. The curtain pulls back, decades of internalized shame and feelings of worthless began its dismemberment. This process of deconstruction begun so long ago, yet took decades in its arrival, like a long-delayed rain to a scorched earth, waiting for release that finally presented. I formed my constructs of the world through experience. This is my living and breathing constructionist epistemology, with which foundation I found comfort and peace to all I am and all I am becoming and who I yet will become. The person who realized I am more than my LD diagnosis and all my internalized feelings of shame that I constructed my identity out from, this breaking and deconstruction of privilege.

MY IDENTITY

Ethnic Identity

I am a third generation Croatian American who is also part German. My Croatian family values also shaped my identity formation through helping others and being my best self. Being known as a Boskovich and all the family pride connected to my last name plays a role in my identity. My favorite Great Aunt Annie told me when I was 18 that, "I too would make a name for myself as a Boskovich, just as the family business stands as a leader in the agricultural industry as Boskovich Farms". I also cannot ignore my standing as a woman of privilege. I do not necessarily define myself. I see myself through the lens of being a whole person not through the lens of being White.

Thoughts on Privilege

As a White woman pursuing a Ph.D. in education, I acknowledge my own sense of privilege while still remaining keenly aware of White males who hold privilege over me. It is my responsibility as a researcher to be aware of how my privilege as a White female may be interpreted by others. I believe we as people, as individuals, are responsible for our interactions and how we form the ideas held on race and privilege. My views of normality are based upon all the experiences in my life as I continue interacting in society. The terms I use do: "control our perceptions, shape our understanding, and lead us to particular proposals for improvement" (Haberman, 2000, p. 203). My best self is the self that continues to grow and challenge my assumptions of White privilege. As I continue asking the following internal questions: What is my role as a woman with the benefits of white privilege? How does this privilege unconsciously impact my daily life? I acknowledge the existence of racism in U.S. society and in education (Milner, 2007). In my research, I am aware of the interplaying and connecting factors as a White woman as I continue my engaging and evolving praxis as an educational researcher. I as a White woman have tremendous privilege, I acknowledge this. This self-reflection stands upon the shoulders of all who have walked before me. This process requires critical reflection, so my actions can transform reality (Freire, 2008).

Intersectionality of Identity

The development of identity is complex process. There are personal questions to be asked and answered (Erickson, 1959/1994). How is identity constructed? What is the evolving process in the intersectionality of identity and learning disability? Identity and labels wrap around us, like slots marked in chosen ink, not always by our hand. Across the page did the nip of the pen sail, without thought or hesitation; its course set to true north. Who are we? How do the intersectionality of identity and labels mark us? Perhaps, the dependency rests upon the shoulders of the labels receiver not the giver of possible identity? Still, experiences of marginalization cannot be ignored or downplayed as they occurred in both our educational settings. What happened when my invisible disability played a role in my identity formation and intersected with my other identities?

Lisa's Experience of Disability Oppression

Labeled
Test scores determined
An LD in Perceptual Organization
What if the test scores were wrong?
What if they only represented a fraction of truth?
A slice of a fraction,
½ of a lie,
Wasn't I a whole person?
How was that missed?
This inner question
Persists.
Accommodations felt like separation

Visual you are different
Tests taken elsewhere set me apart
I didn't want to be separate
But needed quiet and more time
Produced Deficit feeling
DSPS advisor watching
Through a closely guarded lens
I was so much more
Than a graph
Representing LD test scores.
(Boskovich, 2013)

My Accommodations

My accommodations during my undergraduate years, both at the community college and undergraduate level, granted me services. However, those specific services of extended time and a separate room for quiet resulted in feelings of marginalization and experienced ostracism. I was not separate from my learning challenges. They are as much a part of me as my gender or the color of my eyes. This separation failed to recognize disability as a living entity of self: dis/ability as pride and identity. The whole person or self-moves freely inside disability. Was I the only person for whom accommodations were made? The whole supposition of disability accommodations is to strive for equal opportunities. However, it still excludes those it strives to serve by segregating individuals in special separate test-taking rooms. I asked not to be isolated in my difference but to be embraced as being different.

Invisible Disability

Invisible or hidden disabilities, according to Lingsome (2008) and Valeras (2010), are impairments combining able bodied appearances with disability, resulting in few visual identifiers. Valeras (2008) defined "a "hidden disability", one unapparent to outside observers, defies the outward social construction of disability (p. 1). After I received my LD diagnosis, I experienced feelings of confusion and feelings of learning inferiority (Olney & Brockelman, 2003). The privilege of another, the LD specialist, to label me and my later breaking free of the chains of diagnosis and her privileged positionality. The positionality of help while under her glances for four years and my desperate wanting to be perceived as intelligent and worthy. This presentation of self-began to crack eroding and chipping deeper away as the years changed from one to another. This process is challenging for those who identify with a hidden or invisible disability. Still this intersection remains one of fluidity and I call upon my internal aspects of resiliency in learning acquisition and disability negotiation. The formation of identity is a lifetime and multifaceted progression.

The Voice of Self

My voice is expressed through the discourse that "truth or meaning, comes into existence in and out of our engagement with the realities of our world. There is no meaning without a mind. Meaning is not discovered, but constructed" as a Constructionist (Crotty, 1998, pp. 4–5). This epistemology supports an individual's right to make choices and encourages their own journey of meaning making (McWilliams, 2016). This voice of self, framed after hours of thoughts and experiences expressed through words written in narrative, poems and in academic assignments, I found the pathway to freedom and release.

While writing my master's thesis I wrote the poem *Continuous Variable*. My inner dialogue was beginning to mirror my exterior dialogue. The first moments of freedom had begun to arrive.

Continuous Variable
For once there is no documented evidence
No test scores
No scatter plots or bar graphs
To measure me against another
No standard deviation away from the mean to compute

$$\sigma = \frac{\sum (x - \mu)^2}{N}$$

My choice to define
My choice to explain
Just what it means to be me
I claim my own self now
I am my own Qualitative variable
I am n-1 degrees of freedom
The student's t-Distribution
I am my own measure of central tendency
Not defined by anyone
But by me
My own Bell-Shaped Curve
The Entranceway to Reclaiming Self
(Boskovich, 2015)

Victor

Quietly the moments of truth stack up like dominions waiting for that final push, the final movement to descend. Those hours turn into days as day turn into the accumulation of years. How many teachers and professors does it take before we can make a shift in identity? How many classroom hours did I spend wondering what was wrong with me? The direct answer would amount to thousands and many hundreds of thousands. The sky began to clear as the cobwebs began shifting around their decadence like water dripping down into a puddle. It happened through many conversations I had with my mentor in graduate school during my Master in Special Education degree. Those conversations helped me realize my LD diagnosis was contained in pieces of paper, a folder with statistical graphs, whose picture was incomplete. Those graphs failed to tell my whole story. They were only a fraction of a pie not the entire picture.

One-Evening

One evening I heard this inside of my mind, "I am no longer – a victim". I am worthy. I am intelligent, and I have the capacity to help others. This is part of my journey teaching fellow educators by my life experiences. Individuals who have an LD learn differently; however, we are not different. This is the hegemony of normalcy at work, not something "wrong" with me. Every individual is unique and their inner journey out of pain requires so much time, effort, energy, and the steadfast belief in self. This rise of resiliency as a greater capacity to heal from the years of doubts and pain. The moments only known to self and the privileged structures schematically set in place kept me in a LD box. The box where being a victim was an option I took on due to the master narratives of LD. I had no idea there was another way. It took a shift inside to realize I was never at any point a victim. I had taken on the positionality of victimhood supported by the very supports and accommodations my LD gave to assist my learning acquisition. The moment I realized I was no longer a victim, it was as though the earth shifted on its axis.

Questions

In seeing myself as a victim no longer, how will this shift change the perceptual lens in how I view and construct the image of self? How will this shedding impact the internalized view I had to hold? The ability to change the perception we hold of self is a testament to the inner modalities of resiliency we as individuals usher forth. I drew upon the voice of self who finally after years was heard and embraced as valid. I was the only one who could validate myself.

DAVID'S EMOTION-LADEN TALK

How Can I Heal?
My body and mind and spirit are connected
I am healed through theory
I am healed through being myself
I am

I am healed through my utterances
I am healed through listening
I am healed through music
I am healed through my ways through words

I am healed through critical emotion praxis
The pain just beneath the surface
I am healed through my movements of my body
I am healed through reading critical theory

I am healed through allowing my words to express how I feel
I heal through teaching
I am healed by following my spirit
By following my spirit I am my consciousness

I am healed through releasing through language and emotion
Emotion is epistemological and not something to be tamed
I am difference at the epistemological, ontological, axiological and etiological
Foundations that make up who I am

How we talk to each other matters
What we say and how we say it at the emotions and language
What we say to ourselves, not in an individualistic way that reinforces the medical
model
But a psycho-emotional disablism that is cognizant of the intersections

The intersectional disability discourses at the structural level
How we make feeling-meaning making together
How we love each other and ourselves for equity, justice and liberation
For all

I am; we are
Critical emotion praxis for consciousness transformation
Listening to our hearts and minds
Past, present and future
For emotion language use that is non-violent to other and self

My pain and privilege
My male privilege; my colorism privilege
My going to a well-resourced school privilege
My having an education from UC Berkeley privilege

My having a Ph.D. privilege
My having confidence privilege about certain areas of my life, but having
psychological damage regarding the symbolism of a Learning Disability and
Special Education
My having a job privilege and having had a loving mom privilege

My having loving brothers and sisters privilege
My having gotten my US citizenship privilege
Having privilege and having cultural humility about how we construct ourselves and others is of paramount importance since it is creating our worldview/our ideological understanding of the world and our place and relationships within it

However, are these privileges or social constructions that produce particular critical emotional hegemonic orders that divide us from ourselves and each other?
How can we discard such systems of power, privilege, and difference
For individual and societal transformation within the hegemonic order?

Who am I? Feelings of emptiness and violation come to mind when I think about my "LD". People made fun of me. My teachers yelled at me and made me feel worthless. These feelings of worthlessness are a few of my associations with special education and LD that weigh heavy on my heart and soul. I'm tired of carrying it all just beneath the surface. "I have a part in having been labeled with an LD", the master narratives of LD would say (Hernández-Saca, 2016). It's both biological and due to my social interactions within the environment and others. The pain is on my skin and in my bones; body, and mind, and unfortunately, my soul and heart. However, my own reason tells me, "It's for your 'own good;' it's your 'civil right', you are privileged to have been labeled with an LD and provided the services of special education and you should not be complaining". The question, "Who I am?" gets lost in this sea of negative automatic thoughts that lead to feelings of pain, worthlessness, and shame. Where is my true voice and wholeness? Pain and privilege became the double-edged sword I wake to everyday, ever since I learned that I was labeled with an auditory LD and began to experience the stigma of being in special education with all of its intended and unintended consequences.

Going to one of the top school districts in the Bay Area, California, especially for students with disabilities and needing special education services, did not help my self-advocacy and self-determination as it related to my processing of my special education label of LD. Being a first-generation immigrant to the U.S. and growing up a Spanish and English bilingual should not have felt like social locations that made me vulnerable to inequality. This inner world of confusion, pain, and hurt propels me to quest for answers that I know I can only answer, but I have yet to find solace in questions such as: why was I not provided with a culturally relevant education that took my multidimensional ethnicities (El Salvadorian and Palestinian), and other emergent identities into account, but only allowed the hidden curriculum of White-abled-psycho-emotional-bodied-upper-middle class to be the socializing norm that mediated human interaction in my K-12 schooling?

LD Pain

The mental and spiritual drama I experience on a daily basis regarding the stigma of being in special education and LD is the pain I wake to and navigate in order to remain human. The invalidation about my sense of self presented by the labeling and socializing mechanisms within special education is soul crushing. The pain has been with me for a very long time. Within therapy sessions, I close my eyes and I am taken back to my middle-school resource room and the building is on fire. The door is on fire. Feelings of powerlessness come to mind and heart. I know that is in the past and what saves me is coming back to the present moment. Differentiating that this pain is in the past and that I am not the pain helps me move forward and be resilient. Resiliency, however, privileges a psychological perspective and does not consider or disrupt hegemonic structural inequities that did not originate in me or others labeled as such. Who created the master narratives of LD? The majority of those who construct LD in a particular way have hardly engaged in critical emotional reflexivity about issues of power and privilege or how these narratives and texts represent and construct a particular sociocultural milieu that becomes a sticky object (Ahmed, 2004) for those labeled as such. The sticky object (Ahmed, 2004) of LD has objectified me to myself. However, from a Disability Studies in Education approach to dis/ability that foregrounds the psycho-emotional disablism that I experience due to the master narratives of LD, I receive a level of distance to that pain (Hernández-Saca, 2016; Hernández-Saca & Cannon, 2016). From an autoethnographic approach, what I am experiencing and "my" emotionality – my LD pain – is not necessarily my own (Ahmed, 2004). Dominant cultural assumptions about the nature of emotionality constrain those experiencing stigma and other mental health categories as situating the problem within their neurology and bodies, as opposed to reframing how we conceptualize the relationship between dis/ability and emotionality more broadly. This frame helps me come to a different horizon and critical emotional consciousness about my LD pain to release it. However, why does it come back?

Privilege

What is privilege? Privilege positions one internally and externally as being superior to others. This is not only at the discursive and material levels, but at the emotional level, and I would argue, part of the spiritual dimension of being human or not. Privilege comes in many shapes and sizes – economic, social, cultural, and psychological, both real and imagined. These each funnel to instating the status quo within a society and lead to a particular (re)presentation about who one is and who others are. This dialectic creates the "Other" and has led throughout her/history to physical and symbolic violence among human beings. The self is not singular. The self is multiple and intersectional (Crenshaw, 1989; Hernández-Saca et al., 2018) and experiences the structural, political, and personal levels of the social structure in qualitatively different ways and in spiritual, affective, and emotionally radically different ways (Hernández-Saca & Cannon, in press; Erevelles, 2011; Erevelles & Minear, 2010).

My history with LD can be considered a double-edged sword. On the one hand, I am mad, in the Mad Studies sense (Menzies, LeFrançois, & Reaume, 2013), and feel the pain of my LD as a haunting that just won't go away; but at the same time, I feel trapped in a liminal space that has imprisoned me to the power of LD's negative stigma. As I write, my neck stiffens, and heart begins to beat faster as I remember the invalidations from colleagues and "mentors" who minimized my pain. However, I can no longer give power to those in authority, when I am the authority of my life and the framing of who I am. Who I am has become conflated with my LD pain, history, and structuring socialization of being in a resource room that to this day I hate and, in the past, hated. Expressing these feelings is important; if we keep our emotionality about any topic inside it creates a disturbance – however, the canon of special education would have it that then, I deserve to be in special education. Given that you are "emotionally disturbed" – nothing could be further from the truth. My soul was shattered by the labels and symbolism of special education such as the "privilege" of accommodations, having a "least restrictive environment", having one-on-one help and being socialized into being a "special needs" kid. When I recall my 7th grade special education room and special education teacher, my mind sees the room filled with fire. My soul is split into pieces. I will not be silent any longer about how my teachers yelled at me and did not see my humanity.

To learn is a privilege. The affective atmosphere within educational contexts, and especially within stigmatized spaces such as the special education basement and, in turn, its place within society's "mind" left me utterly dehumanized and feeling worthless. The canon of special education would say, "Oh, you have these emotional issues, then you are a kiddo in need of being found" (e.g., "child find"). Did anyone ask me if I wanted to be found? Or was it how I was found that created a sense of inferiority about my abilities? Our voices or emotion-laden talk matter to enter into a new space of liberation given how society and educational spaces have constructed the meanings and feelings of being students with LD. We sense it. We feel it in our bones – our otherness and exclusion – both physical and psychological. This represents the social construction of LD and LD emotions – that do not originate within sentient beings such as human being who are on a journey of learning. Yes, learning, not learning differently or learning disabled – *learning*. We are not incomplete, we are whole just the way we are regardless of our cognitive dis/abilities.

My Intersections

As a gay, Palestinian and Salvadorian immigrant to the U.S., and as a fairly recent U.S. citizen, who is bilingual in Spanish and English, I sense my otherness every day from the dominant cultural ways of being, doing, and feeling within institutions such as educational contexts. This is not only what is visible but invisible as well. Assumptions about each of these attempts to kill my spirit and denies who I am on a daily basis. However, my cultural and social practices from my family have formed who I am today. Coming to the U.S. as a refugee due to the civil war in El Salvador during the 1980s has shaped how I experience dominant experiences that rendered my intersectional identities invisible due to the hegemonic structure of abled-bodied, heterosexual, White-upper-class and English-speaking norms within the U.S. This is due to the fact that the law does not take an intersectional approach. This erasure positions me and those like me without a recognition of such experiences being valid within the social and emotional imaginary of the law in general, but within special education law even more. My intersectional identities would situate my writing within the larger educational system as experiencing what has been known as a high-incidence disability such as LD (Artiles, 2013; Blanchett, Klingner, & Harry, 2009; Hernández-Saca & Cannon, in press). Where was my bilingual education? Where was my multicultural education? How were my funds of knowledge activated to help me develop my intersectional disability identity? Nowhere and None. Given the medical model of disability institutionalization within U.S. society and education, my development of a critical consciousness about my auditory LD and special education history did not occur until I was an undergraduate.

LD at the Intersections

Special and general education can no longer ignore the salience of other identity markers that historically marginalized youth and their families at the intersections bring with them to school. This is only so because of the Whiteness at the intersections, which is the bloodline of the history of U.S. schools (Tyack, 1974) and special education (Artiles, 1998; Artiles et al., 2016; Patton, 1998). The structural ways dis/ability at its intersections is constructed in the minds of others is of paramount significance. The neoliberal and capitalist underpinnings that structure relationships in society contributes to these structural ways. Human interactions and relationships at the nexus of dis/ability with other historically marginalized identities should be aligned with radical true love for self, other(s), and the world through *care, knowledge, human dignity, and freedom* (Fromm, 1956). This is what I attempt to do on a daily basis, so I won't lose my humanity and so my spirit and soul are not completely destroyed. Writing about my disability at my intersections is healing. I must continue to write. I cannot let the fear in/of my LD destroy hope to live, to not be afraid any longer. Undoing and unlearning my LD at my intersections will be my life journey but with radical love, community, friends, and colleagues such as Lisa and others who have helped me find the courage to keep going. I know I can heal. I can't lose hope for a better tomorrow.

Intersectional Dis/ability Bullying

During my early childhood, I remember being made fun of and called a "retard" and "LD" by my siblings and school peers. The cruelty with which we treat one another based on assumptions regarding disability rips at our souls and does not allow us to be spiritually healthy. All the false messages about who I am were thrown at me, as if I was not even there. I can't hold in all of my thoughts about how I was treated any longer. My spirit just wants to keep writing in order to heal. Being reminded about all of the negative ways my Salvadorian and Palestinian ethnicity are part of the matrix of oppression (Collins, 2000) within the U.S. social imagination leads to a loss of identity. We can't conflate my rich sociocultural experiences that created my intersectional identities, sense of self and who I am with how I was treated and how the hegemonic order constructs students and people at my intersections as such. Being in special education sucks! It positions one as the "Other" and the vulnerability is ever-present.

Stepping towards Healing

Stepping towards healing represents my current intentionality to transform my relationship with LD. For the past several years, I have gone to therapy to talk about my LD. In retrospect, this has been a safe space for me to talk about my LD and grapple with, even if I want to claim LD as an identity. Obviously, the system of special education gave me a label of auditory LD. I have come to rationalize this as due to having had convulsions when I was younger and then being put on anticonvulsant medication. Reading Ignacio Calderón-Almendros and Rafael Calderón-Almendros' (2016) article about a resilient young musician, Rafael, who happens to have Down syndrome. However, like me, he decided to put that label aside and just be himself as opposed to internalizing the negative messages that society has about his dis/ability (e.g., Calderón-Almendros & Ruiz-Roman, 2015). His story helped me step forward toward healing and that I am not just making this up, that others feel and sense the same way as I do about the labels and pathologization that takes place with the dominant ways individuals with disabilities are socially constructed in society. As I was writing this piece, I realized that theory is important to me given my fear and trauma due to my labeling of an auditory LD and being in special education. Theory has served as a way to heal and put everything in context.

DISCUSSION

Historically, marginalized voices have been silenced by tools of exclusion that included the very language and knowledge about what counts as Learning Disabilities (LD). LD has been myoptically understood as an individual and neurological entity, as opposed to being explicit about how power, privilege, and difference have structured the experiences of people with LD. How one experiences any social identity marker is qualitatively different to who they are, but at the same time connected to the common sense cultural assumptions about their social group and identities. McDermott, Goldman, and Varenne (2006) have studied the role of culture and LD and posit how culture both affords and constraints individual students. In particular, those at the intersections of disability, class, and race within educational contexts that have pre-determined understandings and categories for what each of these feel like, look like, sound like, and the educational trajectories would be. Our narratives and emotion-laden talk involved how dominant structures of compliance, behavior management, and overall structures of a White-abled-psycho-emotional-bodied-upper-middle class ways of being, doing, and feeling have constructed society's understanding of what is normal. Historically, LD, public special education, and general education have ignored the role of sociocultural factors in how children and young adults with disabilities at their intersections experience the arrangements and sociocultural contexts of schooling, both internal and external (Connor, 2008). We can no longer conflate the rich sociocultural milieus that students come to school with them as "deficit" and something to be "fixed", controlled, predicated, remediated, and intervened (Taylor, Ferguson, & Ferguson, 1992).

Our Unique Journeys

We each come with our own biographies, emotions, feelings, histories, social identities, among others – in short, our own pain and privileges at the intersections of LD, race, ethnicity, language, and social class. Each of these structured our experiences, in both positive and negative ways, within society and educational contexts as it related to hegemony. To reflect on our experiences is to enter into a *third narrative and emotion-laden talk space* to be meta-affective, meta-cognitive, meta-emotional, meta-narrative, and meta-spiritual to heal through the writing process and speaking our truths regardless of the fear within. The latter of which did not originate in us but are those perceptions and assumptions others have socially constructed in their head about us at our intersections. To gain power over our own lives about who we are is emancipatory and liberatory in nature that should always be critical of hegemonic assumptions structured in relationship that lead to dehumanization of self and others. Due to the power of the medical model at its intersections along other systems of oppression, our unique stories illuminate how pain and privilege worked through others to constrain our view of ourselves within situated contexts. Nevertheless, we were always ourselves; our unique selves unfettered at our core that told us a different story about who we were. This reality has pushed us to resist; to deconstruct to construct a counter-narrative and emotion-laden talk that leads to our authenticity, so we do not lose our humanity.

"You Are in Pain. Therefore, You Are"

Tuck and Yang (2013) discuss Gayatri Spivak's question, *Can the Subaltern Speak?* as it relates to the relationship between decolonizing research methods. This book chapter illustrates our beginning journey to this question as an affirmative: *yes, we can*. Nevertheless, Tuck and Yang (2013) caution researchers who are working with indigenous communities to not speak for and misrepresent not only answers to this question, but what and how the pain of indigenous communities have been used. They state:

> The costs of a politics of recognition that is rooted in naming pain have been critiqued by recent decolonizing and feminist scholars … Guthrie (1976) traces

65

the roots of psychology to the need to "scientifically" prove the supremacy of the White mind. The origins of many social science disciplines in maintaining logics of domination, while sometimes addressed in graduate schools, are regularly thought to be just errant or inauspicious beginnings – much like the ways in which the genocide of Indigenous peoples that afforded the founding of the United States has been reduced to an unfortunate byproduct of the birthing of a new and great nation. (p. 228)

As historically marginalized people at our intersections, we are cognizant of the importance of voice within our discipline and as it relates to social science research. We are aware that we don't want to (re)produce the exploitation of our own voices and pain within the academy. This has been the relationship that social science research has had with historically marginalized youth and communities regarding their social problems and suffering. This has been problematic when those who construct knowledge about our experiences do so without considering the real lives behind those labeled as such at the intersections. The flip side of pain is well-being and happiness through healing. How can we turn towards healing?

CONCLUSIONS

To Heal through the Power of Mentoring

To heal is a choice and a process; it requires a steadfast belief in self that inner change is possible. This healing process looked into the feelings and face of pain, experiences of marginalization and the drive to understand self. To recognize that I (Lisa) was indeed a whole person, not a determination based on learning disability charts and results, freed my soul. This is the challenge for many individuals who have been diagnosed with a LD, how to walk the road? How does one decide to look at painful experiences that shape the interior landscape of self? It begins first with the acknowledging of the circumstances that brought the pain to the surface. It was the role of mentors in my life that continue to an impact my journey of healing. One sentence from a mentor impacted my life soon after my LD diagnosis. Alison Williams said, "Lisa, you do not have an LD in perceptual organization; your brain learns differently, and we are going to find a way for you to learn" (Boskovich, 2015). However, it was years later I (Lisa) understood the full impact of her words. To heal is to recognize the worth of self while trusting the journey.

The process of identity negotiation is filled with twists and turns, nights of contemplation filled with questions that drive our souls and mind. Who am I? How does my disability impact my life as an individual? How does the power of diagnosis offer and provide opportunities for growth? Who I am is ever changing and evolving. The acceptance of having a LD takes time and the belief that overcoming self-doubt is not only a possibility but a reality. Our experiences of marginalization impacted the formation of our identity. The negotiation of identity requires an honest looking into the deep passage ways of self. This negotiation requires a throwing off of the false self -acquired through LD diagnosis combined with our internal feelings of difference and fear. These internalized fears have the potential to shut down an individual's forward growth motion. I (Lisa) and David looked in the mirror and after years of false beliefs, we reclaimed ourselves and in doing so redefined our multiple identities and healed.

"Resistance, When Balancing the Scale, Becomes Resilience"
(Calderón-Almendros & Ruiz-Román, 2015, p. 255)

When teaching, it is important to remember that all children and human beings are within processes of becoming. Freire (2000) would remind us that everyone is in the vocational process of becoming human, given the dehumanization processes within structural relationships that are embedded with power, privilege, and difference. Students are aware, especially those at the margins of society and within hegemonic structures, both internal and external, of "normality", and who are valued and who are not (Delpit, 1988). We can no longer interpret "deviance", "misbehavior" or "difference" as something to be tamed. Individual and collective expression, freedom, interdependence, and unity, are fundamental human, emotional, social, cultural, and spiritual dimensions of teaching and learning for all students, especially for individuals labeled (or mis-labeled and non-labeled) at their intersections. The balance between one's autoethnographic self within master narratives at the intersections of LD, language, race, ethnicity, social class, and other social locations, positionalities, and relationships – that are cultural in nature – is developing and enacting one's voice and in so doing engaging in *"resistance ... [in] balancing the scale"* (Calderón-Almendros & Ruiz-Román, 2015, p. 255) and in turn embodying *a lived, in the now resilience*. This resilience should not be interpreted from a traditional psychological way but one that comes out of the sociocultural, economic, political, emotional, and spiritual life worlds of children at their intersections. This resilience in turn provides individual and social justice that can lead to healing for individual and societal transformation.

IMPLICATIONS

We hope that this book chapter has added to the body of knowledge regarding LD diagnosis and the impact upon the intersectionality of identity. The implications from this duo autoethnographic study are both personal and professional. At the personal level, we both were able to grow and share our individual experiences to reflect and create new knowledge as it relates to LD at our intersections of pain and privilege. We were able to grow as it relates to our self-concepts or what Gee (2001) would call our core-identities. Our personal-trajectories and self-narrativizations within big D Discourse such as within educational contexts and the academy. Sharing our experiences as both personal and political contributed to our understanding of the political nature of such ideological and emotional constructions such as LD, race, social class, language, and emotionality. At the professional level, this study contributes to both theory and research about the emotional impacts of LD labeling and diagnosis at the intersections. There has been a lack of personal narratives from those living with LD at their intersections. The lived experiences of those at the intersections of LD and other historically marginalized identities should ground the LD knowledge base, practices and policies of school systems. Policies and practices should not be from a medical model only but one that accounts for students with LD sociocultural contexts and identities and emotionalities. This study contributes to beginning to reimagine what it means to experience LD pain and privilege at the intersections. Autoethnography helped us situate our experiences not only as our own but to speak back to our socialization within the system to transition into a new self and system understanding that is more life-giving as opposed to pathological. In so doing, we were agentive within the master narratives of LD at their intersections.

Based on our intersectional and mixed identity experiences and LD, there are several implications for the middle school years that historically marginalized youth and students with LD at their intersections. Middle school years is a time of transition, growth and identity development. How might middle school special and general educators better teach and be fully present to youth with LD at their intersection with the similar pains and privileges that we outlined above? From our DSE, sociohistorical and interdisciplinary approach it would be of paramount significance to emphasize the importance and lack of attention given within the canon and practice of special education and general education to the (1) intersectional disability development, (2) importance of understanding intersectional oppression and trauma on the internal and external lives of children with disabilities in a highly formative time period of middle school years, (3) the importance of situating a psycho-emotional and relational model of dis/ability that foregrounds the emotional and social context of teaching and learning as involving emotionality and the importance of using inclusive pedagogies and philosophies such as Universal Design for Learning (e.g., Provide Multiple Means of Representation [the "what" of learning], Provide Multiple Means of Action and Expression [the "how" of learning], and Provide Multiple Means of Engagement [the "why" of learning]) (see the National Center for Universal Design for Learning at http://www.udlcenter.org) and neurodiversity. According to Armstrong (2012):

> The neurodiversity paradigm suggests that we take the positive attitudes and beliefs that most people hold about biodiversity and cultural diversity and apply them to differences among human brains. We don't look at a calla lily and say that it has "petal deficit disorder"; we appreciate its beautiful shape. We don't say that a person with a different skin color from our own has a "pigmentation disability"; that would be racist. Similarly, we shouldn't label students as ADHD or as learning dis-abled, for example, just because they

have different ways of paying attention or learning. Instead, we ought to honor and celebrate those differences. (p. 12)

Through the neurodiversity paradigm special and general educators, and we argue, all stakeholders, system-wide, can focus on students with LD at their intersections *strengths as resilience* towards pain and oppression due to how the system has structured the status quo along privilege. One way of doing this is by using cumulative files (Armstrong, 2012). Armstrong (2012) explains that cumulative files would focus on their interests, abilities, talents, and strengths. Pre-service and in-service special and general education teachers can do this through (transition) portfolios with samples of work, photos, DVDs or YouTube videos of students' accomplishments, person-centered Making Actions Plans (MAPS) (see http://pcp.sonoranucedd.fcm.arizona.edu), Planning Alternative Tomorrows with Hope (PATHs) (see http://pcp.sonoranucedd.fcm.arizona.edu) etc. Student-led Individual Education Programs (IEPs) meetings or appreciative inquiry IEPs. There is a growing body of literature on student-led IEPs that foreground the voices of students with disabilities as opposed to foregrounding the voices of their parents or the adults in the room (see Cavendish, Connor, & Rediker, 2016). Armstrong defines appreciative inquiry IEPs as "a method of focusing individualized education program (IEP) meetings on strengths, hopes, and interests" (p. 13). In other words, overall, each of these implications would assist in creating special and general educators to design and develop authentic and genuine relationships between students with disabilities at their intersections, that ground a systems critique to the macro, mess, and micro interactions and communications that s/he has with students with disabilities at their intersections and their families.

Each of these implications can work in tandem as educators on the ground make important moment to moment decisions as they engage in communication with students with disabilities at their intersections and their families for a positive inclusive praxis within educational systems, that is, critical reflection between they act, in the broad sense of the term. This would include being sensitive to the range of both positive and negative emotions, feeling, and affects that students experience and allowing students to feel safe and be who are and becoming as they engage in what it means to be a student with LD at their intersections. This is critical when traditional habits of mind and dispositions tend to constrain students' agency within educational contexts and unfortunately reproduce the status quo in and outside of schools. Allowing students to be themselves and in turn self-determine and self-advocate (e.g., have a say in academic, social and emotional decision making in short and long-term goals) through such implications would be a way to operationalize our sociohistorical approach/lens. In doing so, our work is descriptive of how "schools" can look like, sound like, and feel like, for the larger purpose of operationalizing inclusion within local contexts.

Although we point to specific "solutions", "strategies", and "practices" is it of critical importance to conceptualize practice as praxis, critical thinking before one acts within educational contexts that are sociohistorical in nature at the intersections. However, there are models out there such as middle grades philosophy. Middle grades philosophy is a model to educate young adolescents as outlined within the *National Middle School Association* (NMSA, 2010) position paper executive summary and chart, *This We Believe: Keys Educating Young Adolescents Essential Attributes and 16 Characteristics.* Although the movement started around the 1960s in the U.S., the philosophy itself and its ideals have nevertheless been around since 1893 (Ellis Hurd, personal communication, May 18, 2018). However, we resist "prescribing" a middle school philosophy that would be a one-size fits all approach. As our reflections about pain and privilege have taught us there is a need for a systemic and pedagogical approach through praxis. This approach places the emphasis on critical reflection on ourselves within the system and on the system as system critique for continuous improvement of our intersection and communications toward a more perfect inclusion of all! In other words, our study and its implications are getting to the question of what counts as being a human within educational systems that label and sort in order to answer our research questions, actually.

Pre-service and in-service general and special education teachers' development of critical consciousness about serving students with LD at their intersections is of paramount significance for providing students with their free and appropriate education and implementing their least restrictive environment according to IDEA. Moving forward policies and practices cannot ignore the emotional life of children and adults with LD at their intersections and how "experts" interact with them within educational contexts. In particular on not causing psychological damage which (re)produces psycho-emotional disablism and other forms of isms given student's unique constellations of identities that they come to school with. Future research should engage pre-service and in-service general and special education teachers with professional development training that allows them to critically reflect on the lived experiences of students and adults with LD at their intersections so that their praxis – critical thinking and action – is life-giving as opposed to hegemonic.

NOTE

[1]   By dis/ability, we foreground the social construction of both ability and disability from a Disability Studies in Education (DSE) approach. A DSE approach to disability takes a social model of disability as opposed to a medical one. A medical model of disability understands the impairment or the problem within the mind and body of the individual and presumes a need to control, fix, and "normalize" that individual; whereas a social model of disability understands "disability" as natural and the disabling factors are society's assumptions, arrangements, and ideologies about what counts as normal being mechanism of ableism that happens to individuals with disabilities. The social model foregrounds the role of impairments as existing, but, again, constructs real "disability" as sociopolitical, economic, and cultural. Within this study, we take it one step farther, as DSE scholars such as Shakespeare (2006) and Thomas (1999). We understand disability as psycho-emotional disablism. By psycho-emotional disablism Thomas (1999) means "a form of social oppression involving the social imposition of restrictions of activity on people with impairments and the socially engendered undermining of their psycho-emotional well-being" (p. 604).

REFERENCES

Ahmed, S. (2004). *The cultural politics of emotion.* New York, NY: Routledge.

American Psychological Association. (2016). Retrieved from http://www.apa.org

Anderson, L. (2006). Analytic autoethnography. *Journal of Contemporary Ethnography, 35*(4), 373–395. doi:10.1177/089124160528044

Andrews, M., Squire, C., & Tambokou, M. (Eds.). (2008). *Doing narrative research.* London: Sage Publications.

Annamma, S. A., Connor, D., & Ferri, B. (2013). Dis/ability Critical race studies (DisCrit): Theorizing at the intersections of race and dis/ability. *Race Ethnicity and Education, 16*(1), 1–31.

A Person-Centered Arizona: An information and resource site for person-centered thinking, planning, and practices. Retrieved May 21, 2018, from http://pcp.sonoranucedd.fcm.arizona.edu/resources/person-centered-planning-tools/map

Artiles, A. J. (1998). The dilemma of difference: Enriching the disproportionality discourse with theory and context. *The Journal of Special Education, 32,* 32–36.

Artiles, A. J. (2011). Toward an interdisciplinary understanding of educational equity and difference: The case of the racialization of ability. *Educational Researcher, 40*(9), 431–445.

Artiles, A. J. (2013). Untangling the racialization of disabilities: An intersectionality critique across disability models. *DuBois Review, 10,* 329–347.

Artiles, A. J., Dorn, S., & Bal, A. (2016). Objects of protection, enduring nodes of difference: Disability intersections with "other" differences, 1916–2016. *Review of Research in Education, 40,* 777–820.

Artiles, A. J., King-Thorius, K., Bal, A., Waitoller, F., Neal, R., & Hernández-Saca, D. I. (2011). Beyond culture as group traits: Future learning disabilities ontology, epistemology, and research knowledge use. *Learning Disability Quarterly, 34,* 167–179.

Bamberg, M. (2004). Considering counter narratives. In M. Bamberg & M. Andrews (Eds.), *Considering counter-narratives: Narrating, resisting, making sense* (pp. 351–372). Amsterdam: J. Benjamins.

Boskovich, L. (2015). A narrative and poetic exploration into self-defining Asperger's: Ceasing to be X-1. *Educational Studies Dissertations, 3.* Retrieved from https://digitalcommons-chapman-edu.libproxy.chapman.edu/ces_dissertations/3

Burdell, P., & Blue Swadener, B. (1999). Book reviews: Critical personal narrative and autoethnography in education: Reflections on a genre. *Educational Researcher, 28*(6), 21–26.

Calderón-Almendros, I., & Calderón-Almendros, R. (2016). 'I open the coffin and here I am': Disability as oppression and education as liberation in the construction of personal identity. *Disability & Society, 31*(1), 100–115.

Calderón-Almendros, I., & Ruiz-Román, C. (2015). Education as liberation from oppression: Personal and social constructions of disability. In F. Kiuppis & R. Sarromaa Hausstätter (Eds.), *Inclusive education twenty years after Salamanca* (pp. 251–260). New York, NY: Peter Lang.

Cavendish, W., Connor, D. J., & Rediker, E. (2016). Engaging students and parents in transition-focused individualized education programs. *Intervention in School and Clinic, 52*(4), 228–235.

Chang, H., Ngunjiri, F. W., & Hernandez, K. C. (2012). *Collaborative autoethnography.* Walnut Creek, CA: Left Coast Press.

Crotty, M. (1998). Introduction: The research process. In M. Crotty (Ed.), *The foundations of social research: Meaning and perspective in the research process* (pp. 1–17). Thousand Oaks, CA: Sage Publications.

Danforth, S. (2009). *The incomplete child: An intellectual history of learning disabilities.* New York, NY: Peter Lang.

Delpit, L. (1988). The silenced dialogue: Power and pedagogy in educating other people's children. *Harvard Educational Review, 58*(3), 280–299.

Denzin, N. K., & Lincoln, Y. S. (Eds.). (2000). *Handbook of qualitative research* (2nd ed.). Thousand Oaks, CA: Sage Publications.

Dudley-Marling, C. (2004). The social construction of learning disabilities. *Journal of Learning Disabilities, 37*(6), 482–489.

Ellis, C. (2004). *The ethnographic I: A methodological novel about autoethnography.* Lanham, MD: Rowman Altamira.

Ellis, C., & Bochner, A. (2006). Analyzing analytic autoethnogaphy: An autopsy. *Journal of Contemporary Ethnography, 35*(4), 429–449.

Erickson, E. (1959/1994). *Identity and the life cycle.* New York, NY: W. W. Norton & Company.

Ferri, B. A., & Connor, D. J. (2010). "I was the special ed. girl": Urban working-class young women of colour. *Gender and Education, 22,* 105–121.

Ferri, B. A., & Gregg, N. (1998). Women with disabilities: Missing voices. *Women's Studies International Forum, 21,* 429–439.

Freire, P. (2008). *Pedagogy of the oppressed.* New York, NY: Continumm.

Gallagher, D. (2010). Hiding in plain sight: The nature and role of theory in learning disability labeling. *Disability Studies Quarterly, 30*(2). Retrieved from http://www.dsq-sds.org/article/view/1231/1278

Gee, J. P. (2001). Identity as an analytic lens for research in education. *Review of Research in Education, 25,* 99–125.

Goodley, D., Liddiard, K., & Runswick-Cole, K. (2018). Feeling disability: Theories of affect and critical disability studies. *Disability & Society, 33*(2), 197–217.

Haberman, M. (2000, November). Urban schools: Day camps or custodial centers? *Phi Delta Kappan, 82*(3), 203–208.

Hatt, B. (2016). Racializing smartness. *Race Ethnicity and Education, 19*(6), 1141–1148.

Hernández-Saca, D. I. (2016). *Re-framing the master narratives of dis/ability through an emotion lens: Voices of Latina/o students with learning disabilities* (Doctoral dissertation). Temple State University, Arizona.

Hernández-Saca, D. I. (2017). Re-framing the master narratives of dis/ability at my intersections: An outline of a research agenda. *Critical Disability Discourses/Discours critiques dans le champ du handicap, 8,* 1–30. Retrieved from https://cdd.journals.yorku.ca/index.php/cdd/article/view/39723

Hernández-Saca, D. I., & Cannon, M. A. (2016). Disability as psycho-emotional disablism: A theoretical and philosophical review of education theory and practice. In M. Peter (Ed.), *Encyclopedia of educational philosophy and theory.* New York, NY: Springer Publishing.

Hernández-Saca, D. I., & Cannon, M. A. (in press). Interrogating LD and SLI epistemologies: Towards collective dis/ability intersectional emotional, affective, and spiritual autoethnographies for healing. *International Journal of Qualitative Studies in Education.*

Hernández-Saca, D. I., Kahn, L. G., & Cannon, M. A. (2018). Intersectionality dis/ability research: How dis/ability research in education engages intersectionality to uncover the multidimensional construction of dis/abled experiences. *Review of Research in Education, 42,* 286–311.

Heshusius, L., & Ballard, K. (1996). How do we count the ways we know? Some background to the project. In L. Heshusius & K. Ballard (Eds.), *From positivism to interpretivism and beyond: Tales of transformation in educational and social research (The mind-body connection)* (pp. 1–16). New York, NY: Teachers College, Columbia University.

Horn, J. H., & Moss, D. (2015). A search for meaning: Telling your life with learning disabilities. *British Journal of Learning Disabilities, 43*(3), 178. doi:10.1111/bld.12093

Hurd, E. (2012). The reflexivity of pain and privilege. *International Journal of Critical Pedagogy, 4*(1), 36–46. Retrieved from http://libjournal.uncg.edu/ojs/index. php/ijcp/article/view/151

Lemke, J. L. (2013). Thinking about feeling: Affect across literacies and lives. In O. Erstad & J. Sefton-Green (Eds.), *Learning lives: Transactions, technologies, and learner identity* (pp. 57–69). Cambridge: Cambridge University Press.

Leonard, Z., & Broderick, A. (2011). Smartness as property: A critical exploration of intersections between whiteness and disability studies. *Teachers College Record, 113*(10), 2206–2232.

Lingsom, S. (2008). Invisible impairments: Dilemmas of concealment and disclosure. *Scandinavian Journal of Disability Research, 10*(1), 2–16. doi:10.1080/15017410701391567

Liu, J. J., Reed, M., & Girard, T. A. (2017). Advancing resilience: An integrative, multi-system model of resilience. *Personality and Individual Differences, 111,* 111–118. doi:10.1016/j.paid.2017.02.007

Madigan, J. (2005). The intersection of gender, race, and disability: Latina students in special education. *Multiple Voices for Ethnically Diverse Exceptional Learners, 8*(1), 45–60.

McDermott, R., Goldman, S., & Varenne, H. (2006). The cultural work of learning disabilities. *Educational Researcher, 35*(6), 12–17.

McIlveen, P. (2008). Autoethnography as a method for reflexive research and practice in vocational psychology. *Australian Journal of Career Development, 17*(2), 13–20. Retrieved from http://eprints.usq.edu.au/4253/1/McIlveen_2008_AJCD_Autoethnography.pdf

McWilliams, S. A. (2016). Cultivating constructivism: Inspiring intuition and promoting process and pragmatism. *Journal of Constructivist Psychology, 29*(1), 1–29. doi:10.1080/10720537.2014.980871

Menzies, R., LeFrançois, B. A., & Reaume, G. (2013). Introducing mad studies. In R. Menzies, B.A. LeFrançois, & G. Reaume (Eds.), *Mad matters: A critical reader in Canadian mad studies* (pp.1–22). Toronto: CSPI.

Merriam-Webster Dictionary. *Victim.* Retrieved December 1, 2017, from https://www.merriam-webster.com/dictionary/dictionary

Moir, J. (2005). *Moving stories: Emotion discourse and agency. Frontiers of sociology.* In Proceedings of the 37th World Congress of the International Institute of Sociology, Stockholm, Sweden.

Morrison, G. M., & Cosden, M. A. (1997). Risk, resilience, and adjustment of Individuals with learning disabilities. *Learning Disability Quarterly, 20*(1), 43–60. doi:10.2307/1511092

Nash, A. (2008). Victims by definition. *Washington University Law Review, 85*, 1419.

National Middle School Association (NMSA). (2010). *This we believe: Keys educating young adolescents essential attributes* (Position paper executive summary).

National Middle School Association (NMSA). (2010). *This we believe: Keys educating young adolescents 16 characteristics* (Position paper executive summary chart).

Olney, M., & Brockelman, K. (2003). Out of the disability closet: Strategic use of perception management by select university students with disabilities. *Disability & Society, 18*(1), 35–50. doi:10.1080/0968759032000044193

Patton, J. M. (1998). The disproportionate representation of African-Americans in special education: Looking behind the curtain for understanding and solutions. *The Journal of Special Education, 32*(1), 25–31.

Petersen, J. A. (2009). "Ain't nobody gonna get me down": An examination of the educational experiences of four African American women labeled with disabilities. *Equity & Excellence in Education, 42*, 428–442.

Polkinghorne, D. E. (1991). Narrative and self-concept. *Journal of Narrative & Life History, 1*(2–3), 135–153.

Prior, M. T. (2016). *Emotion and discourse in L2 narrative research.* Bristol: Multilingual Matters.

Ravitch, T., & Riggan, E. J. (2012). *Reason and rigor: How conceptual frameworks guide research.* Thousand Oaks, CA: Sage Publications.

Reid, D. K., & Valle, J. W. (2005). The discursive practice of learning disability: Implications for instruction and parent-school relations. *Journal of Learning Disabilities, 37*, 466–481.

Rutter, M. (1987). Parental mental disorder as a psychiatric risk factor. In R. E. Frances & A. J. Hales (Eds.), *American psychiatric association annual review* (Vol. 6, pp. 647–663). Washington, DC: American Psychiatric Press.

Rutter, M. (2012). Resilience as a dynamic concept. *Developmental and Psychology, 24*, 335–344. doi:10.101017/S095459412000028

Taylor, S. J., Ferguson, D., & Ferguson, P. M. (1992). *Interpreting disability: A qualitative reader.* New York, NY: Teachers College Press.

Trahar, S. (2009). Beyond the story itself: Narrative inquiry and auto-ethnography. *Intercultural Research in Higher Education, 10*(1), 1–10.

Tuck, E., & Yang, W. K. (2013). R-words: Refusing research. In D. Paris & M. T. Winn (Eds.), *Humanizing research: Decolonizing qualitative inquiry with youth and communities.* New York, NY: Sage Publications.

Valeras, A. B. (2010). 'We don't have a box': Understanding hidden disability identity utilizing narrative research methodology. *Disability Studies Quarterly, 30*(3–4). Retrieved from http://www.dsq-sds.org/

Valle, J. W., Connor, D. J., & Reid, D. K. (2006). Editors' introduction IDEA at 30: Looking back, facing forward – A disability studies perspective. *Disability Studies Quarterly, 26*(2). (Online)

PART 2

SUPPORTING YOUTH WITH MARGINALIZED IDENTITIES

HWA PYUNG YOO

4. THE UNIDENTIFIED NATIONALITY

Navigating Middle School as a Third Culture Kid

DISCLAIMER

The account that I am about to give is based on my personal experiences and is not meant to speak on behalf of others. In this narrative that depicts my experience navigating middle school as a third culture kid (TCK), it is important to acknowledge the intersectional nature of identities. I cannot seek to isolate the specific effects of my identity as a TCK on my middle school experience. While other factors such as my ethnicity, gender, and socioeconomic status undoubtedly affect such experiences, in taking these factors into account, I seek to provide an account of this overarching experience through a TCK lens. In doing so, I hope that readers, especially educators and researchers in the field, will have more of a basis from which to engage other TCKs and learn more about them. Having lived for my first year in middle school with my family in which the culture promoted within the household was much different from the one promoted within my classroom, and then with host-families whose culture was the same as the one in my classroom for the rest of middle school, my story stands out as a unique one even amongst my TCK peers. However, I believe that the particularity of this experience helps me reflect more carefully and more in-depth the different aspects during this time, while still maintaining the common thread of a TCK navigating middle school throughout the reflection.

THIRD CULTURE KID, ADOLESCENT, KOREAN AMERICAN

Coming into Fort Wayne, Indiana in fourth grade, I had known from the start that I would eventually be leaving. But that was something I had grown used to ignoring. Instead, I allowed myself to get attached to the unending cornfields, the one mall that served as the popular (and only) hangout spot, and the people I had befriended. So, when I came face to face with the fact that our family was moving back to South Korea, it was no grand reveal. It was a reality that I had ignored until then, but it was also a reality that by that point in my life, I had learned to accept. After all, that was what I was used to: coming and going.

Constant movement. That is in many ways what seems to encompass being a TCK for many people, even though that may not be the direct definition. For me at least, the moving has become an integral part of what it means to be a TCK. After

© KONINKLIJKE BRILL NV, LEIDEN, 2019 | DOI:10.1163/9789004393813_004

a while, it stopped being about me following along as my parents relocated, and simply became me seeking it out myself. Change being the one constant in my life, whether this is just a matter of moving within a country or across continents, I have learned to deal with the pain that accompanies it and to see it for the boundless potential that it encompasses. But at that point in my life, I did not see it like that. For some reason, things felt different this time around. Despite having moved schools nearly every year, I could not shake away the heavy heart from which I was typically able to move on.

The Year Leading Up

Just like everyone else. Fourth grade to sixth grade. That was the longest I had ever stayed in one school region. With a middle school that was in the same building as the elementary school I had attended, I was somewhat nervous, but also confident. I had my friends. I was coming in having established a good relationship with my teachers. I was doing well in school, and I was excited to be going *back* to a school, which did not happen often for me.

Regardless of whatever the common assumption might be of the U.S. middle school experience of an adolescent from a non-Western background, my experiences and particularly my sufferings were much more subtle and longitudinal than what one might suppose. Despite the more obvious loneliness that I sometimes felt and the frustration I experienced constantly moving between two cultures, the pain I endured was not one that I could explicitly place at the time being because of my identity as a TCK. In fact, some of the sufferings did not emerge until much later which I have come to attribute to the particularity of my experience as a TCK, going through adolescence in a majority White American European context.

Coming into middle school, I spoke fluent English and had assimilated into U.S. culture. As such, what others may consider to be the conventional experience of a TCK feeling ostracized was not really the case for me. I had no problem "fitting in" and felt relatively … at home? At that point in my life, that was how I thought I felt, but the problem was, I also had no idea what it meant to "feel at home". Having established myself in the community and that I was fine where I stood, I was not regarded in any ways as a TCK, or as the type of student that needed to have their cultural ambiguity addressed. In fact, my teachers and friends in nearly all circumstances gave no particular attention to my Korean identity. Why should they? I was just like everyone else. I would go about my everyday experiences in the classroom just like all of the other students. I came to class by 8:15 and put my bag in my allotted cupboard space. I went and sat down at my desk, socializing with some of my friends and casually chatting with my teacher. I paid attention in class, as much as a chatty teenager could, actively participated, and did my homework. I sometimes got in trouble for talking too much or for doing things that I should not have been doing, but that was just like everyone else. I went to soccer practice during the first half of the year and then to track practice for the second half. Just like how I had gone through other years of my schooling experience in the U.S., I was oblivious to the differences between me and the other students, and others seemed to be as well.

The double identity. Going from the classroom to my home, I was juggling two different identities: my 'Korean identity' and my 'American identity'. At home, I was constantly encouraged and taught to embrace my Korean side and instilled with collectivist values. On the other hand, I would use the school as the platform for me to explore my individualistic identity, while disengaging my Korean side. In having compartmentalized the two identities, I once again saw no difference between the others and me. The flip from one identity to another was one that seemed to happen naturally for me, and as such, I never really consciously pointed it out to myself. The more I separated my two identities, the more the people around me seemed to disregard this far-off idea that "I am Korean". And the more my teachers and friends disregarded my Korean side, the more I started to disconnect with it. At that point in my life, it was not a matter of overcoming racism and racial divides; I was simply convinced that I was not a part a minority group of which I needed to be conscientious. There were other Asians that may have needed to be conscientious of this, but for me, I was in the clear. I had established myself, and I had somehow transcended my 'Asian-ness', or so I thought. I had convinced myself that I was just like everyone else and that everyone else saw me as such. But the more I became convinced of this, the more my Korean identity seemed to fight back. Even at this point, with the clash between the two identities, I was still not explicitly aware of the dichotomy I had created for myself. From this, my frustration started to bubble over from this personal clash into one that encompassed everyone that was involved in reinforcing my Korean identity.

With the mood swings of a prepubescent teenager, I was beginning to grow increasingly frustrated towards a family that was not able to accommodate to my 'American' side. I assimilated more and more into a culture that seemed contradictory to the one at home, and furthermore, I developed it in a classroom that did not validate this other cultural identity. And yet, it did not occur to me that the suffering of my Korean identity was significant in any way. Rather, at a point in my life in which I was discovering my social identity and finding my validation through the media, friends, and teachers (Brown & Knowles, 2014), I channeled my anger towards those who did *not* validate my American identity – my family. As I continued fostering the identity necessary to fit the U.S. culture and found approval from my peers, *that* was the part of me that I increasingly began to embrace and prefer. And yet again, none of this was explicit to me at the time as it is now in retrospect. Rather, it was simply a matter of the context in which I felt most validated.

As my social identity began to take a bigger place in my life, the culture in which I felt most validated as a human being began to be the culture in which my social identity was the most validated. In recognizing the various forms of identity development that takes place during adolescence, such as academic, ethnic, and social (Brown, 2016), it is also important to recognize the interconnectedness with which they can (and likely do) develop. My family could not provide me with the validation I sought, and as my classmates were able to do so, I began to believe that I had found myself in my American identity.

Of course, like many other teenagers, being moody was a part of puberty (Larson, Csikszentmihalyi, & Graef, 1980). However, the problem was that the lack of recognition towards my cultural identity from my classroom gave me a place to channel my anger. Every incompatibility was simply more kindling to the flame. Particularly channeled towards the parents who struggled most in adjusting to this foreign environment, I would often lash out for reasons that even then, I knew were unfair towards them. I loved my parents and my family, more than anything, but not knowing how to deal with my hormonal mood-swings or where to direct my ambiguous frustrations, I found myself channeling all of it towards my family, often regretting it a few moments later and even more so looking back now.

At the same time, I also knew that in many circumstances they were trying. I remember to this day the moment I told my parents about the tooth fairy. After having lost a tooth during class in fourth grade, my teacher promptly asked me whether she thought the tooth fairy was going to visit. Having no idea what she was talking about, I asked her what that was, and learned about a nifty tradition in which a fairy would provide money in return for taking my tooth. Although I knew by then that something like this would undoubtedly have to be orchestrated by parents, I could hardly sit still on the school bus thinking about this fun tradition in which I would get to participate. The moment I got back home, I told my parents about my lost tooth and carefully instructed them on how they were to go about as the tooth fairy. I would place the tooth under my pillow before going to bed. Then, they were to come in while I was sleeping and swap out the tooth for money.

Carefully placing the tooth underneath my pillow, I went to bed with excitement. I woke up the next day a bit nervous that my parents might have forgotten because they were too tired and reassured myself it would be alright if they had. I lifted my pillow, and to my surprise and excitement, I found that my tooth had been replaced with a crisp twenty-dollar bill. Even as a child I knew that this was way too much, especially for a family that was already financially struggling, and for a kid that really did not have much on which to use the money. I quickly ran over to my mom, with a giant smile on my face, telling her that they gave me too much money, but still very content with the way in which I had gotten to participate in this American tradition.

Every time I think back on this story, I am reminded of the love and effort my parents put in trying to make me happy, while still making sure that I did not lose sight of my Korean roots. Although my efforts were still very much shortsighted, even then, I still acknowledged how hard they were trying. In recognizing this, I would often also direct the frustration towards myself, frustrated at why I could not be more grateful while brooding over why my family could not just be more like the White families. Even when I was not directing my dissatisfaction directly towards my parents, I allowed this mindset to dominate my attitude. I wondered why we could not have the sorts of relationships that my friends' families had and seemed to be the norm based on our classroom discussions. As Brown and Leaman (2007) note, "Culturally and ethnically different students may experience feelings of frustration during the moratorium (active exploration) period based on the discrepancies they note between their lives and those of the majority White European American Culture" (p. 221).

Looking back, it fills my heart with unbearable sorrow at how shortsighted, entitled, and ungrateful I was. Additionally, I cannot express enough my gratitude for everything they have done for me and in ensuring that I maintained my Korean roots throughout our time together in the U.S. The sacrifice that my parents made, not only in working tirelessly to provide for my two brothers and me, but also in having already given up so much back at home is a story that rings as a familiar one for many TCKs and their immigrant families. The story is the one of unending sacrifice, the struggle to fit into a society that somehow seems like another planet, and the countless obstacles that parents must go through to provide for their children. In this way, my story is not just meant for TCKs, but also for the immigrant parents that go through so much in raising TCKs and give all of themselves in the process.

A racial awakening. As I had established the double identity for myself, the first time I had a direct encounter with racism was a rude awakening. The first direct encounter I can recall was in fifth grade. I had dealt with snide comments or micro-aggressions from my classmates in the past (Pierce, 1970), but I did not put any thought into it. Whether it was in asking me about China despite knowing I was from Korea or in purposely mispronouncing my name (see Kohli & Solórzano, 2012, on the importance of names for ethnically diverse student), I would dismiss them from my mind just like any other casual insult that friends might say to one another. Similarly, with my appearance, I was blissfully unaware, or at least unaware of the significance, of the racial differences that distinguished me from my White peers. In fact, I would look into the mirror every now and then as a child and wonder why and how people could be so dissatisfied with their faces. I was perfectly content with the way I looked. As I tried to pick out the parts of my face I would change, I could not bring myself to pick a single part. As narcissistic as little Hwa Pyung may sound, it was not necessarily that I thought I was untouchably handsome; it was simply that I was content with everything I had, and I could not imagine myself any other way. As puberty began to hit and I started to become increasingly aware of my racial differences, all of this changed.

Sooner or later, the snide comments, not just from the friendly faces whom I knew did not mean it to be hurtful, but also from strangers, started to dig a bit deeper, and then a bit deeper. I could not locate why exactly the comments were getting to me so significantly. After all, I had taken my fair share of insults from two older brothers who showed me no mercy. But for some reason, no matter how much I tried to just ignore the hateful words coming from complete strangers, every word burned straight through me no matter how much I tried to resist, whether it was in the library while I was looking for a book or walking through the mall to meet up with a friend. I did not understand – I was a part of the community just like everyone else, wasn't I? Even after accepting that my Asian identity was something that separated me from the sea of white faces that I generally saw, I still could not understand how their words were having such a powerful impact on me. Why should the words of people I do not know hurt me so much? When I reflect now on why racist comments leave such a strong impact on me, it seems to me that it is in the dehumanizing power of the words and gesture that is what makes me feel so defeated. That in the senselessness of such seemingly irrelevant string of words, people rationalize them with a hatred towards you whom they do not know. That the humiliation that accompanies a random stranger throwing insults at you with no context, for some reason still makes sense. That with just a few words, someone is able to strip me of my humanity and reduce me to my skin color and facial features.

Although these were not the thoughts that ran through my mind in middle school when I faced racist comments, what I did know was that I was starting to become more conscious of the ways in which my race set me apart from the people around me. When I looked in the mirror, I began to notice all of the things that I wanted to change. When I interacted with people for the first time, my attention would immediately go to my eyes that were too small or my nose that was too flat, and I would start drilling all of the negative possibilities into my mind. I would wonder with worry whether this person I had just met would be able to look past my Asian-ness or not. The more I became conscious of my race, the more my Asian background became something from which I sought to remove myself. The culture that I had hoped to distance myself from before, no longer became a matter of passive drifting, but one of active separation. At a time when I should have been developing my identity, whether ethnically or socially, others chose my identity for me. I could not bear to explore an identity of which I was eager to abandon. To compensate for the worries that my racial and cultural disparity would prevent me from fitting in, I would often go above and beyond to gain approval from others. Regardless of whether this got me in trouble or whether it jeopardized my grades, I became more reckless in seeking approval from my peers. While my teachers saw this as inappropriate behavior stemming from what I can only assume they thought was a rebellious teenager, I cannot help but wonder how my behavior may have been affected if my ethnic identity had been promoted and validated enough to teach me that who I am was enough. Brown and Knowles (2014) state that "all students must seem themselves in the curriculum and be a vital part of the discourse" (p. 49). As I began to see the ways in which people perceived my culture to be intertwined with my race, I began running further from my Korean identity, containing it within my household as much as I could. As this was also not very explicit for me then, I believe I lost the opportunity to humanize myself and to find validation in myself by not understanding the forces guiding my identity development.

A Fading Cultural Identity

As sixth grade came to an end, it was time for my family to move back to South Korea. Having attended the same school for more than two years for the first time, I had grown quite attached. My fellow classmates and I were hardly able to keep it together for what we thought would be our final day together, as tears flowed down our faces. Fast-forward a few months. I was back with the people in whom I had found friendship, beginning our seventh and eighth grade years. For my parents, it was the grueling decision of recognizing the difficulty of a transition if I were to attend Korean school, the greater set of opportunities that would lie ahead if I continued school in the U.S., and most importantly, my desperation to go back to a school in which I had found stability.

Without going into the details of my experiences living away from my family on which I could undoubtedly write a completely separate chapter, it was a difficult but memorable experience. I enjoyed middle school and even succeeded, graduating as valedictorian. I continued to develop the bonds with my friends and to foster my American identity. However, this time, I was completely immersed. With no home to return to in which I would switch to my Korean identity, even the slightest bit of validation I had been receiving towards my Korean side was starting to fade. For me, it had never been this interaction between my Korean identity and my American identity that should have formed an amalgamation. It was a constant switching back and forth in which I would assume one identity in certain contexts and the other identity in another. So being in a majority White, homogenous school with no venue for me to explore my Korean identity and returning to a home in which I was once again surrounded by the White American European culture, I began to lose track of my Korean identity. As I mentioned before, I was coming into the classroom speaking fluent English and having adapted to the White American European culture. Doing well academically and socially, the teachers saw no reason to actively try and encourage me to explore my other cultural identity. Why should they? Is this not what justice looks like with regards to people of color? That even for ethnically diverse students, we can be treated simply as 'American' like everyone else in the classroom. That was how I made myself seem and that is how they saw me. The problem was that I am not American. That was a part of who I was, but that was not *all* of me.

The longitudinal effects. Whenever we think about needing to engage with someone's culture or being culturally sensitive, we seem to only look for the obvious signs: the accents, blatant cultural barriers, or the tangible isolation. However, for me, for a TCK who during the process of my identity development had already become familiar with the White American European culture, the other part of my cultural identity was one I was hiding and without active encouragement, was not ready to explore. During that time, I felt no immediate repercussion of such decision and was content with where I was. In response to this, my teachers, peers, and others around me did not seek out conversations about my 'other' cultural identity; nor was I presented with many opportunities in which I felt validated enough to engage this other identity. The notion that adolescents in middle school should have a supportive environment in which they are encouraged to explore their phase of identity development is one that I strongly believe should also be expanded to include cultural identities (Brown & Knowles, 2014).

I may not have necessarily felt the effects of this cultural identity deprivation right then and there, but it is something that I strongly believe has impacted the way I engage with my Korean identity, and even other cultures, today. While I may have been content with my American identity in the U.S., the problem was that I would not always end up being in the U.S. My life as a TCK was and continues to encompass not just living in a culture different from a 'home' culture, but also one of constant movement. For me, being a TCK is about being able to adapt. However, my failure to stay in touch with my Korean identity and the hegemonic White American European identity I adopted for myself has made my endeavors of connecting with other cultures, particularly my Korean one, a harder process than it needs to be.

After being in an environment in which I had neglected my Korean identity for so long, I was able to feel a sense of completion that I had not felt before once I returned to South Korea for high school. As I saw faces that looked like mine, heard the language with which I had grown up, and connected with people who had related with me in stories and experiences, a part of me was filled that my U.S. friends had not been able to complete. Yet my mindset was so fixed on my American perspective that I nonetheless had a hard time getting past my American identity to engage with my Korean roots. In fact, it was not even a matter of getting past my American identity to switch back to my Korean identity. Even when I tried to engage them together, so much of myself felt barred by a mindset I had established for myself in thinking that they were incompatible.

Today, I have learned (and continue to learn) what it means to accept and navigate an identity of a TCK. The process becomes a balancing act that for many TCKs can involve more than two cultures. For me, it is mainly composed of the balance between my Korean and American identity. The term 'Korean American' is often used to describe people like me to encompass the dual identity that is embodied by one identity. However, this phrase has always felt like a cheap-way-out for me, to say that I have not foregone my Korean identity while still indulging myself in what seems to be a mostly American identity. While I find myself connecting to the Korean culture in ways that I was not able with American culture, I am also constantly torn by a cultural-guilt that tells me that I am not "Korean enough". I am somehow too American to truly ever settle into a Korean identity. I believe that as the phrase *third* culture kid depicts, a TCK should be able to find a balance between different cultural identities that in their interaction forms a unique, third identity. However, this is only possible if TCKs are given the space and encouragement to do so in a healthy manner. These ideals of space and encouragement can vary widely depending on the context, but I will provide some suggestions for starting points.

As I continue to build on my Korean American identity in the way in which I feel is appropriate, an incredibly difficult aspect has been in navigating the biases I have learned. Much like for other students of color, these biases come from a variety of sources, such as media images or social events (Brown & Leaman, 2007). For me, these sources seem to bias one identity over another. While those around me saw a passive position when I was in middle school, as one that would give me the independence to explore the cultural identity I wanted, the biases that took hold of my mind provided me with no independence. In the face of a tipping scale that seemed to favor the Western perspective, what I needed was active encouragement rather than passivity. Seeing how I acted contently seemed to signal to others to remain on the sidelines when it came to my ethnic identity development. However, educators should be actively promoting the engagement and exploration of other ethnic identities for TCKs, even if it may not be so obvious that the adolescent needs it. It is not enough for teachers to simply 'treat them like everyone else', as this may be failing to recognize existing power structures (Hurd, 2012). This is not to be done in an overbearing way for the TCKs, so that they start to feel entrapped by a surrounding that only sees them as a TCK; but in a way so that they can feel as though have autonomy in exploring their choices while also being supported and validated enough to explore those other choices.

One way to do this is through personal conversations. Brown and Knowles (2014) suggest that teachers facilitate personal conversations with their ethnically diverse students during the school day, inquiring into their language, cultural celebrations, or their family's country of origin. These sorts of discussions that help students open up on ethnic identity development could come from the Carnegie Council on Adolescent Development's suggestion of 'teaming' (as cited in Brown & Knowles, 2014). Rooted in the notion that middle school students should have a small, stable group of adults on whom they can rely, Brown and Leaman (2007) report how teaming is as an effective method of fostering meaningful relationships between the students and adults. This would help to provide a strong student-to-teacher foundation on which teachers can validate TCKs' experiences and ethnic identities. The personal discussions could help teachers better understand their ethnically diverse students' lives, the context from which they are coming as learners and adolescents, and ultimately their particular needs (Brown & Leaman, 2007).

Additionally, it is important that discussions entail sensitive issues, such as racism, which can help in developing a healthy ethnic identity (Brown & Leaman, 2007). Brown and Leaman note the importance of educators explicitly addressing ethnically diverse students' challenges in the classroom in order to aid them in integration (p. 223). Although these discussions may be difficult, particularly in considering the disassociated backgrounds of the majority of teachers (Hurd, 2012), the explicit recognition of these challenges could help students feel as though these challenges are not their faults or the fault of their ethnic identity, thereby helping them engage in healthier ethnic identity development.

On the other hand, educators could also design lessons to spark students' interests in other cultures, thereby sparking organic conversations between TCKs' and their peers. Such conversations could help TCKs feel supported enough to share their cultural backgrounds and to explore their ethnic identities. Brown and Knowles (2014) point to the importance of educators devising lessons that honor all students' voices and in ensuring that curricula reflect diverse ethnic identities. In their reference to the Association for Middle Level Education's (formerly National Middle School Association) (NMSA, 2010), suggestion of exploratory curriculums, Brown and Knowles cite the importance of providing students with a curriculum that allows them to explore their interests. Exploratory curriculums could help ethnically diverse students grow more comfortable with their ethnic culture and their peers to develop an interest in such culture.

> Two intended purposes of exploratories are to provide students with opportunities to develop socially and to pursue a variety of personal cognitive interests that may coincide with traditional curricula or stretch beyond the boundaries of required curricula … Exploratories can be specifically designed to give students a chance to examine issues of ethnicity and diversity personally, among the student body, and throughout the community. (Brown & Leaman, 2007, pp. 228–229)

For more suggestions on the implementation of exploratory studies, Brown and Leaman (2007) offer some example suggestions on how they can be implemented.

Particularly in an age of increasing globalization, the idea of promoting internationally minded students is an important one (e.g., Bunnell, 2006; Cambridge & Thompson, 2010; Kamens & McNeely, 2010). Whether it is through social media, mobility between countries, or global issues such as climate change, the importance of intercommunication continues to grow. Even for those that are not TCKs, it is important that students are able to engage with other cultures in an appropriate and respectful way. Barratt Hacking et al. (2017) discuss a conceptualization of international mindedness that is relational; one that requires 'reaching out' to others and their different perspectives while also 'reaching in' to ourselves to understand ourselves better in relation to others. It seems that early adolescence, as a period in life of searching for and developing an identity, is a timely stage of development for educators and other adults in their lives to actively promote a healthy cultural identity.

However, considering the bias for Western and Euro-centric perspectives, even for programs and curricula that claim to be international (James, 2005), it is important to validate and provide respectful spaces of identity exploration particularly for non-Western cultures. This is crucial not just for the non-Western TCKs, but also for the non-TCK students as they learn to engage with non-Western perspectives. It is on this healthy cultural identity and respect towards other cultural identities that students can 'reach out' and 'reach in. In a research study I recently conducted evaluating the effectiveness of a particular school program in fostering international mindedness, interviews and surveys from students at international schools showed that they felt that they gain the most international mindedness through interactions with other culturally diverse students (Yoo, 2018). As such, TCKs offer an incredible opportunity for non-international classroom settings to foster international mindedness in their sharing of other cultural experiences when given the environment to do so. If this is done in a way where too much of the pressure is placed on the TCK, it may restrict them from even wanting to share their experiences. However, if TCKs are actively presented effective opportunity to share in their journey of exploring ethic identities, other students in the classroom could benefit as well.

CONCLUSION

In hearing my story about experiencing middle school as a TCK, I hope that the message is not one of directed blame towards anyone or any group of people. I recognize the many ways in which my personal shortcomings may have affected this journey. Additionally, I am tremendously grateful for everyone in my life, whether my parents, teachers, or the librarians that often graciously took me under their wings as I was growing up. Throughout my adolescence, they have done so much to help me develop in the best ways they knew possible. However, the issue was that most people, including myself, were not aware of the need for these other ways. If we are to support the healthy development of adolescent TCKs, regardless of where the blame falls, we must all take the responsibility to support our adolescents' identity developments.

Particularly in considering the ways in which institutions may be encouraging certain ethnic identity developments while failing to validate others (e.g., James, 2005), it is important to recognize the ways in which we can better support adolescent TCKs to explore their sense of cultural belonging. This is not only for the immediate effects, such as their social and academic identity (Brown & Leaman, 2007), but also in the potential longitudinal effects such as those I describe above. I also recognize that just like for any other country, a student that assimilates into American culture after having moved to the U.S. is a positive thing. However, we must also acknowledge the other aspects of their identities that are an integral part of who they are for so many TCKs. Phinney and Devich-Navarro's (1997) revised notion of *blended biculturalism* suggests level of ethnic identity development in which ethnically diverse youths can navigate different cultures congruently (as cited in Brown & Leaman, 2007). In alignment with the goal of blended biculturalism, I strongly believe that rather than being guided to develop two separate identities, having a space in which I could allow my two identities to interact would have been particularly helpful. It is easy to ignore the need to provide adolescents with the space to explore other ethnic identities when their cultural diversity is less noticeable, but we should seek to promote such a space proactively rather than reactively. If we are to take on the responsibility of promoting a society that better engages cultural diversity, no matter where we are in the world, we ought to look to those at the forefront of the journey, the TCKs, and hear and learn from their stories.

REFERENCES

Barratt Hacking, E., Blackmore, C., Bullock, K., Bunnell, T., Donnelly, M., & Martin, S. (2017). *The international mindedness journey: School practices for developing and assessing international mindedness across the IB continuum*. Retrieved from https://www.ibo.org/globalassets/publications/ib-research/continuum/international-mindedness-final-report-2017-en.pdf

Brown, D. F. (2016). Identity development. In S. B. Mertens, M. M. Caskey, & N. Flowers (Eds.), *The encyclopedia of middle grades education* (pp. 199–202). Charlotte, NC: Information Age Publishing.

Brown, D. F., & Knowles, T. (2014). *What every middle school teacher should know*. Portsmouth, NH: Heinemann.

Brown, D. F., & Leaman, H. L. (2007). Recognizing and responding to young adolescents' ethnic identity development. In S. B. Mertens, V. Anfara, & M. M. Caskey (Eds.), *The young adolescent and the middle school* (pp. 219–236). Charlotte, NC: Information Age Publishing.

Bunnell, T. (2006). The growing momentum and legitimacy behind an alliance for international education. *Journal of Research in International Education, 5*, 155–176. doi:10.1177/1475240906065600

Cambridge, J., & Thompson, J. (2004). Internationalism and globalization as contexts for international education. *Compare: A Journal of Comparative and International Education, 34*, 161–175. doi:10.1080/0305792042000213994

Carnegie Council on Adolescent Development. (1989). *Turning points: Preparing American youth for the 21st century*. New York, NY: Carnegie Corporation.

Hurd, E. (2012). A framework for understanding multicultural identities: An investigation of a middle level student's French-Canadian Honduran-American (Mestizo) identity. *Middle Grades Research Journal, 7*, 111–127.

James, K. (2005). International education: The concept, and its relationship to intercultural education. *Journal of Research in International Education, 4*, 313–332. doi:10.1177/1475240905057812

Kamens, D. H., & McNeely, C. L. (2009). Globalization and the growth of international educational testing and national assessment. *Comparative Education Review, 54*, 5–25. doi:10.1086/648471

Kohli, R., & Solórzano, D. G. (2012). Teachers, please learn our names!: Racial microaggressions and the K-12 classroom. *Race Ethnicity and Education, 15*, 441–462. doi:10.1080/13613324.2012.674026

Larson, R., Csikszentmihalyi, M., & Graef, R. (1980). Mood variability and the psychosocial adjustment of adolescents. *Journal of Youth and Adolescence, 9*, 469–490. doi:10.1007/BF02089885

National Middle School Association. (2010). *This we believe: Keys to educating young adolescents*. Westerville, OH: Author.

Phinney, J. S., & Devich-Navarro, M. (1997). Variations in bicultural identification among African American and Mexican American adolescents. *Journal of Research on Adolescence, 7*, 3–32.

Pierce, C. (1970). Offensive mechanisms. In F. Barbour (Ed.), *The Black seventies* (pp. 265–282). Boston, MA: Porter Sargent.

Yoo, H. P. (2018). *Evaluating the effectiveness of the International Baccalaureate Diploma Programme in fostering international mindedness within different sociocultural contexts*. Unpublished raw data.

PALOMA E. VILLEGAS

5. MIS ROOTS

I come from frijoles and chile and corn
The holy Mexican trinity
   Used to make enchiladas and sopes, and tacos
        Not "crunchy tacos" or Taco Bell,
But tacos filled with any and every available foodstuff
Including sopa de arroz, espaguetti etc.
Who cares about committing carb on carb crimes?

I come from Jalisco, Guadalajara, Los Altos, Arenal
I come from places evacuated by emigrants
Where agriculture is an expensive reality
And a distant memory for many
Places built through remittances, those who stayed behind, those who returned and
those who were forcibly returned

I don't come from Puerto Vallarta, or Cancun, or "Cabo"
From all-inclusive deals, with margaritas and "guac"
[when did it become a thing to shorten people's food? I don't call a hamburger
"ham" or a grilled cheese "grillc"]

I don't claim to come from exoticized women
   "dicen que las mujeres de Jalisco son muy bonitas …"
   presumed to come from European heritage
No, I come from Mestizxs whose indigenous roots have all but been forgotten
Or forcibly erased
Or incorporated into a "Mexican" hegemonic identity
That often refuses to see race as a determining factor in people's lives

I come from family
From a strong woman who worked and worked until her body wanted to break
From a father so tied to his roots and anger that he became immobile
From *dignidad* and *respeto* and *educación*
From Braceros and returnees
From domestic violence and intergenerational resentment

© KONINKLIJKE BRILL NV, LEIDEN, 2019 | DOI:10.1163/9789004393813_005

I come from the north-east San Francisco Bay
Where my love for burritos developed alongside varicose veins
I got both from working in hot taco trucks, and deteriorating restaurants
Where the pay was low and the conditions sometimes unfriendly
Where I was expected to waitress and cook and translate,
    But where I also learned to cook *carnitas*, *salsa*, and *caldo de camaron*

I come from terms like self-deportation and repatriation,
Illegalization
Which have been marked on my body
They've burrowed deep within me and blistered
The blisters often pop and seep with anxiety and fear
With tears and anger that fuel new blisters

I come from multiple migrations,
Making my way up north
To the "promised land" that did not lead to milk or honey
But that was not fruitless either

I come from the realization that as we travel through time and space
things don't change
    and yet they do

I come from language and theory
I come from dirt and seeds
I come from color
Rich browns and deep oranges
Cool blue nights
Yellow green *nopales*, deep purple *tunas*

And,
as painful as it is to take a step
I travel toward hope
And the *apapachos* that await
To heal the blisters
And plant the seeds

SUSAN Y. LEONARD

6. A DIFFERENT KIND OF ASIAN PERSUASION

"She's Asian – no offense". My friend is not racist, but his words are. They trigger a multitude of questions, as I try to figure out what he means and how to respond. My maiden name is Susan Minkiewicz. My parents are a white,[1] heterosexual couple who were born and raised in New York. My father became a doctor and my mother left her teaching position to became a housewife and caretaker of three children. We lived in suburban neighborhoods with other white people. I attended religious, public, private, and boarding schools throughout childhood, with almost all white students and teachers. We were mostly holiday Catholics, attending mass on Christmas Eve and Easter Sunday with white congregations. Oh, and I'm Korean.

Following his comment, and for the millionth time, I find myself wishing my physical features matched my mentality. I am a white person trapped in an Asian body. Adopted from birth, I was raised with the cultural characteristics of a white person. However, everyone I will ever meet will always see me first as Asian. I did not realize this would become problematic for me until I was exposed to mostly negative interactions about my race throughout childhood and adolescence, making it more difficult as an adult to discern whether people's comments about my race stemmed from a positive or negative place. I did not realize it was bad to be Asian until my peers taught me so. However, my immersion in and access to whiteness enabled me to *other* myself from *real* Asians by distancing myself from stereotypes to create moments in which I temporarily "transcend" my race. A lifetime of interactions with white persons about my race led me to begin filtering their comments onto a continuum with three benchmarks: curiosity, ignorance, and racism. Where I determine their words fall on this continuum informs the response I deploy to assuage personal discomfort and persuade them that I am, really, white like them. However, I know that I will never gain complete membership in either culture. Now, as an educator, I think about what educators can do to provide structures that foster positive interactions between the diverse, unique populations of students they serve. This chapter will describe the ways in which my transracial identity developed through continuous experiences of pain and privilege and how it informs my thinking and work as an educator.

HISTORICAL CONTEXT

Historically, people in power constructed race as a means to categorize people and keep them in boxes. If they don't fit neatly in a box, they must justify themselves (Nakashima, 1992; Shih & Sanchez, 2005; Spickard, 1992). Race is not a biological construct; it is a political-social one. All people belong to the same scientific categories. It was not until people added subcategories that race began dividing people based on physical and geographical characteristics (Spickard, 1992). As people in power built these racial categories, they also structured them hierarchically with Whites at the top defining race – and power and positionality – for everyone below and subsequently allowing institutions, groups, and individuals to define race for us (Chang & Kwan, 2009). Given that race is defined by society, and society changes throughout time, so does the concept of race (Omni & Winant, 1994).

Concepts of race affect people's psychologies and contribute to our funds of identity. Esteban-Guitart (2012) defined funds of identity as "cultural products, inseparable from the social, institutional, geographic, and cultural forces" (p. 173) that are "transmitted and internalized through social interaction and participation in contexts of life and activity" (p. 178). Ratner (2009) claimed that, as a result, structural, ideological, and individualistic ideologies about race create unconscious, cultural psychologies that are enacted through behaviors, resulting in unintended, collective biases. Together, Esteban-Guitart and Ratner (2011) theorized a macro cultural psychology of identity that serves to both embody and support culture and generate behavior considered socially appropriate. Formed through political struggle, a macro cultural psychology of identity eventually filters down into micro level, interpersonal interactions (Esteban-Guitart & Ratner, 2011). Consequently, an aspect of society such as racism can form individuals with oppressed and oppressive psychologies (Ratner, 2009), insidiously working its way into our societies and the discourse of our everyday lives to maintain harmful, and often inaccurate, ideas about groups of people. Thus, "oppression works from inside us, through our cultural constituted psychology to animate our behavior" (Ratner, 2009, p. 263). The ways in which we interact and speak with each other carry meanings that have historical and cultural locations (Jones & Woglom, 2016) that we must consider if we are to realize the effects those meanings have on everyone's lives, not simply persons of color.

Asian Americans adopted into white families may develop oppressed psychologies when they feel like they are not fully accepted into either their native or adopted culture (e.g. Hollingsworth, 2008), a characteristic that also seems possible for any person who has any type of mixed identity. Adopted Asian Americans may experience a variety of self-perceived failures that result in a lack of belonging in one ethnic or racial group. Adoptees raised in a white environment often feel shame and embarrassment for their physical differences (Lee & Miller, 2009) and may develop oppressed psychologies as a result. In other arenas, Asian Americans may feel shame when they fail to live up to the model minority stereotype, which situates Asians as economically and academically successful due to hard work and adherence to Asian cultural norms (Lee, Wong, & Alvarez, 2009). On the other end of the spectrum, adopted Asians may be rejected by Asian communities because they are not *real* Asians (Lee et al., 2009). To cope, some adopted Asian Americans may not choose one identity or the other but rather create a third identity that will constantly have to defend its existence (Simon, 2018). It is a common experience of multiracial individuals to have to justify their identity choices to society (Shih & Sanchez, 2005). For all of the things I read about mixed, biracial, multiracial, and transracial identities, and for the many ways that I could relate, the literature lacked discussion of how adopted Asian Americans could develop oppressive psychologies as a result of their oppressed psychologies. Ratner (2009) claimed that "oppressed psychology is oppressive psychology. It oppresses individuals through their own subjectivity and behavior" (p. 240). This is the space my story seeks to explore and analyze. However, because psychologies are constructed and controlled by the culture in which we live, ideology has the power to control our psychologies. My own "personal experience is not a guide to liberation ... liberation is only illuminated by sophisticated, scientific, complex analysis of social conditions" (Ratner, 2009, p. 265).

WHY I FEEL WHITE

As a person who was adopted from birth and became a naturalized American citizen in a white family, I have grown up with a transracial identity of a white person with Asian features. This transracial identity comes with a price. Access to white privilege involves giving up all customs, traditions, and cultures (Wise, 2011). The stipulation of "giving up" is tricky. The only thing I brought with me from my native country was my middle name, Yoon Ae Im, chosen for me and kept by my adoptive parents as an attempt to maintain ties to my heritage and culture. Growing up, I had the choice to inquire about my story, but my context naturally fought this. I was surrounded by American whiteness. My own household was the quintessential epitome of what it means to be white and the privileges that come with that. Except for having Asian children running around the house (though many may say adoption is an example of white privilege), whiteness was natural and normal to me. It was my life. In fact, except for when I look in the mirror or see pictures of myself, I literally never see myself as Asian. I don't see Korean in the books I read, the words I write, the way I speak, the food I eat, the places I go, or the people with whom I interact. But for everyone else, Korean is the first thing they see in me. What a complication.

This disconnect of being a minority raised in a white household weaves pain and privilege together and forces me to constantly be aware of how others perceive me. It puts on me a responsibility to translate for others what they see in order to find common ground on which to move forward. Korean people have tried to speak to me in Korean and then realized I don't speak Korean. Awkward. One man even gave me a look of disapproval when he realized that I am a fake Asian, or "Fasian". Alternatively, I feel an invisible sigh of relief from white people when they realize that I am not fresh off the boat, so to speak. Navigating these spaces is a full-time job, and it can be humorous, interesting, frustrating, and exhausting.

Since childhood, I have tried to make it easy for people to see me as white. My adoptive mother made attempts to familiarize me with Korean culture. We would sometimes have Korean meals, and she once gave me a CD of Korea's most famous popstar. But other than in my home, there was no authentic space for me to build on this part of my heritage. Had I shown up to school with a Korean lunch or CD in my backpack, I surely would have received strange looks and been made fun of either privately or publicly or both. So, I gave it up, and it wasn't even all that hard. In fact, I do not ever remember feeling a loss. I easily gave up my culture in order to convince my peers through my words and behavior that I was white like them; that I deserved to be a part of the club, if they could only forgive my face and skin for not assimilating as well.

OTHERS CHALLENGE MY WHITENESS

I first began to realize that I was not in the "white club" when I was an elementary student. Teachers took us into the cafeteria for an assembly. We sat in rows, sitting cross-legged and packed together, when a fellow student behind me tapped my shoulder and asked me a curious question: "What are you?" It didn't even occur to me to think that the way the student phrased the question was weird. I certainly did not realize it would be a question that people of all ages would ask me for the rest of my life. It is almost comical that this specific question is the first time I recall my identity coming into question, since it is *the* question every "foreign" looking person gets from white people. I cannot remember a time I did not know that I was Korean, but I do remember not knowing it was something that could be used against me. I responded with a smile, "I'm Korean". The student then proceeded to correct me, saying, "Nuh uh, you're Chinese". Confused, I politely corrected him. "No, I'm Korean". "Nuh uh, you're Japanese!" This time, he was practically shouting it, and I found myself in the spotlight, with every white student sitting around me watching the show. Suddenly, I realized that I was not in a safe zone.

Later in elementary school, I was sitting in a circle with classmates. Out of nowhere and from across the room, a student asked me, "Are you an alien?" Well, damn. I vaguely remember explaining to that student – and the entire class watching – that I am a naturalized citizen. I was so young that I struggle to remember anything else about that event, or maybe I blocked it out of my mind. Honestly, I am impressed that I was able to use the term "naturalized citizen" at that age and know what it meant. Kudos to my mother and father. What I do clearly remember is that no teacher stepped in to facilitate and mediate this interaction as a "teachable moment". Instead, it was just allowed to happen, which was in itself a lesson to all of the students present that day. The inability of my teachers to mediate and my parents to teach me how to advocate for myself culminated in my self-hatred for this face that fooled people into thinking that I was different from them, when deep down, I felt I was the same.

WEAVING IN WHITE PRIVILEGE

Following these interactions, I began to realize that being Asian was a detriment, but I still did not quite realize that I did not fit in. My proximity to whiteness maintained this veil. There are many ways that this proximity gives me access to white privilege. It first appears in my name, Susan. A name that reached its height of popularity in the 1950s, it is a solid white name. I would have much preferred a name like Sarah or Ashley, but that was not my choice. Still, people experience a clear moment of confusion when they see my face and hear my name. They often share this shock with me as if they are the first to ever see an Asian with a non-Asian name. Once, I introduced myself to a white man with his wife and two young sons and he exclaimed, "Susan!? That ain't no Japanese name!" My last name sealed the deal. Minkiewicz, a Polish last name. More difficult to pronounce than the most common Korean surnames like Kim, Park, and Lee, but it still beat having an Asian name. My name is white privilege, always working for me to continuously remind and convince people to believe that I am not a *real* Asian. Every time someone says it, we all hear whiteness, myself included.

My parents being white also privileged me. At school events, I would see them with all of the other parents standing or sitting together – in a sea of whiteness – as I stood among their white kids. This likely narrowed the gap that others saw between them and me. Yes, I'm Asian, but I have white parents and if my parents are white like them, I likely act white as well. It quickly explained why I dressed like a white person and brought "white" food (instead of authentic ethnic food) for lunch. I believe these factors encouraged people to interact with me in ways that they may not have interacted had my parents been Asian.

Still, these privileges were not enough to convince people that I was not Asian. Negative interactions regarding my race persisted throughout middle and high school. Reflecting on those years, I see whirlwind reels of different experiences: people curiously asking about my adoption, making ignorant comments, and laughing or saying nothing when I was the brunt end of a racist joke. Often, people unknowingly damaged my self-esteem with their words regardless of their intent. It became difficult to differentiate curiosity from ignorance from racism. This happened with one of my closest friends in high school. We were just released from the cafeteria, where we waited in the mornings before the first bell rang. The cafeteria funneled everyone into a single hallway that led to an intersection where we would diverge to head to our various classrooms. Walking among the herd, my friend turned to me and excitedly asked, "You know how people call Chinese people Chinks?" "Yeah?" I responded curiously. She delivered the punchline, laughing as she said, "I'm going to call you a Korink". Oh, a Korean version of Chink. I get it. It is the first time I recall a good friend's ignorance resulting in a joke at my expense, oblivious until the end that she was being offensive. I did not know what to say. My immediate reaction was uncertainty, hurt, confusion, and anger. Up until that moment, I had forgotten I was not white and the veil that my friends saw me as white was lifted. At the same time though, it was because of my proximity to whiteness that my friend dared to say this to me. She was not trying to be hurtful, and I doubt she would have said that to an Asian who was not her friend. So, I found myself in two places – white enough for her to include me in a racist joke about my ethnicity but not quite white enough to not make a joke in the first place. Throughout the rest of the day, I contemplated saying something to her about it but in order to do so, I would have had to confess that it bothered me, that I could not take a joke, and that I was too sensitive. I have found that the default reaction for people whom I have confronted about their racism towards me is to put fault onto me for being unable to correctly interpret their intent and make me feel guilty for their offense. White privilege is amazing in that way. It often becomes the burden of the oppressed to make the oppressor feel better about being oppressive. If I could not laugh at her white joke about Asians, I felt that I was admitting that I identified with my Asian ethnicity. It would *other* me from her and subsequently *other* me from whiteness. So, I said nothing. She went about her day never knowing what she had done to me, and I spent the rest of my day wondering why I was born Asian.

My race continued to be a source of pain for me in high school, but it was also an ongoing source of privilege. Americans often have a stereotypical image of Asians as being smart and hardworking (see, for example, Lee, 2015). The Horatio Alger, pull yourself up by your own bootstraps mentality (Sullivan, 2014), argues that being smart and hardworking will get you to college, which will get you a job, which will get you a nice home and nice things, which will all culminate into a nice life. However, that's only one piece of the puzzle. In order to access such success, you have to make sure you get put on the "right" track academically (Oakes, 2005). Having white parents helped me with this. Well-spoken, my father always showed up to school events and meetings dressed in the professional clothing that doctors wear; my mother having previously been a teacher; and the knowledge that they were wealthy – all of that contributed to my teachers' perception that I, too, was destined for success. My mother and father knew what questions to ask and how to advocate for the advanced classes, in keeping with Laureau's (2011) work on class differences in parents' information and interventions in the lives of their children. Combined with my Asian genes that my teachers may have seen as providing me with "inherent" intelligence established by the model minority stereotype (Lee, 2015), it was no problem to get me into every advanced class there was. While I belonged in the advanced English classes, it is a stretch to say that I belonged in the advanced science and math classes. In retrospect, I am certain that my math teachers knew this. I am absolutely terrible at math.

CREATING THE ASIAN PERSUASION

Curiosity and ignorance were easier to navigate than straight up racism. When someone said something with the intent to be racist, regardless of the content of their words, it would generate the same physical and emotional reactions and still does to this day. My heart begins pounding so hard that I can feel it in my fingertips. My throat becomes dry and breathing becomes mechanical. A sort of deafness occurs. I can see the person in front of me speaking and even hear noise around me, but it is unintelligible, and I am unable to keep up with the conversation. It feels like my brain shuts down, and no specific thought runs through my mind. I am powerless, and I have to just wait until it passes. When I can finally get away from the situation, I feel stunned, like I experienced something that my brain could not translate. I feel completely isolated and trapped in feelings that I cannot describe to myself much less someone else.

By the time I finished high school, I had heard most of the usual questions, comments, and jokes over and over again. It was rare that someone could say something to me that I had not heard before. Yet, each time I heard them, I was no better at responding. Albert Einstein shines wisdom on us, saying that "the definition of insanity is doing the same thing over and over again, but expecting different results". I expected people to be nicer and smarter as I got older, but this did not happen. Grown adults were asking the same dumbass questions as third graders. Engaging with the same types of interactions over and over and expecting people to be different made me start to feel a bit insane and hopeless about my future. I was not doing anything differently, so every interaction was able to make me feel the same way. Something had to give.

Enter, the model minority stereotype. I consider it my cheat sheet – better yet my playbook – for engaging with people about my identity. In order to anticipate the things people might say in any given situation, I simply had to know the possibilities of phrases they may defer to when they meet someone who is Asian. Fueled by movies and media and enacted through the curious, ignorant, and racist remarks I have heard throughout my life about my race, I compiled all of the perceptions that make up Asian stereotypes into a bank of potential things people may say to me. I began to feel that I could take control of my identity by using them to prove that my face is just a mask and that I am, in fact, the farthest thing from Asian that they could imagine. It's a different kind of Asian persuasion. I wanted to determine my identity for others not the other way around. I wanted to take away people's power to make me feel the shame, humiliation, and anger that had plagued me throughout my childhood. I decided that my best bet at protecting myself from the discrimination was to deploy it first.

Let me persuade you. If you comment that something is difficult to see, I will make a comment about how I understand because I have naturally limited eyesight (slanty eyes). If you ask a question related to doing math, I will respond that I'm supposed to be naturally good at math, but I was raised here by white people, so I suck at it (good at math). Tell me that you love spicy food, I'll be sure to point out that I'm a terrible Asian because I can't tolerate spicy food. When I show you a tip for how to do something on a computer, know that I will credit my family's business of making computers as my source of knowledge (tech geeks). I'll prove that I'm not Asian when I flawlessly parallel park (bad drivers). Ask me if I made my leftover hibachi food, and I'll tell you I made it in my wok at home, with some bits of Chihuahua and calico cat (eats dogs and cats). Do I like Thai or Chinese food better? Eh, they're all the same, am I right (all Asians are the same)? By the way, I need the training pieces for chopsticks because I don't know how to use them.

See? Not Asian. I'm not just fighting off Korean stereotypes. I'm fighting off a continent's stereotypes, but that's okay. I'm game. I can't help but think of the final scene of the movie, *8 Mile,* with Eminem. He steps up for a rap battle – a white speck amid a crowd of black people – on a stage historically reserved for black people. In a shocking move, he uses his mic time to make fun of himself for things that his opponent might target him for (e.g. "I do live in a trailer with my mom".). He drops the mic and his opponent steps up, only to have nothing to make fun of Eminem for and ending with Eminem's victory and the love of the crowd.

At my graduation from my preparatory college boarding school, the dean and teachers honored students with various awards of recognition and excellence. We had several international students. Our Valedictorian was from Korea. I was Salutatorian. Other Korean students received the other high awards. When the ceremony was over, a fellow graduate came to me and couldn't wait to share a funny story. She told me that her parents had commented on how it was all Asians that won the high awards and that her sister had responded to her parents, "Nuh uh, Susan won awards, too!" That was the greatest honor I took from that day.

My transracial identity most privileged me when I applied to college. As an Asian person, I emphasized my ethnicity in order to appeal to the university's desire to host "diverse" populations. The model minority says that Asians are smart, well-behaved, and grow up to be money makers (Lee, 2015). I was smart enough, behaved within a range of normal behaviors associated with my age group, and I planned to make enough money to make a living. But, as far as the university was concerned, I was going to bring Korea to a college town in the southeast United States. The first section of my college application asked me for my basic information. I wrote my white name down. Privilege. Next, the application asked for "Optional Biographic Information". I wanted to check White and Asian but felt it would be lying. Pain. Ironically, I checked Asian and thought about how I was grateful for the face that allowed me to check a box other than "White". Not checking the White box meant that I might have an advantage with the minority card. Privilege. The application proceeded to asked me for my birthplace. I was born in Korea but have a California birth certificate because I was adopted from birth and naturalized as a citizen at three months old. I do not know what to put and do not want to lie. Pain. The next question asked about my parents' highest level of education and occupation. Privilege. When my acceptance letter arrived in the mail, I was ecstatic.

At some point in college, I was out with a new friend and his group of friends, when one of them caught me off guard with an Asian joke that I no longer remember. Because this person was not in my group of friends, I took the comment as an attack. Caught off guard, I reacted by making a scene and leaving, though my friend begged me to stay. I was humiliated – not because of the racist comment that was said but because I had let everyone know it bothered me. Talk about an oppressed psychology. The next day, the joker sent me an apology in a Facebook message. Explaining that he had Asian friends with whom he joked all the time, he said he did not realize that I would not appreciate the jokes in the same way. He stated that, if

I would accept his apology, he would never again make those kinds of jokes around me. He ended with the disclaimer that if I wanted to hold a grudge, there was nothing he could do. At the time that I read the message, I was still angry and hurting, so I read it with a tone I had heard all too many times. I was too sensitive. It was my fault that I could not take a joke. I was the angry person holding the grudge. I was not in a place to hear what he was saying, so I completely missed what he meant. I missed his reflection that he realized ethnic jokes with friends are different than with strangers. I failed to acknowledge that I operated with my friends in the same way. I missed the sincerity in his offer to be more considerate of what he says in future interactions. I did not realize what I missed until years later. In retrospect, I am sad about losing that opportunity, because it is one of the only times that a person has sincerely apologized for offending me with a racial comment. More importantly, it is the only time I can remember someone sharing a commitment to changing the way they interact with others as a result of their experience with me. Had I been able to have that conversation with him, maybe we would be friends today. Maybe I would have discovered a more positive way to resolve the tension that arises when people outside of my circle engage me about my race. Instead, I never again spoke to or saw my friend, the joker, or the rest of the people who were present that night. Instead, I decided to make the Asian persuasion tactic a full-time job. That night, I had let myself forget that I was Asian, and it made me susceptible to someone's words. It is one of the last times I can remember allowing myself to not think about my race in a new social situation.

Constantly keeping my race on my mind allows me to anticipate opportunities to avoid pain and continue to access whiteness in ways that I could not if not for my upbringing. I can laugh about Asian stereotypes because they are so far from accurately describing me. People in my life also recognize this to be true, so when stereotypical conditions arise, we can name them and laugh with each other. I feel safe and understood in these spaces and my jokes and comments do not serve as a defense. Stereotypes exist whether we choose to acknowledge them or not. People think of them whether they want to or not. For every comment that arises about my race, I know there are comments that either are not spoken or shared with me. Because I was raised in white American culture, I can identify opportunities for Asian jokes at times when *real* Asians might be oblivious. My ability to identify these moments and say what white people around me are thinking – but are too polite to say – is my way of clearing the elephant in the room and aligning myself with whiteness. Rather than risking them sharing the thoughts with each other behind my back, I can say it and create a space where we can laugh together. It is when I am with people who do not know me that I will use the stereotypes either to disarm anyone who might try to use them to hurt me or to convince others of who I am and who I am not. I do not intend to use stereotypes to persist harmful narratives about Asians, though I know I do. However, it is the only solution that effectively relieves the tensions I experience when around groups of white people, and that makes it invaluable to me.

S. Y. LEONARD

AS AN EDUCATOR

After graduating from college, I began working as an eighth-grade history teacher. It was interesting to enter this arena where I almost always felt marginalized and my self-hatred for my ethnicity reached its height. As an authority figure, I was much less likely to encounter racism as often or as harshly as when I was a student, but as long as my face is ethnic, people will engage me in conversation about it. However, I certainly did not feel comfortable deploying my Asian persuasion tactic at a student. A student once asked me, "Do you speak Asian?" I responded, "I don't know. Do you speak White?" The student digested that response, laughed, and then threw his hands up, saying, "No, I speak English!" Enlightening people about how to talk to me about my race while also preserving their dignity often made it difficult to decide which approach to take. Get too serious, and students will be afraid to speak to you. Embarrass them, and they will never ask you anything again.

I have answered students literally, in hopes that they will think about how to convey what they want to say. A student once asked me, "What are you?" *The* question took me back to my childhood, back to the first time someone asked me to explain my face. But that time, I did not excuse the improper phrasing. I replied, "Human". The student laughed. "That's not what I mean". Okay, there's a start. I helped her out. "Do you mean, what is my ethnicity?" "Yeah". "Oh, I'm Korean". Student comments about my ethnicity could immediately pull me back to a place and time where my race was a source of bullying and self-hatred for how I looked. To this day, I struggle with knowing how to navigate these feelings. I have experienced these types of interactions throughout my entire life, and I have not mastered how to react or act in a way that will liberate the speaker and myself from a deficit mindset about people who are not white. As the child of white parents and student of white teachers, no one modeled how to discuss this issue with me. So, I never learned how to navigate them for myself. How could I expect my white teachers to know how to? How do I expect myself to do so for my own students?

In the time that has passed from when I was a child to an adult of 30 years, kids and adults are still asking the same questions. From a student asking me if I was an alien to my own students asking me what I am – students are learning about other places in the world but may not be learning how to engage with the diversity of the world being present in their own communities. Despite America claiming itself to be a "melting pot", students do not seem to know that this means Americans may not be white. They still associate facial features and skin color with single stories (Adichie, 2009). Perhaps this is because the American melting pot is simply an idea that obscures the fact that, while many people of color may live in this nation, they are still marginalized and treated as outsiders. I still fear the dangerous and real effects that racism has on my life.

I worry about the dangers of being Asian. The day after Trump was elected, I was driving to work and realized that I left my license at home. I texted a couple friends, facetiously writing, "I left my license at home. If I get pulled over, know that I am a naturalized citizen and my passport is in a drawer in my office". While it was something we all laughed about, deep down I worried about what would have happened to me if shit really hit the fan[2] and the United States had ended up at war with North Korea, under his administration. During World War II, Japanese-American citizens were herded into U.S. internment camps after the bombing of Pearl Harbor. Every person who had Japanese blood was held responsible for the actions of the Japanese government. Worse, this policy was enacted by President Roosevelt with an executive order, completely suspending those Americans citizens' protections under the Bill of Rights. By the way, I didn't learn about this part of the U.S. involvement in World War II in any history class. Any time tension with North Korea came up on the news, I would ask myself, *What will happen to me if the U.S. goes to war with North Korea and Trump decides to issue an executive order that does the same for Americans of Korean descent? Will I, like so many other people of color, experience yet another way that the U.S. Constitution fails to protect Americans who are not white? Will I find myself in fear of being hauled off to an internment camp?* It amazed me that, in 2018, these were legitimate fears for me. It frustrated me to have to experience those fears due to racial characteristics tying me to a culture to which I cannot at all relate. Should a day like that ever come, I believe I will be grateful for having put in a lifetime's work of *othering* myself from *real* Asians. I will hope that every effort I made to prove my whiteness will protect me. But, deep down, I know that my face will always speak the loudest. I will never fit in both communities completely, and I will be assigned to one as society sees fit. My identity will always be at the mercy of others.

MOVING FORWARD

When conflict about my identity arises with others, the macro cultural psychology theory of identity asserts that I am actually fighting societal oppression that is represented and enacted through people's minds and behavior (Esteban-Guitart & Ratner, 2011). People's beliefs are constructed from larger dominant narratives that are culturally and historically located (Jones & Woglom, 2016). When I ask people why they think it is offensive to call someone Asian, most of the time they do not know why they say or believe that it is offensive and I sincerely believe them. My experiences lead me to believe that people need opportunities to stop in moments like those and analyze our thinking, to engage in what Dewey calls reflective thinking (1910/1997). Dewey contends that reflective thinking includes both "(a) a state of perplexity, hesitation, and doubt; and (b) an act of search or investigation directed toward bringing to light further facts which serve to corroborate or nullify the suggested belief" (p. 9). Reflective thinking is a practice we must cultivate from childhood, when we start to ask these questions, so that as adults, we can engage with each other in positive ways. We must also learn to *act*, though, and develop what Paulo Freire (1970/2000) calls *critical consciousness* that will empower us to advocate for ourselves and others. In his "Letter from Birmingham Jail" (1963),

Martin Luther King, Jr. wrote, "Injustice anywhere is a threat to justice everywhere. We are caught in an inescapable network of mutuality, tied in a single garment of destiny. Whatever affects one directly, affects all indirectly". By engaging in critical reflection and action, we can encourage thinking about ourselves and others within the context of the larger society and build the efficacy to make our own decisions about how we will act in the world rather than allow dominant discourse to designate those decisions for us. We can plant seeds in others' minds that may grow through time and experience and serve to liberate us from both visible and invisible systems of oppression.

Implications for Education

Founded in Paulo Freire's (1970) framework of dialogical action in *Pedagogy of the Oppressed*, critical consciousness has been defined in various ways but those definitions share common components: reflection and analysis of a challenge or issue and action to change it (Diemer, Rapa, Voight & McWhirter, 2016; Jemal, 2017; Smith, 1975; Thomas, 2007; Watts, Diemer, & Voight, 2011). While reflection is well-established as a necessary component of teacher development, it is unclear whether teacher education and in-service teachers are trained to critically reflect on their own practice, which is vital to their professional development (Sari & Steh, 2017). One way that schools can support in-service teachers in developing and building critical consciousness is through ongoing *critical professional development*. Currently, traditional professional development tends to frame educators as all-knowing figures who deposit information into students who know nothing, much like money is deposited into a bank (Freire, 1970). By definition, the amount of knowledge students gain is capped at the teacher's level of knowledge. All too often, professional development seems to sustain this "banking" model of education (Brown, 2012) when it positions teachers as learners, too, the recipients of deposits of knowledge. Trainers identified as experts outside of the school will be pulled in to provide mandated professional development to teachers in targeted ways that often align with the school improvement plan. This top-down, outside-expert approach prevents teachers from being able to address the issues that arise in their classrooms and for their students (Worsham, 2015). The frustration that stems from teachers articulating challenges in class and being met with responses that passively acknowledge their struggle without any offer of support for finding a solution may contribute to teacher turnover (Carver-Thomas & Darling-Hammond, 2017).

In stark contrast, critical professional development "positions the teacher as researcher, disrupting the traditional power relationships" (Thomas, 2007, p. 30) and pushes back against the banking practice by giving teachers the space to question the inequities they see in their classes. In keeping with the call for middle grades teachers who know their students well and can serve as advocates (e.g., Andrews, 2011; Brinegar, 2010; Jackson & Davis, 2000; National Middle School Association, 2010), social justice teaching demands a dialectical stance that continuously focuses on knowing our students (Ayers, 1998) and is also reflective of teachers' identities (Thomas, 2007). Kohli, Picower, Martinez, and Ortiz (2015) theorized critical professional development with four major tenets: providing collaborative space, building unity through availability to all teachers rather than those in the same grade or subject area, organized by teachers rather than administrators, and teachers making decisions and planning actions responsive to their contexts as opposed to using prescribed models.

These tenets might also be applied to preservice education programs, where modeling critical reflection on practice and context can disrupt the commonly held belief that teaching is objectifiable (Gay & Kirkland, 2003) and that "same" means "equal". By "using inquiry teaching techniques and helping [preservice] students develop the habit, skills, and spirit of criticalness as habitual elements of their learning experiences" (Gay & Kirkland, 2003, p. 182), preservice teachers may go into the classroom positioned as change agents who can push back against standards-based curriculum and high-stakes testing by building the same habits of inquiry embedded in critical consciousness into their own students' learning experiences. How might this change the next generation of preservice teachers who come through education programs? I wonder how my identity might be different had my teachers built such habits and modeled them in my classes.

Developing critical consciousness is not solely for the sake of having a positive attitude towards different races and cultures. It is vital that educators continue the quest to integrate critical pedagogies into the learning experiences for students of all ages. Educators' critical consciousness enables them to enact social justice through investigating issues and challenges in education that can reveal harmful narratives and discourses that oppress students. As a result of changes in thinking, educators may positively affect student engagement, achievement and test scores, attendance, and civic engagement as well as reduce behaviors that result in loss of instructional time. Social justice is not something we simply perform. Social justice is the way we think and engage with each other. It seeps into the ways we speak to and for each other, our beliefs about what we are capable of and our capacity to be change agents, and the structures and policies that we support in our society.

NOTES

[1] APA format dictates that racial and ethnic groups be designated by proper nouns. However, I choose to use lowercase letters when referencing skin color and capital letters when referring to ethnicity or origin.

[2] I considered using other terms to describe this situation, but there is no substitute for how this phrase can capture my feelings.

REFERENCES

Adichie, C. N. (2009). *Chimamanda Ngozi Adichie: The danger of a single story* [Video file]. Retrieved from https://www.ted.com/talks/chimamanda_adichie_the_danger_of_a_single_story

Andrews, P. G. (2011). Middle grades education policy: Stagecraft to strategy. *Middle School Journal, 43*(2), 54–63.

Ayers, W. (1998). Foreword: Popular education–Teaching for social justice. In W. Ayers, J. A. Hunt, & T. Quinn (Eds.), *Teaching for social justice*. New York, NY: The New Press & Teachers College Press.

Brinegar, K. (2010). "I feel like I'm safe again": A discussion of middle grades organizational structures from the perspectives of immigrant youth and their teachers. *Research in Middle Level Education Online, 33*(9), 1–14.

Brown, P. M. (2012). *An examination of Freire's problem-posing pedagogy: The experiences of three middle school teachers implementing theory into practice* (Unpublished doctoral dissertation). University of Georgia, Athens, GA.

Carver-Thomas, D., & Darling-Hammond, L. (2017). *Teacher turnover: Why it matters and what we can do about it*. Palo Alto, CA: Learning Policy Institute.

Chang, T., & Kwan, K. K. (2009). Asian American racial and ethnic identity. In N. Tewari & A. N. Alvarez (Eds.), *Asian American psychology: Current perspectives*. New York, NY: Routledge/Taylor & Francis Group.

Dewey, J. (1997). *How we think*. Mineola, NY: Dover. (Original work published in 1910, Chicago, IL: DC Heath).

Diemer, M. A., Rapa, L. J., Voight, A. M., & McWhirter, E. H. (2016). Critical consciousness: A developmental approach to addressing marginalization and oppression. *Child Development Perspectives, 10*(4), 216–221.

Eminem. (2002). Lose yourself [Recorded by Eminem]. On *8 mile: Music from and inspired by the motion picture* [Audio recording]. New York, NY: Shady Records.

Esteban-Guitart, M. (2012). Towards a multimethodological approach to identification of funds of identity, small stories and master narratives. *Narrative Inquiry, 22*(1), 173–180.

Esteban-Guitart, M., & Ratner, C. (2011). A macro cultural psychological theory of identity. *Journal of Social Distress and the Homeless, 20*(1–2), 1–22.

Freire, P. (1970/2000). *Pedagogy of the oppressed: 30th anniversary edition*. New York, NY: Continuum.

Hollingsworth, L. D. (2008). Effect of transracial/transethnic adoption on children's racial and ethnic identity and self-esteem: A meta-analytic review. *Marriage & Family Review, 25*(1–2), 99–130.

Jemal, A. (2017). Critical consciousness: A critique and critical analysis of the literature. *Urban Review, 49*(4), 602–626.

Jones, S., & Woglom, J. F. (2016). From where do you read the world? A graphica expansion of literacies for teacher education. *Journal of Adolescent and Adult Literacy, 59*(4), 443–473.

King, M. L. (1963). *Letter from Birmingham Jail*. Philadelphia, PA: American Friends Service Committee.

Kohli, R., Picower, B., Martinez, A., & Ortiz, N. (2015). Critical professional development: Centering the social justice needs of teachers. *International Journal of Critical Pedagogy, 6*(2), 7–24.

Laureau, A. (2011). *Unequal childhoods: Class, race, and family life* (2nd ed.). Berkeley, CA: The University of California Press.

Lee, R. M., & Miller, M. J. (2009). History and psychology of adoptees in Asian America. In N. Tewari & A. N. Alvarez (Eds.), *Asian American psychology: Current perspectives*. New York, NY: Routledge/ Taylor & Francis Group.

Lee, S. J. (2015). *Unraveling the model minority stereotype: Listening to Asian American youth* (2nd ed.). New York, NY: Teachers College Press.

Nakashima, C. L. (1992). In M. P. Root (Ed.), *Racially mixed people in America*. Newbury Park, CA: Sage Publications.

National Middle School Association. (2010). *This we believe: Keys to educating young adolescents*. Westerville, OH: Author.

Oakes, J. (2005). *Keeping track: How schools structure inequality* (2nd ed.). New Haven, CT: Yale University Press.

Omi, M., & Winant, H. (1994). *Racial formation in the United States: From the 1960s to the 1990s* (2nd ed.). New York, NY: Routledge.

Ratner, C. (2009). The cultural psychology of oppression and liberation. *Journal for Social Distress & the Homeless, 18*(3–4), 231–268.

Saric, M., & Steh, B. (2017). Critical reflection in the professional development of teachers: Challenges and possibilities. *C.E.P.S Journal, 7*(3), 67–85.

Shih, M., & Sanchez, D. T. (2005). Perspectives and research on the positive and negative implications of having multiple racial identities. *Psychological Bulletin, 131*(4), 569–591.

Simon, N. A. (2018). Mixed identity: The invisible majority author(s). *The Journal of Museum Education, 34*(3), 249–253.

Smith, W. A. (1976). *The meaning of conscientizacao; The goal of Paolo Freire's pedagogy.* Amherst, MA: Center for International Education, University of Massachusetts.

Spickard, P. R. (1992). The illogic of American racial categories. In M. P. Root (Ed.), *Racially mixed people in America.* Newbury Park, CA: Sage Publications.

Sullivan, T. (2014, June). Where have you gone, Horatio Alger? *Harvard Business Review, 92*(6), 134–135.

Thomas, A. B. (2007). Supporting new visions for social justice teaching: The potential for professional development networks. *Penn GSE Perspectives on Urban Education, 5*(1), 18.

Watts, R. J., Diemer, M. A., & Voight, A. M. (2011). Critical consciousness: Current status and future directions. In C. A. Flanagan & B. D. Christens (Eds.), *New directions for child and adolescent development* (pp. 43–57). San Francisco, CA: Jossey-Bass.

Wise, T. (2011). *White like me: Reflections on race from a privileged son* (2nd ed.). New York, NY: Soft Skull Press.

Worsham, B. W. (2015). *How middle school teachers construct understandings of their job-embedded learning experiences* (Unpublished doctoral dissertation). University of Georgia, Athens, GA.

HANNAH R. STOHRY

7. TRANSFORMATIVE CONSCIOUSNESS RAISING QUESTIONS

Are we "woke" or awake or aware to what is happening around us? What is it that transforms us? What is it that makes us change? Change comes when we learn or challenge ourselves to think outside the boxes we place around ourselves and others. We must wonder about where to start when it comes to making changes. It usually starts with something that catches us, makes us think. As a social worker and a social scientist, I come from the mindset that knowledge can come from the seemingly simplest places, not necessarily from unsolvable mathematical equations. We could sit with the meaning of a word and how it is applied. Why does this matter in the context of middle education and the nature of this book and our narrative expressions of our middle level experiences and how to create consciousness and change moving forward?

The following are a list of questions to which educators and activists can refer to evaluate self, raise consciousness for self and others, and these may impact one's action in moving forward. Change can happen. It usually starts within; our children and students feel our care, enthusiasm, and sincerity of our character and values in our teaching. We are not as sanitized as we think, despite being and feeling constricted by standards and school culture. We can make small changes and spark change, especially in this day and age where difference (especially for those holding many intersecting identities) is considered deviant. We can no longer conform. Feel free to explore and sit with what comes during reflection. We can sit with (dis) comfort. Again, the social worker in me is sharing that taking moments to accept and commit to non-judgment is important when sitting with something, perhaps, just one question. I imagined over 100 questions that I myself pondered. Pick a question and ponder over it, in whatever way you usually can in your reflective spaces.

The section offers starter questions for raising consciousness for self as well as for our youth and students, to create inclusive environments, to facilitate healthy identity development directed by students, from a teacher-learner stance. These questions question what we are doing in the classroom and why we do them. These come from my own process of writing a chapter for this book, in Part 5, titled, Raising Consciousness for Multi-Racial Third Culture Kids. Please refer to that chapter for more context on the generation of these questions. These questions were just something I started to think about that lead to more questions. I thought they might be helpful for educators and administrators to think about, though, they can really

© KONINKLIJKE BRILL NV, LEIDEN, 2019 | DOI:10.1163/9789004393813_007

be applicable to anyone and everyone. It is okay to have questions, and to discover what comes up when we are trying to understand something and that this is a part of the consciousness raising process where we are critically examining something and potentially taking it to learn more and act on it, or create change for self and others, to create a better society.

Q: What are my positionalities? (I can ask myself this over and over again because sometimes this positionality changes and reflecting on this leads to humility of place, power, and privilege.)

Q: In what ways do my positionalities influence my pedagogy, teaching philosophy, teaching practice, curriculum, activities, and students in the classroom?

Q: In what ways do those privileges manifest in my job and relationship with others, not just in the educational spheres?

Q: In other ways, am I practicing what I am preaching to my students?

Q: Why do we do the things we do?

Q: Do the images I present in my class activities and curriculum reflect and represent the diverse experiences of my students? Why or why not?

Q: Have I used the heteronormative binary (n)either/(n)or framework in my communication with students and families and in my teaching pedagogy?

Q: In what ways do I encourage students to use the both/and framework in their lives?

Q: Do we teach the mind/body/spirit connection?

Q: Why do we stay away from teaching spirituality in the classroom?

Q: How effective are the reflective classroom activities I use? What does reflection look like for different students? Can we encourage ourselves and students to express reflection in various activities?

Q: In what ways can I utilize a critical spirituality framework to reflect on my teaching practices and act as a result?

Q: Who is benefiting from this lesson/framework? In what ways am I benefiting?

Q: In what ways are my students and their families benefiting/suffering as a result of this lesson/framework/teaching method?

Q: In what ways can I adopt the teacher-learner stance in today's classroom?

Q: In what ways can I give power to my students that they do not feel outside the classroom? Can we facilitate activities in the classroom where students can connect to their communities?

Q: How can I learn more about the diverse experiences of my multi-racial TCK students? Or, students with diverse experiences?

Q: What is a humanizing pedagogy?

Q: How can I incorporate humanizing pedagogy in the classroom?

Q: In this humanizing pedagogy, can we teach our students compassion for self and others?

Q: Can we deal with the suffering, discrimination and reproduction of the subjugation/subversion of humanity as a result of these constructs?

Q: Can we accept humans as people who have flaws or make mistakes, yet as whole, spiritual beings?

Q: How do we continue to create a fair and just society as a result?

Q: How do I teach compassion?

Q: In what ways do we recognize compassion in our students?

Q: How often do we recognize the empathy and compassion and goodness in our students?

Q: Can we extend this compassion across a micro, mezzo, macro and global scale?

Q: What does consciousness raising really look like? Will we ever be truly aware of our situation? What does inner change actually mean? Can societal change that which influences inner change?

Q: In what ways can you challenge the curriculum you use?

Q: Can you use the existing curriculum and engage students in the critique of the knowledge they are tested on versus the interpersonal knowledge that they use every day?

Q: How can we engage students in examining the capital that they exchange every day on those micro, mezzo, macro, and global levels?

Q: What is raising consciousness?

Q: What kinds of consciousness raising exist?

Q: When it comes to learning/teaching theories and putting them into action, how do we make this happen?

Q: Am I teaching just to teach?

Q: How did I get to this place?

Q: Since race is a social construction, how can we ask students to (re)imagine how their own personal identities have been constructed? Asking students to connect it to other ideas or topics that have been socially constructed and how would they (re)construct them into something that is better and more socially just.

Q: What kind of a difference can we and our students make on the micro, mezzo, macro/global levels?

Q: Can we anticipate the implications of difference?

Q: In what ways can I utilize critical pedagogy?

Q: In what ways can I utilize contemplative pedagogy?

Q: What has (not) worked in my classroom curriculum?

Q: What are critical questions educators can ask of ourselves, our work, and how our schools approach inclusivity?

Q: What messages are we sending/receiving about student identities?

Q: How would I celebrate multi-racial TCK ambiguity?

Q: What would it look like for me to sit with ambiguity/discomfort/dissonance?

Q: What kind of classroom assignments can celebrate the both/and instead of (n) either/(n)or?

Q: What does fusion mean?

Q: Can I create a fusion food assignment where I encourage students to pick several ingredients that might not seem to work well together and create a new ambiguous dish, something that represents the student's intersectional identities?

Q: What about storytelling and literary assignments?

Q: What influences what stories we tell?

Q: Why do we do the things we do?

Q: Am I willing to be vulnerable to talk about difficult subjects like race?

Q: What influences this vulnerability?

Q: How do I engage families in their children's lives and expression of identities?

Q: What about a family's history (and influence/in relation to culture) assignment that students can design to seek their heritages?

Q: To what extent has race/ethnicity/culture (or other intersections) influenced my identities?

Q: What would critical training look like for schools and educators?

Q: Where did I start in the classroom?

Q: Where can I start in the classroom?

Q: How can what I am doing in the classroom transcend these students' lives outside of the classroom?

Q: In what ways am I using a deficit lens?

Q: In what ways can we refuse the deficit lens?

Q: In what ways are we using the strengths-based approach in our personal lives?

Q: How do we grow the strengths base?

Q: Have I ever been a non-majority? Why or why not?

Q: What did it feel like to be Othered?

Q: Have I Othered somebody else? Why or why not?

Q: What are the motivators or barriers to speaking against Othering?

Q: How can I take these Othering experience as an example for how to live my life?

Q: What has worked for me in the classroom? Why or why not?

Q: What has not worked for me in the classroom? Why or why not?

Q: In what ways am I empowering my students?

Q: In what ways am I empowering my students to challenge stereotypes?

Q: How do I share what works or does not work in my classroom with others?

Q: In what ways am I inviting students to explore the intersection of their identities?

Q: Am I inviting students to participate?

Q: How do I know that I am empowering my students?

Q: What are the cues that I am empowering students?

Q: Is there another way to look at student empowerment?

Q: What was my perspective 5 years ago?

Q: What could my perspective be in 5 years?

Q: When was the last time I fact-checked what I am teaching?

Q: When was the last time I challenged my students to consider another perspective in the classroom and in our classroom texts?

Q: How do I go about teaching intersectional identities to my students?

Q: In what ways have I contributed to the dominant narrative and White privilege?

Q: Who am I?

Q: Who are you?

Q: What makes me "me" and you "you"?

Q: In what ways are we different and similar?

Q: Does it matter at the end of the day? Why or why not?

Q: How would you (de)construct race and ethnicity?

Q: How would you encourage your students to (de)construct race?

Q: How can you raise consciousness by externalizing from the self and engaging students in activities where they are thinking outside of self?

Q: How can you engage students in using their creative skills (e.g. art, music, dance) to express their identities, in ways that encourage all styles of learning?

Q: For an activity suggestion: Create a television show that shows your story. How would your family be (re)presented on a popular television show? What parts would you include and leave out? Who would join your family on television? Why or why not? Would those other characters look like you? Why or why not?

Q: How do I include images and narratives in my classroom that links curriculum with the here and now and represents ambiguous identities?

Q: How is what I am doing relevant to myself and my students today?

Q: How can characters (like the capybara animal) co-exist when their existence and value placed on them is that they are in existence in opposition to others?

Q: Do we teach co-existence?

Q: Am I a leader?

Q: What is a leader?

Q: What is transformation?

Q: What is transformational leadership?

Q: In what ways do I invite transformation in the classroom?

Q: In what ways do I encourage others (students?) to explore and adopt leadership?

Q: How can oppositional forces (or difference) or similarities bring people together? In the food example, using a prompt of asking students to pair a flavor that would be oppositional to another ingredient and create something that goes together.

Q: How can we take the word "map" and make an activity out of it? Try by examining maps and countries and how they are situated and the history of how those countries became one. Look at varying countries that live in opposition with each other. Know our personal relationships to certain countries and why. Take an influential leader who has not fit the norm and examining what makes them and in what ways they live in conflict.

Q: How do we work with other administrators, educators, teachers and students and encourage critical thinking?

Q: What does shifting perspective mean?

Q: How is shifting perspective different from raising consciousness?

Q: How do we engage students in shifting perspective (on any issue)?

Q: Or, how can you have a student look at issue from several different perspectives?

Q: How do you know you have shifted perspective?

Q: How do you know that they have shifted perspective? Is this something you can measure (pre- and post-test opportunities?)?

Q: To what extent are you allowing the student to take the lead in their own perspective-shifting and raising consciousness journey?

Q: How involved are you in your students' journeys? Why or why not?

Q: What does it look like when we are telling our story through our eyes?

Q: How do we tell our story through someone else's eyes?

Q: What would narratives look like for students?

Q: Can we have them design their own assignments/activities?

Q: How can you craft an activity that blurs the lines and challenges those borders/limitations?

Q: What would counter-narratives look like?

Q: At the risk of being redundant and using the word "unpacking", what would box unpacking look like for students?

Q: What happens when a student resists in the classroom?

Q: Besides disciplinary regulations being broken, what is a healthy amount of resistance that a student can express in the classroom?

Q: What would it look like if you resist binary or dichotomous boxes in your own life?

Q: What would it look like if a student calls you out about your putting them in boxes?

Q: What were to happen if we were to just sit with the questions?

Q: What happens when we accept living without answers?

Q: What were to happen if we were to be okay to muddy the waters and refuse to conform?

Q: What has been working for me in my classroom that celebrates this raising consciousness and how can I share it with others?

PART 3

EXPLORING THE CONVERGENCES OF IDENTITY AND CULTURAL RESPONSIVENESS

RAYMOND ADAMS

8. WILL I EVER BE ENOUGH?

An African Louisiana Creole's Narrative on Race, Ethnicity, and Belonging

INTRODUCTION

The sociolinguistics and cultural identity of Louisiana Creoles, specifically those of African descent, have been an intricate part of Louisiana culture for countless decades; yet with this rich heritage, their cultural mixture is contentiously viewed among members of the African American community as a form of privilege. For example, due to this inter-racial combination, some Louisiana Creoles of Color are found to be more aesthetically (e.g., White) in comparison to darker complexions. Using his own lived experiences, the author will present a counter-narrative that aims at decontextualizing the struggles of this particular ethnocultural group. Such counternarratives are imperative given the racialized experiences of Louisiana Creoles of Color. Historically, this ethnocultural group has been categorized as a composite of racially mixed individuals from African, Native American, European, and Spanish descent. This amalgamation of races represents the influence of the socio-political power exerted through White colonialism within the lives of Louisiana Creoles of Color. This same power differential has been recapitulated in various forms in present day Louisiana Creoles of Color. In this chapter, the author maintains a reflexive awareness, while exploring his positionality as a self-identified Louisiana Creole native, negotiating the sociolinguistic and cultural differences between non-Francophone speaking African Americans and Francophone speaking Louisiana Creoles of Color in Louisiana. Using a social constructionist perspective guided by the Critical Race Theory (CRT) and Collins' (2015) Theory of Intersectionality (TOI) the author, through narrative inquiry, analyzes factors germane to Louisiana Creoles' experiences in relation to race-based issues that are present within the community where the author resides and enacts inquiry.

A SITUATED IDENTITY

Cope and Schafer (2017) describe "the polysemous term, *creole*" as a word that was "used at different times and in various geographical regions to describe diverse identities, languages, peoples, ethnicities, racial heritages, and cultural artefacts" (p. 2653).

© KONINKLIJKE BRILL NV, LEIDEN, 2019 | DOI:10.1163/9789004393813_008

This description of the word *creole* best describes my identity as a Francophone speaking Louisiana Creole of Color in Northeast Louisiana. For months, I have struggled with writing my "counterstory" (Solórzano & Yosso, 2002) of being bilingual among non-Francophone speaking African and White Americans within a system where English is the norm. This system in which I received a majority of my formalized education forced me to compartmentalize in many ways my ethnic identity as a Louisiana Creole. Interestingly, my "double consciousness" (Du Bois, 1897), in being racially African but ethnically Louisiana Creole, supports Dubois's definition of the term as a "sense of always looking at one's self through the eyes of others, of measuring one's soul by the tape of a world that looks on in amused contempt and pity" (Du Bois, 1897, p. 1).

Nonetheless, I, as a Louisiana Creole of Color, ethnically identify my maternal descendancy through "the *gens de couleur libres*, the free people of color or "colored Creoles" (Dubois & Melançon, 2000, p. 238). In that same vein, understand that contemporarily, a majority choose to identify as African American; in addition, recognize even fewer speak Louisiana Creole French often referred to as *"kouri-vini"* (Adams, 2016, 2017; Cope & Schafer, 2017; Gilmore, 1933; Louden, 2000). It is also important to note that the Creole identity encompasses other racialized groups (e.g., Acadian French (Cajuns), Native Americans, Haitians, etc.); however, this narrative will be spoken through the lens of a cisgendered male Louisiana Creole of Color from Northeast Louisiana. Having defined what is meant by Louisiana Creole of Color, I will now move on to discuss how the two theoretical frameworks: Collins' (2015) Theory of Intersectionality (TOI) and Critical Race Theory (CRT) will contextualize my perceptions and experiences as a Francophone speaking Louisiana Creoles of Color among non-Francophone speaking African Americans. By providing a brief overview of each theory dichotomous identity experiences as a Louisiana Creole of Color can be culturally situated within a frame that speaks authentically to my lived experiences.

BRIEF OVERVIEW OF CRT AND INTERSECTIONALITY

Before proceeding to examine CRT, it will be necessary to briefly chronicle its development within the body of Critical Legal Studies (CLS) in the mid-1970s (DeCuir & Dixson, 2004). CRT arose due to Derrick Bell's critique of how CLS scholars excluded race and racism from the legal discourse (Taylor, Edward, Gillborn, & Ladson-Billings, 2009). It was this exclusion which catapulted Bell to speculate the ways in which "public problems are defined can influence how laws and policies are constructed and interpreted" (Tate, 1997, p. 218). Along with other notable CRT contributors (e.g., Richard Delgado, Angela Harris, Mari Matsuda, Kimberle Crenshaw, & Patricia Williams), they conceptualized the basic five tenets of CRT (Delgado & Stefancic, 2012; Taylor, Edward, Gillborn, & Ladson-Billings, 2009; Harris, 1993). These five core tenets of CRT have transformed the ways in which various disciplines (e.g., sociology, law, education) problematize issues around equity and equality for minoritized groups (Ford & Airhihenbuwa, 2010; Ladson-Billings, 2003; Ladson-Billings & Donnor, 2005; Ladson-Billings & Tate, 1995; Salter & Adams, 2013). It is also important to note that other CRT scholars have theorized concepts outside the Black and White binary (Brayboy, 2005; Solorzano, 1997, 1998; Solorzano & Bernal, 2001). Nonetheless, CRT, as a theory, according to Dumas and Ross (2016) "attempts to make sense of and respond to institutionalized racism, as this racism is experienced and endured by Black people" (p. 418). With that understanding, Solorzano and Yosso's (2001) proposed description of the basic five tenets of CRT will undergird this counternarrative:

> (1) The centrality of race and racism and their intersectionality with other forms of subordination; (2) The challenge to dominant ideology; (3) The commitment to social justice; (4) The centrality of experiential knowledge; and (5) The transdisciplinary perspective. (pp. 472–473)

Each tenet is described in such a way that will reveal the ways I negotiate my racial, cultural, and social identity(ies) with that of the oppositional collective identities that exist within the context of our society. In conclusion, the proposed five CRT tenets seek to deconstruct the ways I experience and perceive my ethnic identity as a Louisiana Creole of Color in a post-racial society. Let's now turn toward TOI, a theoretical frame, originally coined by Kimberle Crenshaw, a Black feminist legal scholar, to explicate the multiplicative ways in which race, gender, and class can affect Black women within the realm of law (Crenshaw et al., 1995; Crenshaw, 1991, 1989). However, in this narrative, I want to expand its analytical premise to my situated racial identity as an African male who ethnically self-identifies as a Louisiana Creole of Color. Therefore, I will adopt Collins' (2015) TOI which states that it's "the critical insight that race, class, gender, sexuality, ethnicity, nation, ability, and age operate not as unitary, mutually exclusive entities, but as reciprocally constructing phenomena that in turn shape complex social inequalities" (p. 2). As such coupled with CRT, TOI will allow for readers to understand how race, power, oppression, and ascribed identity roles have either positively or negatively influenced how I saw myself as a bilingual African male from Louisiana existing in a monolingual society and varied systems.

I am of the firm belief that the White majoritarian interpretations of race and racism both historically and contemporarily have significantly contributed to the disillusion that race no longer has any bearing on our everyday lives or interactions. This fallacy fuels not only the Black and White binary; in particular, among Black Americans but also obfuscates those of "mixed identity" (Hurd, 2012) to the point where they feel ostracized despite their racial membership within the African diaspora. As mentioned earlier, CRT and TOI will become the analytical lenses in which I utilize to narrate on the binary opposition I experienced as a way to re-story the ways in which my race, ethnicity, gender, and identity intersected within various systems of this society.

The Centrality of Race and Racism and Their Intersectionality with Other Forms of Subordination

Regarding the intersection of race and racism, CRT is uniquely positioned to expound unapologetically on its role within the lives of minoritized groups (e.g., Africans, Asians, Latinos); yet, how can it be utilized to interpret its role among ethnocultural groups (e.g., Louisiana Creoles of Color)? I have always understood race to be socially constructed (Ladson-Billings & Tate, 1995). With that said, both my parents, were intentional about educating me early on how my race and ethnicity would be interpreted within a racist White society and educational system. For instance, on June 25, 1953, Jet Magazine, a notable Black news magazine published the following article entitled: "Are Creoles Negroes". This query, though saturated with colorism, allowed for a wider discussion on who gets to dictate membership within an ethnocultural group? Granted, I was not born during this period. However, it offers a lens in which to discuss the intersection of race and racism within my lived experience as a Louisiana Creoles of Color. So as to have a clear understanding of how colorism will be defined, I will utilize Hunter's (2016) description which is as follows: "colorism describes the way skin tone, within racial groups, affects the intensity of that discrimination, the frequency, and the privileges that the lightest-skinned experience" (p. 55).

Colorism, in general, makes a permanent psychological indentation on how inter-racial individuals view their overall identity as they try to co-exist in a Black-White binary society. Although, I am well aware of and closely identify with my Senegalese ancestry, "skin-color bias" (Hunter, 2016) are direct by product of White colonist standards of beauty. Such biases were formalized through the legacy of African slavery and were perpetuated through the practice of plaçage in colonial Louisiana (DeGruy, 2005; Dominguez, 1977; Hunter, 2016; Thompson, 2001). For clarity, plaçage, was a state-sanctioned practice in where White slave owners would enter into contractual marriages with enslaved African women before taking on a more "socially appropriate" marriage. This practice is believed to have institutionalized the "color hierarchies" (Hunter, 2016) thus perpetuating the divisiveness between the present-day descendants of enslaved Africans and *"gens de couleur libres"* (Dubois & Melançon, 2000).

In my youth, I saw ugliness in my African identity; as a result, I would often ask my Black mother, "Why am I not light-skinned like my eldest brother or my grand-mère paternelle (i.e., paternal grandmother)? Though her tender-hearted reflections were genuine, I remained perplexed as to why I was darker than my grand-mère paternelle yet of similar complexion to my grand-mère maternelle (i.e., maternal grandmother). Even though, both possessed the same inter-racial heritage, my grand-mère paternelle, was passé blanc (i.e., passed for White) while my grand-mère maternelle possessed the typical phenotypical features of a person directly descended from enslaved Africans.

As an illustration, when I first socialized with my grand-mère paternelle I assumed she was a White woman with a very decent accent; however, it wasn't until I had further dialogue with my biological father I was illuminated to the reality of her racial heritage. Above all, both my belated grandmothers, closely identified racially as African American women yet ethnically as Louisiana Creoles of Color. It was through their counternarratives I learned more about how our sociolinguistics varied significantly from other African Americans. For example, my first encounter with racism occurred during a learning exercise in middle school where a White teacher made a derogatory comment about my accent and bilingualism in front of my peers (Adams, 2016). This racialized experience generated feelings of exclusion not only from a group where I hold a racial membership but also confirmed that the Black and White binary will always be a factor in my identity formation.

At that moment, I recognized how Black and Brown's folks stereotype even be prejudicial toward individuals of inter-racial identities within their racial group. Also, how White males utilize race and racism to inform identity politics for those historically oppressed. Collins (2015) espouses that "intersecting identities produce distinctive social experiences for specific individuals and social groups" (p. 12). Expressing my identity as a Louisiana Creole of Color through the lens of CRT and TOI showcases a way how one can express their inter-racial heritage without subscribing to one element of their identity for societal appeasement. Expanding the discourse of how I re-interpret my personhood, identity, race, and gender serves as a way of disrupting "the master narrative" (Ladson-Billings, 1998) which is explained by Woodson (2015) as "the social mythologies that mute, erase, and neutralize features of racial history and struggle in ways that reinforce ideologies and practices of White supremacy" (p. 5). In the next section that follows, this CRT theoretical construct undergirds how my counternarrative challenges the historic debate of "Are Creoles Negroes".

The Challenge of the Dominant Ideology

As described on the previous page, "the master narrative" (Ladson-Billings, 1998) the United States has historically perpetuated through the conflation of race, nationality, and ethnicity is primarily aimed toward maintaining the White status quo; in spite of this, race, ethnicity, and nationality have been reframed by well-known race scholars so as to speak truth into power of how this conflation impends racial equality and equity.

Therefore, it becomes crucial we utilize definitions that best articulate the way in which each term is understood in this counternarrative so as to "challenge the dominant ideology" (Solorzano & Yosso, 2001). Let's first begin with the way race is defined by Burton, Bonilla-Silva, Ray, and Buckelew (2010) as "the assumption that individuals can be divided into groups based on phenotype or genotype and that those groups have meaningful differences" (p. 440). As I continue the dialogue in regards to the 1953 Jet article entitled "Are Creoles Negroes" this definition captures not only the core of my main argument but also as a whole how our society conceptualizes race. In the same like manner, this racial conceptualization captures the ways my ethnic identity as Louisiana Creole of Color is regulated in the Black and White binary discourse.

Through my interpretation, the discussion proposed in the original publication offers a one-dimensional depiction of the ethnicity known as Louisiana Creole. By conflating and propagating the racial label, *"Negro"*, as a generalizable term for all members of the African diaspora reflects the master narrative in where Whites viewed African descended folks as inferior biologically, genetically, and culturally (Espino, 2012). As stated earlier, I was not born during this period; thus, viewing the neutrality of the racist label *Negro* among those within the African American population remains a very foreign concept to me; however, my narrative seeks to problematize the way in which it reproduces negative interpretations of whose eligible for racial membership within the Africa diaspora. To be specific, let's examine the concept of the "one-drop rule" (Khanna, 2010) which implicitly denotes, "if a person of whatever age or gender is believed to have any African ancestry, that person is regarded as Black" (Winthrop, 2014, p. 99). In fact, Garroutte (2001) stated, "Up until 1970, Louisiana state law defined as Black anyone possessing "a trace of Black ancestry. The legislature formally revised its definition of racial identity in that year, declaring that only those possessing more than one-thirty-second degree "Negro blood" were to be considered Black" (p. 231).

This master narrative is a pervasive historical reminder of White supremacies' ideological influence over those with interracial identities such as Louisiana Creoles of Color. Sadly, historically oppressed groups' (e.g., African Americans, Africans, Caribbean, and Dominicans) abject acceptance of such White supremacist ideologies further compound and delegitimize expressions of ethnicities inherent within the African diaspora. Admittedly, White colonialist influences exacerbated such beliefs; however, we, as a people must continue to actively repel how we reproduce anti-Black narratives of membership. First and foremost, Shriver and Kittles (2004) remind those descended from enslaved Africans that "From approximately 1619 to 1850, tens of millions of indigenous West and Central Africans from 7 coastal regions were kidnapped and transported to the Americas" (p. 612).

Through this deracination, racial and ethnic identities were decimated, traditions and customs lost, and our African tribal affiliations erased primarily because of the Trans-Atlantic Slave Route. Before proceeding to examine ethnicity, it will be necessary for me to reiterate how I express my racial composition. As a naturalized American citizen who was born to two parents of "Senegambia ancestry" (Richard, 2013), as such, I fully embrace and celebrate the intersectionality of my ethnic membership (Wolof and Louisiana Creole) as a self-identified African-American male. This affirmation neither dilutes nor minimizes my racial affiliation rather confirms that "notions of race and ethnicity and their intersections are fluid, dynamic and context-specific (Thornton, Taylor, Chatters, & Forsythe-Brown, 2017, p. 507). Bearing this in mind, it moves the conversation to the term ethnicity which as interpreted by Burton, Bonilla-Silva, Ray, and Buckelew (2010), "refers to a subset of people whose members share common national, ancestral, cultural, immigration, or religious characteristics that distinguish them from other groups" (p. 440).

To this end, ethnicity is not extrapolated genuinely within historically oppressed groups nor within the majority of our White educational systems (e.g., PreK-12; colleges, universities). Alridge (2006) alluded to this fact when she stated, "that American history textbooks present discrete, heroic, one dimensional, and neatly packaged master narratives that deny students a complex, realistic, and rich understanding of people and events in American history" (p. 662). This purposeful extraction prevents many from seeing the significance of ethnic minorities' cultural contributions historically. Earlier I spoke of my Senegambia ancestry; interestingly, archaeologists have demonstrated through archival research that early enslaved Senegambians; in particular, the ethnic group known as Wolof contributed significantly to the Africanising of colonial Louisiana (Richard, 2013). Though only equipped with a 6th-grade education, before her passing in 2010 my grand-mère maternelle, by in large, instilled the importance of educating me of this fact through the art of storytelling.

I, as a younger man, would regularly enjoy sitting on her front porch in Northeast Louisiana and listen as she shared her lived experiences with her brothers and sisters on their ancestral farm in South Louisiana. It was during one of these story sessions while we ate our traditional Sunday meal of seasoned catfish, hot-water cornbread, and collar-greens, which I better understood why race and ethnicity are partialized during discourse around Louisiana Creoles of Color. Sadly, according to Lynn (2006), "African Americans have, more often than not, been pathologized and viewed as a homogenous group" (p. 106). It is because of this homogenous interpretation African Americans who possess an intersectional identity are left with no recourse of how best to process their entire identity. Ray, Randolph, Underhill, and Luke (2017) speculate, "Research is needed to assess how minorities from different racial backgrounds and social structural locations understand diversity (p. 6).

Based on narratives from individuals within my own family of origin and those outside, I believe these scholars' assertion to be accurate. This lack of understanding as well as exploration around diversity; in particular, African American diversity, stifles broader discussions of how our intersectional identities can coalesce. I am of the belief for us to achieve real inclusivity we much rebuke exclusionary denunciations such as "Can Louisiana Creoles of Color call themselves Black given their enmeshed White ancestry" especially given our current socio-political climate (e.g., Trump administration). Despite this, little progress has been made in exploring the extent, we as a society, have politicized nationality to justify ignorant rhetoric that seeks to remove any historical or contemporary dialogue about the ways ethnicity, race, and racism have historically intersected in American Society let alone how they are expressed culturally.

As I unabashedly begin to offer experiences to such ignorant rhetoric, I want to reiterate my ethnocentric beliefs toward my race, ethnicity, and culture can't be conflated to surmise my lack of appreciation for my national origin (e.g., American citizenship). "Calling a thing a thing", a favorite colloquial of mine, challenges the ways we reinforce our paternalistic relationship to "the hegemony of Whiteness" (Sleeter, 2016, p. 5) on an individual and structural level. Individually, some Black and Brown folk have reinforced Whiteness to the point where their conversations and interpretations about language, race, ethnicity, and nationality closely align with White Supremacy. To illustrate, I can recall a conversation between myself and my maternal cousin in where we spoke French as we waited for our meal at a local restaurant in here Louisiana. Our conversation at that time was twofold: (1) we wanted to practice our language proficiency for class, and (2) strategize how we were going to secure permission and funds to travel to Ghana as a part of a study abroad from our parents with our other white counterparts.

Unbeknownst to us, a middle age, African American male approached us and stated, "You all need to learn how to speak English, don't they teach you that in school, and here in America we speak English". For context, my following response was that of a 13-year-old who at the time did not have the maturity nor the appropriate lexicon to address this stranger's ignorance of bilingualism; thus, my response was emotional, not rational plus it occurred a week after the incident with my White middle school teacher's act of racism towards me (Adams, 2016). Though we both rose up in anger, somehow my voice was elevated to the point of me uttering in perfect English, "You first can kiss my Black ass and go to Hell; second it would be in your best interest to step off from us before you get tore up from the floor up!" In recognizing his disadvantage, as my cousin was bigger and taller than him, the stranger eventually conceded and walked away.

Structurally, this vivid memory of a Black Americans' misaligned interpretation of our "supposed" linguistic deficit as Black youth speaks to the ways internalized racism and linguicism intersect on a national scale. Choi (2017) wrote, "linguicism normalizes native (monolingual) speaker values, beliefs, and experiences as those dominant and thus legitimate" (p. 668). Along the same lines, Pérez Huber (2016) discusses how "racist nativism framework articulates how perceived racial differences construct false perceptions of People of Color as "non-native", and not belonging to the monolithic "American" identity—an identity that has historically been tied to perceptions and constructions of Whiteness" (p. 220). This legitimacy leads me to discuss why I have adopted an intersectional social justice frame not only as a part of my CRT pedagogy but also to counter motifs that affirm regardless of race, ethnicity, the nation of origin, gender, class, or creed all Americans are treated equally. Unfortunately, the latter is the furthest from the truth; as such, the section that follows will expound on why Solorzano and Yosso's (2001) proposed description of "the commitment to social justice" (p. 472) is especially important not only for individuals and groups with interracial heritage but also as we look to survive under the Trump's administration.

My Commitment to Social Justice under a Trump Administration

One of the most important events of 2017 according to Ray, Randolph, Underhill, and Luke (2017) was how "Donald Trump's election has shattered the collective hallucination of postracialism" (p. 1). On January 12, 2018, President Donald J. Trump described Haiti and Black countries in Africa as "shithole countries". His crude pronouncement can only be interpreted as dog-whistle politics which camouflages both his racist hostility for Black people as well as his belief that these countries are inferior in social and economic structures in comparison to the United States as well as Norway. In essence, he tries to justify his Eurocentric immigration policies by claiming that people from these countries lack what it takes to be productive as well as useful to America's overall society.

In redefining how a person's worth is established, President Trump consciously engages in acts of social injustice. Such statements are germane to my own ethno-racial identity (e.g., African/Louisiana Creole/Wolof) given my African ancestry. Nonetheless, such defamatory proclamations by our 45th President are not surprising, given President Trump's disdain for Black people. His hate, in general, for "People of Color" (Pérez Huber, 2016) is calculated which make him extremely dangerous given his new political position.

The evidence of his hate can be clearly seen in the case of the Central Park Five in where he took out a newspaper ad provoking violence against them in the late 80s, then by his denial of housing based on race through his rental property, and his most recent declaration of the social justice activist, Colin Kaepernick, as a "son of a bitch" because of his silent protests against police brutality. The dismissal of President Trump's anti-Black rhetoric by his base perpetuates the illusion that social injustices among Black and Brown folks are not as severe; however, Pérez Huber and Solorzano (2015) makes it plain, that "without a structural understanding of the racism that manifests in the everyday lives of People of Color, it remains an elusive concept that becomes difficult to 'see' in any tangible way" (p. 7). As a result, we live in a society, where we are unable to acknowledge or remedy the problem. To that end, for us to establish social justice Gillborn (2015) demands CRT scholars begin to "explore how raced inequities are shaped by processes that also reflect, and are influenced by, other dimensions of identity and social structure" (p. 278). With that in mind, allow me to expound about the ways identities such as race and state serve as key motivating factors in my commitment to social justice under this current administration.

Recently, Bracey (2015) synthesized CRT alongside the six core tenets of Omi and Winant's (1994) Racial State Theory (RST) "racialization of the state; state as white institutional space; instrumentalism; interest convergence; fluid boundaries; and permanent racist orientation" (p. 555). In doing so, he moves past a broad CRT theorization and more towards directly addressing what he describes as "a CRT of State that views racial conflict as foundational, institutionalized, permanent, and a perduring guide for the development and racial character of state structures" (Bracey, 2015, p. 555). To enumerate, President Donald J. Trump's politicizing of racial conflict contributes to the moral bankruptcy of the state; in other words; his acts of social injustice (e.g., repeal of DACA); namely, towards Blacks, Hispanic, and Latinos, directly speaks to why Bracey (2015) suggests "it is reasonable to conclude that state power will primarily reside in the hands of people apathetic or hostile to antiracist projects" (p. 562). Anti-Blackness is often inherent in institutional structures; as a result, making it not only possible for this sort of racial apathy but also antipathy. Consequently, while I am aware that no form of Black centered protest whether written or oral has ever met the mass approval of Whiteness; its paramount those from interracial heritages especially given our history with the institutionalization of miscegenation laws in various states of the union (White, Love, DeBose, & Loprieno, 2015) to rebel against racist state structures which deny social justice for those seeking freedom.

While it may be true, "People of Color live in a world where race is salient, where racism is alive, and where there is no shortage of reminders of the racism around them" (Atwood & López, 2014, p. 1135) remaining ignorant to the dangers of such racialized state structures makes us complicit in the ways Whites deny other Black and Brown folk their basic humanity and rights.

Dismantling these structures of oppression through counterstories is a tool prized by a wide array of CRT and TOI scholars (Covarrubias, Nava, Lara, Burciaga, Vélez, & Solorzano, 2018; Gillborn, 2015; Matias & Liou, 2014; Solórzano & Yosso, 2002; Sleeter, 2017). For this purpose, the next section unfolds as brief counterstory to the ways I closely identify with Matias' (2012) belief that "Race, gender, and class become definitive markers that impact researchers' identity, agenda, and analysis" (p. 122).

The Centrality of Experiential Knowledge

To be honest, when I read Atwood and López (2014) state the following, "the luxury of living in a deracialized world is not afforded to People of Color" (p. 1135), I genuinely felt like "Damn somebody finally really gets it". Here are at least two scholars willing to say, without fear, what many People of Color have had to endure across their lifespan. Even Audre Lorde (1977) corroborates by saying, "I have come to believe over and over again that what is most important to me must be spoken, made verbal and shared, even at the risk of having it bruised or misunderstood" (p. 40). These inspirational quotes give voice to why it's crucial I release any and all cares about Whites' comfortability with my unapologetic counterstory.

As such, I make it known; it is not my responsibility nor that of those with interracial identities to nurture racial politics that suggest we must compromise our visceral experiences with race and racism so as to be palpable for White nor scholarly consumption. How we share our lived experiences with race and racism must be honored and respected as our intersectional narratives uncompromised. It is through our intersectional narration we genuinely explore the ways "identity politics" (Collins, 2015) intersects within various social systems of our society for individuals of "mixed identity" (Hurd, 2012).

As an illustration, CRT scholars in teacher education have explored how constructs of Whiteness, race, and racism are interpreted and experienced among not only teachers but also Black and Brown students (Lynn & Parker, 2006; Mark & Pennington, 2003; Matias, Viesca, Garrison-Wade, Tandon, & Galindo, 2014; Vaught & Castagno, 2008). In that same vein, I utilize my lived experiences as a master-level social work practitioner who self-identifies as Francophone speaking Louisiana Creole of Color to inform my CRT pedagogy within my role as a tenure-track professor. Through my role, I educate students on the ways in which my "experiential knowledge" (Solórzano & Yosso, 2002) gives voice to my pedagogical stance on why we must acknowledge and validate different "social identities such as age, sexuality, race, gender, ethnicity" (Collins, 2015) to reveal how it intersects with others inequities. Specifically, I require my students "to examine how these categories of oppression and privilege act to structure their own lives, and then to understand how they shape the opportunities granted or denied to diverse communities" (Edmonds-Cady & Wingfield, 2017, p. 435). To simulate deeper dialogue, I utilize my intersectional identity as a Xennial, bilingual, dark -skinned, cisgendered male Louisiana Creole of Color teaching and existing among monolinguistic African and White American counterparts in a post-racial society where Whiteness is consciously celebrated and normalized as way to demonstrate how Collins' (2015) intersectional perspective "provides new angles of vision on social institutions, practices, social problems, and other social phenomena associated with social inequality" (p. 3).

In spite of my transparency, and espousing empirically based facts on the ways race and racism intersect for minoritized groups, I encounter on a yearly basis "White student resistance to alternative ways of knowing and theorizing with the social world" (Evans-Winters & Hoff, 2011, p. 465). Scholars such as Matias and Liou (2014) allude to this rebellion in how students' subject faculty of color "to White aggressions (e.g., student petitions attempting to get us fired, emails with foul language, and ceaseless emotional outburst claiming race is no longer an issue because of the election of the nation's first African American president" (p. 3)). Nonetheless, I stand in solidarity with Milner and Howard's (2013) assertion that "CRT recognizes the experiential knowledge of People of Color as credible, highly valuable, and critical to understanding, analyzing, and teaching about racial subordination in all of its facets" (p. 539). In this section, it has been explained that tacit knowledge construction is a poor substitution for knowledge building given the multiplicative ways individuals of interracial heritage and People of Color choose to live out their truths and identities. This section that follows will attempt to showcase how I utilize Howard and Navarro's explanation (2016) of how "CRT scholars believe that the world is multidimensional, and similarly, research about the world should reflect multiple perspectives" (p. 259).

The Transdisciplinary Perspective

Graham, Brown-Jeffy, Aronson, and Stephens (2011) reveals that at its core CRT encourages "investigators think and write about their connection to research subjects and their work overall" (p. 88); in doing so, CRT scholars "challenge "ahistoricism and the unidisciplinary focus of most analyses" (Solórzano & Yosso, 2001, p. 473). Quite simply, CRT necessitates "literature from a variety of disciplines must be drawn on and incorporated" (Graham, Brown-Jeffy, Aronson, & Stephens, 2011, p. 91) to respect the multidimensionality of those within and outside the Black and White binary. In my own life, I think of the ways I was "othered" (DeCuir & Dixson, 2004; Gillborn, 2005) because of my interracial heritage and bilingualism especially by those who are White as well as those racially members of my group. Thus, as an emerging scholar, I take in account how germane language, race, gender, an even educational level is before I even conduct a "contextual and historicized analysis" (Graham, Brown-Jeffy, Aronson, & Stephens, 2011) of any minoritized or non-minoritized group.

This form of theorizing requires I remain intentional in making sure my epistemological and ontological frames are not fixed so as to not obscure "racism's primacy as an empirical, personal, and political aspect of critical race scholarship" (Gillborn, 2015, p. 278) due to my inflexibility to learn other disciplinary interpretations and inquiries. Recently, according to Wing (2016) "A very new development for CRT is critical race theory and empirical methods ('Ecrt')" (p. 52). Conceptualized in 2010 eCRT is "the melding of sophisticated social science research methods with the analytical elegance and political power of critical race theory" (Paul-Emile, 2014, p. 2954) an approach that Carbado and Roithmayr (2014) found only "a small group of empirical critical race theorists has begun to mine the potential of this intersection more systemically" (p. 150). In a sense, this is contributory, from the standpoint, it adds further validation into the ways CRT can illustrate how race, gender, and class intersect within the systems of law. Honestly, I am reluctant to truly celebrate this development as I feel it divorces itself to a certain degree from CRT's acknowledgement that "positivism has contributed to the apartheid of knowledge because it strives for a universal science of society, rooted in Western/Eurocentric epistemology" (Malagon, Huber, & Velez, 2009, p. 260). Contemporarily, hierarchal positivist standards of quantification within academic discourse when amplified by the general public's propensity to woefully choose not to understand the ways race, gender, and social class are nuanced within power structures in relation to People of Color and those of interracial heritage does nothing more than justify asinine rhetoric that CRT is a "race baiting", "divisive", even "anti-patriotic" philosophy.

Take for instance how Freeman (2011) highlights Farber's and Sherry's (1997) contention "that CRT represents 'radical multiculturalism' and seeks to overthrow the foundation of American legal thought and its institutions" (p. 185). It's this type of White hypersensitivity to the ways CRT scholars investigates race and racism that precludes any real and honest conversation of how transdisciplinary scholarship could revolutionize real social change in American society. This misguided belief that CRT is somehow a "threat" to the fabric of our society is about as fatuous as how CRT specifically targets "Whites". Gillborn (2005) addresses this fallacy by stating, "critical scholarship on Whiteness is not an assault on White people per se: it is an assault on the socially constructed and constantly reinforced power of White identifications and interests" (p. 488). For all these reasons, it's imperative we remain committed "to deconstruct and expose the research paradigms that ignore the role of the observer in the construction of social reality and thereby fail to consider the historical and social conditions that distort and ignore the experiences of People of Color" (Malagon, Huber, & Velez, 2009, p. 260).

In short, a Eurocentric form of analysis can *never* fully extrapolate how People of Color and those of interracial heritage have lived and are living out their storied experiences. As stated by, Freeman (2011) "the voices of people of colour are unique and must be heard to understand how structures of power actually work. Marginalized voices are sometimes more effective in comprehending both the intended and unintended consequences of laws or actions by public bureaucracies" (p. 185). So, to conclude, to authentically story individuals Hurd (2012) describes as "mixed identity" CRT's transdisciplinary perspective must be celebrated as a mode of analysis by both those in academe and the public sphere.

CONCLUSION

Throughout my counternarrative, Jacques Derrida's (1978) theory of post-structuralism, undergirds sentiments shared by myself of how one's way of interpretation privileges categorization of meaning while eradicating the other. For too long the dichotomous identity experiences of individuals Hurd (2012) describes as "mixed identity" have gone unvoiced; as a result, are enmeshed in a society where their racial ambiguity is seen both historically and contemporarily through a lens of Whiteness. The pain of not feeling apart of one's racial group, the feelings of being unloved by that same group, and to see the way the world hates People of Color and those of interracial heritage dictates the how we choose to navigate a race-conscious social world. Dunn and Lavender (2016) report individuals Hurd (2012) describes as "mixed identity" have often resorted to "amplifying" one identity over another, compartmentalizing identities when possible, or abandoning one identity entirely" (p. 139) to psychologically deal with society's racialized identity politics.

Such identity politics are germane to individuals of interracial heritage as a study conducted by Ho, Roberts, and Gelman (2015) found that "in the context of race, category discreteness implies that people who endorse racial essentialism understand that someone could have one Black parent and one White parent, but their rigid concepts of race result in a tendency to categorize this person as Black rather than both Black and White" (p. 2). To have a mono-racial person dictate my Blackness not only affected my self-worth but also my ability to define myself along with my journey of self-discovery. Such acts of racism are termed by Harris (2017) as "monoracism" in where its "horizontally perpetuated by communities of color, vertically perpetuated by white communities, and may also be internalized and maintained by multiracial individuals" (p. 433). In closing, what is never taken into consideration by a majority of mono-racial individuals is that "each time multiracial individuals are asked 'What are you?' they are simultaneously reminded that there are existing racial structures and that they do not fit neatly into those structures" (Anderson, 2015, p. 16).

REFERENCES

Adams, R. D. (2016) The influence of R.A.C.E. mentoring on a Black Man's journey navigating White spaces in academe. In M. Trotman-Scott, D. Y. Ford, M., R. B. Goings, T. Wingfield, & M. Hensfield (Eds.), *R.A.C.E. Mentoring through social media: Black and Hispanic scholars share their journey in the academy* (pp. 93–103). Charlotte, NC: Information Age Publishing.
Adams, R. D. (2017). The lived experience of a francophone speaking louisiana creole of color in Northeast Louisiana in an English-speaking school system. *Multiple Voices for Ethnically Diverse Exceptional Learners, 7*(1), 1–15.
Alridge, D. P. (2006). The limits of master narratives in history textbooks: An analysis of representations of Martin Luther King, Jr. *Teachers College Record, 108*(4), 662.
Anderson, C. R. (2015). What are you? A CRT perspective on the experiences of mixed race persons in 'post-racial' America. *Race Ethnicity and Education, 18*(1), 1–19.
Atwood, E., & López, G. R. (2014). Let's be critically honest: Towards a messier counterstory in critical race theory. *International Journal of Qualitative Studies in Education, 27*(9), 1134–1154.
Bracey, G. E. (2015). Toward a critical race theory of state. *Critical Sociology, 41*(3), 553–572.
Brayboy, B. M. J. (2005). Toward a tribal critical race theory in education. *The Urban Review, 37*(5), 425–446.
Burton, L. M., Bonilla-Silva, E., Ray, V., Buckelew, R., & Hordge Freeman, E. (2010). Critical race theories, colorism, and the decade's research on families of color. *Journal of Marriage and Family, 72*(3), 440–459.
Carbado, D. W., & Roithmayr, D. (2014). Critical race theory meets social science. *Annual Review of Law & Social Science, 10*(5), 149. doi:10.1146/annurev-lawsocsci-110413-030928
Chapman, T. K. (2007). Interrogating classroom relationships and events: Using portraiture and critical race theory in education research. *Educational Researcher, 36*(3), 156–162.
Cho, H. (2017). Racism and linguicism: Engaging language minority pre-service teachers in counter-storytelling. *Race Ethnicity and Education, 20*(5), 666–680.
Crenshaw, K. (1989). Demarginalizing the intersection of race and sex: A Black feminist critique of antidiscrimination doctrine, feminist theory and antiracist politics. *University Chicago Legal Forum, 140*, 139–167.
Crenshaw, K. (1991). Mapping the margins: Intersectionality, identity politics, and violence against women of color. *Stanford Law Review, 43*(6), 1241–1299.
Crenshaw, K., Gotanda, N., Peller, G., & Thomas, K. (Eds.). (1995). *Critical race theory: The key writings that formed the movement.* New York, NY: The New Press.
Collins, P. H. (2015). Intersectionality's definitional dilemmas. *Annual Review of Sociology, 41*, 1–20.
Cope, M. R., & Schafer, M. J. (2017). Creole: A contested, polysemous term. *Ethnic and Racial Studies,* 1–19.
Covarrubias, A., Nava, P. E., Lara, A., Burciaga, R., Vélez, V. N., & Solorzano, D. G. (2018). Critical race quantitative intersections: A testimonio analysis. *Race Ethnicity and Education, 21*(2), 253–273.
DeCuir, J. T., & Dixson, A. D. (2004). "So when it comes out, they aren't that surprised that it is there": Using critical race theory as a tool of analysis of race and racism in education. *Educational Researcher, 33*(5), 26–31.
DeGruy, J. (2005). *Post traumatic slave syndrome: America's legacy of enduring injury and healing.* Portland: Uptone Press.
Delgado, R., & Stefancic, J. (2012). *Critical race theory: An introduction.* New York, NY: New York University Press.
Derrida, J. (1978). *Structure, sign, and play in the discourse of the human sciences: Writing and difference* (A. Bass, Trans.). Chicago, IL: University of Chicago.

Dominguez, V. R. (1977). Social classification in Creole Louisiana. *American Ethnologist, 4*(4), 589–602.

Du Bois, W. E. B. (1897, August 1). Strivings of the Negro people. *Atlantic Monthly, 80*, 1.

Dubois, S., & Melançon, M. (2000). Creole is, Creole ain't: Diachronic and synchronic attitudes toward Creole identity in southern Louisiana. *Language in Society, 29*(2), 237–258.

Dumas, M. J., & Ross, K. M. (2016). "Be real Black for me" imagining BlackCrit in education. *Urban Education, 51*(4), 415–442.

Dunn, B. J. L., & Lavender, D. (2016). Culture, race, and the self: How mixed-race Alaskan people counter micro aggressions, stigma, and identity dilemmas. *Journal of Sociology, 4*(1), 134–145.

Edmonds-Cady, C., & Wingfield, T. T. (2017). Social workers: Agents of change or agents of oppression? *Social Work Education, 36*(4), 430–442.

Espino, M. M. (2012). Seeking the "truth" in the stories we tell: The role of critical race epistemology in higher education research. *The Review of Higher Education, 36*(1), 31–67.

Evans-Winters, V. E., & Twyman Hoff, P. (2011). The aesthetics of white racism in pre-service teacher education: A critical race theory perspective. *Race Ethnicity and Education, 14*(4), 461–479.

Ford, C. L., & Airhihenbuwa, C. O. (2010). The public health critical race methodology: Praxis for antiracism research. *Social Science & Medicine, 71*(8), 1390–1398.

Freeman, D. (2011). Teaching Obama: History, critical race theory and social work education. *Patterns of prejudice, 45*(1–2), 177–197.

Garroutte, E. M. (2001). The racial formation of American Indians: Negotiating legitimate identities within tribal and federal law. *The American Indian Quarterly, 25*(2), 224–239.

Gillborn, D. (2005). Education policy as an act of white supremacy: Whiteness, critical race theory and education reform. *Journal of Education Policy, 20*(4), 485–505.

Gillborn, D. (2006). Critical race theory and education: Racism and anti-racism in educational theory and praxis. *Discourse: Studies in the Cultural Politics of Education, 27*(1), 11–32.

Gillborn, D. (2015). Intersectionality, critical race theory, and the primacy of racism: Race, class, gender, and disability in education. *Qualitative Inquiry, 21*(3), 277–287.

Gilmore, H. W. (1933). Social isolation of the French speaking people of rural Louisiana. *Social Forces, 12*(1), 78–84.

Graham, L., Brown-Jeffy, S., Aronson, R., & Stephens, C. (2011). Critical race theory as theoretical framework and analysis tool for population health research. *Critical Public Health, 21*(1), 81–93.

Harris, C. I. (1993). Whiteness as property. *Harvard Law Review, 106*, 1707–1791.

Harris, J. C. (2017). Multiracial college students' experiences with multiracial microaggressions. *Race Ethnicity and Education, 20*(4), 429–445.

Ho, A. K., Roberts, S. O., & Gelman, S. A. (2015). Essentialism and racial bias jointly contribute to the categorization of multiracial individuals. *Psychological Science, 26*(10), 1639–1645.

Howard, T. C., & Navarro, O. (2016). Critical race theory 20 years later: Where do we go from here? *Urban Education, 51*(3), 253–273.

Hunter, M. (2016). Colorism in the classroom: How skin tone stratifies African American and Latina/o students. *Theory into Practice, 55*(1), 54–61.

Hurd, E. (2012). The reflexivitiy of pain and privilege. *The International Journal of Critical Pedagogy, 4*(1). 36–46. Retrieved from http://libjournal.uncg.edu/ojs/index.php/ijcp/article/view/151

Ladson-Billings, G. (1998). Just what is critical race theory and what's it doing in a nice field like education? *International Journal of Qualitative Studies in Education, 11*(1), 7–24.

Ladson-Billings, G. (2003). It's your world, I'm just trying to explain it: Understanding our epistemological and methodological challenges. *Qualitative Inquiry, 9*(1), 5–12.

Ladson-Billings, G., & Donnor, J. (2005). The moral activist role of critical race theory scholarship. *The Sage Handbook of Qualitative Research, 3*, 279–301.

Ladson-Billings, G., & Tate, W. F. (1995). Toward a critical race theory of education. *Teachers College Record, 97*(1), 47.

Lorde, A. (1977). The transformation of silence into language and action. *Sister Outsider: Essays and Speeches*, 81–84.

Louden, M. L. (2000). African-Americans and minority language maintenance in the United States. *The Journal of Negro History, 85*(4), 223–240.

Lynn, M. (2004). Inserting the 'race' into critical pedagogy: An analysis of 'race-based epistemologies'. *Educational Philosophy and Theory, 36*(2), 153–165.

Lynn, M., & Parker, L. (2006). Critical race studies in education: Examining a decade of research on US schools. *The Urban Review, 38*(4), 257–290.

Malagon, M. C., Huber, L. P., & Velez, V. N. (2009). Our experiences, our methods: Using grounded theory to inform a critical race theory methodology. *Seattle Journal Social Justice, 8,* 253.

Marx, S., & Pennington, J. (2003). Pedagogies of critical race theory: Experimentations with White pre-service teachers. *Qualitative Studies in Education, 16*(1), 91–110.

Matias, C. E. (2012). Beginning with me: Accounting for a researcher of color's counterstories in socially just qualitative design. *Journal of Critical Thought and Praxis, 1*(1), 9.

Matias, C. E., & Liou, D. D. (2015). Tending to the heart of communities of color: Towards critical race teacher activism. *Urban Education, 50*(5), 601–625.

Matias, C. E., Viesca, K. M., Garrison-Wade, D. F., Tandon, M., & Galindo, R. (2014). What is critical whiteness doing in OUR nice field like critical race theory? Applying CRT and CWS to understand the White imaginations of White teacher candidates. *Equity & Excellence in Education, 47*(3), 289–304.

Milner, H. R., & Howard, T. C. (2013). Counter-narrative as method: Race, policy and research for teacher education. *Race Ethnicity and Education, 16*(4), 536–561.

Parker, L. (2015). Critical race theory in education and qualitative inquiry: What each has to offer each other now? *Qualitative Inquiry, 21*(3), 199–205.

Paul-Emile, K. (2014). Critical race theory and empirical methods conference. *Fordham Legal Review, 83,* 2953.

Pérez Huber, L., (2016). Make America great again: Donald Trump, racist nativism and the virulent adherence to White supremacy amid US demographic change. *Charleston Legal Review, 10,* 215.

Pérez Huber, L., & Solorzano, D. G. (2015). Racial microaggressions as a tool for critical race research. *Race Ethnicity and Education, 18*(3), 297–320.

Pérez Huber, L., & Solorzano, D. G. (2015). Visualizing everyday racism: Critical race theory, visual microaggressions, and the historical image of Mexican banditry. *Qualitative Inquiry, 21*(3), 223–238.

Ray, V. E., Randolph, A., Underhill, M., & Luke, D. (2017). Critical race theory, afro-pessimism, and racial progress narratives. *Sociology of Race and Ethnicity, 3*(2), 147–158.

Richard, F. G. (2013). Thinking through "vernacular cosmopolitanisms": Historical archaeology in Senegal and the material contours of the African Atlantic. *International Journal of Historical Archaeology, 17*(1), 40–71.

Salter, P., & Adams, G. (2013). Toward a critical race psychology. *Social & Personality Psychology Compass, 7*(11), 781. doi:10.1111/spc3.12068

Sharma, A. (2015). Teacher activism: Got post-structuralism? *Journal for Activist Science and Technology Education, 6*(1), 27–36.

Shriver, M. D., & Kittles, R. A. (2004). Genetic ancestry and the search for personalized genetic histories. *Nature Reviews Genetics, 5*(8), 611–618.

Sleeter, C. E. (2017). Critical race theory and the whiteness of teacher education. *Urban Education, 52*(2), 155–169.

Solorzano, D. G. (1997). Images and words that wound: Critical race theory, racial stereotyping, and teacher education. *Teacher Education Quarterly, 24,* 5–19.

Solorzano, D. G. (1998). Critical race theory, race and gender microaggressions, and the experience of Chicana and Chicano scholars. *International Journal of Qualitative Studies in Education, 11*(1), 121–136.

Solorzano, D. G., & Bernal, D. D. (2001). Examining transformational resistance through a critical race and LatCrit theory framework: Chicana and Chicano students in an urban context. *Urban Education, 36*(3), 308–342.

Solorzano, D. G., & Yosso, T. J. (2001). Critical race and LatCrit theory and method: Counter-storytelling. *International Journal of Qualitative Studies in Education, 14*(4), 471–495.

Solórzano, D. G., & Yosso, T. J. (2002). A critical race counterstory of race, racism, and affirmative action. *Equity & Excellence in Education, 35*(2), 155–168.

Tate, W. F. (1997). Chapter 4: Critical race theory and education: History, theory, and implications. *Review of Research in Education, 22*(1), 195–247.

Taylor, E., Gillborn, D., & Ladson-Billings, G. (2009). *Foundations of critical race theory in education.* New York, NY: Routledge.

Thornton, M. C., Taylor, R. J., Chatters, L. M., & Forsythe-Brown, I. (2017). African American and Black Caribbean feelings of closeness to Africans. *Identities, 24*(4), 493–512.

Thompson, S. (2001). "Ah Toucoutou, ye conin vous": History and memory in Creole New Orleans. *American Quarterly, 53*(2), 232–266.

Vaught, S. E., & Castagno, A. E. (2008). "I don't think I'm a racist": Critical race theory, teacher attitudes, and structural racism. *Race Ethnicity and Education, 11*(2), 95–113.

White, T. R., Love, S. M., DeBose, H. L., & Loprieno, D. M. (2015). The changing landscape of race, culture, and family life: Interracial couples' contribution to the conversation. *World Journal of Social Science Research, 2*(1), 24.

Wing, A. K. (2016). Is there a future for critical race theory? *Journal of Legal Education, 66*, 44.

Woodson, A. N. (2015). "There ain't no white people here" master narratives of the civil rights movement in the stories of urban youth. *Urban Education, 52*(3), 316–342.

JESSICA SAMUELS

9. SIKA

INTRODUCTION

I always knew I was different than my mommy. She had long silky straight to wavy strawberry-blond hair and pinkish light skin. My hair was short, dark, and kinky. My skin tone varied with each season. When I was young, I would get dark in the summer, but now I stay an even shade of honey brown. I remember sitting next to her on the couch and slapping my little brown hand against her big pale upper arm, as it jiggled. I often thought how beautiful she was and how I wanted to look like her.

*Figure 9.1. My mother pregnant with me in
California in 1975*

People always commented about how I looked like my father. When I was young, I assumed I was Esskahpo, Nimiipuu and or Nez Perce Indian, as colonization renamed my dad's people. My dad is 31/32nd "Nez Perce", almost full-blooded Native American or Indigenous. But like most of us Americans, he too has "white" or European blood in him. As I got older, I began to sarcastically question in my head what people really meant when they said I looked like my father.

I was five years old when I learned my dad was not my biological father; I was so devastated. My older cousin and I had gotten into an argument when she told me. I clearly recall the numbing shock and confusion I felt. I went to my mother crying with questions. "Was my dad my dad? Was I a little 'nigger-bitch'? What is

© KONINKLIJKE BRILL NV, LEIDEN, 2019 | DOI:10.1163/9789004393813_009

a 'nigger-bitch'? And why did you give away my White sister?" Things were never the same from that day on.

Before the age of five, I was aware and accustomed to all the eyes staring and glaring at our family. We lived on the Nez Perce Indian Reservation in a predominantly White, small, rural logging town in Northern Idaho. I also noticed people were nice to my mom when we were alone, then rude when my dad was with us. As I got older, it became apparent that some people were nice to us when we were alone, until they learned that my mom was my biological mother and that I was not adopted. I witnessed faces go from a smile to disgust at the thought of her with a Black man. The looks were like the ones we received when my dad was with us, sometimes worse.

Figure 9.2. Me and my little brother and sister about a year after I learned my dad was not my biological father, 1982

I also knew at that age there were members of my mom's "White" family that didn't like me and my dad because we were "Brown". And my dad's family did not like that my dad married a "White bitch", as I would often hear. Nor were they happy that she came with "a little nigglet", as I have been called in the past. But what I didn't know, realize, or understand until after that day was that my biological father was a Black, Puerto Rican which made me Black. You see being Puerto Rican does not dictate your race; just like being American does not dictate your race.

I had never been "White" and can never be White (phenotypically speaking), as passing is not an option for me based on my skin-tone and hair texture. You should see people's faces when I say my mother was Hungarian, Norwegian, and probably Irish. I was no longer Indian or Native, at least not to some. That day, I became Black to my mom, a Mulatto to my grandmother, Colored to my great grandmother, and sometimes a nigger to my great grandfather, aunts, uncles, cousins, strangers and even siblings. But today, when I am asked, my typical response is mixed.

Figure 9.3. First wing dress made specifically for me

I am mixed. Don't get me wrong. I have a dominant racial identity, which is Black. While some claim they do not see race, when I look in the mirror I see a Black woman. A medium skinned Black Woman which shapes how people engage me. Most assume my Blackness, but as they get to know me, their confusion over my racial and ethnic identities becomes apparent. I frequently hear things like: "Where are you from?"; "But there are no Black people from Idaho?"; "Really, your mom was White?"; "What? You're not Indian? But I thought you were Black and Indian?"; "Aren't your siblings Indian?"; "Wow, you speak Spanish?"; "I didn't know Black people spoke Spanish?"; "But you are Black, right?"; and "Don't Black people just say their Puerto Rican, so they don't have to be Black?"

I'm constantly caught in an in-between realm, I always have too much of one to fully identify with the other. I have been teased that my speech, where I grew up, where I live, as well as my musical selections are too White. While others insist that my hair, my passion, my anger, my enthusiasm, my tone, my temper, and or general expression through clothes, music, and more are also Black. Then there are the times when my deep cultural ideals, beliefs, values, and norms come out as too Indigenous, as I prefer sweat lodge over church for prayer, and healing among other things. I even conversationally learned Spanish out of respect, duty, and obligation to my Puerto Rican heritage, because of the values and beliefs enculturated into me by my indigenous upbringing. The irony is that, while visiting Puerto Rico, I was promptly met with questions as to why I look Puerto Rican and sounded Mexican.

As an Academic Success Counselor at an Inland Northwest University, I am very privileged to have finished a Master of Public Administration degree and to be working on a PhD in Political Science. On the surface, it may seem that I come from a life of privilege, as I use standard English and I am educated. I grew up hunting, fishing, hiking, swimming, boating, berry picking, four wheeling, and riding horses in the mountains of Northern Idaho during the summer; while my winters were spent playing in the snow and baking with my grandmother. I've fished with my dad at Rapid River and "The Fish Ladder" in Ahsahka. I have danced in Pow Wows, participated in ceremony, I bead, make good fry bread, meat pockets, and salmon patties.

Yet things are not always what they seem. Life was not and is not easy. I live in a constant negotiation at home with family, in my professional life, and within the communities that I live in and belong to. People's assumptions of who I am and where I come from are always incorrect, yet these assumptions influence how they interact with me. I can recall once spending four months in Louisiana. Certain White people were rude and abrupt with me, until they heard me speak. Then they would ask me where I was from. Once I told them I was from Idaho or when they heard me speak Spanish, they instantly became curious, hospitable, and appeared to have a desire to prove race didn't matter to them. Yet I had the opposite experience when I interacted with Black people in Louisiana. I was always greeted with a smile that many times changed to indignation when they either heard my Idaho accent or they over heard me communicating in Spanish, to my Mexican ex-husband. When I am not at work, people rarely assume that I am educated. When they learn that I am educated, then they assume that my parents are rich, I was adopted, or my school was paid for because "I'm part Indian and get Indian money". None of these are true.

My dad (stepfather who raised me) worked in cedar mills; we lived in a tribal house and received commodities. There were times when we lived on welfare, times I lived in a foster home, and there were times I was molested. My mother and grandmother died when I was 19, and I was left to co-parent my four younger siblings with our alcoholic dad (my stepfather) and our grandfather (stepfather's dad). While all those events contribute to who I am and who I have become, I believe it is the pain and privilege of my mixed racial and ethnic identity that has made me strong and given me the resilience needed to overcome all barriers.

Figure 9.4. Dad (Stepfather) Dworshack Dam, 1984

Every time I went to my mother crying about someone calling me a nigger, my mother would say that "a nigger just means a worthless person" and that "it had nothing to do with skin color, so prove them wrong". Then she would confront them no matter what the cost. I thank the Creator every day for blessing me with my mixed race and ethnic identity and a mother that was able to teach me to embrace my heritage and fight ignorance and injustice.

Therefore, this chapter will explore my personal experiences regarding my mixed racial and ethnic identity. When I initially envisioned writing this chapter, I thought of all the racial encounters I had growing up. I thought of the ones I had that other mixed-race people could identify with, as well as what makes my experience unique. I also thought about how I could best explain and express the contrast of my experience. But upon further reflection, I felt that it was more important to reflect upon recent encounters. These experiences that I wish to explore with you are reflective and exemplify the dichotomy that I live daily.

LANGUAGE OF THE LAND

In February of 2017, just after taking a job in a new department on campus, I came across a flyer on the bulletin board above the copy machine. It was for the annual Palouse Language & Culture Symposium and it was set to be held in April of 2017. It was being hosted and co-sponsored by the college my new department was in. I thought it would be a good chance to meet and interact with some of my new colleagues.

When I arrived that day, I was happy to find a few presentations directly related to my new position, as the Project Director of the Indigenous Knowledge for Effective Education Program (IKEEP). I was hired to recruit and assist Native American

Students through teacher Preparation at the University. Prior to that I was an Academic Success Counselor in Student Support Services for three and a half years. Unfortunately, IKEEP received budget cuts from the Federal Government; thus, the program had to cut back on administrative costs and I returned to Student Support Services at the beginning of 2018.

As I looked over the symposium program, I became intrigued and excited about the workshops. I was excited about the one on tribal immersion schools because I was working to recruit a student interested specifically in starting an immersion school for her tribe. I was intrigued by one entitled, "Literacy of the Land / Alphabet of the People". I was interested because I had met the presenter a few times in passing and thought she was very sweet. I knew she taught literacy, but I did not know she had a specific interest in Indigenous or Native peoples.

As I entered the class to hear the presentation, I sat up front as I always try to do, so as not to get distracted. As the presenter began to introduce herself, it happened. For some reason, she introduced me to the rest of the workshop attendees and said that I was Native American. I quickly interjected and corrected her, startled by both the introduction and the declaration of my heritage. I said, "I am not Native American, my family is". She looked at me confused and said "but". Part of me understood her confusion of my identity, as she is not the first to make that assumption. Yet I was irritated by her need to introduce me, label me, and declare my heritage without really knowing anything about me. I felt compelled to interrupt, so that we could move past her confusion and her "but" statement. I explained that I grew up on the reservation in a Native American household, as my stepfather and four younger siblings are all enrolled tribal members, so most of my family members are Native.

The confusion left her face, and she replied, "Oh well, same thing".

I was furious. I thought to myself, what do you mean, "Same thing". Native people are not the same thing as me. They were murdered and colonized. The fortunate ones who survived and were lucky enough to sign treaties or gain recognition from the Federal government ceded away many of their rights and most of their land. I have too much respect for their history and legacy to try to claim it as my own. I believe our country should truly respect and observe the law of the land and the treaties it signed with Indigenous peoples. Growing up, I had crushes on native boys; but I never pursued a relationship with any because I understood the necessity to maintain and preserve the rights reserved for Native people to continue to be Native people. While I hate the oppression and division blood quantum places on Native peoples, I respect the heritage and legacy it represents. Blood quantum is a colonial concept introduced to tribal peoples that sets a minimum blood limit standard acceptable to be recognized or enrolled as a tribal member of a federally recognized tribe (Canby, 2009). It almost forces Natives to marry their cousins to maintain some cultural practices like hunting, fishing, and possession of an eagle feather for ceremony as descendants are not afforded and guaranteed the same rights as enrolled tribal members. The book American Indian Law in a Nutshell (Canby, 2009) explains that for many "statutory purposes it is not enough that an individual be regarded as an Indian by his or her community; the person must be considered a member of a federally recognized tribe" (p. 10).

"It is not the same thing", I kept thinking to myself, as I tuned out most of the presentation ... as my mind raced on with all the ways the Indigenous experience is not the same thing as mine. Our experiences may have similarities and correlations. But to equate our experiences as the same is disrespectful to both their ancestors and to mine; as we are an extension of their legacy and our future generations are an extension of us. I am privileged to have grown up in an Indigenous family, as I was enculturated to see that everything is connected, that it is important to be humble but proud of where I come from, to give respect to my ancestors and elders, to forgive, but remember, and to give back to my community. Yet, the pain that I endured for not being Indigenous based on my blood or biological ancestry is forever a scar I will bear. Similar but different, I imagine, to the wound of an Indigenous person, raised in an Indigenous community, but without enough blood quantum to be enrolled or "recognized" by both the Federal government and the Tribal government as being a citizen of the tribal community from which they descend.

Finally, I calmed my mind and turned my attention to the presentation. As I began to thumb through the power point handout, I found it ironic to see slides entitled, Culturally Responsive Teaching, Cultural Literacy, and Cultural Sensitivity. Then the presenter explained she had an activity that called for volunteers. I thought to myself, "Oh no. I am not doing this". I began to focus harder on the power point handout and tried to avoid eye contact. As she began to call up volunteers, she handed them a script, stating that they would be reading aloud a "Reader's Theater" skit that she had adapted, based on the "Trail of Tears". She explained that it was a depiction of "The Cherokee Removal" and it was from an Indigenous perspective. She needed one more person and of course she called on me.

I cringed as she said, "You get to be the Little Old Indian Woman" and handed me the script. Irritated but not wanting to prolong the moment and make a show of myself, by declining her request, I took a deep breath, accepted the script, and went to the front of the room with the other seven readers. I scanned the script for the "Little Old Indian Woman" but noticed it only read, "Old Woman". As I took a closer look at the script, "Oh Lord", I thought to myself! This depiction was supposedly from an "Indigenous perspective" and featured: President Jackson, General Scott, the Secretary of War, two military men, two narrators, one chief, and one "Little Old Indian Woman". The old woman and chief spoke one time, each!

When the torture was over, I got out of the classroom as fast as I could. It took me days and weeks to process the entire event. I know her intentions were not malicious. However, her assumptions of my background and misrepresentations of Indigenous perspective were offensive and disrespectful on many levels. As a University teacher preparation instructor, presenting at a language and culture symposium, she probably never even considered that her actions were damaging and had perpetuated the status quo of ignorance concerning Native Americans, Culturally Responsive Teaching, as she lacked both Cultural Literacy and Cultural Sensitivity.

Tribal Member

On Thursday June 8th, 2017, exactly two months after the symposium incident, I drove the IKEEP scholars down to the Nez Perce Indian Reservation. We were nearing the end of the third week of an Indigenous Pedagogies Institute. IKEEP had arranged for the scholars to visit Lapwai Middle School and High School for practicum. It happened to be the last day of school before summer vacation for the district. When we first walked into the school and spoke to the staff that greeted us, I felt a little nervous, as I was not acquainted with them. My nerves eased, and a big smile crept to my face when the principal appeared. I thought, "Yes, someone I know", as she is a distant cousin on my dad's / stepfather's side of the family. We quickly embraced and exchanged greetings. Our family is very proud of her. She welcomed the IKEEP scholars and invited us to join the school for their end of the year awards assembly taking place later that day, before dispersing us to the practicum class rooms.

As the time for the assembly drew near, we regrouped and walked over to the gymnasium. As our group entered the gym, I could see lots of familiar faces in the crowd. Students, parents, grandparents, aunties, uncles, and cousins where sitting in the bleachers smiling, clapping and cheering. I felt warm inside seeing extended family members and friends in the audience cheering on their children and grandchildren. For a moment, I became nostalgic as some of the people I hadn't seen since high school or at family members' funerals. It was good to see so many had taken time out of their day to see these high school students receive recognition for their dedication and efforts in school.

A couple of the scholars sat on the bleachers with the rest of the spectators while the rest of us remained standing near the door. We planned to only stay for about 15 to 20 minutes of the awards assembly, as we had to get back to the university. I was thinking to myself how grateful I was to be there and how awesome it was to see my cousin in action. As the principal, she was moderating the assembly. When I usually run into her, it's off the job, at a Pow Wow or university event. At that moment, I felt privileged and honored to witness one of the few PhD holding female Native American public-school principals, bringing together a community to honor high school students. I could feel the pride in the gym as the students walked up to accept their awards.

Lost in my thoughts of what an amazing and memorable experience I was having, I became aware that the principal was looking at us and pointed our way as she acknowledged collaborations between Lapwai School District and my university. She further welcomed the IKEEP teacher preparation scholars as guests. Then panic and fear ran through my body, as she referred to me as a tribal member. I don't know how many other people heard it, registered it, or thought anything about it. I stood there dumfounded for a minute and thought, "Oh, Fuck".

The assembly continued and after a minute or two; I slid out the door hoping no one could read my face or my thoughts. In my mind, I could picture a couple of my dad's (stepfather's) sisters and distant cousins. My head echoed with all the things I could imagine them saying when it was recounted, that I was referred to as a tribal member. In my head, I heard them say, "Oh, Sika's up there in Moscow trying to pretend like she is Indian, fucking nigger-bitch! She's not Native. I bet that's how she got that job; they should have hired a real Native for that position!"

I was only outside of the gym for a few moments, when the IKEEP scholars started trickling out to join me. They mistook my escape from the gym as a signal that it was time to leave. As we made our 45-minute drive back to campus, I pondered many things. Did she know I was not an enrolled tribal member? Yes, she's family and of course she knows. Man, I wonder who all caught that? Did my students notice? I knew I had made it clear to them, during orientation, that most of my family is native but I am not. Oh man. I hoped what she said didn't get up river to some of my dad's family, to fuel the speculation that I am pretending to be Indian and that's how I got the job or fuel the commentary that a real Indian should have that job instead of "that fucking nigger", more specifically me.

As soon as I got home, I called my little sister to help me process it. I was not upset with my cousin; part of me was honored that she would referred to me as a tribal member and acknowledge my relationship in the tribal community. Unlike the presenter at the symposium, her introduction was not based on unknown assumptions categorizing me and disregarding and disrespecting our ancestors' plight. Rather this was a bold statement of acceptance based on knowledge of my family, upbringing, and my commitment to uplift tribal peoples. She was not the first tribal member to claim me as a member and I know she will not be the last. The difference is typically when a tribal member asserts my tribal affiliation, it is during a one on one personal conversation affirming and reassuring me of their individual personal acceptance of me as one of them. Those conversations are always meaningful and special. Many of my "deep cultural norms and values"[1] are indigenous and my race is Black, but I see my ethnic identity as mixed. My mixed identity is a legacy that has been shaped and is a result of three things: (1) what was inflicted upon my ancestors like slavery, racism and discrimination; (2) dominate societal beliefs like manifest destiny, capitalism and White supremacy held by my mother's family and others; and (3) the choices my ancestors made, like my mother and biological father choosing to have me.

Unfortunately, my historical trauma would not allow me to enjoy and accept this beautiful privilege and honor of my cousin's public acknowledgement. When I say historical trauma, I am not talking about some far off ancestral experience and plight. Although systemically, the historical baggage I carry could be traced back to colonization and slavery. The reality is that my historical trauma and baggage is a result of my own lived experiences, not my ancestors. When people think of the words historical trauma and baggage, they immediately think that those things were in the past. They think that minorities are just referring to slavery, Jim Crow, the Indian Removal Act, Termination Era, Japanese internment camps, or other historically traumatic events. It's more than that to me. It's those day-in and day-out traumatic experiences I have had, that stem from those historic beliefs and ideologies which led to those historical tragedies. In my life, I cannot count nor recall all the times I have been called a nigger, nigger-bitch, nigger-baby, a jungle bunny, a coon, a jig-a-boo, a hatchet packer, a wagon burner, a prairie-nigger, Oreo, a monkey, Oprah, Blacky, or negrita by my Native, White, Black and Latinx community members. Further, members of each of those communities have on numerous occasions made it clear that either they do not accept, or they question my lineage or connection to those communities. I always have something in me that makes me different and not belong.

"BLOOD"

Over the past decade, social media has become a major way that many people remain in contact with friends and family (Amedie, 2015). For some of us, it may be the only way we keep abreast of what is going on with those that are supposedly close to us and care about us. At times, it can be enlightening, divisive, or reaffirm things you already know. And sometimes, it may even change your opinion of someone.

In January of 2017, I was scrolling through my Facebook feed, disappointed by chatter over our new (Trump) administration's priorities. As I was scrolling, I came across a podcast post on a friend's page with whom I had attended elementary through high school. I had not physically seen this person in years. I'm not the type of person that normally listens to podcasts; I barely know what one is. The podcast caught my attention because it was called "Doubt it with Dollemore". Dollemore I thought, like Dollemore from back home? It made me think of one of my best friends that passed away from Leukemia, as she used to date him. I knew his family, our moms had been friends at one time; but I never really cared for him, as I had heard the word nigger slip out of his mouth on a couple of occasions.

However, my curiosity made me listen, and to my surprise he changed my whole outlook on him. My heart was filled with joy; I was inspired and renewed with faith that there is a chance to reach people and help them come to terms with and resolve their hatred and bigotry. I quickly added him to my list of friends.

A few months later, on November 28, 2017, I decided to share a video which featured Dollemore describing president Trump calling Senator Elizabeth Warren Pocahontas as "only the latest example in Trump's Long History of Racism".[2] Trumps choice of timing and place was completely inappropriate and disrespectful! But even my siblings and I would have found it sarcastically funny in the right setting, as her actions of saying she was Native American and or appropriating a heritage or lineage can be just as disrespectful, violent, and hurtful. But that was not why I posted the video.

It was more than that; the video highlighted more instances of which I felt truly illustrated Trump's intolerable ideologies which perpetuate racism and discrimination. There is one piece specifically that cannot be denied as Trump being racist. The scene highlighted Trump being questioned about saying an American Judge from Mexican descent could not do his job because he was Mexican. So, I posted the video. Now when I post, I typically don't comment. I just share things. Rarely do I add commentary. I like things to speak for themselves. And in this case, I did the same; I just shared the video, without any commentary.

Shortly after, I received a Facebook response. It was from my aunt, my mother's oldest sibling and only sister. She is also my mother's only living biological sibling, as my uncles had passed after my mother and grandmother. I don't even usually talk to her. I occasionally run into her at one of her grandchildren's birthday parties. My siblings and I invite our cousin, her daughter, to our gatherings; but we never invite her. We have grown weary of her racist jokes and regular racial slurs, like "beanner, wet back, nigger and FN Indians". As a (mixed) Black woman with four native siblings and three children from a Mexican, I prefer keeping my distance. After 41 years of being silent, when she spewed her venom, I snapped and responded. It might not have been the best thing to do, but I was blunt and honest.

I then logged off Facebook for a few minutes to cool down, so that I didn't say anything worse. Over the years, I had grown to really dislike my aunt; but blood is supposed to be thicker than water, so I have tried to avoid conflict with her by avoiding contact. But this day, her "shut up" comment just hit me wrong. And my response must have hit her wrong, too, as I logged back in to find three consecutive response posts from her. Her posts basically said that my mom was White, and that I was being a racist, stirring the "shit pot" by posting the video. She further questioned if I hated myself for being half-White.

Part of me said, "What the hell is this crazy lady talking about"! The other part of me said, "You have held your tongue too long; tell that crazy bat off". Yes, I did it. I responded. Maybe I should not have, but I did. Then I logged off of Facebook. And of course, when I logged back into Facebook a few hours later, there were three more consecutive response posts from her. These were just as crazy as the first three. I couldn't even respond. Her last post said it all! She finally released her subconscious beliefs and ideologies. She informed me that I should quit trying to cause trouble because White people are going to "stick together" and where does that leave my "DUMBASS".

Of course, my action of pointing out discrimination and racism was twisted into an act of racism against her which happens all too frequently. Her own daughters did not defend her nor rebuke me for telling her the truth. However, her son-in law who did like her post said, "Your mom would tell you to quit stirring the shit pot". I know he is not a racist. He is a Trump supporter. But I also know that his comment would not have been my mother's response. My White mother stood by my dad and encouraged him to protest, alongside other Nez Perce Fishermen when the state of Idaho attempted to infringe on their people's reserved treaty fishing rights, during the early 80's.

*Figure 9.5. My mother at the standoff between Nez Perce
Fishermen, and state and federal officials*

I didn't need to respond, though. Instead my other aunt did. She is not my aunt by blood; rather, she is my aunty by love. I can remember her smile and shiny blond hair; when I was a child, she was always so kind and loving to me. She was the prettiest of all my uncle's girlfriends or wives. I think she was his true love, the one that got away, and that's why he had so many after she left. When I was young, my aunty by love, my mom, and my mom's sister had all been close.

My aunty by love responded, "Dear Jessica, can you say 'gaslighting'? You're a strong, intelligent woman; and I know you see 'your aunt's' comments for what they are. Don't ever be silent in the face of discrimination. Silence is complicity. Love you girl!" Tears welled up in my eyes, as I read my mother's words, through the response of my aunty by love.

CONCLUSION

My race and mixed Nez Perce, U.S., Afro, Latina ethnic identity revealed to me deep hatred and inflicted deep pain from all directions. It has emphasized to me that discrimination is alive and well in all our communities, not just amongst "White people". It has allowed me the privilege to see great beauty and experience relationality because, at the core of my Indigenous upbringing, I know that we are all one community, and each of us is needed to sustain our ecosystem. We all need to examine ourselves for bias and discriminatory behavior and stand together as one community, against the ideologies that sustain racism, exploitation, and oppression.

My mixed identity has developed in me an understanding of people that encourages me to identify and empathize with other people and their struggle by truly listening to their stories. Historical trauma is not just trauma endured by our ancestors but is something that many of us experience on a regular basis. It is inflicted upon us by the reoccurring ideologies, systems, and beliefs that once gave birth to injustices like slavery, internment camps, and the slaughter of millions of innocent women and children. Moreover, it taught me that it takes courageous people, like my White mother, to stand with people whose rights are being violated, even though it didn't directly affect her, despite what her family may think or say.

NOTES

[1] "Deep culture refers to the unconscious meanings, values, norms and hidden assumptions that allow us to interpret our experiences as we interact with other people" (Shaules, 2007, p. 11).

[2] https://www.facebook.com/OccupyDemocrats/videos/1810943005665412/

REFERENCES

Amedie, J. (2015). The impact of social media on society. *Advanced Writing: Pop Culture Intersections, 2*, 3–18. Retrieved from http://scholarcommons.scu.edu/engl_176/2

Canby, W. C. (2009). *American Indian law in a nutshell* (5th ed.). St. Paul, MN: West Publishing.

Shaules, J. (2007). *Deep culture: The hidden challenges of global living.* Great Britain: Cromwell Press.

PART 4

INTERRELATED HOMILIES (MOVEMENTS) OF MIXED IDENTITY: AN INTERNATIONAL LENS

LYNNETTE MAWHINNEY

10. BEING AMBIGUOUSLY BROWN IN AFRICA

An Autoethnography of Biracial Identity in Three Acts

INTRODUCTION

Taxicabs in New York make me uncomfortable. I appreciate the hard work of taxicab drivers. But whenever I hail a taxicab by myself, without fail, the driver asks, "What are you?" Like many other biracial people, I continue to dread this bold question (Lewis, 2006; Mawhinney & Petchauer, 2013), which I am often asked in taxicabs, as many drivers were born outside the United States. I usually respond, "My father was African American and my mother is White". They invariably respond, "No way! You look [insert ethnicity here]". The conception of racial identity in America is often binary in nature (Funderburg, 1994; Rockquemore & Brunsma, 2002; Rockquemore, Brunsma, & Delgado, 2009). I found that my brown-skinned ambiguity and struggle with identity took hold in the early stages of my adolescent life in the United States (Mawhinney & Petchauer, 2013).

However, being ambiguously Brown (as my mixed-race friends affectionately call this "complex") has proven complicated when traveling internationally as an adult. Race is a social construction, and is often "not useful as a biological construct", yet "social race remains a significant predictor of which groups have greater access to societal goods and resources and which groups face barriers – both historically and in contemporary context – to full inclusion" (Smedley & Smedley, 2005, p. 22). This is frequently why, wherever I travel, my identity shifts according to the historical, political, and social context of the country that I visit.

This chapter explores how my biracial identity and social construction of race shifted in complex ways during my time in South Africa, Egypt (North Africa), and Kenya (East Africa) (see Figure 10.1). In each country, I experienced and took part in "a losing system by being mixed, unable to fully identify (e.g., experience no tension) within a singular racial, social, or cultural group" (Hurd, 2012, p. 41). This chapter travels to each country, unpacking the racialized ambiguity of each in three acts. Act I explores being denied Blackness (although I identify as Black) and having no real racial identity in South Africa. Act II explores being considered Egyptian in Egypt, even though I am not Egyptian. Lastly, Act III explores being considered White in Kenya, and having my Blackness denied by the people of that country (see Figure 10.1).

© KONINKLIJKE BRILL NV, LEIDEN, 2019 | DOI:10.1163/9789004393813_010

NOTES ON AUTOETHNOGRAPHIC MEMOIR

This chapter has been constructed using the autoethnographic approach outlined by Ellis (2004) as "writing about the personal and its relationship to culture" (p. 37). Written in memoir style, photographs and Facebook entries were the catalyst for scribing the chapter, and at times, were used as a data set. The representations of Facebook data are presented verbatim. For instance, emojis were not deleted from the quotes, as they provide an extra layer of context to excerpted statements. Moreover, all typos and mistakes have been left intact to maintain the information's original representation.

Figure 10.1. Lynnette's socio-racial constructions in Africa

ACT I: SOUTH AFRICA

I was a new faculty member at an institution that has educational summer programs around the globe. These programs are designed for teachers, who are often employed at American international schools, to pursue teaching certificates or master's degrees. It is a rare opportunity in the educational field to have these international programs, and I was elated when my colleague who directed the Johannesburg, South Africa program asked me to join the team for the summer.

I identify as Black, and I have always viewed Africa as the "motherland". I had never been there before, and I hoped that this chance to visit would provide an opportunity to have a deeper connection with myself. Moreover, I was slated to teach two graduate courses that were specific to dealing with justice-oriented approaches in classrooms. Since the graduate students were from Zimbabwe, French Cameroon, Canada, and South Africa (to name a few), I knew that the dialogue around race, class, and gender would be unique and enlightening, given the various contexts of the students' understanding.

And the class provided just that. One gentleman, born in India but raised in Zimbabwe, discussed the complexities of his identity and immigrant status. An Afrikaans woman cried when she told us about her family leaving South Africa at the end of apartheid (called the "chicken run" – when all the Whites fled South Africa), and was embraced by a Zulu man affectionately calling her sister. The class brought forth love and healing in ways that were intentional in my class design, but this love and healing reached deeper than I had expected. Yet outside the safety of my classroom, I was quickly hit with the reality of the wounds of apartheid.

A (Too) Brief History of Apartheid

It is important to briefly outline the history of apartheid in South Africa. Apartheid, which translates as "apartness" in Afrikaans, was established in 1950 ("South African History Online", 2018) with the Population Registration Act (Thompsell, 2017). Apartheid laws were akin to America's Jim Crow laws and legislated strict separation and segregation among the three declared races: (1) White, (2) "native" (Black), and (3) Colored (usually not considered either previously mentioned category, this included mixed race and Southeast Asian individuals) (Thompsell, 2017). The political party behind the design of apartheid, the National Party, studied the histories of countries with successful racial segregation (America, the Netherlands, and others) to design these racist and White supremacist laws (Noah, 2016). It dictated where South Africans could live, whom they could and could not marry, the jobs that they could obtain (if any), and even more. In short, the White supremacist doctrine in South Africa vastly hurt and marginalized all people of color. Finally, in 1991, President F.W. deKlerk repealed the last legislation that formally institutionalized the South African governmental doctrine of apartheid, and shortly afterward, Nelson Mandela was elected president in 1994.

The Reality of Wounds

Our teaching team consisted of an African American woman, an African American man, a White woman, and myself. Needless to say, it was a rarity to find such a diverse group of individuals at restaurants or shopping in South Africa. I would often go into stores with the other African American woman, Bianca (all names

151

are pseudonyms), whom I affectionately call AWM (At Work Mom). We would enter a store, which was often run by a Black South African woman. Bianca and the employee would have a wonderful and jolly conversation. When I would enter the conversation, the employee would roll her eyes at me. When I would walk into stores to ask questions, Black South African women would ignore my inquiries. Often, Bianca had to serve as my voice, asking my question to get the answer I needed. The irony is that Bianca, like me, identifies as African American, and is also mixed race (Black and Puerto Rican), but is more Black presenting than I am.

These behaviors only occurred among Black women, and they were repeated each time I stepped out of the classroom. I would leave these interactions wounded, discouraged, and ultimately confused. Bianca, who spent each summer for over 20 years in South Africa, was just as perplexed about this situation as I was. I found myself racially microaggressed (Pierce, Carew, Pierce-Gonzalez, & Wills, 1978; Sue, 2010, 2016) by people who I considered the same as me, but who did not see me in the same way. The concept of racial microaggressions was coined by counselor Chester Pierce in 1978 to describe how African Americans experience the daily "subtle, stunning, often automatic exchanges which are 'put downs' of [B]lacks by offenders" (Pierce et al., 1978, p. 66). Over the years, the term has been applied to all people of color as the "brief, everyday exchanges that send denigrating messages to people of color because they belong to a racial minority group" (Sue, Capodilupo, Torino, Bucceri, Holder, Nadal, & Esquilin, 2007, p. 273). In these instances, racial microaggressions were being used to minoritize me.

One day during our lunch break in class, I was in the back kitchen heating up my food. One of my graduate students, Jorge, was also in the back kitchen. Jorge is Colored from South Africa (Malaysian and Dutch), is married to a White American man, and is the father of two adopted Zulu girls. If anyone could explain why I was being treated so horribly by Black women, it was Jorge. Without predication or even context, I turned to Jorge and blurted out in anger and frustration, "Jorge, what the f**k is happening to me here?!" The underlying subtext of my question was: Why were Black women in South Africa treating me horribly? Jorge did not need me to explain further or to provide clarification – he knew exactly what I was asking. He explained, "During apartheid, there were tensions between Colored and Black women. The Black women thought they had it harder than the Colored women, which was true in some instances, but they forget that the Colored people had to rise up and protest, too, in Cape Town. But the tensions continue, though".

Although this brought more clarity to my situation, I still felt confused. "But why, when I open my mouth and they can hear that my accent is not from here [South Africa], does the treatment continue?" Jorge stated, "It doesn't matter that you're American. The wounds of apartheid are deep". And with that, it all became clear.

Jorge's statement profoundly demonstrated how movements and history shape cultural values and identity. Black South African women considered my ambiguously brown skin as Colored (although Colored women would never see me as such). Although I returned to South Africa the following year, and the racial microaggressions continued, I tried to be more conscious and understanding of how my ambiguously brown skin was a trigger for the memory of the pain, torture, and history that still lingers today.

ACT II: EGYPT

The same program afforded me the opportunity to travel to North Africa. This provided an entirely different context for my ambiguously brown skin. The second I deplaned in Egypt, I was mesmerized by how similar I looked to everyone. My *café au lait* skin and curly brown hair seamlessly blended into the busy, crowded streets of Cairo. In America, people often do double takes as I walk by, trying to figure out – "What am I?" But in Egypt, no one seemed confused by my appearance because it looked like I belonged. And I felt like I belonged. For the first time in my life, I knew what it felt like to look like the majority.

This was often confirmed in people's interactions with me. When I would approach Egyptians, I was never ignored, as I was in South Africa. Often, when I was engaged in discussion and dialogue, I was seen as a fellow Egyptian. They did not immediately realize that I was not fluent in Arabic. Switching to broken English, I was often asked, "You Egyptian?"

I would respond, "No".

This was often followed by, "No? You dad, he Egyptian, right?"

"Nope. Sorry".

"You mother. She Egyptian".

My response was often laughter. These interactions contrasted starkly with the daily question, "What are you?" that I experienced at home. In Egypt, the question was why I did not belong, even though I looked like I belonged. Honestly, this was a more comforting question, as I felt like the collective instead of an outlier from the collective.

What often followed this series of questions was what I called the "Egyptian Dissertation". Often, Egyptian men took their time discussing all the ways in which I looked like an Egyptian. One time, I finished teaching and took two days to vacation in Sharm el-Sheikh, which is located near the Red Sea. The gentleman working behind the breakfast bar conducted a 20-minute "Egyptian Dissertation". It started out like this – "You see, your skin. You see, your skin looks just like us. And your eyes. You have brown eyes just like us. Your hair. It is curly and the same color as us. Now, the ladies might not have curly hair [indicating that most Egyptian women style their hair straight], but don't be fooled, you have hair just like us …". For once, I felt like I belonged.

Othering in Egypt

The teaching site in Egypt, unlike the diverse South African site, is primarily composed of Egyptian women teachers working at American or Canadian international schools. On occasion, there were one or two American or Egyptian-American students, but this was very rare. Interestingly, since my looks and gender often matched that of most my graduate students, they felt free to talk more candidly about justice-oriented practices in the classroom.

Since Egypt has a very patriarchal society, the main focus of our discussion of marginalization and othering was gender. One day, I opened a dialogue about race in class. Hoda, a graduate student in the class, quickly replied, "That's an American problem. We don't have that here". Now, a majority of taxi drivers and other low-income workers in Egypt are often Nubians. As a people, Nubians originate from Southern Egypt. They tend to have darker skin and coarse hair, similar to the rest of the African continent. Nubians are often channeled into low-income positions, and this was very clear to my outsider perspective. So, I countered Hoda, "I don't believe that to be true. Why are all the taxi drivers Nubians?" With that, the whole class took pause and fell silent. I was worried that I had shut the conversation down, but another student, Mariam, responded, "Actually, you're right. I never thought of that before".

In this instance, and in many others, my ambiguous brown skin was a strength that promoted candid conversations in the Egyptian classroom. Because I looked like my students, I was able to push their understanding and lack of awareness around racial social constructions that were usually masked by larger issues such as gender and faith. Since writing this chapter, I have visited Egypt 12 times in eight years. Each time I visit, I feel empowered by the space of those who look like me and embrace me, while also utilizing my ambiguity to highlight the ills of those who are othered in Egyptian society.

ACT III: KENYA

I sat down at the desk across from Kyle, my powerlifting coach. Kyle's mother is biracial (Black/White), just like me, and Kyle looks like he could pass as my younger brother. He is one of the few people in my life who understands the "reflexivity of pain" (Hurd, 2012) and the struggle of my ambiguously brown skin. As I had not seen Kyle for one year while I was living in Kenya and working as a volunteer at an orphanage there, he immediately asked, "How was Kenya?"

People have asked me this question time and again. I usually answer, "Oh, Kenya. It was rewarding, challenging. You know, all the things you expect living in a new culture". But that day, I answered with my truth. I bluntly explained to Kyle, "I was considered White there. They called me mzungu [White person] all the time". He replied, "That must have set you back like five years". With a sigh of relief at his understanding, I said, "You have no idea".

White on Black

I took a sabbatical from my institution to write a book. I can only write for about four hours a day, and I realized that this left an enormous amount of time to volunteer my services. I decided to move to Kenya for the whole academic year to volunteer at an orphanage. From the very minute that I exited the airport, I was often greeted with the term *mzungu*. This is a Kiswahili word that is very commonly used in most parts of East Africa. The term translates as "wanderer", but is often reserved to call out White people. The term has various applications. It could be used by people selling goods on the side of the road to get my attention, or by people addressing me in a derogatory way.

At the orphanage, even though the children knew my name, they would often call me mzungu instead. Being called "White person" multiple times a day would often get under my nerves. I did not identify as White, yet mzungu was synonymous with my name. As I cyber-logged my experiences throughout the year on Facebook, this early post clarified my feelings of frustration and perplexity about being considered "White":

> Culture shock #1: Everyone here thinks I am "mzungo" (white person – I know, it's a first) and they call and stare at me everywhere I go. Almost into a third week of this, and it's starting to get under my skin. Today on my 3-mile walk, a lady was telling me why I wasn't a Black American. Later on there was a black sheep on the side of the road and it starting "bah-ing" at me. I'm like, "WHAT?!?! I'm not Black enough for you either!!! Fall back son!" Clearly not a great conversation between sheep and I 🐨. (Facebook Post, November 14, 2016)

This is a clear representation of my frustration and transition to this new construct of my ambiguously brown (or in this case, white) skin. But this experience was not unique to me. My friend, a Kenyan living in America, married a White man. She has two biracial children of her own, and explained in a reply post:

> My own family call [sic] my kids mzungu despite the fact that I am their mother and of course I am their daughter and sibling. It's just that you are lighter than them all and they see you as white. Just roll with it for now and try and educate them. They are very considerate people and if you tell them it hurts they will correct it and help educate others. Am sorry love but enjoy the sticks [implying I lived in a rural area] and smile lots! Xoxoxo. (Facebook Reply, November 17, 2016)

It took about two months for the children at the orphanage to finally call me by my name. Each time that a child would call me mzungu, I would ask, "What's my name? You know my name". Over time, they affectionately began call me "Lynnettie", which was more heartwarming than "White". Although in the space of the orphanage, the children may not have called me White, they still viewed me as such. All I had to do was to step outside the orphanage grounds to be reminded of that.

After a year of living in Kenya, I learned to react less harshly to being considered "White". I knew that the tides had changed when I met my Kenyan finacé's cucu (grandmother) for the first time. I reached out my hand to shake hers and said, "It's nice to finally meet you. I'm Lynnette". Instead of taking my hand, she leaned over to her sister and said, "mzungu". In essence, she used this term to define who I was, and I actually laughed about it. In Kenya, my ambiguously brown skin learned to let go just a little bit and to focus on my purpose. This was best stated by my friend's mother, who is a light-skinned African American. She had the same experience while in Kenya. She explained, "I completely understand ☺ [your perspective]. I get the same response, didn't understand what was going on at first. I'm like okay now, do what I have to do ☺". I did just that – I focused on the children and my purpose as a volunteer in the country.

CONTEXT IS EVERYTHING

This Facebook discussion brought forth a rich dialogue including other biracial people's voices and their experiences living in and traveling to different countries.

For example, Nick, a friend who is Latinx/White American and who lives in Thailand, explained his perspective:

> Every person in the world will find places where their appearance/ ethnicity is marginalized and also where it is lauded. Everybody. What marginalizes your particular experience in the USA and Kenya would offer an opposite response in places like Cuba or Brazil. Just some perspective … as a mixed person myself I would say that Brazil is the only place where my ethnicity hasnt [sic] been an issue whatsoever. In Thailand, i'm [sic] considered French. Not because they think i'm [sic] from France but because all european-esque [sic] people are called French. (Facebook Response, November 16, 2016)

Nick's story aligns deeply with mine and the other voices of biracial/mixed heritage people. Being ambiguously Brown is a reality of social construction, although it is one that does not receive much discussion in the literature.

Yet, it is this context that caused me to experience various racialized and minoritized perspectives in Africa. South, North, and East Africa have all painted my racial constructions differently. I recently ordered a DNA test to pinpoint my African roots. It is interesting how science has created this new element of racial and cultural identity. My most recent test indicates that all my African roots stem from West Africa: 20% Ivory Coast/Ghana, 10% Nigeria, 2% Benin/Togo, 3% Mali, and 3% Senegal. Although I have never been to West Africa, I have to admit that I am purposefully delaying the experience. I finally have evidence of my "Blackness" to hold on to, and I am worried about how my racial identity will be perceived in West Africa. Will they see me as one of them? Will West Africans reject me as their own? Only time will tell as I continue to traipse through this world as an ambiguously Brown woman.

IMPLICATIONS

My socio-racial experiences around the world stem from the deep historical context of American racial identity juxtaposed with the historical context of each country.

Being a professor of teachers in these countries, as well as in the United States, reinforces the importance of how biracial or multiracial children are viewed and embraced in the schooling context. Yet, mixed race youth are often left out of the discussion, as they are slated to the binary standard of monoculturalism. In the United States, this monocultural socio-racial construction of youth and adolescents often starts in the school. Tutwiler (2016) explains, "educators tend to view mixed-race children as children of color, regardless of how individual children might self-identify racially" (p. ix). Sadly, there is a lack of knowledge on this issue among teachers, and this becomes more complicated during adolescent development. Tutwiler (2016) further clarifies:

> There is a chasm between teacher knowledge about this highly diverse group of students [mixed race youth] and the unique educational support they may need. The way of multicultural educational practices and related texts has been slow to fully address the unique experiences and educational needs of mixed-race children. (p. x)

Sleeter (2008) posits that this rift of knowledge can be traced to neoliberal assaults on teacher education. Now more than ever, in many countries, teacher education programs are struggling to maintain a program focused on diversity and equity (Harber & Serf, 2006; Sleeter, 2008). Often, teacher education programs are pressured from top-down influences (e.g., government, funding sources, accrediting bodies) to prepare teachers to be technicians. Without a focus on equity and justice, teachers are ill-equipped to deal with the diverse classroom. Moreover, teachers are asked to "become actively aware of the larger world, asking significant and relevant questions about the world and wrestling with big ideas and questions for which there may not be one right answer" (National Middle School Association, 2010, p. 1), yet they are not taught *how* to do this in their training. The demands of the increasingly culturally diverse classroom, along with the realities of the profession, further strengthen the argument that teacher education programs should implement equity- and justice-oriented educational standards.

Conklin and Hughes (2016) offer a pedagogical framework for critical teacher education that creates an important space for multiracial youth to be considered. The framework, which proposes a "compassionate, critical, and justice-oriented teacher education" approach, revolves around four guiding principles and practices:

> (a) facilitate the development of relationships and community; (b) honor preservice teachers' lived experiences and existing attitudes; (c) introduce preservice teachers to multiple perspectives of viewing the world; and (d) provide a vision of equitable, intellectually challenging teaching and learning. (p. 47)

Each of these principles and practices are analyzed and described in three areas: representations, decompositions, and approximations. Conklin and Hughes (2016) further specify each description as:

157

(a) representations of practice: the multiple ways teaching practices are represented in K-12 and teacher education classrooms and what these representations make visible to preservice teachers; (b) decompositions of practice: the ways teacher educators break down practice into essential parts for the purposes of teaching and learning; and (c) approximations of practice: the types of practice preservice teachers have opportunities to engage in that are more or less proximal to the practices of teaching. (p. 49)

Educators of teachers can use this framework in each individual course, as well as program-wide, to ensure a justice-oriented approach to teaching that includes the multiracial perspective in the curriculum.

REFERENCES

Conklin, H. G., & Hughes, H. E. (2016). Practices of compassionate, critical, justice-oriented teacher education. *Journal of Teacher Education, 67*(1), 47–60.

Ellis, C. (2004). *The ethnographic I: A methodological novel about autoethnography.* Walnut Creek, CA: Altamira Press.

Funderburg, L. (1994). *Black, White, other: Biracial Americans talk about race and identity.* New York, NY: Quill.

Harber, C., & Serf, J. (2006). Teacher education for a democratic society in England and South Africa. *Teaching and Teacher Education, 22*(8), 986–997.

Hurd, E. (2012). The reflexivity of pain and privilege. *International Journal of Critical Pedagogy, 4*(1), 36–46.

Mawhinney, L., & Petchauer, E. (2013). Coping with the crickets: A fusion autoethnography of silence, schooling, and the continuum of biracial identity development. *International Journal of Qualitative Studies in Education, 26*(10), 1309–1329.

National Middle School Association. (2010). *This we believe: Keys to educating young adolescents* (White Paper). Westerville, OH: Author.

Noah, T. (2016). *Born a crime: Stories from a South African childhood.* New York, NY: Spiegel & Grau.

Pierce, C. M., Carew, J. V., Pierce-Gonzalez, D., & Wills, D. (1978). An experiment in racism: TV commercials. In C. Piece (Eds.), *Television and education* (pp. 62–68). Beverly Hills: Sage Publications.

Rockquemore, K. A., & Brunsma, D. L. (2002). Socially embedded identities: Theories, typologies, and processes of racial identity among Black/White biracials. *The Sociological Quarterly, 43*(3), 335–356.

Rockquemore, K. A., Brunsma, D. L., & Delgado, D. J. (2009). Racing to theory or retheorizing race? Understanding the struggle to build a multiracial identity theory. *Journal of Social Issues, 65*(1), 13–34.

Sleeter, C. (2008). Equity, democracy, and neoliberal assaults on teacher education. *Teaching and Teacher Education, 24*(8), 1947–1957.

Smedly, A., & Smedly, B. D. (2005). Race as biology is fiction, racism as a social problem is real: Anthropological and historical perspectives on the social construct of race. *American Psychologist, 60*(1), 16–26.

South African History Online. (2018). *A history of Apartheid in South Africa.* Retrieved from http://www.sahistory.org.za/article/history-apartheid-south-africa

Sue, D. W. (2010). *Microaggressions in everyday life: Race, gender, and sexual orientation.* Hoboken, NJ: John Wiley & Sons.

Sue, D. W. (2016). *Race talk and the conspiracy of silence: Understanding and facilitating difficult dialogues on race.* Hoboken, NJ: John Wiley & Sons.

Sue, D. W., Capodilupo, C. M., Torino, G. C., Bucceri, J. M., Holder, A., Nadal, K. L., & Esquilin, M. (2007). Racial microaggressions in everyday life: Implications for clinical practice. *American Psychologist, 62*(4), 271.

Thompsell, A. (2017). Racial classification under Apartheid. *ThoughtCo*. Retrieved from https://www.thoughtco.com/racial-classification-under-apartheid-43430

Tutwiler, S. W. (2016). *Mixed-race youth and schooling: The fifth minority*. New York, NY: Routledge.

MARIANA LEÓN AND GUILLERMINA-ITZEL DE GRACIA

11. IDENTITY PERCEPTIONS OF YOUTH IN MIDDLE AND HIGH-SCHOOL

Beyond Being Mestizo

INTRODUCTION

Mestizo is the best word to specify a combination that I do not know. (12th grade student)

An individual's identity is constructed throughout the life cycle. That construction is a permanent process and will depend on the sociocultural environment of the individual. "The space of every-day life, not abstracted from its belongings, its situations, relationships and influences, by means of processes of production and social reproduction in which the subject participates, and becomes multiple, into innumerable elements of social order that incorporate as reference points for the subject; as identity adscriptions to which the subjects adhere" (Reyes Juarez, 2008, p. 148).

This chapter presents the results of a preliminary research project about the identity perception of youth during their high school education. The results of a survey applied to upper middle and high school students[1] in Panamá indicated that they had not seriously thought about the ethnical group they belonged to until that moment. Most students identified themselves as Mestizos. The respondents believe that the information they receive in their schools regarding the different ethnic groups is vague but has reinforced their identity to a certain measure.

MULTICULTURAL IDENTITY CONCEPTUAL FRAMEWORKS

Identity Development Frameworks and Models

Poston (1990) explains that racial identity development is important for the following reasons: "It helps shape individuals' attitudes about themselves, attitudes about other individuals in their racial/ethnic group, attitudes about individuals in other racial/ ethnic minority groups, and attitudes about individuals from the majority; and it dispels the cultural conformity myth, that is, that all individuals from a particular minority group are the same, with the same attitudes and preferences" (p. 152). Poston proposes a biracial identity development model with different levels and specific attitudes that are associated with each level of development. The levels are: personal identity, choice of group categorization, enmeshment/denial, appreciation, and integration.

If adolescents are not provided with sufficient opportunities to accomplish a healthy identity formation, they may face clinical implications such as identity confusion, self-hatred, substance abuse, suicide, delinquency, alienation, denial of self, gender identity confusion, and feelings of guilt and disloyalty (Gibbs, 1987).

Sue and Sue's (2016) racial and cultural identity development model (R/CID) serves as framework to better understand the attitudes and behaviors of culturally diverse individuals. This general model is helpful in being able to discuss various stages of building racial or cultural identity for teachers or others who require a peripheral understanding of the process.

> The model defines five stages of development that oppressed people experience as they struggle to understand themselves in terms of their own culture, the dominant culture, and the oppressive relationship between the two cultures: *conformity, dissonance, resistance and immersion, introspection,* and *integrative awareness* (p. 367).

A survey applied to adolescent students attending public school in Panamá demonstrates that these students are still in the conformity stage of this development model. Their responses indicate that they are not truly immersed or have a deep understanding of their ethnic background, and are therefore unable to reach a stage of introspection and integrative awareness. Instrospection can be facilitated if schools provided the discussion opportunities for students to deeply understand and reflect on their identity, including their ethnic identity.

Hurd (2012) also presents a framework that looks at how "adolescents of mixed heritage live in and negotiate between worlds form within oppositional (double/ dual) lenses" (p. 29). Hurd suggests that both pain and privilege are experienced by individuals of mixed identity, that these elements are interrelated.

Erikson's Stages of Psychosocial Development

When adolescents have a deep understanding of their ethnic and cultural identity, they are better able to experience positive youth development. This study is relevant because it explores identity formation of adolescents in a country that, because of its history and geographical location, is a multiethnic and multicultural amalgamation. Erikson (1959) proposes eight stages of psychosocial development that span from infancy through late adulthood. Each stage presents a conflict or crisis that must be resolved in order to move to the next stage. When these developmental crises are resolved adequately, they result in the formation of a healthy personality. The eight stages are: *trust versus mistrust, autonomy versus shame/doubt, initiative versus guilt, industry versus inferiority, identity versus role confusion, intimacy versus isolation, generativity versus stagnation, and integrity versus despair* (Erikson, 1959).

According to Erikson (1959), adolescence (youth between the ages of 12 to 18) is when youth face the conflict of identity versus role confusion. During this time, they are creating identities, affiliations, and a sense of moral compass. They will also explore different roles, ideas, and identities in an attempt to better understand who they want to be as adults. A successful resolution of the identity versus role confusion stage will result in an adolescent who has a strong understanding and feeling of identity and is able to maintain that identity when faced with problems and criticism from other people (Erikson, 1959). Furthermore, if the individual is not able to successfully construct an identity during this stage, they will struggle to achieve this as an adult (Erikson, 1959).

Erikson's (1959) work highlights the importance of conducting a study regarding the ethnic identity of adolescent individuals. High schools are spaces in which adolescents can formalize and reaffirm how they see themselves, both as individuals and in a social context. In the specific case of Panamá, with a history of country formation tied to a reaffirmed colonization,[2] there is a certain tendency to overlook or deny certain characteristics that tie us with indigenous and Black ethnic groups.

The study presented in this chapter will explore the ethnic identity perception of adolescent students in three different schools in Panamá City, Republic of Panamá, as well as how they perceive their multicultural and ethnic education.

RESEARCH METHODOLOGY

The methodology employed for this study is a mixed method, through the application of a survey with both closed- and open-ended questions, which provide quantitative and qualitative data. Quantitative data were collected through closed-ended questions which provided a description of the demographics of the sample population, as well as a measure of certain attitudes and perceptions through questions with a Lickert scale value. The closed-ended questions were analyzed through the use of descriptive statistics, which are displayed in averages, percentages, and frequencies. Qualitative data were collected through open-ended questions which focused on participants' perspectives, and extracting meaning from their responses (Creswell, 1998). The use of vignettes will help better describe and draw the reader to understand the case (Creswell, 1998).

Procedures

This research applies a descriptive survey from the perception of the student in relation to his or her construction of identity in adolescence. Descriptive surveys are designed with the objective to characterize a population or geograhic context as a function of the selected variables (Bowers, 2008; Hernández-Sampieri, 2014), in this case ethnic identity among adolescents attending public school in Panamá City,

Panamá . The use of this survey is useful to help portray the different dimensions of a phenomenon, system, process, or mechanism (Hernández-Sampieri, 2014).

We implemented the survey – containing 19 questions – during the month of March 2018 to a total of 212 students of the three large public schools located in the City of Panamá. The survey was applied electronically, using tablets, to the students while they attended extra-curricular English classes at a local English institute. We took field notes regarding comments and discussions that were generated as a result of the application of the survey. Some of the field notes are included in the results section of this chapter. The use of field notes in this study is important because it provided context that helped inform the data analysis (Phillipi & Lauderdale, 2018). Since the study was conducted in Panamá , field notes may help the reader better understand the country, its history, the national school system, and the students within this system. Furthermore, field notes "prompt researchers to closely observe environment and interactions" (Phillipi & Lauderdale, 2018, p. 382). Field notes helped the researchers in this study pay close attention to side conversations that occurred while students were answering the surveys, for example.

We divided the survey into two parts: general information and environment. The general information portion of the survey included demographic information such as respondents' age, grade, address, and ethnic identification. Questions regarding environment included education quality, ethnic group education and information distributed in school, and ethnicity perceptions at home and at school.

In order to obtain the information for this study, we applied a survey with questions related to students' ethnic identity and ethnic identity formation. One of the questions asked the students what ethnicity they most identified with. The options provided were:

- Black with White.
- Indigenous with Black
- Black
- Colonial Black
- Antillian Black[3]
- White
- None
- Other

Population and Sample and Communities

We applied the survey to students between the ages of 15 to 19, attending three different public schools in Panamá City, Panamá. The schools will not be named to preserve the anonymity of the institutions and its students. The three schools were considered large schools and offered education from Kindergarten through 12th grade. School A had 2733 students in total, and 68 students responded the survey. School B had 2500 students in total and 99 students responded the survey. Schools C had 1800 students and 33 students responded the survey.

The majority of respondents were between 16 and 17 years old, with 54.25% (n=115) and 31.13% (n=66), respectively. Of this number, 7.08% (n=15) of the respondents were 15 years old, 6.60% (n=14) of the respondents were 18 years old, and 0.94% (n=2) of the respondents were 19 years old. There were no respondents younger than 16 or older than 19 years of age. Of this same number, 55.66% (n=118) of the respondents were in 11th grade and 43.87% of the respondents were in 12th grade (n=93). Only one respondent was in 9th grade.

The presence of 15 year olds in 11th grade is not unusual in the Panamanian context. The school year in Panamá runs from March to December, and this survey was applied at the beginning of the school year, in the month of March, meaning that some of the students in the sample who will graduate 12th grade with 17 years of age have not yet turned 16 but will turn 16 at some point during their 11th grade school year.

The majority of respondents were female: 57.55% (n=122), and 42.45% (n=90) of the respondents were male. This data is similar to the overall gender distribution of high schools in the country, which also reflects a tendency for there to be more girls than boys in school. Panamá's National Institute of Statistics and Census (NISC, 2017) reported 101,377 students attended high school in 2015, of which 52.4% were female and 47.6% were male.

Panamá is a small country with roughly 4 million inhabitants, and more than 2 million inhabitants live in the metropolitan area of Panamá City. At the time of this study, most of the respondents lived in Panamá City, and those who did not lived in nearby cities of San Miguelito and Arraiján. Respondents reported over 30 different areas where they resided. However, roughly a quarter (25.9 percent) of the respondents were concentrated in two neighboring areas, called Las Cumbres and Omar Torrijos. Both areas were towards the north of the city, Las Cumbres part of Panamá City and Omar Torrijos part of San Miguelito City. Both areas were mostly inhabited by working middle class. The three schools that respondents attend were located in central Panamá City, meaning that the students faced long commutes to and from school daily, ranging from 30 minutes to two hours each way.

RESULTS AND DISCUSSION

This section provides a description of the findings of the study, with a focus on questions related to ethnic identity. Vignettes are used to provide the reader with a complete understanding of the open-ended responses to questions that asked the respondent to think about how they explain why they identify with a specific ethnicity. Furthermore, we discuss some interesting findings regarding the education quality perceptions of students and the role of the school environment in identity formation.

Thirty-eight percent of the students who identified as "Black with White", also referred to as "Mulato".[4] On the other hand, 13% of respondents consider themselves a mix of "indigenous with White, also referred to as "Mestizo".[5] Why is it that more than 50% of the respondents identify themselves with a mixed identity? It can be supposed that youth in their majority perceive themselves as mixed because for them the concept of ethnicity is tied to a racial matter that is above all phenotype. In addition, the information that youth receive in their homes and schools further embeds the concept of Panamá as a "crisol de razas".[6]

To obtain in depth information regarding identity perception, we asked respondents to justify their answer to the previous question about what ethnicity they identify with. Below, we provide examples of some of the comments, in which most respondents referred in a generalized manner to the phenotype of their parents:

My mom is Black and my dad is White and I feel part of both.

Because of the color of my skin, I have a cinnamon-like color, also because of my descendants, on my father's side, there is Antillian blood and on my mother's side White.

My father is purple 'cholo'[7] and my mother is a mix of Spanish and Black.

Because I deal a lot with both (Black and White), because I have parents on both sides.

My mother is of Spanish descent, but I have aunts that are daughters of indigenous leaders.

My mother is White and my father is 'trigueño'.[8]

My mother is White and my father is Brown.

Because my mother's skin is white and my father's skin is brown.

Because in my family we have all the colors.

The reason for which I feel identified with that ethnicity is because in my family there is a great diversity of color, both Whites and Blacks.

Another revealing result is that the respondents considered that there is a direct link between the places of birth of their parents with a certain ethnic group. Take as an example the following responses:

My grandparents are of different ethnicities, on behalf of my father one is indigenous from Guna Yala and my grandmother is from Veraguas, her parents were from Spain. I love my indigenous origins.

My mother's side are Whites (Panamá City and Veraguas) and my father's side are Blacks (Colón).

My grandmother is 'chola' and the father of my grandfather is Spanish.

My father is Brown (from Chitré) and my mother is White (Panamá).

My mother is from Darién and my father is of Spanish descent.

I identify with Black and White because my family comes from China and Haiti.

My family has Spanish traditions but has even more Afroantillian traditions.

These findings seem to align with Hurd's (2012) pain and privilege framework, which establishes that it is expected for Mestizo adolescents to not be able to fully identify with a singular race, culture, or social class.

Iriarte Esguerra (2000), in her article "A look from the diversity to the hypothesis of mestizaje", points out that "the complexity of the processed of integration of communities and the particularities that respond to pluricultural contexts require a look from research, that highlights the differences and recognizes the different cultural competencies from which a new identity is constructed, based on the social organization of diversity" (p. 83). This statement holds true when applied to the results of this survey where the topic of identity implies a complex process, especially when the research takes place in Panamá which possesses such a diverse society and with rich history of mestizaje.[9] A revision of televised images in Panamanian television demonstrates the way Panamanians boast a society conformed by diverse ethnic groups that are pluri-ethnical and multicultural. This provides an idea of how complex and, at times, absurd is the picture in which the research is conducted.[10]

On the other hand, it is contradictory that for many it is difficult to understand what it really means for Panamá to be considered a melting pot, and that contradiction is demonstrated by one of the respondents through the argument that "Panamá is a melting pot, so basically I am a mix of many races", without having to provide further explanation that, from her perception, Panamanian society is constituted by many races, and is therefore a Mestizo country. Where the affirmation stems from, and why the same thing is always repeated doesn't have an explanation.

There is a portion of the respondents that on a few occasions had thought consciously about the topic of identity. It is also interesting that 9% did not identify with any ethnic group and argued their response in the following way:

Simply because we are a race that has a lot of variety and we can't identify exactly what we are.

I feel identified with all ethnicities that my country holds. I love all ethnicities, I like the culture and customs of each one.

What influenced the respondents to look at reality in this way? It is likely that the respondents did not have spaces in their homes, neighborhoods, or schools where they could have meaningful dialogues about this topic. Furthermore, Hurd (2012) explained that "Mestizo adolescents experience pain and privilege by travelling between and negotiating within racial, cultural, or social groups and oppositional collective identities" (p. 25). The responses for this question seem to demonstrate that adolescents have to constantly negotiate between different heritages, cultures, traditions, and identities that come from living in families that have mixed race and ethnicity.

School and Its Role in Identity Formation

What role do high schools play in the process of identity formation? Schools must, through education, facilitate the process where the students construct or reconstruct their identity. For this, it is necessary that academic programs include a discourse regarding identity and how it is developed. The definitions and links related to ethnic groups must be clarified and reinforced, and cultural perspectives of Mestizaje from different points of view, including the biological and phenotypical points of view, must be tackled. For many students, high school is a space for the creation of interpersonal relationships of friendship, partnership, freedom, and escape from the reality of the home. It is also a space where they can relax, creating a useful educational place (Reyes Juarez, 2009).

Banks (2015) identified factors and variables that all need to occur and work together to produce a total school environment that fosters multicultural education. This model confirms that the responsibility does not lie on one factor alone, such as teachers or the curriculum; rather, the interconnection of a variety of elements, such as teachers, community, training, counseling, curriculum, produces the total school environment. In order for this environment to be created and sustained requires commitment and engagement from the government, the community, the families of students, administrators and school leaders, teachers, counselors, and students. Involvement of the civil society in such an initiative is paramount because the community and the parents need to understand and value the importance of multicultural education. If this occurs, multicultural learning will not only occur within the classroom, but will also be encouraged at home or within the community.

We also asked participants to rate the quality of their education. Of the total, 55% of students qualified their education as good, 29% as very good, and only a 7% as excellent. Identity is constructed and reconstructed through time. Several factors impact the process of identity formation in youth, but the existence of a social environment allows the person to elucidate in what society they are immersed and what place they occupy within that social structure. Ideally, teachers should have received trained in culturally responsive teaching and be able to practice "cultural scaffolding", embedding cultural experiences into the learning process to facilitate an improvement in academic performance (Gay, 2002).

We believe this result reflects a certain apathy and denial to deeply reflect on the reality of the quality of their education. If the quality of Panamanian education, measured through learning evaluation, is benchmarked with other countries, it ranks as one of the last in the world. PISA scores are very controversial topic of discussion in Panamá . Our last participation in Pisa was in 2009. Panamá ranked 71st in mathematics, 68th in science, and 69th in reading, out of 74 participating countries (USA ranked 31st, 23rd, and 17th, respectively).

Reyes Juares (2009) considers that "high schools are not just spaces where the heterogeneous, multiple, diverse, and changing character of expressions and ways of the adolescent condition is manifested, but it constructs and reconstructs students as youth subjects" (p. 152).

Following with the analysis of this same question from the preceding section, the respondents considered that they received a lot of information from the White ethnic groups. To what do we owe this perception? It's possible that it is related with the contents that are covered in the classroom. If you take as an example the lesson plans, it is possible to see how educators or schools approach the concept of identity[11] and, in many cases, it is linked mainly to teaching Republican history of the country and the conformation of Panamá as a nation (1903 to 1999).

The education that students received in the classroom may have helped or hindered their identity formation, and because of this we added a question in the survey asking how much information they considered they received at school for White groups, indigenous groups, and Black groups. An analysis of the data reflects that respondents received "some" information, meaning that they knew "some information regarding Blacks (39%), Whites (35%) and indigenous (34%) groups. This mid-level response may also indicate neutrality on behalf of the respondents towards this question, where they did not feel strongly about receiving little information or a lot of information on the subject. This response may be attributed to the lack of transformative civic education in schools, threaten to generate a lack of reflective nationalism among the Panamanian population where the individual will not have the "commitment needed to function within a range of ethnic and cultural groups within his or her nation" (Banks, 2015, p. 37). These actions discourage multiculturalism and negatively affect educational institutions.

According to Nieto (2008), multicultural education and education are one and the same. It is important for schools in Panamá to take advantage of their naturally occurring, multicultural environment to promote a total school environment (Banks, 2015) and the highest level of multicultural education support (Nieto, 2008). Hurd (2012) reflects on the role of teachers in multicultural education, commending their efforts in working with multicultural and multiethnic adolescents, while also lamenting the "unfortunate practices" that continue to exist within some schools.

The results obtained in this study allow us to further explore the process by which the following question is posed: Are Mestizos born or are made? When a student perceived him or herself as Mestizo, certain responses emerge that ensure that it stems from a strong physical component. Consider the following examples:

I don't know, because of the color of my skin. I am of black descendancy, but I am light skinned.

My skin is light, but with curly hair, thick lips and prominent cheekbones.

Because my skin is white, but I have afrodescendent features.

However, we found the respondents did not have a clear concept of their identity and of their mestizaje, but for their experiences they linked with ethic groups with certain cultural characteristics. So, it seems that they are conscious that any form of identity be adopted has a cultural component and thus conflate ethnicity and culture with racial identifications. As an example, we provide the following participant example, "I feel identified with all ethnicities that my country encompasses. I love all ethnicities, I like each and every culture and tradition".

My Neighborhood Is Mestizo

The environment that surrounds students influences the way in which they perceive their identity. Because of that, we included two questions in the survey with the objective to invite thought regarding the different ethnic groups with which participants identifies in their schools and in their neighborhood.

The students considered that in their schools there was a population that was Mestizo in its majority. Of the total, 66% of the students perceived that their classmates were within the combination of Black with White (50%), Indigenous (6%) or Indigenous with White (10%).

However, they specified that in their schools there was "a little bit of everything" and that within that variety there was "a good balance". It seems that they did not have concepts such as identity and ethnicity clear, and the perception of the students falls into the phenotypical conception to provide their classifications.

This also seems to happen when they were asked: What is the ethnic group that you consider is the majority in your neighborhood? Of the total, 60% considered that in their neighborhoods the population was located within the mix of Black with White and indigenous with Black.

CONCLUSIONS

This study presents a first approach to a complex topic, and presents the cultural identity perceptions of a group of adolescents in their final stages of school completion. The results shed some insights regarding these perceptions but also generate additional questions that become opportunities for future research. It is important to continue to explore whether or not the education that these Panamanian students receive appropriately integrates spaces for students to explore their identity and develop positive identity perceptions.

The results of this study show that students who completed the survey had not consciously considered to what ethnic group they belonged. These results reflect some of the contradictions of the education the students receive, where the school calendar of activities dedicates the month of May as Black Ethnicity Month, with the objective to vindicate the afro-descendant history of Panamá. However, field notes from informal conversations with the students demonstrate that these activities do not create spaces for students to have significant discussions and reflections about their cultural identity. Students mentioned that they "dress black" during these activities in order to obtain a grade and feel that they are not provided with the necessary information to elucidate the objective of this celebration.

However, it is clear that these festivities without any debate about their meaning reinforce the preconception that the students have to associate ethnic groups solely by their phenotype and does not help them gain a deeper understanding of the different horizons involved within the cultural characteristics that also make a part of our ethnic identity.

NOTES

[1] The grade configuration for the Panamanian school system is slightly different than the system in the USA. In Panama, Grades 1 through 6 are called "básica", which is similar to the USA's elementary education. Grades 7 through 9 are called "pre-media", or the USA's middle school. Grades 10 through 12 are called "media", which is USA's high school. Given the fact that there is an overlap between Panama's high school and USA's middle school, it can be inferred that, developmentally, Panama's high school is similar to USA's middle school. Therefore, for purposes of this chapter, research literature about identity formation in middle schoolers applies to the context of the survey respondents featured in this chapter.

[2] Panama is a multicultural and pluriracial nation. We are a mix of towns and cultures and a great variety of ethnic groups have left profound imprints among us. With the arrival of the Spanish, Portuguese, Italians, Dutch, French, German, Irish, besides many Amerindians from other parts of the continent, and with Colonization also arrived people from Africa. Colonization was our first big jump towards multiethnicity and biological mestizaje. The second jump started in 1849 when Oriental, Irish, North American, and Afro-Antillian military arrived. Many of them stayed to enrich our culture and diversify mestizaje even more. After came the French canal and once more myriads of immigrants flooded our beaches to work or to stay. Our national identity has been nurtured not just from history, but from that cultural multiplicity" (Castillero Calvo, 2003, p. 258).

[3] Panama has established a difference between the Colonial Black, that speaks Spanish, it baptized as Catholic, and was brought under the system of slavery since the 16th Century, and the Antillian, which speaks English, Creole-English, or French, predominantly Protestant, and arrived to Panama from the Caribbean, Jamaica, and Barbados, with the construction of the Canal throughout the 19th Century and beginning of the 20th Century. This last was focused mainly in the cities of Panama, Colon, and Bocas del Toro" (Pulido Ritter, 2018).

[4] We must keep in mind that they terminology used has its origin during the Colonial Period and corresponds to how colonizers denominated the different combinations of ethnicities. "Once the process of mestizaje has been consummated, we find ourselves upon new circumstances, new men, new names, new skins [...]. The product of the mix of White and Indigenous is denominated Mestizo [...]. In this way, the mix of Indigenous and Black produces Lobo, Zambo [...]. And we find, at last, infamous qualifications".

[5] This data is important because it is aligned with the results of genetic research that have been conducted in the last two decades in Panama. It leaves as a reference some publications of national newspapers that echo this information (see Arias, 2001).

[6] A historical analysis of the concept "Crisol de Raza", can be read in the essay of Pulido (2012). See also Porras (2009). The basic idea and translation into English is that of a crucible of races, more commonly known today as a melting pot of peoples. Crucible of races, or pot, are expressions used to refer to how seemingly heterogeneous societies gradually become homogeneous societies, thus the term "crucible" or mixture of those people from different cultures, races, ethnicities, religions, etc. forming a multi-ethnic society.

7   According to the Royal Spanish Academy (Real Academia Española), the term "cholo" can be defined as a Mestizo of European and indigenous blood. Also, when the Mestizo has more indigenous features, but has lost or does not speed their language.
In the Panamanian context, the concept of "cholo" can also be reinforced with Arias' (2001) study regarding the genetic background of the cholos of the Cocle province in Panama. Arias (2001) states: "after the cross of the Cocle (indigenous that came from the center of the country) with whites and blacks were originated the cholos. Although the Cocle are genetically similar to the Ngobé indigenous peoples, they are not identical, due in part to the contact of the Coclé with their neighbors in the East, the Cueva. The linguistic evidence is very important and the Cocle, who were evolving towards the cholos when they lost the language, spoke a variation very similar to ngoberé, the guamíe from Penonomé".

8   According to the Royal Spanish Academy (Real Academia Española), trigueño refers to an individual of Black race or very dark skin.

9   Alfredo Castillero Calvo in his already cited article "Estructura demográfica y mestizaje" sustains that "The biological and cultural mestizaje constitutes a fundamental factor of the history of Panama and this story will be difficult to understand without knowing which have been its characteristics, how it evolved, and what normatives regulated it, what biological and cultural forces have pulled it throughout the centuries".

10   Dr. Patricia Pizzurno has touched a subject perhaps a bit explored by historians in Panama and in his essay Memories and Imaginaries of identity and race in Panama in the 19th and 20th Century. She makes an analysis of how Panamanian society emphasizing in concept as invisible identities (indigenous and farmers), but above all deepening the topic of identity embedded in a historic context with the emergence of Panama as a Republic.

REFERENCES

Arias, T. D. (2001). Los cholos de Coclé: Origen, filogenia y antepasados indígenas ¿Los Coclé o los Ngobé? Un studio genetico-histórico [The cholos of Cocle: Origin, phylogeny and indigenous ancestors. The Cocle or the Ngobe? A genetic-historic study], *Societas, 3*(1), 55–88.
Banks, J. A. (2015). *Cultural diversity and education: Foundations, curriculum, and teaching* (6th ed.) Boston, MA: Pearson.
Bowers, A. (2008). *Encyclopedia of survey research methods: Field survey.* Thousand Oaks, CA: Sage Publications.
Castillero Calvo, A. (2003). Estructura demografía y mestizaje [Demography structure and mestizaje]. In *Historia General de Panama Tomo I.* Panama, Panama: Comité Nacional del Cententario de la República.
Erikson, E. H. (1959). *Identity and the life cycle: Selected papers.* New York, NY: International Universities Press.
Gibbs, J. T. (1987). Identity and marginality: Issues in the treatment of biracial adolescents. *American Journal of Orthopsychiatry, 57,* 265–278.
Hernández Sampieri, R., Fernández Collado, C., & Baptista Lucio, P. (2014). *Metodología de la investigación* [Research methodology]. México D.F.: McGraw-Hill.
Hurd, E. (2012). A framework for understanding multicultural identities: An investigation of a middle level student's French-Canadian Honduran-American (Mestizo) identity. *Middle Grades Research Journal, 7*(2), 111–127.
Iriarte Esguerra, G. (2000). Una mirada desde la diversidad a la hipótesis del mestizaje [A look from diversity into the hypothesis of mestizaje]. In *Mestizo Yo? Diferencia, identidad e inconsistencia.* Colombia: Universidad Nacional de Colombia.
National Institute of Statistics and Census. (2017). *Educación premedia y media* [Middle and high school education]. Retrieved from http://www.contraloria.gob.pa/INEC/Publicaciones
Phillippi, J., & Lauderdale, J. (2018). A guide to field notes for qualitative research: Context and conversation. *Qualitative Health Research, 28*(3), 381–388. doi:0.1177/1049732317697102

Pizzurno Gelós, P. (2011). *Memorias e imaginarios de identidad y raza en Panama siglos XIX y XX* [Memories and imaginaries of identity and race in Panama centuries XIX and XX]. Panama: Editorial Mariano Arosemena.

Porras, A. E. (2009). *Cultura de la interoceanidad: Narrativas de identidad cultural (1990–2002)* (2nd ed.). Panama: Universidad de Panama. Instituto de Estudios Nacionales.

Poston, W. S. C. (1990). The biracial identity development model: A needed addition. *Journal of Counseling & Development, 69*, 152–155. doi:10.1002/j.1556-6676.1990.tb01477.x

Pulido Ritter, L. (2012). Armando Fortune y la identidad cultural panameña [Armando Fortune and Panamanian cultural identity]. *Tareas, 140*(1), 83–106.

Real Academia Española [Royal Spanish Academy]. (2018). *Diccionario virtual* [Virtual dictionary]. Retrieved from http://dle.rae.es

Sue, D. W., & Sue, D. (2016). Racial/cultural identity development in people of color: Therapeutic implications. In D. W. Sue & D. Sue (Eds.), *Counseling the culturally diverse: Theory and practice* (7th ed., pp. 355–388). Hoboken, NJ: Wiley & Sons.

FRANCISCO J. VILLEGAS AND PALOMA E. VILLEGAS

12. BORDERED LIVES

An Autoethnography of Transnational Precarity

INTRODUCTION

For most of our lives, undocumented status has been a key part of our identity, alongside being Mexican, students, members of a family, and scholars. Our experience has consisted of pain, privilege, heartbreak, and opportunity, opening new paths to pursue both academically and personally. Because of this, it is always difficult for us to answer the question "Where are you from?" In fact, while we have consistently had a tenuous relationship to borders, the nature of that relationship has varied. We have gone from being undocumented in the U.S., to holding different statuses in Canada that were marked by degrees of precarity but also included relative safety and privilege (international student, permanent resident, citizen).

In this chapter, we engage in an autoethnographic account of our experience as transnational border crossers. This reflection includes not only the act of crossing physical borders, but also the mixed identity produced through crossing class locations and privileged statuses. Through that discussion, we highlight the resilience of borders and the ways race, gender, class, geographic location, and non-citizenship ameliorated or exacerbated our relative precarity, particularly our recognition of deportability and the pursuit of a livelihood.

A CHRONOLOGY OF UNDOCUMENTEDNESS: THE EARLY YEARS

1991

We sat in the back of a truck at the Mexico-U.S. border, anxiously awaiting what would happen. While we both swore to stay awake to mark the moment when we crossed *al otro lado*, we promptly fell asleep. The border at that time was a construct for us, something with little material consequence. Little did we know it would become attached to our bodies, follow our every move, and become the lens through which we see the world. 1991 was also 5 years after the Immigration Reform and Control Act passed, allowing a number of undocumented migrants to receive permanent residence. If our parents had only migrated to the U.S. in the early 1980s like they had planned, we might have had papers, we might have been born in the U.S., and benefitted from a "birthright lottery" akin to property inheritance (Shachar, 2009). Our experience would have perhaps been completely different.

© KONINKLIJKE BRILL NV, LEIDEN, 2019 | DOI:10.1163/9789004393813_012

As we reflect on that crossing, the memories are fuzzy. Our age protected us a bit from the violence that borders enact. However, it did not protect our mother, who crossed separately. We do not provide much detail in describing our experience crossing the border in an attempt towards protection. As Anzaldúa (1999) reminds us, the borderlands can produce a gaping wound on the land. They also produce trauma and violence, which, for many, is carried out prior to crossing. For us, the trauma manifested through the knowledge that crossing the border did not signal safety; instead it meant the possibility of finding our family in different sides of the border if anyone were to encounter *la migra*. To this day, anytime we read the word immigration, even while "documented", it makes us anxious.

1994

The year is often marked in U.S. history through the passing of the North American Free Trade Agreement (NAFTA). We barely noticed. We noted that our aunt lost her job working at a coffee factory around that time, but the consequences were less apparent, particularly as our mother's employment had always been unstable. What was more pernicious was the passage of Proposition 187 in California, where we lived at the time. Proposition 187, also known as the "Save our State Initiative" (SOS), passed 59 to 41 percent on November 8, 1994 (Proposition 187, 1994). Supporters sought to take over what they felt the federal government had failed to do, "protect" their state, by excluding undocumented migrants from accessing state funded services such as public education, healthcare and public assistance. For our family, 187 produced fear and led to a deeper understanding of what it meant to be undocumented. Parents kept their children from school and many families including ours chose to keep their immigration status quiet, leading to social isolation.

Growing up, things were financially difficult. Being undocumented meant our mother was not legally eligible to work. She had been able to get a driver's license because policy was less stringent then, but, the only work available to her was domestic labor. This feminized and precarious labor produced embodied effects. Cleaning houses everyday meant a constant exposure to chemicals, physical effects to her hands and nails due to the wearing of rubber gloves, and chronic pain from moving vacuum cleaners and other supplies around middle class Bay Area households. As a polio survivor, her relegation to this type of work also meant a further breakdown of her body, a literal process of backbreaking labor. Cleaning houses also involved a dehumanizing oscillation between maternalism from employers who felt pity for her situation and saw her as "one of the family", to demands for physical and emotional labor, tasking her with listening to their stories and complaints when they desired, and finally pretending to be invisible when they reminded her to "know her place" (Hondagneu-Sotelo, 2007; Romero 1999).

While the context of our daily life is not uncommon within the undocumented experience, we were also fortunate to have familial support. We were lucky to pay low rent because our extended family owned a house they rented to us. This subsidy facilitated a few more freedoms than those afforded to undocumented migrants in similar socioeconomic standing.

Mid to Late 1990s: The High School Years

Prop 187 exposed us to some of the effects of our undocumented status, but we did not fully understand the repercussions of border regimes and migrant illegalization until *major* events occurred in the life of our peers. These events include getting a driver's license, a first job, etc. We emphasize major because at the time it was an important event to all people involved regardless of documentation (Gonzales, 2011). These relative privilege of these spaces – workplaces and driving – facilitated mobility and disposable income. For us these were also spaces of danger, preventing us from engaging in the same activities as our peers and opening suspicions about our status. Therefore, our lack of participation demanded rapid responses to continuous inquiry.

In what follows we provide a personalized perspective on our respective experiences. The topics covered merge and diverge in an effort to describe how the saliency of our experience as siblings can be remarkably different while maintaining significant similarities and being driven by the same process of illegalization.

UNIVERSITY

Paloma

2000. I started my university career wanting to be a doctor – not a PhD, but a physician – to work with the medically underserved. As a hopeful pre-med, I sought to "fake it until I made it". I believed in the meritocracy: that if only I worked hard enough, I would achieve everything I wanted because, after all, my dream was not "selfish". As the too often cited pre-med cliché went: I wanted to help people. I thought that was enough; it worked in high school and got me into college, so why wouldn't my luck continue?

I was not prepared for the shock of reality and it came quick. As an incoming freshman, I had to contend with the fact that the California school system had not prepared me for the science courses I was required to take for my major. More importantly, my dream of belonging came crashing down when I was told I had to pay three times the regular tuition fees because although I grew up twenty minutes from campus, I was considered an "out-of-state" student. I did not have a plan B and did not see this coming, so I decided to pursue strategies to alleviate the situation.

I remembered one day walking through the student center, I saw a flyer for the student advocate office, a group of pre-law or law students who volunteered their time to help students with legal problems. I met with one and she told me not to worry; I just had to get some paper from immigration that said I had been living in the U.S. for a long time and had an outstanding immigration application (my mother was being sponsored by a family member and as her dependents her children were included in the application). What she was asking seemed huge, but she was so nonchalant about it that I believed her. I had not yet learned that people, even with the best intentions, do not always know what it means to be undocumented, both legally and emotionally, despite the fact that as a wise person once told me, "everyone considers themselves an immigration expert". I had fought so hard to avoid any contact with anything that remotely sounded like immigration and now I had to come face to face with it. I did it anyway.

My aunt took me to the Immigration and Naturalization Services (INS) offices. Later she would tell me that she had been scared the whole time, imagining agents coming by and arresting me. Fortunately, that did not happen. We waited for hours. Finally, I arrived at the front of the line. I was nervous but had practiced what I would say many times. The man asked me what I needed, and I told him that I had been accepted at a nearby university, but they were charging me out-of-state fees. I had proof that an immigration application had been submitted on my behalf and I wanted to prove to my school that I was not out-of-state. The man only smirked and quickly brushed me off saying that the application did not matter until it was processed, adding "you're nothing until then, you're nothing".

You're nothing. You're nothing.

That phrase would echo in my mind for a long time. Later on, I would connect it to Coutin's (2003) theorization of the legal nonexistence some undocumented migrants experience, not being able to prove their presence, employment, and housing history. But for me, that lens did not quite get at the dehumanization I experienced that day. Logically, I understood that I was not legible to the immigration regime yet, unless it was for the purposes of deportation. Emotionally, the phrase dug into my psyche, nourishing itself through my self-doubt.

My hope had been that my denial of the differences and exclusions undocumented migrants experienced would somehow carry me in a cloud over all my troubles. When this did not happen, I was at a loss. I contemplated dropping out of school because my budget – comprised of a loan from my grandmother – barely covered regular tuition. Again, later I understood I would not be 'dropping out but pushed out by the system (Dei, 1997). However, at that time I thought about letting everyone down. How could I drop out of school, and if I did, what would I do? My emotional investment in my education as my only "savior" was the only thing I could hold on to, even if it was at a preposterous price.

2001. Things changed when California Assembly Bill 540 became law. AB 540 allowed undocumented immigrants, including myself, to pay in-state tuition at California institutions if we attended a California high school at least three years and signed an affidavit stating we would "regularize" our status as soon as possible. Being considered a California resident for "tuition-purposes" allowed me to finish my undergraduate work. I was one of the lucky ones because I could prove that I attended a California high school and could fund my education through family loans and part-time jobs. This was no easy feat given rising tuition rates and the fact that my loan accrued interest at a higher rate than my peers' financial aid packets. However, I knew others ineligible to enroll in a community college because they had only attended a California high school for two years.

Throughout my undergraduate studies, I felt isolated and guarded in a way that I did not experience in high school. Because I did not feel comfortable revealing my status to most of my friends in school, it was difficult to relate to others' experiences. My status held me back from doing a number of things and I was resentful because wasn't college supposed to be a time for experiencing new things, meeting new people, going to new places? My status did not only mark me as different, it limited and bound the spaces I could enter while demanding a constant sense of surveillance about the potential dangers of it becoming known.

During this time, I was also employed precariously at a number of service sector food businesses. I had to juggle the emotional and physical work of serving people food while navigating sexual harassment as an undocumented racialized woman, with little recourse to complain or change jobs (Brunner & Dever, 2014; Clark, 2004).

Then another shock. My brother and I aged out of the application for residency my family submitted to the then INS. This meant that we had little chance of adjusting our status through our family, something we had believed would happen eventually. Given our mother's income and immigration backlogs sponsoring us was near impossible and we were left without options.

While I continued my university studies, I did not take the Medical College Admissions Test (MCAT) nor apply to medical school because I knew I could not fund it. Even if I had had the money, I was told by a medical school administrator that medical schools were discouraged from accepting undocumented immigrants, "but there were many attractive people on campus, so why didn't I just marry one of them?" His comments shocked me in two ways. First, through the realization that I had relatively no chance to pursue medical school. This was the early 2000s, right after 9/11 when immigrant students, particularly those from the Middle East and South Asia were being asked to report themselves to immigration authorities. Working towards a medical profession would have led to more scrutiny and visibility. Second, as a feminist, I did not want someone to tell me my problems would be solved through marriage. I repelled the idea that my worth was related to my level of attractiveness and the devaluing of my potential contributions to the medical field and community at large. Furthermore, the use of this trope did not recognize the gendered and race-related power dynamics involved with sponsorship.

2004. Although I had enough credits to graduate, I had no real promise of obtaining a job. What else was I to do? Even with experience, would anyone have hired me without a social security number? I still wanted to study medicine, but I was beginning to realize my path would not be linear. I now refer to this as a *Cantinflada,* in reference to the Mexican actor and comic Mario Moreno Cantiflas' non-linear stories. This was 2004 and versions of the Dream Act, which would effectively adjust the status of undocumented students who planned to attend college, the military, or were already in college, had been proposed in Congress since 2001 We hoped one of those versions would pass. So, my brother and I did what we had done all our lives: stayed in school.

My brother designed the strategy: apply to graduate school. As a first-generation university student, my university experience has involved two key factors: the lack of a roadmap and improvising on the spot. I did not research many schools because I knew I could not afford to go far, and I ended up applying to only one program, without even thinking through the consequences of attending graduate school. I do not know what I would have done had I not been accepted ... but I was.

Similar to my undergraduate experience, the university administration for my graduate program was not well versed in issues concerning undocumented immigrants. I received letters demarcating me as an international student and requiring me to register with immigration services. I had to "teach" administrators about AB 540 and fight to be categorized under it. They were not very open to being incorrect however, and it took a lot of phone calls and emails for them to classify me correctly.

I had to reconceptualize my ideas about the future at that point. What allowed me to become excited about a program outside of the sciences was my experience as an undocumented Mexicana. I realized that I could bridge my interests in healthcare and immigration in a Gender Studies program because of its interdisciplinary, intersectional, and transnational focus. Therefore, although I still did not feel comfortable revealing my status to fellow classmates and professors, I felt that part of my experience was finally coming through in my studies. I was finally learning to think critically about issues, to think for myself instead of taking things for granted. A blurring of boundaries – of disciplines and interests – continued for me because effectively, by writing about access to healthcare for undocumented women I was writing about myself.

The Dream Act did not move along in Congress. Once again, I did not know what I would do after receiving my degree. I could not afford – financially, emotionally and in terms of a future career – to keep going to school without the possibility of obtaining employment. It was time to repay all the hard work and sacrifices my family invested in my education. But what did I have to show for it? Two nice pieces of papers, ironically signed by then California governor Arnold Schwarzenegger.

During the second year of my master's program, my brother brought up the idea of applying to doctoral programs outside of the U.S. where we could have the opportunity of obtaining funding. We discussed it with our mentors who advised us about appropriate programs in Canada. However, I felt reluctant to leave what I had called my home for almost fifteen years. To me, it felt like we were giving up and, if only we tried a little harder, we could make it in the U.S.

Applying to doctoral programs was similar to applying to my master's program, a great big fumbling in the dark. Although I researched the schools more extensively,

I did not feel confident about the likelihood of admittance. It was difficult to explain my non-linear academic trajectory.

One morning I received an email from someone telling me she was my advisor and congratulating me for my acceptance to the department's doctoral program. I did not know what to do. My brother was in the other room and I screamed to him, "I got in, I got in!" The problem was that only I had heard from that school, and both of us applied, making me feel uncomfortable and guilty for my excitement.

Then, not an hour later, the phone rang. It was a faculty member from the same institution giving my brother the same good news. I felt a huge release in me, but at the same time, a question kept nagging me: Would I really do it? Would I really leave my family, the place that I called home and my life and accept that it was very likely I would be unable to return for a long time?

2006. It was the biggest decision of my life, and I did not realize that the consequences and reverberations would continue for many years. Leaving felt like a dream. Perhaps it was for the best that it was sudden because I do not know if I would have been able to make the same decision if I had had time to really think about it. We had to contend with not only leaving home, family, and especially our mother, but also with the fact that we might not be able to even attend our new school. We realized that we had to go to Mexico to obtain a study permit, because we had to apply from the country where we held legal residency or citizenship. However, we did not know how to explain our long stay in the U.S. We could not lie and say we had been studying there with permission because we did not want to jeopardize our application. At the same time, how would revealing the whole truth look to the immigration authorities of another nation? I had all the necessary documents to obtain a study permit, but I lacked confidence because I knew the process would be subjective and I would have to convince someone that my undocumented "record" would not influence me to overstay. The question changed from what will I do after I graduate if I cannot use my degree, to what would I do in a country I had not visited in fifteen years if the application was rejected?

Francisco

I always tell my students that higher education was never meant for us. We were not supposed to enter the halls of academia, much less serve as educators within it. Although I was very lucky to attend the university, the consistent hopelessness I experienced affected my performance and psyche. While California's AB 540 provided me the opportunity to attend the university paying resident tuition, the financial and emotional impact was still costly.

1997. I completed high school at an early age. My mother, because of polio could not walk long distances and while we lived in Mexico, enrolled me at the age of 4 in a nearby elementary school instead of traveling to a faraway kindergarten. After high school graduation I was lost. I knew I could not afford to go to college and it was also a location that was alien to me. I was fortunate to have friends show me the way and similarly, I was very lucky to have family able to invest in my education. Because of my undocumented status, I was unable to receive financial aid and experienced severely limited scholarship options. I highlight the word luck because a number of factors facilitated the possibility for my attendance to higher education. First, my family did not require my income as a full-time worker to survive, allowing me to focus on schooling, and second, family members had the ability to request loans on my behalf. This, however, did not mean I did not have to worry about finances; I was constantly reminded of my need to pay back the money and high interest rates. Furthermore, at the end of every quarter, in between worrying about finals and how to make the rest of my money last until the next amount was available, my aunt consistently brought up the possibly of not getting the loan necessary for the next quarter of study, causing me additional stress concerning the possibility of continuing my education.

One effect I attributed to undocumented status was the fear of asking questions in situations with a potential for disclosure. While I was thinking about where to apply to complete my undergraduate, I contacted a few universities regarding my possibility of attending. I called a local California State University and was told my application could not be reviewed without a social security number which at the time was erroneous information but served as the deciding factor to apply elsewhere.

My entire time in higher education I confronted individuals working at the university with little or no knowledge about people like me. One example still fresh on my mind was my attempt at activating my library card at the university. At the time, it was necessary to fill out a form, of course requiring a social security number. This was a moment of dissonance: I had been accepted to this university without a social security number and now this requirement stared me in the face. I asked the student worker about the possibility of not filling in the requirement and, as is often the case in bureaucratic institutions, they had to speak to their superiors. While standing in the middle of the library, all of a sudden, a librarian emerged from an office and charged at me in a very loud voice asking how it was possible that I did not have a social security number, telling me that I was mistaken, and demanding that I call my parents to get the number. In retrospect, the response is not surprising. The normalization of documents is not rare and years later, I would find the same behavior when working to enroll undocumented students in K-12 in Canada (F. J. Villegas, 2014). To date, I don't know how I should have reacted given the apparent power differential and immediate danger placed on me by my status. At the time, it felt like a flight or flight moment . To be clear, I don't mean fight or flight, as my instinct was to leave as soon and as discreetly as possible. My choices were either run away, so all eyes in the library would be staring at me, or meekly tell her I was sorry for wasting her time and that I would call my parents to find out. I did the latter. I conceptualize this as a moment of survival and my response as utilization of the "weapons of the weak" (Mclaughlin, 2010), particularly the appearance of meekness as a means of finding relative safety.

~2002: Hopelessness.   In the middle of my undergraduate, I realized that because of my undocumented status in the U.S., I could not use my degree to obtain employment. This caused a sense of hopelessness, where I continuously wondered about the purpose of attaining a degree if I could not hope to use it.

I experienced depression in my undergraduate mainly due to financial difficulty and my inability to secure employment to fund myself. Although my partner at the time helped me tremendously by sharing her meal card with me, it was still an embarrassing situation and one I could not share with people at home because they already worried about me.

A dubious coping mechanism I developed, and later found other undocumented students also used, was rationalizing. I often found the need to rationalize why I could not partake in different activities in which my peers normally engaged. If there was a job in tech support, which at the time I enjoyed, I explained I found the job boring and did not want to get bogged down with it. If people asked why I had no license, it was because I could not afford insurance and without it, a license would do me no good. If people wanted to go to Tijuana, I was not interested because it took so long to get back through the checkpoints. The majority of these rationalizations were not spontaneous but rehearsed since my time in high school; and while they protected me from potentially disclosing my status, they also served to remind of the barrier placed upon me by my immigration status and made me wonder if I would ever partake in those activities. In this way, my status became a phenomenon that followed me everywhere and mediated my actions.

In graduate school, hopelessness manifested in my growing concern over the possibility of using my degree. I questioned the importance of such an expensive piece of paper when all I could do is look at it. Applying for a doctorate was difficult, I was insistent in not spending any more money unless there was a possible way to use the degree. I knew that was impossible in the U.S., so I started searching abroad.

2002–2006: My two Dr. JCs.   Above I mentioned the effect luck had on my education. However, mentoring also played a tremendous impact in this process. Mentoring is an important theme in the experience and success of Latinx students (Gonzales, 2000–2001; Hurtado, 2003) and it was further enhanced by my undocumented status. For my undergraduate, I attended a university with a very small Latinx population and overworked Latinx faculty. As far as people I met within the university, I attribute my survival to three people, my partner at the time, and two mentors. My first academic mother, affectionately referred to here as my first Dr. JC, was a driving force in my navigating academia. She provided me with avenues to meet people in the fields in which I was interested, taught me how to conduct research, included me in her research team, and was the first person on campus to learn about my undocumented status. This was a sign of trust because at that point time, there were only a handful of people who knew about my status outside my family. Although often overworked in her position as the only Latinx mentor on campus (or so it often seemed), she always took the opportunity to smile your way, to call you *mijo*, and to remind you how much she believed in you. The path to her office was often filled with a line of bodies eager to speak to her. We would wait outside her door sitting on the floor waiting to tell her about something new and exciting that just happened to us or to seek comfort about yet another terrifying fear or experience. The response was always the same, a commitment to share in both our pains and joys, to ensure our survival in a cold campus environment, and to aid in the continuation of our studies into graduate school. To this day, one of my biggest fears is disappointing her. To do so is equivalent to disappointing my mother. In order not to do so, when I felt I had not acted to the full of my abilities in whatever class, project, or activity, I would "disappear" from locations I knew she frequented, often taking the long way around campus to avoid her office. Then, when I felt I had done whatever I had to do, I would make an appearance and with a knowing smile, she would look at me and tell me, "You've been avoiding me; oh, you didn't think I knew about that? Dr. JC knows everything". I still smile at these memories.

Following her outstanding mentoring method, Dr. JC encouraged me to continue my education and provided me with a wealth of information regarding the process of applying to graduate school and possible institutions. However, reminiscent of my experience in high school, we did not fully understand the consequences of my undocumented status. I was introduced to various recruiters to doctoral programs and the experience filled me with hope about a future. This all took a turn when we found out I was ineligible for most funded programs. My undocumented status deterred me from receiving any type of federal assistance, and the majority of the programs used that to fund their students. In fact, one university representative told me not to bother applying because they could not legally accept me, mirroring my sister's experience above. I have in the past theorized the undocumented experience as a continuous tension between hope and hopelessness and my sister has described the difficulties in planning for a future when systemic exclusions maintain and further precarity (Villegas, 2006; P. E. Villegas, 2014). In this case, while the option of pursuing a doctoral program in these schools was an impossibility, the promise of the DREAM Act materialized as a possibility, and I pursued a master's close to home where I could minimize cost and wait for this piece of legislation to bring me to the promised American dream. There would be more disappointments in the future.

I met my second Dr. JC (Dr. JCR) in graduate school in 2004. She taught the first class I took in graduate school. The class took place on Saturdays and because it was held every other week, it was six hours long. Coming from a university where the first day of class consists of handing out syllabi and excusing you from class, I did not expect to be there the entire time; perhaps more surprising was the fact that I enjoyed the six hours. Dr. JCR is blessed with the best storytelling skills of anyone I have met. It is impossible not to be captured during her talks. Her class introduced me to my first reading of Chicana feminist writings, a fact that sadly I did not experience from other professors in my program. Dr. JCR embraced me and upon learning of my undocumented status, provided a list of resources available to undocumented students, sharing networks and social capital often not available to us (Enriquez, 2011; Trivette & English, 2017).

My Master's program was a joy. My cohort was very close and developed a deep loyalty for each other, prompting various professors to declare us the closest-knit cohort they had seen. This was important. It was the first time I found a group of scholars that saw their intervention in the world from a similar starting point, while pursuing vastly different projects. I also found a support group for students like me. Immigrants for a College Education, (ICEd, a pseudonym used in my thesis) is a campus organization involved in supporting undocumented students through community interaction, campus activities, and the dissemination of information relevant to their experiences (Villegas, 2006). ICEd was not made up solely of undocumented students, it received much support from students with full status as well. ICEd offered me as an undocumented student the same benefit my cohort provided as a graduate student: a shared experience. Although we were all in hopeless situations, the group delivered members comfort in an increasingly anti-immigrant campus, a sense of belonging in an institution with a chilly climate towards Latinx students, and resources within the university and the community at large. I have never met more courageous individuals than the members of ICEd. I was constantly scared of disclosing my immigration status to anyone, and yet these students were often in the front lines making a case for the inclusion of undocumented students in the university. I sometimes wonder how different my undergraduate would have been if I had met them then rather than feel I was the only undocumented student in the whole campus.

Finally, Dr. JCR was a fundamental factor for my and my sister's move to Canada. She provided us with information about Canadian universities, helped with the writing of our personal statements, and with the anxiety of leaving everything we knew in the U.S. to return to a homeland we barely remembered and a final destination to an unknown nation. It was through Dr. JCR's efforts that we regained hope that we could use our degrees.

OFF TO A FARTHER NORTE

2006

As Paloma discussed above, leaving the U.S. to apply for our international student permits in Mexico was the most difficult thing we have done in our lives. Leaving the country meant the strong possibility of not coming back, and if we were denied the permit, we had everything to lose. Worst of all, our mother did not come with us because she was still waiting for her residency application to be evaluated (the process actually took 15 years).

We arrived at the airport with no idea what to expect. Our mother, an aunt, uncle, and Dr. JCR, were there to bid us farewell. We had family in Mexico who were very excited to see us again but sadly, we could not share in that excitement until we knew what would happen with our study permits.

The process to receive the permit was not difficult but a bit tedious. Once it was submitted according to a set of meticulous bureaucratic demands, we were told to return the next day. Upon our return, we were called to a window where a man awaited us. He asked where we had been accepted to study, for how long, and how we would pay for the expenses. He also asked us for a medical exam. Living in the U.S. exempted applicants from having to undergo the exam, which was ironic because we rarely visited a doctor there for lack of money and fear that using state services would jeopardize the likelihood of eventually gaining residency via some type of immigration reform. However, in lieu of the exam he wanted proof of continuous presence in the U.S. and asked for a copy of a green card or school records. We thought "okay, we can bring school records, and he does not have to know that we never had green cards". However, the question came: "Were you living there without documents?" We thought about what to answer for a split second. We were concerned that the knowledge of our previous undocumented stay in the U.S. would affect the way they perceived us, but we could not lie about it; we had too much on the line.

We told the embassy official the complete truth and he said it didn't matter. To this day, his response amazes us. No one had ever told us that our undocumented status would not affect us negatively. After running to an internet café to print out university transcripts, we returned to the embassy. Paloma went first and exited with her study permit. Then it was Francisco's turn. The official asked him to convince him we would not stay in the country past the expiration of the permit. This was the easiest question yet. Francisco answered that he knew what it was like to be undocumented, the difficulty in finding work, worrying about health, and constantly experiencing deportation anxieties. The official smiled and in the background, Francisco heard paper printing. A few minutes later, with permits in hand, we stood outside the Canadian embassy alone with smiles nobody could erase, realizing we were finally on our way. At that moment, we felt that we had reached the land of gold and honey. The reality was, however, rather different.

THE BORDER REEMERGES

As racialized, immigrant, and first-generation students, we have experienced consistent messaging about not belonging academia. Given our positionalities, as we move up the rungs, there are less and less people who look like us or share our experiences. We were lucky to do our doctoral program together, but we still experienced instances of insecurity, "impostor syndrome", macroaggressions, and explicit violence. Thus, for us, finishing the PhD was an accomplishment in and of itself. But it was not enough. We also wanted to experience security in terms of status and employment prospects. That is, we wanted to also partake in ensuring a livelihood four ourselves and our families (Olwig, 2003).

While we arrived in Canada with relative privilege as international students and no longer undocumented, this did not mean the absence of immigration precarity. We were not able to return to Mexico because of a visa requirement imposed in 2009 that made it more complicated for Mexicans to travel or return to Canada (Villegas, 2013). And, we could not return to the U.S. because of a 10-year ban imposed on us after having lived undocumented for longer than 6 months (American Immigration Council, 2016). This meant a degree of social dislocation, as we were forced to miss marriages, births, and other important life events, as well as experiencing a social distancing from individuals we could now only contact via phone, email, or internet chat. While the concept of transnationalism often denotes the ability of goods, information, and peoples to move across borders and the "multi-sited" experience of migrants (Basch, Glick Schiller, & Szanton Blanc, 1994), the effects of immigration regimes continued to play an important role in our transnational lives.

While we were living in Canada, our mother eventually received her permanent residence and was able to visit us. After some time, we also received permanent residence in Canada, though the ban to travel to the U.S. remained in place. Following the completion of our PhD, we experienced a difficult job market that was perhaps accentuated in Canada given the small number institutions of higher education in comparison to the U.S. After applying to Canadian jobs for a couple of market cycles, Dr. JCR again counselled Francisco. She suggested applying to U.S. jobs and utilizing the newfound class privilege of a PhD and an invitation to give a job talk at a U.S. university as a means to gaining entrance into the country with a possibility of a tenure track position. Francisco was the first to try in 2014. After applying to a number of schools, he was shortlisted at a California university in a department willing to provide him a number of documents to support an application for a travel visa. Prepared with these documents, as well as a copy of his degrees, proof of permanent Canadian residence, an upcoming citizenship interview, among other "evidence", Francisco showed up at the U.S. consulate in Toronto only to be denied because of the 10-year ban. That is, no amount of capital gained up to that point, what Aurora Chang (2011) refers to as being hyperdocumented, would circumvent the effects of the border. The visit, however, provided a glimpse of hope when the visa officer initiated a waiver of inadmissibility application that would take no less than three months. As expected, given time constraints, the university removed Francisco from consideration from the job and the job cycle would have to wait for another year.

Paloma faced a similar experience. Encouraged by Francisco's interaction, she also applied for a waiver and subsequently jobs in the U.S. However, her waiver review took too long, and she also lost out on interviews.

Our experiences demonstrate borders as "sticky", though a bit different than proposed by Goldring and Landolt (2013). To them, the stickiness of precarious immigration status refers to the consequences of being relegated to informal labor while working to secure permanent status, and the long-term consequences. The stickiness followed us transnationally regardless of our ability to achieve a modicum of social mobility (PhDs, jobs as lecturers in an academic department, a good salary). In this way, the legal production of illegality (De Genova, 2004) affected our ability to secure livelihoods.

Francisco has been fortunate. After receiving the waiver of inadmissibility, he again tried the academic labor market in 2015 and accepted a tenure track position in an institution willing to sponsor his visa application as well as to provide the necessary support towards permanent residence. However, he also entered the U.S. at a time of significant shifts in the immigration landscape, as a result of a new administration in the White House as well as prominent xenophobia among legislators. He remains hopeful.

Strength in numbers. Like many other people we know, our mother is our role model. Although living our entire lives below the poverty line, our mom made us believe we could achieve a university education. It is through this unwavering support that we found the resolve to cope with the systemic violence to which we were exposed. We also served as major source of support to each other. In Canada, it was through one another that we found a connection to home. Tara Yosso (2006) has written about the capital that students of color bring with them to college campuses. In our case, family did not only provide the types of capital that facilitated school survival while going unnoticed by the university, they also insulated us from a dangerous and difficult American landscape where we were discursively constructed as disposable and a drain on society. Finally, the mentoring received throughout this journey has been invaluable. In our respective PhD programs, we were mentored by the same individuals and while it is no surprise that it was once again Latinx women, given the ways mentoring and caring labor is often distributed, they were instrumental in our survival and success in the academic system. Through it all, the effects of borders have limited the availability of options but through the support of key individuals in our lives we have navigated spaces that were beyond reach.

CONCLUSION

Being undocumented is not a desired experience. We recognize this given that writing this chapter has triggered a number of emotional responses. As Ledesma (2015, 2017) notes, undocumented status can impose a "writer's block" given the emotional responses to writing about the subject elicits, as well as the fact that many of us have practiced not speaking about these issues for years if not decades.

Experiences of undocumentedness vary depending on the social and political context. We are not abject victims and through the coming together of luck, familial and community support and our own strategizing, we have been able to piece together careers and identities that disrupt those framings. We have experienced privilege through the fact that our migration at an early age opened up doors for us that were not open for others including some of our family members. Those doors were tricky and painful to cross, but in some ways, we have made it. We both have PhDs and have accessed a class status our parents have never known. However, to end our discussion we want to reject the notion of migrant deservingness or worth. *Dreamers* have been interpellated into a discourse that exalts them in relation to other undocumented migrants. Some willingly embrace it. Others reject it. We identify with the latter. We share our story as a way to continue to visibilize specific experiences of migrant illegalization and how they operate transnationally.

REFERENCES

American Immigration Council. (2016, October 28). *The three- and ten-year bars*. Retrieved from https://www.americanimmigrationcouncil.org/research/three-and-ten-year-bars

Anzaldúa, G. (1999). *Borderlands/ la frontera: The new mestiza* (2nd ed.). San Francisco, CA: Aunt Lute Books.

Basch, L. G., Glick Schiller, N., & Szanton Blanc, C. (1994). *Nations unbound: Transnational projects, postcolonial predicaments, and deterritorialized nation-states*. Basel: Gordon and Breach.

Brunner, L. K., & Dever, M. (2014). Work, bodies and boundaries: Talking sexual harassment in the new economy. *Gender, Work and Organization, 21*(5), 460–471.

Chang, A. (2011). Undocumented to hyperdocumented: A jornada of protection, papers, and PhD status. *Harvard Educational Review, 81*(3), 508–521.

Clark, A. (2004). A hometown dilemma: Addressing the sexual harassment of undocumented women in meatpacking plants in Iowa and Nebraska. *Hastings Women's Law Journal, 16*(4), 139–158.

Coutin, S. B. (2003). Illegality, borderlands, and the space of nonexistence. In R. W. Perry & B. Maurer (Eds.), *Globalization under construction: Governmentality, law, and identity* (pp. 171–202). Minneapolis, MN: University of Minnesota Press.

De Genova, N. (2004). The legal production of Mexican/Migrant "illegality". *Latino Studies, 2*(2), 160–185.

Dei, G. J. S. (1997). *Reconstructing 'dropout': A critical ethnography of the dynamics of Black students' disengagement from school*. Toronto: University of Toronto Press.

Enriquez, L. (2011). "Because we feel the pressure and we also feel the support": Examining the educational success of undocumented immigrant Latina/o students. *Harvard Educational Review, 81*(3), 476–500.

Goldring, L., & Landolt, P. (2013). The conditionality of legal rights and status: Conceptualizing precarious non-citizenship. In L. Goldring & P. Landolt (Eds.), *Producing and negotiating non-citizenship: Precarious legal status in Canada* (pp. 3–27). Toronto: University of Toronto Press.

Gonzales, R. G. (2011). Learning to be illegal: Undocumented youth and shifting legal contexts in the transition to adulthood. *American Sociological Review, 76*(4), 602–619.

Gonzalez, K. P. (2000–2001). Toward a theory of minority student participation in predominantly White colleges and universities. *Journal of College Student Retention, 2*(1), 69–91.

Hondagneu-Sotelo, P. (2007). *Domestica: Immigrant workers cleaning and caring in the shadows of affluence*. Berkeley, CA: University of California Press.

Hurtado, A. (2003). *Voicing Chicana feminisms: Young women speak out on sexuality and identity.* New York, NY: New York University Press.

Ledesma, A. (2015). On the grammar of silence: The structure of my undocumented immigrant writer's block. *Harvard Educational Review, 85*(3), 415–426.

Ledesma, A. (2017). *Diary of a reluctant dreamer: Undocumented vignettes from a pre-American life.* Columbus, OH: Mad Creek Books, an imprint of The Ohio State University Press.

Liladrie, S. (2010). 'Do not disturb/please clean room': Hotel housekeepers in Greater Toronto. *Race & Class, 52*(1), 57–69.

Olwig, K. F. (2003). "Transnational" socio-cultural systems and ethnographic research: Views from an extended field site. *International Migration Review, 37*(3), 787–811.

Proposition 187: Text of Proposed Law. (1994). Retrieved from http://traynor.uchastings.edu/cgi-bin/starfinder/8476/calprop.txt

Romero, M. (1999). Immigration, the servant problem, and the legacy of the domestic labor debate: "Where can you find good help these days!". *University of Miami Law Review, 53*(4), 1045–1064.

Shachar, A. (2009). *The birthright lottery : Citizenship and global inequality.* Cambridge, MA: Harvard University Press.

Trivette, M. J., & English, D. J. (2017). Finding freedom: Facilitating postsecondary pathways for undocumented students. *Educational Policy, 31*(6), 858–894.

Villegas, F. J. (2006). *Challenging educational barriers: Undocumented immigrant student advocates* (Master's thesis). San Jose State University, San Jose.

Villegas, F. J. (2014). *The politics of "access": Undocumented students and enrollment in Toronto schools* (PhD dissertation). University of Toronto, Toronto.

Villegas, P. E. (2013). Assembling a visa requirement against the Mexican 'wave': Migrant illegalization, policy and affective 'crises' in Canada. *Ethnic and Racial Studies, 36*(12), 2200–2219.

Villegas, P. E. (2014). "I can't even buy a bed because I don't know if I'll have to leave tomorrow:" Temporal orientations among Mexican precarious status migrants in Toronto. *Citizenship Studies, 18*(3–4), 277–291.

Yosso, T. (2006). Whose culture has capital? A critical race theory discussion of community cultural wealth. *Race, Ethnicity, and Education, 8*(1), 69–91.

ANNE RYEN

13. THE UBIQUITOUS RANK

Some Reflections on Walking on Thin Ice

INTRODUCTION

When I was a child, my parents brought me along to welcome my father's prosperous American relatives who had emigrated in the 1920s. They were the unfamiliar American dream, waving to us from "the America boat" docking at the local quay, in sparkling colors in Norwegian post-war times (the early 1960s). Relatives from across neighboring regions had all met up to see the huge boat arrive with people in colorful textiles, lilac-haired women doused in a mix of perfume and mothballs, and bringing their big Buicks and Wrigley chewing gum. I became the observing knee-height nobody pre-school girl, watching from below, seeing male shoes with colorfully embroidered white silk socks and bodies in yellow sweaters – not shirts – under strange jackets passing by, an incarnation of the meeting between the known and the unfamiliar.

The observations introduced an invisible line between "ours" and "theirs". The everyday was never quite the same. As my grandfather's sister and brother-in-law they were "one of us", yet not. How little did I grasp the momentum of this story of which I was made a part. Let me proceed on the intricacy of meetings, people, and complexities to reflect on my own life from the outside of being predominantly "classic European", one of many categorizations.

CONFRONTING THE UNFAMILIAR

Meetings

Meetings are endowed with communication. Some are accidental, such as when we bump into someone (Goffman, 1972), others are planned as in business and/ or and in research (Temba, Ryen, & Matotay, 2011); whereas some are involuntary and unpleasant as in war and crimes (Nagel, 2003). Still, others are of a different kind as with institutional practices and decision making that perpetuate the social world in implacable and resilient manners. In their own ways, they are all sources of reflections because people, contexts, and settings imply relations with the familiar, the unfamiliar, and with ourselves as in Figure 13.1.

© KONINKLIJKE BRILL NV, LEIDEN, 2019 | DOI:10.1163/9789004393813_013

Figure 13.1. Kenyan employee

The markers we notice, whether they work with or against us, are structural, cultural, and contextual be it in relation to ethnicity, race or color, class, age, gender, or accent, with some more pervasive than others. We get to see how we resemble and how we deviate from the other by observing, by being astonished, by not getting things right, by enjoying, by celebrating, by being confused, bewildered, ignored or rejected, or by feelings of contempt or by the other's resentment. We may admire by which elegance Americans, as we see it, do street life when they accidentally bump into you compared to others who without an utterance arrogantly proceed, or how tidy the Dutch organize the queues in and out of the train. Is this the same way for all of us? It could also be about the risk of being hijacked in the Ugandan field. Is this the same risk for all of us? Or, the pleasure of enjoying a cold drink out of the Tanzanian midday sun with good colleagues. A cold drink for everyone? Where I live, we rush out to enjoy the sun that constitutes Tanzania into "theirs" different from "ours" as in Said (1978/2003). Tourists do it differently from us locals and may even find my Nordic place exotic. The midnight sun (simply the ordinary sun), moose passing by, or telling from the grass that a deer or a fox has crossed the path, is normal to me; whereas my informant stopped the car to inspect the marks he saw by the road south of Sudan: elephants. If you do run a lodge, you appreciate wildlife. Also, elephants mean business. If the Maasai people steel your cattle, I find it scary that the police tell you to buy a gun, just like seeing the armed police when I was watching the Pride Parade in New York decades back. To me that was scarier than elephants. To others, too. Still, those are different risks. Life is an endless unfolding of such confrontations. They invite reflections: Who am I? Who am I to others? What am I a part of? Do I want that?

Being white in East-Africa and in Norway, a female big band trumpet player, being a member of the majority indigenous population in my country, a professor, a student supervisor, a cancer survivor, a sister and daughter negotiating with welfare state workers to assist caring for my handicapped brother, or daughter of my late Alzheimer's mother, life experiences confronted me with the above questions. Are these fragments from a privileged life? Later my life, too, became more multi-facetted and intricate, such as when things were imposed upon me or my loyalty was under scrutiny.

Classic sociologists have raised such issues for decades as in Baumann's discussion of the exile (2005), Simmel (1950) and Schütz (1944) in their writings on strangers and locals, and Fanon (1952) on being black in a dominant white society, on arguing for colonialism as the foundation of the contemporary world, for advocating the importance of life experiences – and confrontations – to critical reflections. These issues enter our discussions of the universal, such as in Sardar's (2005) Islamic criticism of European research, the impact of the global knowledge hegemony to academia (Ryen & Gobo, 2011), research practice (Atkinson & Ryen, 2016; Emeagwali & Dei, 2014; Said, 1978/2003), and research ethics (Battiste, 2008; Ryen, 2008).

Life is comprised of such meetings, i.e., physical, statistical, in court, on the bus, online, institutional, ideological. These make social scientists concerned with how we make up social life. In post-war Europe, The Frankfurter School called upon social scientists to differentiate between the legal and the illegitimate and fight the illegitimate irrelevant of legal status. With populism on the raise, this call is still valid in times of another call, namely that of ethnic nationalism (Maurras, 1905), with the right-wing political parties on the rise like in contemporary Hungary, Poland, and Italy with Lega Nord into Lega reflecting the party's now national standing (Fukuyama, 2018). At times, flattery becomes humiliating e.g. when the Norwegian Prime Minister during her US-visit flattered President Trump and his "Make America Great Again", because of Norway being a big market for US-produced Tesla cars. This triggered his much-cited, "Why can't we have more immigrants from countries like Norway, and not from these other 'shithole countries'". We felt embarrassed. With his former immigration policy on Muslims, his utterance was heard as firmly positioned within a longer sequence, though the words "Muslim" and "colored" were not explicitly uttered. Micro-aggression, systematically ordered privileges, and the opposite are anchored in structures we need to uncover in our efforts to fight injustice. "Capitalism or communism"? "Shithole-countries?" President Trump is not the only one. In the Nordic countries, young immigrants (primarily 2nd generation women) use storytelling to uncover their own pain, such as in Iraqi-Danish Sara Omar's book, *Dødevaskeren* (2017) (The Death Washer), and Arab-Norwegians' Amina Bile, Sofia Nesrine Srour, and Nancy Herz's book *Skamløs* (Shameless), in their fight against ethnic social control, just as Palestinian-Danish Yahya Hassan wrote from his male perspective in his 2013 book, YAHYA HASSAN. I deliberately refer to their hyphenated status, which is crucial to their intra-ethnic confrontation. They show their strength by fighting inflicted pain as a call to action by unanimous political support just as Pakistani-Norwegian Iram Haq did with her movie *Hva vil folk si* (What will people say). They all write from their own life experiences. Majority members do the same such as young Aleksander Dale in his book, *Arbeidsnever* (2017) (Working hands), as a member of the precariat class. I am unfamiliar with their pain. Growing up in Norway, with privileges here, my normal has become their parents' worries because of what their own people say. We must choose sides, and I choose the side of these young voices to fight the risk that their pain becomes "ordinary".

This brings me over to my own career across 25 years in East Africa. Just as with my quay image, we are reminded that ethnicity and culture are about relationships between *persons*, not between cultures or ethnicities. In the Nordic fairy tale, *The Emperor's New Clothes*, ordinary people along his route compliment the Emperor on his new clothes. Their appropriate performance makes him confident about his new outfit – despite his nudeness. Loyalty may come with a prize detrimental to fighting social injustice though the fairy tale lets us know that resistance can be performed in numerous ways.

On Doing Being Ordinary – or Not

My own life is a mix of north, south, local, global, quite "ordinary" at home or even in a European context, but predominantly White in Black African contexts or in Brown or Indian contexts when my "Norwegianness" becomes quite dim compared to the image of the British as portrayed in Figure 13.2.

Figure 13.2. The author at Mount Kenya Safari Lodge, opened in 1959 with its lavish lifestyle for the international (White) jet set and charter members. After much debate, the lodge accepted my "colored" informant as member

Some of my colleagues and informants who visit my community or campus have been Tanzanian, Ugandan, or Kenyan. This generates a pertinent question: Is being Tanzanian in Norway equivalent to being Norwegian in Tanzania? Hardly. The statuses as "ordinary" or "guest" are contextual constructs rather than some external truth, such as when my Tanzanian colleague worried about the scar on his daughter's leg by his comment "I hope it will become normal again". Black is the Tanzanian normal. Still, for historic reasons, certain statuses are more pervasive than others.

Some of my students and friends have come here as refugees or have been recruited as highly qualified personnel into the Norwegian oil-based industry, or as children accompanying their parents. We have walked some paths together over a coffee or in supervision. Being a white European professor in a rich country with a high score on UN-ranks on gender equality, happiness and trust allow me to be endowed with privileges. Assets ascribed and acquired that others may think of as a mirage, such as free education and health care, enjoying a peaceful democracy with human rights, politicians who have invested our oil surplus money into a fund for future generations' welfare rather than in instant consumption or in somebody's pockets, high trust in the state, bureaucrats and politicians; all of these make us accept a fairly high level of taxes since we experience the money being invested in joint goods such as schools, local youth clubs, and eldercare. To me, these are privileges, though others may see this differently. In my lectures, we discuss the value of a university degree if being female is perceived as "negative capital". What then about immigrant status? If so, then structural inequality is in the lecture hall, not something "out there".

People in the former Soviet Union used to accuse Norway of capitalism, with Americans accusing us of communism. Africans think we have lost the clan-like care and collectivism of Tönnies' Gemeinschaft-community, while Italians find us bureaucratic and cold, with dead faces reflecting a lack of enthusiasm, hugs, and intensity. Being protected from worries about food, clean water, war, pensions, and vaccinations is a privilege. Being associated with the rich, well-organized part of the world is also a privilege as I see it, though at times it is held against the "us" they put me with. Still, I am here and will continue to be.

Being born as – and growing up as a girl was not a worry to my parents. What a relief. That is my normal. My Tanzanian colleague's husband only celebrated when she had a baby boy. It made her so sad. She later founded The Women's Group on her campus. Our other colleague grew up in extreme poverty, but later took her Ph.D. in the Netherlands. A third died from breast cancer, though I survived. I always bring flowers to her grave in Tanzania. My informant was sad because all his children had left East Africa to go to the US on green cards. They no longer cared about the businesses he had developed to pay for their university education, but he told me "they were flying in" to sit by his bed the last week before he died. We said our farewells on the phone, and I am confident Allah was there to meet him and had mercy on his temper. He asked me to forgive him if he had caused me any harm (Ryen, 2008). He prayed to Allah when my elderly mother passed away. We talked about our Alzheimer mothers. He sent me a text message in the middle of the night when his son died from cancer. He saw me and my family as his family. It was a privilege to know Bellah, Mahid, and the others. They said it was mutual and I trust them. We worked together, laughed and basked – especially I – in the unbearable heat. They helped me light the corners.

Let me draw on these sketches to inquire further into pain and privileges, the complexity, the elasticity, and the relational aspects of such phenomena. Our meetings were themselves endowed with both. Ethnomethodologists criticize statistics for allocating people to be externally defined within operationalized categories, such as being ordinary, privileged, or marginalized, rather than exploring the how of this process which offers us to see how things are constituted as relevant or the opposite. We cannot take for granted that such descriptions simply float above as universally valid. Doing being "ordinary" is an active and collaborative accomplishment that every traveler is continuously reminded of when struggling to find out how things are being done "here" as in Figure 13.3.

Figure 13.3. Doing being ordinary in Tanzania

It is contextual as in Tanzania and Norway, and situational when we meet at a bar in Dar es Salaam, although there is a prior history. We need to explore how this is called upon and made relevant. To work for social justice means we need data that can help us nuance and argue. This becomes significant in times of populism and to avoid being trapped in suffering that drains our energy.

Let me elaborate on some of the sketches above to illustrate. I will also point to how the structural and global historic of it may enter our meetings in ways that privilege some members over others, me included.

DISRUPTING SOCIAL ORDER IN THE LIVING ROOM

Let me briefly return to the initial story that unfolded over a 70-year period from before I was born. After three decades, the old US immigrant couple's daughter and grandchildren flew in. She wanted to show them their roots which happened to be in our house. Our joint great grandparents had built the farm in 1850 which was now swarmed over by strangers in what they saw as an accessible public before their next stop in Paris. We dusted off the old rituals. Relatives were informed, cakes baked, and long tables prepared in damask and silverware in all houses. This huge apparatus made old relatives kindly wait with coffee and their homemade menu, assisted by their now grown up daughters, who had taken off from their jobs only to witness a performance in which the visiting matriarch reminded her children of the objects (in one house a woodstove) that their millionaire grandparents had given to the locals, their close relatives, in the 1950s. Though as Mauss (2008) reminds us, the gift-giving ritual is comprised of giving, receiving, and reciprocating. To the locals, these gifts were firmly embedded in the old gift-giving culture and surely appreciated in post-war poor Norway, with hard winters and shortages of food and clothes. The locals, themselves experienced gift-givers, played along with the ritual and refrained from talking about the third element – the expensive silverware they had offered in return (the only acceptable to do at the time independent of household economy).

How much did I regret that I had volunteered to be their interpreter, and felt humiliated when translating to honest hard-working, old people who had kindly opened their homes to descendants of their close relatives. In our own language, we agreed that at times money and etiquette come separately. We were all smiling, both hosts and visitors. However, the performance and storytelling reinforced the host-visitor axis, which acted themselves as agents for us to investigate. What resources did the members draw upon in their interactional process that constituted the ranked relationship? It activated the emotional and embodied childhood experience, but devoid of the warmth with which my lilac "US aunt" had embraced me.

The early quay-experience never left me, as it is activated in meetings. The gaze made me realize about positions and boundary processes, about being and becoming, about self and Otherness, about staging and performing distance and belonging. It also taught me about situatedness and transitions. The chaos made me see life not as linear, but as bunches of spaces in which we navigate. Bauman (2005) points to the gifts nomads bring the locals though they do not always realize. Quite so. He also reminds us that to see, we need to walk slowly on thin ice despite the urge to run to a safer space.

This pervasive image has become a reminder of the inherent potential of meetings whether good or troublesome. Life comes with surprises, and with pain and pleasure in a mix of local and global spaces, always in a transition that drains and nurtures your imagination. To live in a country with statistical top scores on the classic standard of living, trust and gender equality are accompanied by paradoxes that take stamina to navigate within. My path, too, is built on paradoxes and surprises that made me acknowledge we live different lives and that paths evolve as we go. Still, privileges do not relieve us of the obligation to acknowledge pain – also others'.

Foucault writes on the invention of the self as a requisite for reporting from a competent self (Atkinson & Silverman, 1997), with Holstein and Gubrium (2011) focusing on the many selves we talk from. The complex ideas about social realities is linked with identity as more problematic, as in Baumann's *Life in fragments* (1997). A new position, a new gaze, but gazes also collide, such as in the ethnographic field or at home with workable, favorable, unfamiliar, uncomfortable identities constantly changing, evoked and situated, mutually played with, suppressed and twisted, accompanied by pain and pleasure (Ryen, 2008a, 2008b, 2012; Ryen & Silverman, 2000). As referred to, Simmel (1950) captures this condition of being betwixt and between by his metaphor of the immigrant as a "stranger" who inhabits a space, but is not "of" that space or Giddens's concept (1991) of "the trajectory of the self" with the "now" as a liminal phase that permeates the transitions in which we find ourselves.

I also later found this childhood memory highly relevant, though in a new setting. Doing research in East-Africa with African colleagues and Asian (Indian) businessmen made the quay image come back. Who am I to Mahid or to Eulalia – the lady on the boat or the girl watching? I have shared this story, and they have reciprocated with their experiences of working with white people, thereby making color relevant. We have been together in the field, basking in the heat, tired, hungry, happy, grumpy, laughing. Colleagues and friends. Fragments of lives.

As Norwegian/African/local/international, I raise these issues with my multiethnic and -cultural students and invite them along to collaborative activities on campus and beyond. They also attend my course on Multicultural societies, a rather new status for Norway, which has been described as a latecomer immigrant country (Brochman & Kjeldstadli, 2008).

My research programmes in Norway, East-Africa, and Indonesia, in addition to my many seminars and Ph.D. courses with students from across the world and meetings with colleagues at home and abroad, inevitably invite reflections on what storytelling does.

THE SOCIAL PRODUCTION OF ACCOUNTS

Harald Garfinkel, who coined the term ethnomethodology, was concerned with the recognizable patterns of social life, and the problem of social order. This included his interest in the relationship between an established social order and the way in which people account for that social order (Lehn, 2014). This, he claimed, could provide us with a resource to study how actors in situations produce social order, hence the problem of recognizable patterns of social events that took him to his well-known tutorials in everyday settings which shattered participants' trust in the orderliness of the situation. These violations of the taken-for-granted made them respond by jokes or explanations to normalize the situation (Lehn, 2014, p. 75). This made Garfinkel explore sense-making as an intersubjective and observable practice, rather than a cognitive and subjective process. If participants remain able to make sense of a situation, social order does not collapse despite violating the norm. The standardized and standardizing background expectations – seen but unnoticed – are the same that participants use to design their actions in situations, and to make sense of situations that makes encounters intelligible as "appearances-of-familiar-events" (Garfinkel, 1967, p. 36, as cited by Lehn, 2014, p. 76). In this way, Lehn argues, Garfinkel sees social order as continuously produced through actions that make it "observable and reportable", though without revealing the trust that underpins it (Lehn, 2014, p. 75).

When the trust in the orderliness of the situation is shattered, people orient to such crises by "post-hoc" (2014, p. 76) accounts (such as "well, this is her [the matriarch's] first visit here"). Though not always fully accounting for the meaning of the action, they are sufficiently specific to allow the actors to continue to participate in the situation. The reflexive relationship between the meaning of the action and the context of its production becomes important. Ethnomethodology then is concerned with how people make sense of social order as continuously produced and experienced by the actor with methodology as a technique for acquiring data that explicates how some form of the social is created by participants in concrete situations (Lehn, 2014, p. 78). Rather than classic methods, Garfinkel's interest in the everyday is with the production of adequate descriptions of the everyday. The interest in peoples' method to make sense of other's actions in everyday life is different from interpretive approaches of the time. Also, it is not about the symbolic interactionist interest in taking the actor's perspective, but instead it is about a sociological attitude to understand the actor's actions (2014, p. 51).

COLOR TROUBLE AND INSTITUTIONAL ACCOUNTABILITY

Garfinkel's interest in the accounts that people produce in situations to explain their own and other peoples' actions also make us see that people may orient to and experience the social world differently. Based on a prior Rosa Parks personal experience, he used this approach to explore into ethnic segregation in the public transportation in North Carolina when a black young woman enters the bus with a friend and they object to the driver's instruction to sit in the back. The event escalates, and the driver accounts for the late arrival with the classic "color trouble". He refers to the Virginia legislation, whereas the two passengers refer to the American Constitution. They refer to two different normative orders. Color trouble then becomes an external institutional account that undermines the black women's request to be treated as equals. When we refer to the official time-table, we do the same. As participants, we exhibit a social order based on an institutionally legitimized account. He simply demonstrated how the power of institutionally accountability embodied in explanations, "can disrupt and undermine trust relationships between actors in ordinary interactions". By his account, the driver can apply "unjust rules about race without penalty to himself" (Lehn, 2014, p. 32). Garfinkel's analyses of court accounts (1949) showed how the judges and jurors' explanations restored the 1940s' white social order. Could Garfinkel be relevant in Tanzania? Let me look at some experiences from my own work.

FOREIGN "AID"

My university was engaged by the Norwegian embassy in Dar es Salaam, Tanzania to assist in institutional building by converting a former administrative educational institution into a university. To avoid the classic hierarchical structures, we developed a parallel structure on both sides with a parallel structure of research leaders of research clusters organizing joint research projects based on ideas launched on either side. Initially, all the cluster leaders were men. The Gender Group initiative from our female collaborative colleague to start up a gender cluster ended at my desk, the only researcher on our side then concerned with gender issues (well, the only woman in my department). The top leader group contacted me to express their enthusiasm and that they had surplus money to allocate to this idea. I happily attended their meeting just to experience the classic "somebody has been talking" without informing me that they had decided to allocate just a minor part of their budget to research on gender issues. It was this or nothing. They seemed content on both sides and put a junior woman as head of the cluster on the Tanzanian side and with me on our side. There was no budget for Ph.D. students or extensive fieldwork unlike the other clusters, only minor projects for junior researchers (a classic). My co-leader seemed to attend all budget meetings with a pre-fixed budget and without the legitimacy to negotiate. It was rather hopeless, but also informative of how men across continents constructed the status of gender issues and management. Foreign aid has been criticized for exhibiting a "kindness-regime" in the sense that it feeds into a donor's self-perception. It tends to perpetuate the old colonial order. At least, in this case, it perpetuated the gendered order reinforced by the annual ritual celebrations in Tanzania for the senior men, as no one from the gender cluster was ever invited.

This reinstated gender as a low-priority field subjugated under male management, hence the "aid" of "foreign aid". Consequently, the gender group was the only cluster to experience money being illegally removed from our budget in Tanzania, a rather classic incidence in the old southern regime. I called the relevant dean for a meeting, and he had to sit down on one of the two chairs I had arranged facing each other, which was a confrontation beyond the monetary business. It also challenged the gendered order. Nonetheless, the money taken was not for me, but for the Tanzanian junior researchers. I demanded all the money back or I would report it to the embassy. I noticed I was left to do this confrontation on my own, with any support confined to the background. As expected, repercussions were unavoidable. Junior researchers were warned: "She is tough, and, also, she talks like a man". After this, he called me Manka, the name of the second-born daughter in his tribe, the

Chaggas up by Kilimanjaro, known for her strength. Interestingly, he also found an explanation to make sense of the story. The account was anchored in his tribe. As an ethnographer, I was lucky to team up with the larger group of colleagues on campus, where we could exchange stories across our experiences. The accused had seen it as his privilege to put his hand into our budget, a low priority group headed with a hand-picked low ranked local junior member. However, donor money is not quite equivalent to ordinary money, or at least not this time. This reflects the prerogative of the donor over the recipient. On the other hand, I actively drew on this tale to protect the female junior researchers. It gave me a glimpse into how institutions may open or close for activities when done by some and not others. Since I now had proven my fearlessness, juniors now invited me to talk about their vulnerable positions, and how their respect of male seniors held them back from applying for the announced open funding opportunities, in particular targeting juniors. Without junior applications, money would go to the most senior man's project (if a highly ranked man applied, local practice made him the only applicant). The women continuously reported that they benefited from my style because it invited new ways that had been rejected when performed by local female researchers, who would also risk the end of further career opportunities. Again, I had enjoyed my privilege to challenge the local gendered order, though I still had to align with the northern parallel. In my cluster, however, we put such issues on the agenda. This also benefitted institutionally marginalized men not protected by rank in the unofficial back stage activities. A parallel organizational order appeared in which many of us had to navigate, a classic in all organizations though here more accentuated than in my country. This segmentation into layers materialized in numerous ways. Apart from the systematic gendered budgets, there were also encounters constituted in other everyday interactions.

Money Talks

The Toyota trouble. At the end of a data collection with one of my Tanzanian colleagues, the Norwegian male group would pick us up on our joint trip to town. They did so, but told us, that unfortunately, there were only two seats left – one in the back seat with the two others and the other outside in the open air at the back of the car. My Tanzanian male colleague and I were confronted with an impossible choice. No guest can be seated "outside" on display. This was a place for hitch hikers and other free-riders. Also, there was no way a group of white people could drive with a black colleague as the only person outside on the rail. We looked at each other, as both of us had seen this evil act. He insisted I sit inside also because of the apparent discomfort he would feel sitting with the instigators. I agreed out of respect for his politeness, but insisted we change half way. I resented the situation and how openly the funders' white Western privilege – as we both saw it – was played out in the open. We recognized the classic male loyalty test "Whose side are you on?" and the colonial White order "blacks use other entrance".

201

The hotel trouble. In all gender-cluster fieldwork trips, the team always stays together in the same hotel. Good colleagues do such things; joint dinners are excellent for winding up the day's fieldwork and breakfasts for agreeing on the agenda for the new day. And a great option for getting to know each other. However, I came to see that other clusters practiced it differently, such as when I once had assisted one of the other clusters. The team members split up with the Nordic in a higher standard hotel, and with the Tanzanians in a local African hotel, as an opportunity to save money when local wages are low. This meant a lower standard compared with the more Western hotels. Arriving downtown with the Toyota, the privileged group inquired about our hotel for our continued fieldwork. Since this was an African hotel, the group hinted to me in our language of a more private relationship. I hit back and shared with my African colleague, who felt very uncomfortable. They would enjoy better options. However, to stay at local hotels with a medium standard also offers the chance to see what to many other locals would be unavailable privileges, still not attractive to Westerners due to unreliable water support, lack of mosquito nets, and less safe surroundings, though the trick is simply to stay with – and listen to local advice. It made me better notice the nuances of typical local spaces, such as with the standard table of prostitutes that guests could enjoy given they agreed with the pimp's rate. Expensive hotels do it differently. I learned much more since it happened my colleague had done a project with a foreign NGO on prostitution. The next morning, he could also tell me that the manager had contacted him to inquire if it was possible he could get more guests like me here, which would be good for business. I should say that I have no problem enjoying a good hotel standard with a proper shower that works, a spacy desk and a lamp with a working light bulb to write up my notes, employees spraying against mosquitos in the late afternoon, a more varied menu, and better for security reasons after the youth gangs started to appear in cities over the last few decades, but, not if my local colleagues prefer otherwise.

These two stories display how the groups refer to different normative orders. They also show that Garfinkel's interest in accounts is still valid. The analytic is with the actors' use of accounts to provide explanations for whatever they and others do, and how people orient to – and experience the social world differently. Today, there is nothing new in this. The interest is with how their accounts are made to normalize the situation which produce some as norm-abiders as opposed to the troublesome norm-violators. Jokes and harassment strategies associated with bodies are classic sense-making mechanisms. Nagel (2003) reminds us of the ethno-sexual meaning boundaries, as firmly rooted in earlier historical periods, like that of colonialism. She also argues that national borders are specialized forms of moral borders, in which being a citizen or being national is constantly tested and challenged. This makes national symbolic borders into places for producing, surveying, and punishing deviance, which again may revise or produce new definitions of loyalty towards the nation. Being a white European in Tanzania invokes images of the old British colonial rule and works to replace the more restricted "national". The black-white confrontation takes on a moral dimension intricately interwoven with the symbolic values of women's bodies beyond the private. I argue that the two stories illustrate how the participants tacitly draw on the ethnomethodologically available resources that make the color-gender issue relevant. Both are situational and contextual products anchored beyond. The experiences also disrupted and undermined the trust between the involved actors in ordinary interactions. Being "ordinary" is not something we "are", but instead "do". And history has shown that violations produce a noise parallel to Garfinkel's "color trouble". Most of today's states and nations are the results of the modern world system based on a political, economic, and cultural system, where a few states controlled vast territories and which we may make relevant in our everyday lives.

By reference to Garfinkel, this illustrates how institutional accountability is embodied in explanations. It made visible how "color trouble" still worked to restore the white, male social order. It also told me about my gender's vulnerability in the eyes of certain men. If we turn the tables, it also illustrated my colleague's strength to endure both the road trip and the continued fieldwork, since I after all was one of "them". Such life experiences teach us of how historic privileges are powerful mechanisms still in operation, but also that they need to be nuanced and explored. My Tanzanian colleague later supplied drunken Western aid workers' detrimental descriptions of Africans when they were sober.

At times we learn about our privileges in other ways. Once I had asked him if he would be kind enough to possibly book an ordinary hotel for the next fieldwork since he already would be downtown for another project. When I arrived, he had already booked it, so we had no worries when tired at the end of the day. However, he later he told me how much trouble this had caused him in relation to the question: "What kind of hotel would a lady like you prefer?" To find out, he had stopped his car outside different hotels to see if the guests who left and entered resembled persons like me. My concern had been with work efficiency, as I saw it, unaware of the pain I had caused him. I had simply asked him an "ordinary" question since he knew the area better than me. With reference to Harvey Sacks, to be ordinary "takes work, as any other business does" (Silverman, 1998, p. 39).

This is how lived experiences work to uncover the everyday, and to confront undue privileges and pain as well as hierarchies of the privileged social order.

THE PROBLEM OF DESCRIPTIONS

Harvey Sacks was indebted to Garfinkel. He says that "ventures out of being ordinary have unknown virtues and unknown costs" (Silverman, 1998, p. 39); this makes us all work at being ordinary, which makes being ordinary a work. When we observe something, we first look for the ordinary aspects and ordinary explanations to tell us that the non-ordinary was an ordinary normal observation after all. According to Garfinkel, such a routine is embedded in whatever we do (1998, p. 39). This is not about self-consciousness, but about something locally constituted *in situ* as shown in the above observations. Both Garfinkel and Sacks insist that the trouble with conventional social science is the reliance on members' accounts as documenting some underlying reality (1998, p. 38). They both argue that we should treat "findings" as "topics", and since pain and privilege are often discussed in the same vein as culture, it makes sense to mention that Sacks sees "culture" as "an inference-making machine" that social scientists use to identify findings. He says that when statistics or people help to produce "finding", the problem with conventional social science is that they see these "findings" as some underlying external truth. Sacks approaches culture as a descriptive apparatus which is revealed in how descriptions are "administered" and "used" in specific contexts, according to Silverman (1998, p. 50). To agree on accounts or even on inter-coder agreements is not the solution, but rather poses another question about members' ability to see things in common. Our job is not to note down, clarify, or criticize such findings, but to describe them. The job, he says, is not to tacitly use them, but to describe them because they depend on some "pre-scientific, common sense assumptions based on everyday language and employed to sort 'facts' from 'fancy'" (1998, p. 46). The issue is not to study the categories that informants use, but to investigate the categories they use to find the activities in which they are employed. That is, not to understand behavior, but to examine ways people do whatever it is they do and to describe that/these way/s. Let me now draw on some data from the transnational space.

Killing a Monkey

We had a small project in Tanzania on bribes and corruption, a phenomenon not easily approached, and what follows is a small data transcript from our long talk. My colleague and I had invited Ike to what my colleague saw as a safe zone to talk about such issues. It was at an outdoor bar targeting the local market, with some light and some broken chairs after too much activity by the prostitutes as the owner described it; the hook on the door and the bulb in the ceiling of the outdoor privy were no longer there which caused me a great deal of trouble in the dark with the design of my long skirt and handbag when attempting to balance on the two stepping stones, though I managed. The standard was very different from the owner's house which we later visited, reflecting his status as a businessman. After a long talk and enjoying some soda, I started to share a story about a bag that was not there when I picked up my luggage at the conveyor belt at the airport. It was very inconvenient since my job was inland and every time I went back to inquire, the man behind the desk reported it was still missing. The third time I drove back to the airport a young lady told me it had been there all the time. I told the story to Ike without using descriptions denoting what kind of incidence this could be. Ike responded by using this metaphor on killing a monkey. By this he categorized the incidence as recognizable. The metaphor is also sufficiently detailed for me to recognize that I as a foreigner had not noticed the signals he sent me. He communicated he would help me, but I had ignored his invitation. We talk in a relaxed manner, as is usual to recognize the other as a speaker:

Extract 1.

1. I: They, they have a saying in (0.3) in Swahili. They say "when you are
2. killing a monkey a monkey, don't look at it.. a.. a.. at its eyes because it
3. will make you feel ah (0.3) they'll make you sympathize so because I
4. don't know … what they say is … if you are killing a monkey … is it a monkey
5. or whatever, it looks so so sad, so perhaps you might end up not killing
6. A: yeah
7. I: so don't look at the eyes

…

8. A: so that's the way they do it
9. I: that's what they are saying

…

10. A: eh (2.0) I had big problems this time with getting my bag
11. I: mhm mhm
12. A: so I was quite sure they took this trolley to the plane
13. I: that's it

…

14. I: yeah ye (0.2) and then?
15. A: and then
16. I: what did they say? (laughing awaiting my reponse)

…

17. I: ehe
18. A: I mean you hear about it in general, but when you come into it eh you're
19. an amateur so you
20. I: ehe
21. A: don't know how much
22. I: mhmm mhmm yeah even for, you see, even for us, you don't know how much, you don't know how much ehh (0.3) yeah (firm) there is (laughing) one of my own experiences of eh two weeks ago, I think, two weeks back, I went to town …

Let me comment briefly on the relevance to our theme of pain and privilege. First, bribes and corruption are not easily talked about explicitly with strangers despite being widespread. Also, we would not know how it is locally categorized, as employing external categories would not necessarily overlap with local categories. Instead, we could easily reproduce the classic South/West-binary. In her book, Åkerström (2014) explores into how phenomena like small company gifts in Sweden are now closely inspected through a new bribery gaze and the implications to how people orient themselves to familiar phenomena that now introduce unfamiliar risks. She shows how stories work in countries associated with low scores on bribery and corruption. My interest is not with conventional "fact-finding", but with describing and investigating the categories people use and the activities in which they employ them.

The intricacy of bribery is partly captured in how Ike elegantly monitors my "how *they* do it" (line 8) with his casual "that's what *they* are saying" (line 9), just as in his monkey story. He simply employs my own description and refers to other people. In my lines 18–19 I talk about amateurs heard as a description of outsiders and responded to by Ike in line 22 with his "even for us". This illustrates Sacks' insistence that sociologists' primary interest is with the details of interactional and collaborative activities. Second, the ethnomethodologist moral indifference, means that our interest is not with morality, but with how people manage the descriptions they themselves use. Questions about other people's bribery practices convey a hidden message that this is the answerer's problem, not the interviewer's. A question tells you a lot about the person who asks and his or her own assumptions of the other person. To get around this dilemma, I referred to my own experiences. This made Ike share his own experiences, too, as we eventually could speak as equals. My major point here was to discuss how social scientists, despite their care not to inflict pain, may still themselves be the ones to bring it into our studies by the implicit constructions of the answerer as a very different Other. This illustrates the problems with conventional "findings". This does not mean that this kind of extra charges do not exist or is unproblematic to people in their everyday life. They do indeed make life tricky for poor people who may be charged extra for ordinary matters, such as a mandatory signature in the local government to approach the bank for a loan. The ethno-informed interest in analytic details offers to describe the complexity of pain and privilege in ways that otherwise might sadly pass unnoticed. Let me now return to my own campus.

A Practical Joke No More

When Mahid, one of my Asian informants, visited my family I invited him to campus. I called some colleagues and we all went over to the personnel canteen. Mahid looked at me and with reference to our discussions about being brown in a white community (he had previously worked in both Europe and the US), he said, "Let me show you how easily it is done".

We sat down to enjoy the lunch and I briefly introduced everyone to each other. They knew he was an informant, and one of my colleagues started to inquire of him in a friendly way about what he was doing here. "I am looking for a job" he responded, and my colleague continued by asking what kind of job he was looking for. This went on for some time, and eventually my colleague had to return to her office. Mahid looked at me and said with a smile, "You see how easy it is!"

He was easily categorized as a newly arrived ordinary job seeker, and he complimented her "new clothes". She did not see him as the rich businessman he was, with several high-quality businesses targeting both the local as well and the international market. Her available categories, I assume, might have been images of Pakistani working migrants who came to Norway in the 1970s, or one of their oversea relatives now looking for a new job. This could very well have been the case, but the question is: How come she so easily accepted this category or description? What kind of tacit knowledge did she use? Why this, why not another by contesting his explanation? He was very elegantly dressed; his moustache was properly trimmed, and his English was without the accent westerners associate with Pakistani or Indian languages. No bell ringing? How come she did not crack his practical joke that turned into a local drama, which he used to illustrate how easily even supposedly polite Europeans rank non-whites. He was the only non-white person in the personnel canteen. He had already told me a story from the East-African bush with a camp run by a Western NGO that had desperately called for a specialist to help them solve some technical problems. After having driven for hours, he stopped by the gate only to find out they would not let him in. This made him furious. They did not expect the expert to be brown, just as my student from Africa who told me she had agreed to meet one of her African interviewees at campus, but the interviewee had been looking for a white master's student. Sacks says that the trouble with anthropologists is that they rely on their native informants. My colleague did the same. She unproblematically used or adopted the category that my informant offered her, rather than investigating it by looking for the activity in which he employed it. Well, maybe she was simply polite as she saw it, but being unfamiliar with a multicultural society she had few categories available.

After our dinner at a Greek outdoor restaurant in Tanzania with my British and Tanzanian colleagues, I went over to a table by the entrance to compliment the food. When we left, my British colleague asked why did I talk to people like them? I told him they were the owners, though this was my first visit here. He had no knowledge about how to recognize how to be restaurant owners in this part of the world, and simply employed his familiar British descriptions. These instances work to inquire into how categorizations are being produced in our everyday activities. I noticed that my European colleagues, both in Norway and in Tanzania, imported the classic rank or hierarchy rather than to challenge it. My student's interviewee, an immigrant from Africa, did the same at campus when looking for my master's student. These stories describe how people in their everyday talk use and reproduce dominant images.

CONCLUSIONS

Rank is omnipresent, but I argue that the ethno-informed approach invites us to describe how dominant images, pain and privileges, are accomplished and perpetuated, and descriptions employed in recognizable as well as in everyday less recognizable ways in situ. There are historical and political differences between regions when it comes to matters of race, civil rights, and welfare, but ethnomethodology is concerned with how members accomplish the ordinary, how we relate to non-ordinary observations or how members come to agree on things and accounts in different contexts. We explore how the involved do all these activities. At a more practical level, let me add that when the embassy funding ended, I managed to get a quite different and lucrative funding for a four-year programme period – later negotiated with an extra year, and with two female professors as top managers. We skipped the old rituals and focused on research.

In a few decades my city has gone through a transformation from a rather ethnic homogeneous place to a multicultural and-ethnic population from across 120 different countries. Still, the stories show that dominant images are easily made relevant, willingly or not. Going back to Garfinkel and his fundamental question "How is social order possible?", his focus was on the relationship between an established social order and the ways people use to account for that social order. When we make sense of an unfamiliar experience or trouble by reference to a normative social order, we participate in normalizing that social order and in making it legitimate. This implies the accounts we use to explain our own actions and those of others – including the other Toyota passengers. We are reminded of Garfinkel's comment based on his observations of court hearings, that "the processes of trial consist of activities oriented to reinstatement of desecrated communally sanctioned values" (1949, p. 376 as cited in Lehn, 2014, p. 34). By this he points to the power of our everyday activities. To some, they appear as seemingly ordinary troubles, but a closer inspection tells us they are anchored in problematic institutional accountabilities and with a potential to violate trust between actors in ordinary interaction.

My own life experiences, combined with my analytic interest have invited me to explore ordinary experiences also in my own life and their innate power to confront or accept. The contemporary interest in identity made me focus on the classic color trouble, mainly because of my research experiences across the historically loaded European-African axis that show the intricacy of color, culture, gender, pain and pleasure. Rank is indeed powerful and works in mysterious ways – until uncovered. It is our job as social scientists to describe how descriptions work. My concern has been with the *social* organization of it by looking for observable activities around us in our everyday life, in addition to my life as sociologist, to reveal the background expectancies that underpin the social order of the everyday. This makes sense-making serious business. History has proven the power of such ordinary matters as bus-, car- and restaurant seating, so to analyze the everyday of life helps us uncover the intricacy in which we are involved myself included. It has also made me see how.

REFERENCES

Åkerström, M. (2014). *Suspicious Gifts. Bribery, morality and professional ethics.* New Brunswick, NJ: Transaction Publishers.
Atkinson, P., & Ryen, A. (2016). Indigenous research and romantic nationalism. *Societies, 6*(4), 34. doi:10.3390/soc6040034
Battiste, M. (2008). Research ethics for protecting indigenous knowledge and heritage: Institutional and researcher responsibilities. In N. K. Denzin, Y. S. Lincoln, & L. T. Smith (Eds.), *Handbook of critical and indigenous methodologies* (pp. 497–509). Los Angeles, CA: Sage Publications.
Bauman, Z. (1997). *Life in fragments.* Oxford: Blackwell.
Bauman, Z. (2005). Afterthought. On writing; On writing sociology. In N. K. Denzin & Y. S. Lincoln (Eds.), *Handbook of qualitative research* (pp. 1089–1098). Thousand Oaks, CA: Sage Publications.

Bile, A., Srour, S. N., & Herz, N. (2017). *Skamløs* [Shameless]. Oslo: Gyldendal forlag. Retrieved February 3, 2018, from http://www.gyldendal.no/Barneboeker/Boeker-for-ungdom/Skamloes

Brochman, G., & Kjeldstadli, K. (2008). *A history of immigration. The case of Norway 900-2000*. Oslo: Universitetsforlaget.

Dale, A. (2017). *Arbeidsnever*. Oslo: Kolon Forlag.

Emeagwali, G., & Dei, G. J. S. (Eds.). (2014). *Anti-colonial educational perspectives for transformative Change. African indigenous knowledge and the disciplines*. Rotterdam, The Netherlands: Sense Publishers.

Fanon, F. (1952). *Peau noire, masque blanc*. Paris: Les Éditions du Seuil.

Fukuyama, F. (2018). *Identity: The demand for dignity and the politics of resentment*. New York, NY: Farrar, Straus, and Giroux.

Garfinkel, H. (1967). Studies of the routine grounds of everyday activities. In H. Garfinkel (Ed.), *Studies in ethnomethodology* (pp. 35–75). Cambridge: Polity Press.

Giddens, A. (1991). *Modernity and self-identity. Self and society in the late modern age*. Cambridge: Polity Press.

Goffman, E. (1972). *Encounters. Two studies in the sociology of interaction*. London: Penguin.

Haq, I. (2017). *Hva vil folk si* [What will people say]. Retrieved February 3, 2018, from https://no.wikipedia.org/wiki/Hva_vil_folk_si

Holstein, J. A., & Gubrium, J. F. (2011). Animating interview narratives. In D. Silverman (Ed.), *Qualitative research* (pp. 149–167). London: Sage Publications.

Lehn, D. (2014). *The creation and development of ethnomethodology*. Walnut Creek, CA: Left Coast Press.

Maurras, C. (1905). *L'Avenir de L'intelligence*. Paris: A. Fontemoing.

Mauss, M. (2008). *The gift. The form and reason for exchange in archaic societies*. London & New York, NY: Routledge.

Nagel, J. (2003). *Race, ethnicity, and sexuality. Intimate intersections, forbidden frontiers*. New York, NY: Oxford University Press.

Omar, S. (2017). *Dødevaskeren* [The death washer]. København: Politikens forlag. Retrieved February 3, 2018, from https://www.imusic.dk/bound/9788740026979/sara-omar-2017-doedevaskeren-indbundet-bog

Ryen, A. (2008a). Trust in cross-cultural research. The puzzle of epistemology, research, ethics and context. *Qualitative Social Work, 7*(4), 448–465.

Ryen, A. (2008b). Wading the field with my key informant: Exploring field relations. *Qualitative Sociology Review, 4*(3), 84–104. Retrieved July 23, 2016, from http://www.qualitativesociologyreview.org/ENG/Volume11/abstracts.php#art5

Ryen, A. (2012). Assessing the risk of being interviewed. In J. Gubrium & J. Holstein (Eds.), *Handbook of interview research: Context & method* (pp. 477–493). Thousand Oaks, CA: Sage Publications.

Ryen, A., & Gobo, G. (2011). Managing the decline of globalised methodology. *International Journal of Social Research Methodology: Theory and Practice, 16*(6), 411–415.

Ryen, A., & Silverman, D. (2000). Marking boundaries: Culture as category work. *Qualitative Inquiry, 6*(1), 107–127.

Said, E. (1978/2003). *Orientalism*. London: Penguin Books.

Sardar, Z. (2006). *How do you know?* London: Pluto Press.

Schütz, A. (1944). The stranger. An essay on social psychology. *The American Journal of Sociology, 49*(6), 499–507.

Silverman, D. (1998). *Harvey Sacks. Social science and conversational analysis*. Cambridge: Polity Press.

Simmel, G. (1950). The stranger. In K. H. Wolff (Ed.), *The sociology of George Simmel* (pp. 402–408). New York, NY: The Free Press.

Temba, E., Ryen, A., & Matotay, E. (2011). Social security provision and social welfare in Tanzania: Reflections and possibilities for social security to the informal sector. *Tanzanian Journal of Development Studies, 9*(1–2), 34–44.

PART 5

ON BEING MIXED AND MOVING FORWARD

HANNAH R. STOHRY

14. RAISING CONSCIOUSNESS FOR MULTI-RACIAL THIRD CULTURE KIDS

> I am cultured because I am participating in the creation of yet another culture,
> a new story to explain the world and our participation in it, a new value system
> with images and symbols that connect us to each other and to the planet.
> (Anzaldúa, 1999, p. 103)

I was twelve years old, scrawny, shy, and awkward when my family moved to the United States for a new military assignment in 2000 after having spent the last six years living in the Republic of Korea (or South Korea) (three different assignments/ locations) and three years in Italy before that, moving almost every two years since birth. I was thrown into a new physical and metaphysical environment yet again, in what was considered my home country where I would quickly find out was not my home and that I was not truly an not truly an American, as perceived by homegrown Americans. I quickly learned that my being American (in this particular local community) meant that I grew up with the television show *Full House*, had the same friends from kindergarten, ate mayonnaise on my sandwich, drank soda, wore Mudd brand clothes, watched American football not soccer, Adidas was no longer popular in my new community, and that American and Confederate flags adorned many front porches of homes off-base. My American-ness was different from everyone else's American-ness. People no longer looked like me and I did not fit in.

The air in the States breathed differently and my breathing began to change, out of survival, to reflect the rhythm and local atmosphere. I remember the realization that I had that Korea was so far away now and that I was now disconnected from all of my friends and Korean family (this was the age of expensive international phone calling cards and before accessible internet). The physical location of the state was much flatter than the beautiful mountains and hills of Korea, and we now had hurricanes instead of monsoons and typhoons; the landscape was spread out, meaning that buildings were built farther apart and had fewer high-rise buildings, giving the feeling of emptiness. Public transportation was much less accessible. I was introduced to the barrage and myriad of fast food restaurants and strip malls of which I had little knowledge/experience base. I did not know what was on the menu or what tasted good or which stores were hip and I desperately wanted to learn how to fit in and be like everybody else. I had little experience eating out and having to choose American food when on school trips instead of packing a lunch, or what to look for and what shop had what kind of clothing. We still shopped at the Base/Post

© KONINKLIJKE BRILL NV, LEIDEN, 2019 | DOI:10.1163/9789004393813_014

Exchange for our food and clothes instead of the places like Food Lion or outlet malls where everybody else shopped off-base. We attended a local Christian school that was based out of a local church. Some of the students were military families, but no one else lived on base, at least not in my cohort. Everybody's reality was different from mine. I had little connection with my cohort who had never lived overseas or had much exposure to active duty military life. Having to choose school supplies that were solid colors and lifeless and sharing that Korea had cuter stationery stuff (this is relative) did not compute with my new friends and I found myself clinging and hoarding my beautiful things so that I would not run out of supplies.

As a military family, it was common that we moved from base to base, but this move was unlike any other. We moved at what I considered a critical time in my developmental life (conclusion built after reflecting for more than half of my life) to another American base where the physical structures were also very different. This base was bigger with much more military power; we lived in a house where we had a yard (with grass that needed maintenance) for the first time versus apartment-style family housing. A side note is that wherever we lived, my Dad always refused to live in higher-ranking Officer housing, but to live in housing that was similar to other officers who were not in command positions, that was still fit to house families (versus single military members who would live in barracks). My Dad now had a higher position with more people under his command and higher levels of visibility with more people. The sounds of the base were very different from our previous base where we lived; the planes that flew overhead flew more frequently and had a different feel of training than it did in Korea.

Despite having attended international Christian schools through 7th grade and moving to the States for 8th grade and enrolling in another Christian school, I knew immediately that things life would never be the same. I entered a new physical structure with the school being much larger than the schools in Korea that I was used to, with a larger gym and bleachers. This was the first time I had to subscribe to wearing a school uniform. I was no longer surrounded by people who looked like me. I was now in the minority being from a military family, and this family just so happened to be a biracial family (Asian and White), even less common. Many international schools are filled with families who do not usually fit the structure of the host country (White family, four people total).

I immediately began grieving (I did not know this at the time, and perhaps I drift through those stages of grief to this day; once again, this is what I choose to call that phenomenon at this moment) my community because I was no longer in the majority, surrounded by others just like myself (other multi-racial families). I no longer had connections with peers who knew what it was like to grow up in a normative Third Space. I did not know the popular culture lingo or what was culturally relevant. We no longer had as much access to ingredients to make yummy Korean food. I had no idea who I was as a person. I did not even have the language to communicate who I was or where I was from and when I did, it was contested or disbelieved. I had no idea how to describe Korea because it was just a part of me, not something that could be extracted or essentialized into language that my peers could understand. My confusion became a norm, a direct result of people asking me unfamiliar questions and projecting onto me who I was (not) and who I should (not) be and I learned how to feed them the answers that they wanted to hear.

At the lunch table, I understood that I was different when my lunch smelled bad (normative experience, when the basic staples are different) or I brought yellow-colored water (barley water or green tea) and I was embarrassed by my peers' gaze. The fact that we ate fusion food, pairings that do not normally go together in the same lunch box was different and I was embarrassed. I wanted to afford to buy lunch, to have sodas and Bagel Bites and bring kimchi to school because it smelled. Not once did anyone sit me down and talk to me about myself, my intersecting identities, or what it meant to transition to school or to America, outside of what it physically meant to move and what it meant for our physical belongings. Not once did we talk about race, ethnicity, or cultural identities. We had one student from a U.S. territory in my cohort who held an ethnic identity who also had a lot of cultural misunderstandings surrounding his experiences. We had a few other students of color, but race was not addressed at all in school. Not once did we talk about the colonizing effect of the West, family differences and how our People of Color are different/similar. Not once did we celebrate cultural differences at school; I am not even sure we celebrated Black History Month. I had so many struggles that would be later realized when we moved again to the Midwest (where my identity became more limited) when I was 15 years old and as I reflect now, it would have been helpful for educators, the schools, and my family to have recognized identities and taught us how to explore, challenge, and express self. All I remember is that I did not want to be me and the me that I had to be had so many intersecting identities that now conflicted, which haunt and inspire me today.

INTRODUCTION

In this chapter, I validate my existence. From a social research standpoint, I am invalidated by the lack of academic research conducted that represents my experiences of being biracial as well as having grown up as a third culture kid (TCK), growing up in countries/cultures that were not my family's dominant culture. The term "binational third culture" was coined by John and Ruth Useem (1967), when doing research with American families living in India whose lived experiences are defined as "patterns generic to a community of men who stem from two different societies and who regularly interact as they relate their respective societies, or segments therefrom, within the physical setting of one of the societies" (p. 131). It has transformed to a fuller definition for third culture kids made known by Pollock, Van Reken, and Pollock (2017), later described in this chapter. From an interpersonal standpoint, those around me assign me identities that make sense for them that do not represent me or my realities; I belong everywhere yet nowhere. This chapter is my first professional attempt to share how I navigate my identities, race, ethnicity, and cultures. I describe various theories that can be applied to our multi-racial TCK experiences and reflect on the vignette I introduced at the beginning and how educators could have improved my empowered identity formation/expression and experiences in educational spaces. Then, I will introduce Gloria Anzaldúa's mestiza consciousness and raise consciousness for self and for others like myself. I will conclude with a challenge/resources for middle-level educators to raise consciousness for self, for students and their development of their identities, and especially for multi-racial TCKs.

As of early 2018, when I searched for published research journal articles on EBSCOhost (selecting all databases), 731 articles popped up with just the key word "third culture kid". It narrowed down to 352 Scholarly and peer reviewed journal articles. When typing in the keywords "third culture kid" and "biracial", nothing popped up. The same happened when I searched for "third culture kid" and "multi-racial". There are several books available that solely focus on our population but do not seem to be visible in mainstream literary circles and never have I once ever heard about our experiences in mainstream media. The number of TCKs is growing so much so that the online community and number of social media groups (e.g. Facebook groups and YouTube channel) have exploded with such a need to express self and feel community. Such a display of the lack of research on a large population is alarming, so it is difficult to quantify and narrow down areas for recognition (for those of us who live in the world of social sciences).

This chapter serves several purposes: to raise consciousness of educators; inspire and empower educators to work with and for multi-racial TCKs like myself; and to cultivate our own consciousness to challenge the dominant narratives of power and oppression. Throughout, I use "we" when describing our multi-racial TCK experiences in an attempt to align myself and to avoid Othering since we are Othered in majority spaces. My experiences will not reflect every multi-racial TCK experience, but I wish to speak as one of many voices and raise consciousness to start dialogue and empower ourselves to craft our own counter-narratives to the dominant cultures, at least for those of us that need the empowerment. I call for us (as educators of all positionalities) to challenge the next generations to craft their own identities and counter-narratives. I also use the term multi-racial to encompass those of us with more than one racial identity, so as not to limit our experiences to my own biracial identity, again to resist the binary mentality. We do not live in a post-racial society where race does not exist (as much as people claim and believe), so although I know that race is constructed, I will frame our experiences through racial lenses since we happen to be raced. Our very existence as multi-racial TCKs produces experiences where we live on the edge of what it means to be multi-racial and TCKs at the same time. Racial, ethnic, and cultural differences continue to remain at the forefront of conflict on a worldwide scale and continue to persist in our United States of America.

This paper is a call and response from the depths of the adolescent me to the me today, to the other multi-racial TCKs and to all educators/students and has served as a consciousness-raising experiment for myself through the very attempt to tell parts of my story, reconcile my (un)pleasant experiences and strengthen my resolve for moving forward. I argue against dichotomy and binaries and for humanity, although I acknowledge that there are problematic limits since race, ethnicity, and the TCK experience are socially constructed. I fully acknowledge the limitations in attempts to group people with similar experiences because it can lose importance, the importance of the individual story. Again, my experiences do not reflect others' experiences, but this is an attempt to rally those of us who have been Othered and live in an Other reality, in Third (or in-between/among) Spaces.

I will not able to explore Westernization, racialization, sexualization, exoticization, and gendering of multi-racial TCKs and the impact on our lives, but these issues are certainly our realities. Multi-racial TCK journeys are complex, but our identities are reduced (and some dictated) to binary constructs. There is an internal identity shift (and embodiment) that happens when a multi-racial TCK first understands that they are different, that we are the "Other". For those of us who live in those experiences, that first realization can be enlightening and traumatizing. Even as an adult, I can reflect and pinpoint those moments and realize how impactful they were and how they influence me today. This manuscript will critically explore pain and privilege that multi-racial TCKs face on a daily basis (and cannot escape) and the possibilities of a world where our realities are recognized and celebrated on our own terms.

The inspiration for this book chapter has come from a very deep place starting from my own recent consciousness-raising experiences. My journey is impacted by many experiences that I have had and will continue to have. My middle childhood education (inside and outside the classroom, especially the hidden curriculum) was influential in my identity formation and what I am currently exploring and researching for self and for others. The act of writing this chapter is raising my own consciousness and serves as a healing tool and another stepping stone to helping multi-racial TCKs like myself move forward.

EDUCATIONAL EXPERIENCES

In the context of school, I grew up going to international Christian schools until I moved to the States at twelve years old and then attended Christian schools that were affiliated with churches. In the military community, there were many kids who went to base schools or Department of Defense schools or they were home-schooled. Upon reflection in all of those spaces, I am not so sure that I have a recollection of intentionality on the part of our communities or teachers celebrating multi-racial experiences in the classroom. I even sometimes felt out of place at our international schools because my multi-racial counterparts spoke multiple languages at home, whereas we just responded in English with our mother who would speak to us in Korean and we were encouraged/mandated to speak English at school. We adopted my Korean cousin at four years old who we then mandated to speak English at school and home and to this day, she cannot remember her first language. I remember feeling like it was my duty to enforce that because I perhaps had an (un)conscious fear of standing out or that she would experience adverse effects as a result of not being able to speak English or conform. She did stand out; she was held back a year in school when we moved to the States. My sister was made to repeat 2nd grade because her English standards were not up to performance levels at our American school, which is another issue when it comes to transitory students and school transfers. We happened to be privileged to move at the end of the school years so we did not have to struggle with transferring in the middle of the school years like many other families. All of these educational issues are problematic (to me) because I have been living with a deficit lens for so long that I feel the need to go back and correct past wrongs and produce a counter-narrative to prevent such things from happening again and to cultivate freedom of choice to pursue and recognize the beauty of complexity. If I could go back and change things, I would have celebrated hiring teachers who would embrace speaking more than one language. I would have learned to speak Korean in school (if they would have offered it) or at least practiced it with my mother. I would have encouraged my sister to speak Korean at home while learning English. Looking back now, I would have encouraged after-school tutoring or cultural clubs for students to plug into in order to feel connected and express selves that cannot usually be expressed in school. I feel this because I feel like I have contributed to that story that we cannot celebrate what it means to hold more than one identity.

There was this other intersection of military and missionary culture in the middle of all of these things. We had this expectation that we were to uphold protection of our culture and ideals and contribute to safety alongside these countries that we were living in. We were to perform at the highest level since my Dad was usually in a position of power and leadership. Our family was to always be prepared for any situation and the same goes for our performance in church where my Dad was also always in a position of leadership. We were to uphold those standards in our family.

When my family moved to the States, I no longer had connections with peers who knew what it was like to grow up in a normative Third Space with those intersections or layers of cultures. For other military children (who had never lived overseas) in the States, they could not relate to overseas base life and had different understandings of what base drills were, safety levels, or even what life was like off-base in another country.

While my adolescent experiences were far from my first experiences from knowing I was different from everyone else, it was certainly during this time where I felt the difference the most. It was during this time where I began to process my feelings, form defense mechanisms, and proceed to feel confused, even to this day. I spend a lot of time unpacking and in doing so, it has been healing and empowering.

In many ways, I am struggling as an adult unpacking all of the things I experienced as a child, adolescent, and young adult. I had been reproduced and conditioned to believe that everyone was an expert on my life and never that I was the expert. In some ways, I proved to myself that I was not an expert on myself because I was not intentionally taught self-awareness, or self-care in school. What I remember feeling was shame and confusion because my peers and teachers told me I was shy, nervous, insecure, and that I had low self-esteem, which I think was their perception of me when I could not articulate who I was and then I just naturally embodied their perceptions trying to navigate their judgmental gaze. Reflecting now, perhaps that was true that I was insecure, but this was a manifestation of confusion by the questions by others and turned into a cycle and reality of confusion, but they were certainly also reactive behaviors to how I was being treated as an Other (which we will get into). Educators' responses to "fix me" was to become closer to God, to cure my maladies and unhappiness. As a person who still practices faith, I believe in a Higher Power, but I also believe in human connections, communication, and choices that are influenced by that communion with God, and it did not seem that those who Othered had it or had a distorted perception of what communion with God and community really was and how to practically apply it.

IDENTITY

To this day, I still struggle with what it means to hold my many identities in varying spaces. I am pretty secure in my racial/ethnic identities, but I am navigating how to express them, and struggle the most when I am Othered. There are things about the military community that are hidden deep within me, a deep appreciation for duty, protection, and making the system work (and so much more rich culture) but that I do not usually express because everyone has an opinion about the military, rightfully so. I struggle in White spaces in a predominantly White institution (PWI) by passing as a White person who uses her identity to connect and build community. In my American community, I have to pledge my allegiance to America when I express my Korean self. In Korean spaces, although I speak conversational-level Korean (or enough to impress Koreans), I still am not seen as biracial. So, I walk this narrow balance where I have to strengthen one racial/ethnic/cultural identity to build community and validate myself as "one of you". I am obligated to speak Korean, tell Korean people that I studied the language in college and finally tell Korean people that I am half-Korean to have them believe that I am Korean. I am certainly much more aware of how I carry myself, what I say and how I act and to whom, and what kind of results appear. I walk this really strange line of amplifying one identity to validate myself, to be seen, and to advocate for self. So, I would call this code-switching, where I move in among metaphorical languages, something linguists have researched and other disciplines have extended to cultural and interpersonal relationships (Baker, 2000; Krashen, 1985; Brooks & Karathanos, 2009; and Thomas & Collier, 1997). The ideas of code-switching have many hypotheses, but I like the ideas that when someone has a certain level of mastery of one language, they can seamlessly switch to the next language, with(out) ease, which is what many of us who have lived abroad (and hold many racial and intersecting identities) do in our everyday lives. This code-switching also serves a function to build capital in control of our resources as well as the struggle to hold onto our resources merely by manipulating our language and communication (Heller, 1992). It is what most People of Color do in dominant White spaces. This code-switching is a third and unspoken language that we have and of which we may not be aware. I certainly enjoy privileges of my many identities, but it is this fine line of only presenting and expressing parts of myself at a time and denying others because it is necessary for others to feel comfortable. Where this fits in educational spaces is where teachers have a unique opportunity to challenge students to think outside the box in their interactions.

It was not until I was an adolescent that I realized that I was really confused by White Americans asking me "What are you?" At the time, I had understood that they were trying to figure out my race and ethnicity due to my ambiguous physical appearance (broad nose and hazel almond-shaped eyes). It was not until it was late in my college years that I heard for the first time that I could speak back to that question by stating that I was a human being and not a "what". I had never conceptualized that it was a de-humanizing experience, so I experienced anger that I had been so conditioned to not assume and that I was, in fact, dehumanized. I went on to work as a professional for two years as a home-based therapist (I am a social worker) and then, now as I am pursuing graduate school again and throughout the draft-writing process of this chapter, I now realize the deep impact of that question, that the way that it is posed (perhaps un/intentionally) assumes that I am not human or sub-human. Mic drop. This is why I am writing this, so that we can teach ourselves and the younger me that we are all human beings regardless of phenotype or cultural origin or any other non-normative identity presentation.

These questions of "What are you?" or "Which one do you identify with more?" are quite common and are posed by individuals of all ages. The second question was weird, and I had no idea how to respond when I was first posed this question when we moved to the States as an adolescent. It is a perfect example of this binary logic model we live in, that we cannot check more than one box at a time. I just quickly learned to code-switch and came up with a different answer each time depending on which parent I felt most kinship with at the moment or how deeply I felt homesick. TCKs are always in a state of transition and gauging how to respond to the question of "Where are you from?" depending on the level of interest and purpose of the person asking the question. When I was a late adolescent, I learned to make a game out of people guessing my identity (once they projected onto me that they did not know what I was, in their words) and seeing how creative and educated those othering others were while interacting with me. In some un/conscious ways, I understood that choosing one (race) was disingenuous to who I was/am and began to alter my responses to reflect in which ways I ascribed and presented my ethnic heritage (English spoken language, but could understand Korean; eating fusion food and preferring Korean food to American food ... now, this was an affront and at the time, I was produced to believe that everyone else was right and I must somehow be wrong about preferring something other than the dominant normal). I just learned to shove all of my differences aside and conform and stay out of sight because I certainly could not be the expert on my life if I was pointed out for being different and I refused to be wrong all of the time. I had to perform. None of it was intentional at the time (no self-awareness, remember?), but I purely acted to survive on a daily basis.

I hope to have set a foundation by naming my privileges and unique experiences, in order to introduce a framework or theory that has become very important to me in order to move forward from my developmental years. I have finally found language that can be applied to my experiences, in a way that makes sense and is empowering to me. I wish to apply it and transform this mestiza consciousness that I found. First, let me describe how third culture kid experiences are cousins with mestiza experiences and then we can talk about mestiza consciousness.

THIRD CULTURE KIDS

TCKs are people who grow up (during developmental years) outside of their passport country (Pollock, Van Reken, & Pollock, 2017) and live in a Third Space/ Culture (not to be confused with Third World), described as one not fully owning the parent's nor the host's cultures, a shared cultural experience of belonging everywhere yet nowhere. This culture is considered the culture within cultures and I would argue it is a space that is dictated by those of the host or parent culture or others. This definition implies that TCKs come with a first culture (parent's), are introduced to a host culture, and then live in a new culture on the borders of both cultures, at war with attempts to master and navigate both and hold both (or many) identities at the same time. These TCKs are most known for high mobility and cross-cultural living (Lambie & Limberg, 2011). To put it in context, the most notable public figure who holds the multi-racial TCK identity would be former U.S. President Barack Obama who holds two distinct racial/ethnic identities and grew up in Indonesia (Obama, 2004).

This Third Culture is a space that TCKs fall into and can even morph into unsafe spaces, a place where we TCKs feel as though we do not belong. Despite the definition's deficit lens (not fully owning parent's nor the host's culture) with which this lends TCKs and assumptions that we cannot have something that someone else has or that we are not whole, we will use this constructed definition/identity to focus solely on the experience that TCKs have when we are not seen as whole humans, capable of having our own culture. Multi-racial TCKs, like myself, face challenges when others dictate my identity and determine my life's trajectory. I constantly live on the borders of who I am, who I am told to be, and who I desperately want to be. I live with these beautiful intersections that have become unsafe. We will talk about the borders in this paper, or at least attempt to name the limitations that are set on me by others with whole cultures. Queer theory, feminist theory, and Third Space literatures have embraced those persons that do not fit the heteronormative experiences and describe queering spaces or blurring the lines of those living on borders (Licona,

2005). Those theorists and practitioners challenge the dominant narratives and rally in community to advocate for the communities. I cannot do justice to Licona's use of the mestiza third space that accepts and celebrates complexity; these bodies of research accepting the ambiguous and create new norms. Exploring how identities can be queered and the lines of what we know as racial/ethnic identities can also be blurred is worth an investigation but stand outside the scope of this chapter.

MESTIZA CONSCIOUSNESS

My understanding of mestiza frames the experience of a multi-racial woman of the Mexico-U.S. borderlands, a term most widely defined by Gloria Anzaldúa and other Chicana feminists. I am not a mestiza since I am Asian/White and did not grow up on those geographical borderlands, but I will draw from the experiences and embodiment of the difficulties faced with living on the borders in Third Spaces, not fully feeling or being a whole of the cultures on all sides of those borders.

Just as the mestiza has tolerance for ambiguity, so does the multi-racial TCK (Anzaldúa, 1999, p. 101); we tolerate so much everyday moving through different spaces and adjusting ourselves (the strength and resilience of adaptability). This is our norm. We the people are ambiguous, and we tolerate our own existence and must live and tolerate how others tolerate us and demand that we conform to their tolerances of us as multi-racial TCKs. However, in our relationship with others, "the ambivalence from the clash of voices results in mental and emotional states of perplexity. Internal strife results in insecurity and indecisiveness" (Anzaldúa, 1999, p. 100). Anzaldúa (1999) describes this internal strife of the mestiza:

In a constant state of mental nepantilism, an Aztec word meaning torn between ways, *la mestiza* is a product of the transfer of the cultural and spiritual values of one group to another ... and in a state of perpetual transition, the *mestiza* faces the dilemma of the mixed breed: which collectivity does the daughter of a darkskinned mother listen to?...cradled in one culture, sandwiched between two cultures, straddling all three cultures and their value systems, *la mestiza* undergoes a struggle of flesh, a struggle of borders, an inner war. (p. 100)

Much like the mestiza, we can become a hodge-podge product that is produced from this battle. We multi-racial TCKs also undergo that struggle of flesh, literally a struggle on the inside and out, a beautiful concoction of complicated ambiguity. Many of us constantly struggle on the boundaries of what is and what should be (as thrust upon us by those around us) because the majority continues to perpetuate their own norms. We struggle with which voice to listen to and wrestle with the value conflicts that arise when those voices demand something from us that goes against our core values and identities. This is our reality, and the reality of so many that live with so many identities.

So, how can we take my narratives and introduction to theories on race and identity and apply it to the classroom as educators, especially for those in middle-level education? Gloria Anzaldúa (2007) says "her first step is to take inventory" (p. 104), which I take to mean to get down and dirty in the messiness and catalogue the burdens and "baggage" (p. 104), knowing the who, what, when, where, why, and how of the structures that oppress us. The reason she gives is that "this step is a conscious rupture with all oppressive traditions of all cultures and religions" (p. 104). This is a pretty radical step because it starts with our recognition that there is a problem in society, that the rest of society problematizes our existence. This is radical in the way that we start recognizing and opening our eyes to those structures that do not serve us. Anzaldúa (1999) acknowledges the oppressive structures and asks us to acknowledge yet work together and co-exist as humans, across difference. This co-existence is possible by acknowledging our existence, making our needs known and meeting the needs of those that Other us. For multi-racial TCKs to adopt this raising consciousness framework that Anzaldúa (2007) introduces for the mestiza, we can also raise this consciousness for self and others by recognizing and acknowledging "the struggle has always been inner, and it played out in the outer terrains. Awareness of our situation must come before inner changes, which in turn come before changes in society. Nothing happens in the "real" world unless it first happens in the images in our heads" (p. 109). But, what does consciousness raising really look like? Will we ever be truly aware of our situation? What does inner change actually mean? Can societal change that which influences inner change? I think that can depend on the person and what it means to them. What kind of a world can we imagine for ourselves? What kind of world can we imagine where we can express our intersectional identities in ways that are not questioned? What is consciousness? Does it stay? Does it go? Can we come to a place where we can re-imagine what life would be like where we can all be humanized and not dismissed or Othered or be forced to reduce ourselves? Can we come to a place where we humanize and do not dismiss or Other or for someone to reduce themselves?

So, how can this look in the classroom? Keating (2007) takes the educator's stance that we should invite our students to participate in the classroom rather than ordering/demanding participation. I happen to like this because activities and learning can be invitational and intentional and allows the student to lead their education rather than being told what they are told they should learn, or at least to ask questions while learning. This allows self-determination of the individual and gives choices to the student, giving room to question knowledge. However, I will allow a disclaimer that it would have been difficult for me at the time to speak up for self because I had little awareness or self-concept because *ALL* of my cultures held this ideology that I was to accept the authority and that to question would be anti-cultural. This is another educational standpoint that I wish I had been taught, that I could have a little more control over what I could learn and where I could direct the learning. This leads into a bigger question of: How can we quantify learning in classrooms that are dictated by standards measurements and make it difficult to accommodate learning?

From my perspective, having more of an equal status of learning/teaching (teacher-learner stance) in the classroom or in my cultural circles would have been and would still be considered stepping outside one's roles and would require vulnerability on the part of those in authority and would be so radical and disrespectful. However, students as having the ability to decide for self teaches humanity and curiosity rather than forcing students to become robots who compute knowledge and plug them into boxes and thus create output that serves little to no purpose except conformity. Keating (2007) subscribes to the "ethics of openness, reciprocity, and exchange" because of how she perceives humanity and our "interrelatedness" (p. 34). Transformation begins with self, with consciousness-raising and Keating (2007) introduces four lessons to learn and premises that we must adopt in order to teach transformation:

Categories and labels, although sometimes necessary, can prevent us from recognizing our interconnectedness with others" (p. 2); "out of all the categories we today employ, 'race' is perhaps the most destructive" (p. 4); "the oppositional politics so effective in the past are no longer as useful in the twenty-first century; we must develop relational, nonbinary forms of opposition, resistance, and transformation" (p. 6); and "radical, liberatory change – on both individual and collective levels – is urgently needed and in fact possible, although not necessarily easy to achieve. (p. 9)

Teaching without connection with students seems antithetical; for students like myself who did not feel like we belonged would have loved to have felt like we connected with teachers, especially in important areas of racial and cultural identities. So, what would it mean to teach students when we teach them concepts that fit in categories that must be measured by standards? How can we teach students about labels that essentialize and reduce rather than build up and connect us? In American news every day, we have more and more race-related violence and intolerance, so how can we teach our students about difference and connection, especially when it relates to ourselves and our peers in the classroom, that also transcends to our homes and communities and society? How do we teach students resistance that does not fit in boxes that creates change without violence? How do we encourage change among our students that reaches beyond the self and classroom? Does it need to transcend the classroom to provide meaning for self for a student? These are all questions to ask self in order to teach transformation in self and the classroom. However, they are only a starting point from which to begin and for reference to further questions, refer to Part 2's Transformative Consciousness Raising Questions where you can find more comprehensive questions to spark change.

Multi-racial TCKs have also developed a "tolerance for ambiguity", where one "constantly has to shift out of habitual formations ... and toward a more whole perspective, one that includes rather than excludes" (Anzaldúa, 1999, p. 101). We TCKs have learned what is normative and have conditioned ourselves to answer when people ask us to choose our loyalties among cultures. This conditions us. We choose what we want people to hear, and how they feel we should identify, especially in the presence of peers, whom we spend most of our lives with (since school is our life at those ages). We choose according to the dominant culture; we also code-switch among our families. Many of us have figured out how to have that whole perspective by naturally and resiliently speaking out about the complexities of our beings, much like I did in the example where I transitioned to distinguishing which parts of me were related to which racial/ethnic/cultural origin. We have a history of including all in the process of being excluded or silenced. The trick is for us to learn how to teach transformation of self and others.

We have to try by communicating with others. hooks (2013) talks about talking across difference, transcending boundaries by talking openly about issues such as race: "to find a way to move beyond race is not only the goal of critical thinking, it is the only path to emotional longevity, the only true path to liberation" (p. 8). Our lives are much more than race or ethnicity and we have so much potential in fullness of life. We come from diverse and complicated places (figuratively, literally, and metaphorically). Is this even possible in schools where educators are afraid for their lives to talk about sticky issues for fear of being challenged by students?

When I was in middle school and high school, I was terribly unhappy for many reasons. But, one of those reasons was that I was deemed weird for understanding my position in school as a temporary position (knowing I would move again in a few years) and for knowing and wanting to go back to Korea, or to go back to what I consider home. I received the message loud and clear that I was not welcome and that I knew I was not welcome and that I was even more unwelcome for not wanting to connect or feel at home in a place where I knew I could never feel at home. I am still, as of writing this book chapter in 2018 American-shamed, being told I am not American enough and to practice my patriotism by discontinuing to express my Korean-ness. This is a feeling of (not) belonging, and it became a cycle that refuses to stop. I was deemed not a part of the group for not wanting to stay, especially because I did not want to stay because I was unwelcome. Those that Other seem to have difficulty having multiple perspectives. I get that. I empathize. I was not surrounded by others like myself, who did not speak my language (broken English/ Korean/military/TCK/biracial language). As much as I tried to conform, I was never happy and always knew I never would be able to fully be one of them. I am finding my happiness by expressing myself and teaching others to find that, whatever it means for them.

We do what have to do to survive since we adapt and demonstrate our many resiliencies. We as multi-racial TCKs are really adept at surviving and adapting, but we also fully know we will never be one of "them", whoever "they" are. If that means surviving by passing as White (or the dominant culture; I reference White because that is one of my identities) or trying to relate to local popular culture, we did our research and conformed in many situations. My brother immediately began to try to relate with others by playing the same video games and left behind the ones he used to love. I no longer wore Adidas, I wore Nike, despite my preference.

In most places, I can look at the person next to me and lack a shared experience and connection. Unless I intentionally seek out TCK communities, I have difficulty relating to others who grew up in one country; I can align myself with those who have been Othered, but rarely do some of those people share the commonality of being multi-racial and having grown up in a Third Space or Third Culture.

When TCKs move, we must re-learn what is acceptable per community; this sense of belonging can be felt and communicated by those around them, peers, educators, family, and local culture. What would happen if I took a strengths approach and said that multi-racial TCKs were fine adapting to new school cultures but quickly realized they were unwelcome on their first day in school? What were to happen if their buzz was killed even though they had all of the skills of adapting and were ready to conquer their new school environment? Again, can we go back to re-imagining what would life look like if we were just able to express our strengths and multiple perspectives and be accepted and not need to alter ourselves?

I first knew my existence was validated in my mid-20s when I was working at a book store and through a random conversation with a customer, she introduced me to the term "third culture kid". This was the first time that there was language that I could apply to my experience as well as others. It was in late 2017 that I was introduced to feminist Third Spaces and the mestiza consciousness that I find so useful and applicable to describe and move our experiences forward. Why did it take 20+ years to feel validated as a human being?

If educators could facilitate us being able to "acknowledge our complicated places and consciously drift into the abyss beyond dualisms in order to speak a third voice, re-vision third meaning" (Licona, 2005, p. 13), perhaps we would reduce the Othering, instances of being Othered, and assume power over our lives. Our voice being relegated and ranked to a third voice is wrong. We want our voice to be our first voice, the first voice that people hear, or to hear us as we are and not as someone that others perceive us.

In the field of psychological and behavioral health sciences fields, the transtheoretical model of change is used to understand decision-making and behavioral change processes. People can fluctuate through the pre-contemplation, contemplation, preparation, action, maintenance, and relapse stages when it comes to change (Prochaska & Velicer, 1997). An interesting process of change includes consciousness raising, "increased awareness about the causes, consequences, and cures for a particular problem behavior" (Prochaska & Velicer, 1997, p. 39), helps people move through the stages to create change for self. It is this stage that I wish to focus on as an important process of change. As a social worker who has worked as a home-based therapist for two years, I am familiar with clinical approaches to working with clients to self-determine changes we wish to make in our lives. I will not go into depth since we are looking at the middle educational context. However, I bring up the stages of change because I believe that it is important to realize we do have some part and power in decision-making when it comes to making change. We certainly have a bias in thinking that all people will have the same values to eradicate racism and discrimination and we are always at one stage of change in that model. Not everyone will be in the action and maintenance stage of change; we fluctuate through and are in constant flux. We must remember this when constructing narratives and counter-narratives, that people are in varying stages of change and development and must make the conscious choice to change or regress and recognize their privileges in ability to (not) do so. This relates back to the self-determination concept where we allow individuals to be the driving forces and authors of change in their own lives. We all have varying driving forces that push/pull us to make decisions (e.g. family factors, environmental factors, health, peer pressure, media, etc.).

The argument of both/and versus (n)either/(n)or is something that is still new to me. A-ha moments are the most poignant because they not only blow your mind, but they stick with you. Realizing and recognizing that dominant culture has been demanding and continue to demand that I choose an identity based on race and place (either/or) for their gain as well as not being fully something (neither/nor) and that I am (in some ways, let us not go overboard) able to re-define or just simply express who I am as both/and (which is also problematic, but let us glory in the step up). I am *both* Asian *and* White (if we choose to follow the racially inadequate socially constructed race categories), ethnically Korean and German-American, and a third culture kid (having grown up moving around in Europe and Asia and on military bases surrounded by multi-cultural, multi-racial, military, and missionary sub-cultures). Those sub-cultures were my dominant culture. I am all of those and so much more. I just am. I am both/and. And more. I am no longer (n)either/(n)or in the way that dominant culture demands that I be. I will never go back to just accepting what others prescribe to me. Or, at least, I will fight to continue to educate myself and express myself in ways that challenge the dominant narratives and be the expert narrative on my own life, because no one knows me better than myself and my feelings and experiences are valid and worthy.

So, this is where the messiness can be beautiful. Messiness does not equate with muddiness. If so, whatever. The messiness and fluidity for which gender identity and sexuality studies are championing are fearless. Why is it that multi-racial folks, TCK folks, and multi-racial folks cannot/do not have the voice to champion this fluidity of identity? We are certainly raced, gendered, sexed, and discriminated against.

If that was not enough, we are led by others (not just by monoracial people) to ask ourselves about (im)purity of identity by living with more than one "race" and whether we consider mixing communities a good thing. We find a lot of pride in our communities and when you bring more than one community together, it is perceived that you lose some of the other community and become "less than" rather than "more of". This is not the case; we are much more than you which you have reduced.

In all of the research I examined, I found one article on addressing mental health needs of TCKs. Limberg and Lambie (2011) have laid out needs of middle-school TCKs and assign mental health interventions for counselors to meet those needs. As mentioned in a previous section, not a lot of research is done on TCKs, multi-racial TCKs, much less middle-school TCKs who hold multi-racial identities. They attempt to provide psychoeducation on who TCKs are, introduce TCK transitional stages (we do need to also focus on what happens after a TCK goes through the stages) (and, these stages are problematic, but that is for another paper) and suggest those counseling strategies. Those counseling strategies are directed at the stages of TCK transitional stages, focusing on helping the child transition to school and leave the school. The counselors that are referred to are guidance counselors who serve important roles academically guiding students; but what about mental health counselors addressing children's needs?

What is lacking from this one article is the need to address the larger mainstream culture, the culture outside the family, the educational system, the educators, the family, the students (and their voice in their needs), and curriculum needs to reflect the experiences and needs of students during their stay at school. While it is an attempt to get needs met, we should think about how to make change on all levels. My critique is not of the article, it is on the assumption that counselors should hold the sole responsibility of helping TCKs in school, or that TCKs need help, or just meeting the needs of students. Through a case study, the authors in this article outlined the extent to which the school was involved with a student who came and left the school as a TCK and the attention they gave to ensure that the student experienced a "supportive and culturally competent educational environment" (Limberg & Lambie, 2011, p. 53) and not just on the part of counselors. It is the absolute responsibility of everyone in schools to know their students, to know their needs and to be "woke", and present for selves and students. What can be gathered from this article is the necessity to practice ethical counseling and educating by checking bias, having and maintaining competencies/skills, and seeking "knowledge about diverse culture" (Limberg & Lambie, 2011, p. 46). Many of the cues that TCKs are having difficulties manifest like normal behavior problems of children when a child is experiencing difficulty, (e.g. acting out if a child has experienced trauma). The tips for educators and administrators is to look closer and to refuse simple write-offs and diagnosis for what we consider problems. Children are much more than problems or behaviors.

Multi-racial TCKs do not fit in simple boxes, much like people of certain races, gender, ability, and sexual orientation. TCKs have been gendered and racialized, especially if part of our racial identity is White. Just as Asians are exoticized, multi-racial children are exoticized and can sometimes represent cultures who have been Westernized and dominated.

Children spend most of their time in school, and this is where we learn who we are in relationship with self and others. We learn from home, we learn from teachers and administrators and we also learn from our peers. We know that so much happens in the classroom and children are relatively ignored and regulated, taught to sit still and be quiet and schools can even operate similarly to the way that prisons operate.

International schools are not immune to conditioning children. In my experience, they are notorious for celebrating Western holidays, but making efforts to celebrate International Week, mostly celebrating the host culture's holidays or celebrating traditions during that week. Efforts are made to allow other cultures to celebrate during International Day or International Week. This is a good start. For people like myself, I was very confused about what I was supposed to celebrate since

I celebrated a mixture of cultures, mostly military culture. I had no distinct sense of self because the choices of who I could be were limited per space and place. None of that celebration of difference happened at my American Christian schools. We only celebrated American holidays at school and there was no effort (ironic since the school I mentioned in my vignette at the beginning of the chapter was located near two military institutions and had some domestic military families) to incorporate International Day and no room for expression of other cultures. In that case, I would have had no language to express that I was half-Korean because I had no concept of what Korean culture was or how to describe it. For students like myself, I think that educators could have been more intentional in student identity formation and expression of self. I remember staying silent when my one Korean friend at school would answer about Korea on my behalf. My perceptions based on my experiences were different than hers and thus she was an expert, but I had no way to differentiate or describe my own experiences. Raising consciousness of difference as something positive would have decreased the negative associations I felt. I truly had no concept of what it meant to be different until I moved to the States, at least not where it counted. After a few of those instances, I dissociated and then conformed to the dominant White culture, attempting to pass as White and was only different in racial/ethnic identity. I hid my international and military and biracial experiences. The only way I could express that I was different was when I invited my friends over and they enjoyed my Mom's cooking (despite being fusion food and not full Korean spread).

In some ways, that reproduction of knowledge, of being different was cyclical. I hid being different and my friends did not facilitate it and helped me perpetuate my new identity. I had to hide myself to survive. It was not until late in college that I was able to begin to come to terms. My true and realized self began to emerge in graduate school and when I began practicing as a social worker, only a few years ago. I came to terms and began to accept myself and it was through raised consciousness (through psychoeducation of oppressive systems) and expression of decades of frustration and confusion (especially felt in my middle educative years) and finding ways of counter-narrating my experience and advocating for self that I feel like I am coming into myself. I recently attended a Midwest Asian American Student Union conference as a graduate student chaperone and was so empowered to see others (some multi-racial like myself) being empowered to raise consciousness and act upon realized self that I began dialoguing with my younger self and healing.

TOWARD A NEW CONSCIOUSNESS

This mestiza consciousness can be re-imagined as multi-racial TCK consciousness, one in which we raise our voices and tell our stories in ways that make sense for us, and not fit inside the lines of dominant cultures asking us to choose and exercise loyalties between and among racial identities/cultures/ways of being. It is a consciousness in which we accept the ambiguity and complexity, one in which we survive till the end, victors of and for ourselves.

This consciousness "refuses fixed dichotomous structures and their reductive implications for matters of (self) representation" (Licona, 2005, p. 1), encapsulating the freedom I feel after confronting and refusing the reality of what happens when people ask me to choose one racial/ethnic identity or another, without allowing me to be a whole person. This counter-narrative or attempt to educate myself and advocate for myself is an expression that I value myself as a whole person, or at least someone made up of different parts all coming together in one human being. I recognize and realize that I also fluctuate on the depths of my perception of what it means to be human or a whole person who is not spatially rooted dependent upon my surroundings and the extent to which I allow others' perceptions of me to affect my perceptions of me.

Licona (2005) makes the point that lines are drawn that are confusing for us. For those in authority positions, they get to draw and enforce the lines. It becomes even more confusing for children when they are in schools and the lines do not make sense. Our families tell us who we are. Borders divide and delineate. "Revealing multiple (inter)subjectivities is a result of a deconstructive process as it requires a challenge and ultimate dismantling of the identity binary ... the border – not always a straight line – obscures a third space or fertile ground of unrealized potentials" (Licona, 2005, p. 6). This is the opposite of a deficit lens; we often do not take the time (especially majority cultures) to deconstruct and to find the potentials. It takes time and effort to tear down the walls of our ways of knowing.

Children can use their voices now on varying platforms and for many relevant social causes. For example, in early 2018, there was a mass school shooting in Parkland, Florida, where several children were shot by a former student. Through this horrific event, some of the children at the school have had the privilege and ability to advocate against gun violence with national attention. As a result of this visibility around such a polarizing topic, the root message the children are saying is that they do not feel safe and have had such clapback from adults, thus perpetuating this unsafety. These children (across the U.S.) have raised consciousness about who they and their right to safe educational spaces and adults are blaming them and placing social responsibility on the children to keep themselves safe. To take this point back to this chapter, to what extent to we place responsibility on our children to educate us about their complex experiences of what it means to be human and living with many identities? Children/students are fed up with being told who they are and to stay in their lanes.

"But it is not enough to stand on the opposite river bank, shouting questions, challenging patriarchal, white conventions" (Anzaldúa, 1999, p. 100) because it places one in a position of opposition, "a duel of oppressor and oppressed ... a common denominator of violence" this position is "a step towards liberation from cultural domination. But it is not a way of life" (p. 100). The key is that "the possibilities are numerous once we decide to act and not react" (p. 101). Asking that question of "Which culture do you identify with more?" begs the choice, to quantify and assign more importance to one side. It begs opposition. Merely fighting against the dominant narratives is oppositional and may not leave room for progress, it is a dependent position. Shifting one's body or perspective allows for alternatives; one, perhaps, is working together, in parallel lines, moving forward, perhaps in muddy waters. So, how do we act and practice intentionality in the classroom rather than reacting when an issue comes up that challenges our perceptions of multi-racial TCKs or non-normative (what is normal?) student identities?

Just as the mestiza has no country yet claims all countries (Anzaldúa, 1999), multi-racial third culture kids (TCKs) share many of those experiences that come when others do not consider us one of their own. Just as I felt an overwhelming feeling of connection and relief when I found TCKs, I found relief when I read Anzaldúa because she was able to describe a complicated experience in way that was inclusive and action-oriented.

Lisa Delpit (2012) argues for educators and administrators to understand that people of all colors are capable (and deserving) of learning and should not be taught down to. We as educators must believe that children of all diverse backgrounds/ identities are capable of learning and that we can learn together. We have to believe in the basic humanity of people who are different. "These revelations can serve to challenge fixed notions of identity" (Licona, 2005, p. 6) and can serve as a basis for how one's life is lived.

We are all humans and capable of learning and making change (if we need to). Keating (2007) also starts with this premise that students are capable of learning and that "they – like all people – have intellectual/intuitional agency: they can think for themselves and, through careful self-reflection, can choose to alter their beliefs, worldviews, self-definitions, and actions" (p. 34). Sit with that. If we choose to believe that students are humans, with innate capability to think for self and are worthy of learning and thinking critically, we can make change. We can gather that critical consciousness to help children understand the way that the world works to form how we view ourselves and how we socially construct our worlds, and our identities in it.

Critical consciousness illuminates that for some, we do not feel as though we belong because we are divided by borders that people make us straddle or pick sides. "A border is a dividing line, a narrow strip along a steep edge. A borderland is a vague and undetermined place created by the emotional residue of an unnatural boundary. It is in a constant state of transition" (Anzaldúa, 1999, p. 25). For those populations whose status is transitory, having no sense of home in one's own body/ space, it can feel unsafe. It certainly feels unsafe to me, not knowing who I am, especially because people from all mono-racial communities tell me that I do not know who I am and that they do and that I should conform. Living on the borders is unsafe because as soon as I start to express myself in a way that does not conform to a mono-racial perspective of who I should be. It is immediately called out and I am immediately admonished that I am operating outside of the borders. Being on the identity borders is unsafe. Even in some cases, I do not have language to talk about what it means to grow up in other countries because it is just a part of me that I have learned to suppress. My ambiguity is deemed unsafe because it has been recognized as unsafe by others who cannot understand it. It is seen as a threat and my actions demonstrate my need to protect myself.

When we moved to the States, there was a White American kid moved in down the street and I made fun of him because he was counting in Japanese and I thought he was making up words. I had this pre-conception that his Whiteness meant he could not possibly know Japanese and I had no concept that unless he was a missionary kid, he could not possibly have lived overseas. I implied that he was stupid and did not know anything about Asian culture (what did I know, I could not even communicate or express what I knew anyway) because I projected onto him what I thought about him based on my perception of his race and ethnicity. He looked different from myself, and therefore, he could not possibly have experiences like mine. I remember this clearly because he began to become frustrated and insistent that he knew how to count in Japanese and then I began to feel sorry for him and doubt myself. This is quite common. I think that at the time, I was attempting to defend and protect what I perceived to be mockery of Asian culture, but I ended up a part of that dialogue that says "You do not know what you are talking about. You cannot possibly know anything about Japan". I could not even empathize or perceive that he could speak another language or as having had a Third Culture experience like myself. If educators had been around, or if family had been around, I am sure that I would have been put in check much sooner and would have allowed me the opportunity to learn that I was wrong and that his truths were true and that my ideas were not based on fact, but on constructions of realities that had also been projected onto me.

When I disclose to people that I hold a Korean identity and that I lived in Korea from the age of six years old until twelve years old, they challenge me and ask me to say something in Korean. Through my consciousness raising endeavors, I have uncovered that there are implicit messages that I received from this (whether or not this is the intent of those messages is another story). Those messages include: You do not look Korean or Asian, I do not believe you. You are lying. Prove it to me. You must prove your identity, being, and existence. Your response is not good enough. It does not make sense to me that you traveled and lived in another country (and I'm not even going to give you the chance to list the other countries in which you were born and lived because I made you pick your most formative place). You have said you want to go back, then go back. You do not belong. Why would you want to go back? In my head, it is not possible that could live a completely different life in a completely different country where you felt belonging and love. We only parse out love and the feeling of belonging by being rooted and growing up in one location. You do not have a hometown, that makes you weird. How could you not have a hometown? Why would you not want to call our state your home? We are the best and that threatens my sensibilities when you say you do not call this home. You are American. This is your home. My home and neighborhood should be good enough for you, but I would never ever consider that your home would be good enough for me. You need to prove your existence to me. You are not whole and you need to pick and choose your identities to fit my comfort levels and act more White so that we do not think you are weird and pick on you. You will never be one of us. I say that you hold this identity and this is good enough for us, so it is good enough for you. Where and what is Korea? That is strange, that is not a country. I have never heard of Korea. North or South? Here is my opinion on Korea and the military. You are strange and I want to exoticize you by listening to you say something strange. Once I hear you say something strange, this now gives me license to Other you and set you apart. What you are saying does not make sense because you look one way and talk another way.

The power of those messages being heard (un)consciously, of course, became my reality and embodied. Those are my current interpretations of the messages I was receiving and continue to receive. Back then, I was hearing that I was different and that I needed to prove myself and I did not want to stand out and be different. I was an Other. I heard that I needed to be (n)either/(n)or and couldn't be both/and. I hear those implicit messages now, through critical awareness and raised consciousness and now speak back to it or at least question it and demand the audience of the person asking the question to at least listen further than what they originally intended.

Critical exposure to histories and community-building social organizations "lead to the emergence of an empower critical consciousness" and it is this awakening and perspective shift which influences Asian Americans to discontinue perpetuating our experiences of Internalized Racial Oppression (IRO) (Pyke, 2010), this oppression that we internalize based upon our prescribed race (Trieu & Lee, 2018). IRO continues to affect the whole human existence, in individual and collective consciousness. The messages we give and receive can be internalized on all ends of the interactions. What we hear from someone can become a reality and truth for someone else. It is absolutely critical to expose our students to the oppressive structures in our society that continue to marginalize groups of people. It is critical to continue to educate ourselves. For educators who hold teaching licenses and need to obtain Continuing Educational Units (CEUs), perhaps plugging into workshops that train about race, racism, and racial/ethnic identities is a way to accomplish two things at once. I do not believe in making things more difficult than necessary.

This multi-racial TCK consciousness is a good place to start having adolescents question who they are and why we are prohibited and forbidden from which people and spaces and from which reasons. For multi-racial TCKs living and being in their homes, this consciousness can allow exploration of what happens and why and who adolescents are and can be. This ambiguity has no limits; it is a place/space for exploration. Borders are set up to keep people out, to keep people in. It is something that makes sense because we have a knowledge set from which to base this information (Gunaratana, 2011); we are in a constant mindset of processing information and placing them into categories or assigning judgment (good vs. evil; tall vs. short; Black vs. White) so that it makes sense to us. We only know this through raised consciousness.

RACE, ETHNICITY, IDENTITY, AND CULTURE

Markus and Moya (2010) write on race in the U.S.:

Race is a doing – a dynamic set of historically derived and institutionalized ideas and practices that: sorts people into ethnic groups … associates differential value, power, and privilege … and emerges when groups are perceived to pose a threat … to each other's worldview or way of life … and or to justify the denigration and exploitation … of other groups. (p. 21)

So, in this book chapter I have used the word race (and multi-racial) to describe my identity because this is how I was grouped and this is how I am categorized, marginalized and exploited and how others like myself experience day-to-day life. These authors have made a point to distinguish that race and ethnicity are actions and doings, by ourselves and others, and we express and demand expressions to gain power for self or over others.

Patricia Hill Collins (1986) argues through Black feminist thought, which is a "standpoint of and for Black women" (p. S16), and introduces the concept of the "outsider within" (p. S14) status, something for which TCKs can relate. We can also self-define, self-value, understand interlocking (and intersectional) oppression in relation to self and others and stress importance of our culture (through raising our consciousness). Using Collins' (1986) model, we can also utilize our own multi-racial TCK self-definition and self-valuation as active challenge of the dominant narratives and replace those images/definitions with our own and humanize ourselves. We multi-racial TCKs have insider insight into others' intimate cultures yet hold the outsider status, the "outsider within" and it has also impacted our lives much like the historical experiences of Black women in the U.S. Much like Collins (1986) argues that the Black feminist thought is of and for Black women, I argue that multi-racial TCK consciousness and thought can be most poignant coming from our voices and fully representing our experiences.

Once again, I argue throughout this chapter that our experience has been that the dominant cultures assign our identities and do not allow for our own choice and self-determination in our complex identity selection and expression. Perhaps we multi-racial TCKs already have this raised consciousness but are excluded much like Black feminists from dominant conversations/arenas. Collins (1986) makes an argument that the dualistic (n)either/(n)or thinking that domination continues to perpetuate is unstable and that these "dichotomous oppositional differences invariably imply relationships of superiority and inferiority" (p. S20). Collins (1986) expands on Audre Lorde's idea of protection that "Oppressed peoples may maintain hidden consciousness and may not reveal their true selves for reasons of self-protection" (p. S23). This is important since many of us do not have safe places to do this in majority-led classrooms, in our communities. In my many intersections of family culture (and ethnic influence), I am not considered an expert on myself and cannot question elder opinions or dialogue in a way that challenges the elder authorities.

This translated into many of the male-dominated White patriarchal environments and learned to be seen (if that) and not heard. My world was consumed with "You're not Korean enough" or "You're not American enough" or "Why don't you know what *Full House* is?" or "Haven't you ever heard of *Babysitters' Club?*" and "Where did *you* grow up?! You're missing out" and "What's wrong with you?" or "You never hang stuff up on the walls?" or "You must hate moving all the time" and many more.

Johnston-Guerrero (2016) calls for us to embrace the messiness or race and ethnicity using the metaphor of a zipper, where one zipper side is race/racial identity, the other side is ethnicity/ethnic identity and when zipped together, the "student, researcher, or educator has control over how to make sense of the constructs and whether it is best to distinguish and focus on one aspect of development or to combine them" (p. 48). Acceptance of muddiness seems to be the most healthy approach since the opposition dissipates and we can sit and understand it as it is. Keating (2007) practices a great deal of cultural humility when it comes to teaching her students, a vulnerability and admittance that she does not know all of the answers:

I am still learning how to enact this ethics of openness, reciprocity, and exchange in my classrooms, and I probably fail more often than I succeed ... with every classroom encounter, I make the conscious decision to act on our interconnectedness – even when these connections are difficult or impossible to perceive. Using imagination and mindful attention, I posit, explore, and in other ways try to enact interrelatedness. When failure occurs, I remind myself that we are always in process, always open to further change. (p. 39)

This stance of learner-teacher is important since educators are very much a part of student identity development, so identifying and creating space for exploration of race or ethnic and facilitation of development is important; taking an intersectional approach is important to understanding the diverse experiences of students. Johnston-Guerrero (2017) conducted a study on college students and found that they or Others were holders of their racial authority. The point of this is that educators can understand students and who they deem as authorities over their own racial identity and challenge students to assume their own authority and check self and not to project identity. The other point is checking the silencing that we do and experience.

Delgado and Stefancic (2017) introduce Critical Race Theory (building on critical law theory) as "studying and transforming the relationship among race, racism, and power" (p. 3) and find: racism is pervasive and normative; interest convergence happens when racism serves white people, thus preventing address of racism; race is socially constructed; racialization has consequences; and People of Color can and should produce counter-narratives to the dominant narrative. Multi-racial TCKs can and do counter the narratives. However, there continues to be a lack of a multi-racial voice raising awareness for the complexities of what it means to not be considered a full human or impure. We can take inspiration from critical race theory (CRT) to understand the relationship of race and power, through raising consciousness. We

H. R. STOHRY

can take this raised consciousness and CRT mindset to understand and explore the relationship of power and the TCK experience, of who decides where children move, for what purpose, and how to interpret normative behaviors and ideology that are forced on children.

RAISING CONSCIOUSNESS FOR EDUCATORS

Johnston-Guerrero and Nadal (2010) define *monoracism* as "a social system of psychological inequality where individuals who do not fit monoracial categories may be oppressed on systemic and interpersonal levels because of underlying assumptions and beliefs in singular, discrete racial categories" (p. 125) and receive backlash of aggressions directed toward us due to "general ascribed status as a person of color and not necessarily due to his multiracial heritage" (p. 126). We can wrestle with the recognition of microaggressions, decision-making when it comes to address (or not) the microaggression, and how to address it. The call for inclusion of "multiracial issues in multicultural competence models" (Johnston-Guerrero & Nadal, 2010, p. 140) can be applied to educational spaces for all students and there is a call for practitioners (can be applied to educators) and their clients (students) to "be conscious of the ways in which their monoracial identities may influence their biases, assumptions, and attitudes about multiracial persons, while recognizing the privilege that they have as monoracial individuals" (p. 140). When was the last time you checked your privilege and how you race yourselves and your students?

Moving beyond what happens in the classroom, Nadal, Sriken, Davidoff, Wong and McLean (2012) describe the microaggressions within families as manifesting as: isolation within the family; favoritism within the family; questioning of authenticity; denial of multiracial identity and experiences by monoracial family members; feelings about not learning about family heritage or culture; and recruitment by monoracial family members and objectification. This certainly differs per family and cultural group and certainly the context of the Third Culture in which multi-racial TCKS live. For educators to know this when teaching children can be important since expression of self at school may certainly differ from expression of self at school or be an extension of identity.

Let's start by going back to what it means to be human and consider ourselves and our students as humans and our stance where educators learn as they lead, by taking notes from Paolo Freire:

> The only effective instrument is a humanizing pedagogy in which the revolutionary leadership establishes a permanent relationship of dialogue with the oppressed ... a revolutionary leadership must accordingly practice *co-intentional* education. Teachers and students (leadership and people), co-intent on reality, are both Subjects, not only in the task of unveiling that reality, and thereby coming to know it critically, but in the task of re-creating that knowledge. (Freire, 2000, pp. 68–69)

We are extensions of families and systems, but at our core, we are human beings. When it comes to being vulnerable as humans, at the very least, start with Freire's and Keating's ideas that teachers are also learners; in my head, it means lowering one's status to meet students (who are in a position of submission in the classroom and are judged to perform to meet some standard set by society based on what they learn and know) where they are and their identities that they carry. What we can take from the quote is asking ourselves what a humanizing pedagogy means as well as what does it mean to have dialogue with the oppressed. This pedagogy of the oppressed is a "revolutionary" idea (Freire, 2000, p. 68) that students can be the experts and that they are valuable and hold valuable ideas, especially about themselves. Adopting this revolutionary mindset/practice means that your leadership is revolutionary.

APPLICATION OF CONSCIOUSNESS-RAISING

In order to apply the ideas of consciousness-raising I raised in this chapter, what I would have found helpful as an adolescent multi-racial TCK in the classroom would cover anything from changing curriculum to changing teaching style, to variations of exercises incorporating raising consciousness as a process and outcome. I think I would have appreciated the consciousness piece on my part, the part of my parents, family structures, communities and educators/administrators. If I had skills then to explore and understand my identities, how they were being formed by others and how I could have a voice in my own life and identity formation, I would be a different person.

For the school's academic calendar, finding time for representation and celebration could be a start from the top down that shouts inclusion and identity expression. International days/weeks at international schools celebrate other countries and allow students and their families to express love for their home country and celebrate traditions in a space especially for families to express themselves. The schools allow for performances (e.g. dance, music, traditional fighting methods), food celebrations and traditional dress. In attempts to be inclusive, we can advocate for a way for students to celebrate things that have meaning for them, and create space in our schools for those expressions. When planning activities, we must be careful not to essentialize, and to include students in the process.

We can activate a refusal to essentialize as a way to challenge dominant narrative in the educational system when it comes to learning about other cultures and identity expressions and communicating that knowledge to others. How do we engage students in ways that make sense? We can co-create assignments that challenge the (n)either/(n)or for the both/and; Keating (2007) incorporates texts that challenge the dominant narratives. In our case, I would have felt more represented in curriculum seeing people who had ambiguous looks and who grew up in countries that were not their home countries (whatever that means).

Parents and schools fear children resisting. Consider the following questions: What does resistance look like and what does it mean when a child resists? Does it need to be tame for middle-schoolers? Why do we hold a fear of resistance? Why is it so threatening to adults when children can think for themselves and express themselves and challenge the power and authorities that adults have, especially in the classroom? Is resistance troubling? Who gets to determine this? How does this relate to student and educator roles? What role does an educator have to influence a student's identities? These are a few of the questions that you can refer to from Part 2's Transformative Consciousness Raising Questions for further questions to challenge self.

But, to be sure, just take a second to contemplate why it would feel threatening to have your knowledge (position as an educator) challenged. What would it mean if someone challenged your teaching styles, your inclusivity practices (or lack of), curriculum, etc.? So, this fear of resistance threatens our structures that we have set for order and control. To raise consciousness and act as a result means that something is not working and that the dominant narrative must change. This can and will be uncomfortable, to challenge our ways of knowing, to acknowledge our roles in oppressive structure (including schools). Feeling afraid of resistance if this is in response to oppressive structures, we may feel insecure because this certainly means we must give up some of our privilege. This then leads to us exploring our willingness to do so and acknowledge our power, privilege, and positionality.

When we talk about positionality, are we talking about positioning self in opposition to the other? At the same time? Are we talking about the privileges that we have or the things that orient us in our perspectives? Can we position ourselves in a position of togetherness, rather than in opposition? I think that life requires us to continuously position ourselves based on our constructed structures and we cannot always find a way to avoid leaving someone out, but what are the ways in which we can strive to do better by our students with conflicting (this is a projection from dominant culture) identities and be a part of our society in meaningful ways yet not live in subjection to sub-part human existence?

Middle grades philosophy proposes that education that is developmentally responsive; this means that every student can learn and explore their ambiguous identities in relation to self as well as others. According to the Association for Middle Level Education (AMLE) formerly National Middle School Association (NMSA), Keys to Educating Adolescents (NMSA, 2010) include this stance that educators are "prepared" to teach them. While my core social work values call for cultural competence, we have moved from this idea that we can ever be fully competent and instead move toward cultural humility, that we can continuously learn from others. Perhaps there can be a model for supporting transitory students or multi-racial TCKs in general. Perhaps there can be more proper implementation (from the top down) to implement bias training/education that includes the multi-racial person as someone who does not fit the norm and perhaps faces struggles with monoracism.

I do not pretend to know the answers to the problems raised by intersectional identities. The beauty of being an educator (to those of us who intentionally impart knowledge in various settings, not solely the responsibility of teachers) is that we can cultivate consciousness to allow students to explore and choose the roles that they wish. We can cultivate action or contemplative practice/reflection, but why not start with consciousness raising? Educating our educators to be better equipped to recognize that TCKs may have specific challenges, but all the while refusal to relegate or project need onto adolescents.

CONCLUSION

By offering up a personal story at the beginning, my intent was to introduce the complexities of what it means to be a third culture kid intersecting with so many other identities like military/missionary culture and biraciality. Our identities, much like the mestiza, have been dominated by those that Other us and we constantly live on those borders that people set for us.

Many of us thrive and are able to express all of the identities with fluidity. We live in a culture where it does not make sense for us to teach ourselves and children to accept difference. It is difficult to sit with the discomfort when something does not compute when it comes to racial/ethnic/cultural identity. We can change this trend, starting with raising consciousness. This chapter was an intent to share my story, to demonstrate the complex issues that multi-racial TCKs face and the necessity to raise consciousness for students and self. I really wanted to muddy the waters and through raising consciousness create constructive confusion and normalize not having answers to the questions we face surrounding, race/ethnicity/cultural identity and identity development. The question is, what will we do with the ideas we muddle through in this chapter? Let's move forward.

Ponder the path of thy feet, and let all thy ways be established. (Proverbs 4:26, the King James Version Bible)

REFERENCES

Anzaldúa, G. (1999). *Borderlands: La Frontera*. San Francisco, CA: Aunt Lute Books.

Association for Middle Level Education. (2010). *This we believe: Keys to educating young adolescents*. Retrieved from https://www.amle.org/portals/0/pdf/twb/TWB_colorchart_Oct2013.pdf

Baker, C. (2000). *The care and education of young bilinguals: An introduction for professionals*. Clevedon: Multilingual Matters Ltd.

Brooks, K., & Karathanos, K. (2009). Building on the cultural and linguistic capital of English Learner (EL) students. *Multicultural Education, 16*(4), 47–51.

Chang, S. H. (2016). *Raising mixed race: Multiracial Asian children in a post-racial world*. New York, NY: Routledge.

Collins, P. H. (1986). Learning from the outsider within: The sociological significance of Black feminist thought. *Social Problems, 33*(6), S14–S32.

Delgado, R., & Stefancic, J. (2017). *Critical race theory: An introduction* (3rd ed.). New York, NY: New York University Press.

Delpit, L. (2012). *Multiplication is for White people: Raising expectations for other people's children*. New York, NY: The New Press.

Freire, P. (2000). *Pedagogy of the oppressed*. New York, NY: Continuum International Publishing Group.

Gunaratana, H. (2011). *Mindfulness in plain English*. Somerville, MA: Wisdom Publications.

Heller, M. (1992). The politics of codeswitching and language choice. *Journal of Multilingual and Multicultural Development, 13*(1–2), 123–142.

hooks, b. (2013). *Writing beyond race: Living theory and practice.* New York, NY: Routledge.

Johnston-Guerrero, M. P. (2016). Embracing the messiness: Critical and diverse perspectives on racial and ethnic identity development. *New Directions for Student Services, 2016*(154), 43–55.

Johnston-Guerrero, M. P., & Nadal, K. L. (2010). Multiracial microaggressions: Exposing monoracism in everyday life and clinical practice. In D. W. Sue (Ed.), *Microaggressions and marginality: manifestation, dynamics and impact* (pp. 123–144). New York, NY: Wiley & Sons.

Keating, A. (2007). *Teaching transformation: Transcultural classroom dialogues.* New York, NY: Palgrave Macmillan.

Krashen, S. D. (1985). *The input hypothesis: Issues and implications.* New York, NY: Addison-Wesley Longman Ltd.

Limberg, D., & Lambie, G. W. (2011). Third culture kids: Implications for professional school counseling. *Professional School Counseling, 15*(1), 45–54.

Markus, H. R., & Moya, P. M. L. (2010). *Doing race: 21 essays for the 21st century.* New York, NY: W. W. Norton & Company.

Nadal, K. L., Sriken, J., Davidoff, K. C., Wong, Y., & McLean, K. (2012). Microaggressions within families: Experiences of multiracial people. *Interdisciplinary Journal of Applied Family Studies, 62*, 90–201.

National Middle School Association. (2010). *This we believe: Keys to educating young adolescents.* Westerville, OH: Author.

Obama, B. H. (2004). *Dreams from my father: A story of race and inheritance.* New York, NY: Three Rivers Press.

Pollock, D. C., & Van Reken, R. E. (2017). *Third culture kids: Growing up among worlds* (3rd ed.). Boston, MA: Nicholas Brealey Publishing.

Prochaska, J. O., & Velicer, W. F. (1997). The transtheoretical model of health behavior change. *American Journal of Health Promotion, 12*(1), 38–48.

Thomas, W. P., & Collier, V. P. (1997). *School effectiveness for language minority students.* Santa Cruz, CA: Center for Research on Education, Diversity, and Excellence.

Trieu, M. M., & Lee, H. C. (2018). Asian Americans and internalized racial oppression: Identified, reproduced, and dismantled. *Sociology of Race and Ethnicity, 4*(1), 67–82.

Useem, J., & Useem, R. (1967). The interfaces of a binational third culture: A study of the American community in India. *Journal of Social Issues, 23*(1), 130–143.

DAVID I. HERNÁNDEZ-SACA

15. RESISTING LEARNING DISABILTY OPPRESSION

Healing through Dis/Ability Voice

LD PAIN

LD pain
Gripping my soul
Disgust
Yearning for release

LD pain
Stigma on the mind, body, and soul
No longer ashamed to express it
For release of master narratives of LD

LD pain
Inside the body and my story
In the past, present, and future
Core-identity hopeful

LD pain
Is real
Is a sociocultural construction
Healing through dis/ability as the psycho-emotional disablism model

LD pain
Anger
Mistrust
Needing to let go

LD pain
My journey towards healing
The importance of expressing your truth
To transform self and society

© KONINKLIJKE BRILL NV, LEIDEN, 2019 | DOI:10.1163/9789004393813_015

LD pain
Continuous
Communicated
Not heard

LD pain
"Just get over it"
"Stop being so sensitive"
Lost in others' opinions

LD pain
Does not originate in me
This LD as a cancer long leading to LD pain
Releasing and healing by writing, theorizing, teaching, researching, and service for all and myself

SPEAKING BACK TO LD PAIN

Body, spirit, mind, pain, and hurt
So ever present
So-ever felt
So-ever that desire to repel

Desire turned into action
Action accomplished through will
Will to transcend and heal
Heal through presence that is not interpreted as the medical model, but the psych-emotional disablism at work inside and outside of me

How can this theory turn into healing?
Theory and practice as praxis
Breathe as praxis that coupling of critical reflection and action
Towards speaking and being free

Free from the master narratives of LD
Free from psyche-damage of the symbolism of special education and LD
Free from the oppressor of LD
Free from both the oppressor and becoming the oppressor at the intersections

How can we be free from such inequity and our capacity to dehumanize self and other?
Through love
Through compassion

Through the range of positive emotions and feelings, that are social in origin, for human development's sake to and through voice

Voice
Voice
Voice
What is voice?

How can voice help liberate me?
How can voice be sustained?
How can voice relate to language and freedom?
How can voice facilitate: *"Nothing about Us Without Us"*?

"Nothing about Us Without Us"
I have been speaking back
Internally
Externally

No more!
No more!
No more!
(I am) speaking back to LD Pain

LISA A. BOSKOVICH

16. POEMS ON BEING MIXED AND MOVING FORWARD

PRIVILEGE AND IDENTITY

I stood at the doors,
Identity, Learning Disability, and Privilege.
1-handle was rusted and showed
Signs of wear.
The 2nd a new coat of paint:
Representing change, resolution,
and healing shined ever so brightly.
The 3rd stood slightly ajar,
With uncertainty and questions.
Identity.
Learning Disability.
Privilege.
Provide a ratio to experiences
In my life and internal growth.
Intimate are these conversations,
Held in quiet moments,
Of contemplation,
Only the soul knows,
And
The mind responds too.
Identity is a lifetime of
Experiences and junctions.
Its solidness is now taking ground,
More solid than before.
Deep are the layers of self,
Whose innate spiraled circumference,
Continues to respond to and
Carve out layers of new understanding.
To heal the deep stains of Learning Disability,
Marginalization, took time,
And
Help from others.

Privilege,
My role as a White woman,
Continues this inner discourse.
For this road is walked,
Step by step,
Turn by turn,
In and through liminality.

IDENTITY

Identity speaks
To the self we each call I.
This ever-evolving circumference,
Weaves in and out,
Slowly shifting and emerging.
This Enigma code,
Shaped through time,
Through shames filled halls,
Twisted passage ways,
And codes only known to self.
Perhaps we even feel,
We are impostors.
It's a personal fill in the blanks.
Some of these beliefs,
Are false truths,
That we hold deeply inside.
Maybe we fear,
We are not good enough,
Intelligent enough.
Perhaps we never feel understood,
Perhaps we don't feel loved.
Those long held dogmas.
Once spoken,
The Enigma broken.
Dials turned,
As new experiences,
Thoughts,
Challenge,
Long held beliefs.
Who we really are,
Is an ever evolving,
Tapestry of identity.
Some formed,

And some are ever evolving,
As the window of time,
Continues to move me ever forward,
Yesterday's reflection reminds me
Of who I used to be.
This nautilus of self,
Continues evolving,
And sets my soul free.

IMAN FAGAN

17. WALKING THE LINE

IN THE BEGINNING

Imagine being a seven-year-old second grader. You are a student in a classroom with two phenomenal teachers. You have a mother at home who works hard to provide and do her very best and a father who feels barely there throughout most of your days. These four individuals look differently, they speak differently, and act differently; nonetheless, they each play an unmistakable role in your everyday life. In the classroom, there are two faces to greet you each day, a smiling set of team teachers that you admire. At home, there is the sweetest face that you have ever known; you call her mom. You have a dad that you see on occasion, one that you adore and one that adores you, too. Imagine that your world of role models is just that, nothing more and nothing less.

At the age of seven, I did not actively think about the physical traits of the individuals whom I held on the highest of pedestals. The way that my idols looked was not on my scope of importance; instead, it was the way that each of them made me feel. I did not take color into consideration when seeking authority, comfort, or a playmate during recess, until I did.

I vividly recall hearing a voice shout, "I am going to pour this water bottle on you because your mom is White[1] and your dad is Black".[2] Suddenly, my mom became my *White* mom and my dad became my *Black* dad. Tears immediately streamed down my face. I knew what was said, and I knew that it was wrong, but I did not know why. The tears flowed, and my next response was to tell one of my teachers. Rather than telling my White teacher what my classmate said on the playground, I chose to tell my Black teacher. I do not recall the look on her face or the words that exited her mouth. To my knowledge, there was no specific action that was taken in response to this event, and I do not know if choosing to tell her rather than my other teacher was a conscious decision or simply one made based on proximity.

Today, as an undergraduate[3] student of Color in the Department of Education, I am not sure how I would respond if an elementary aged student approached me with tears streaming down his or her face after a fellow student uttered words that would lay the foundation for a future of altered self-perception. I do know that no matter what I would say or do as a result, my response would be minimal in comparison to the events that would follow, as that student wrestles with the realization that skin-color would continue to matter for the rest of his or her life.

As a twenty-three-year-old student, I look back on that event and chuckle. The truth is my mom is White, incredibly white-toned, in fact. My mother has green eyes, fair skin, and freckles. Furthermore, my dad is Black. He has very dark skin, dark brown hair, and dark brown eyes. The information that my second-grade peer was relaying was factual; but the notion that it provoked an overt threat was something that my naively innocent brain could not comprehend. The world continues to be a place where skin-color matters (Cannady, 2005).

Rewind back to second-grade me: I am watching the movie *Tarzan*. There are moments in the movie where the antagonists cannot not fathom a human being raised by wild animals, gorillas specifically. I have a vivid memory of relating to the Phil Collins song, "You'll Be In My Heart". The song plays in the background while Tarzan is with the female that raised him. The female that I am describing is in fact a Gorilla. The scene in the movie is a heartfelt plea toward the antagonists of the story that are insisting that these two characters are different. The characters are pleading the opposite, they are instead asserting that they are the same. There is a line in the song that says,

Why can't they understand the way we feel?
They just don't trust what they can't explain
I know we're different, but deep inside us
We're not that different at all.
(Collins, 1999)

My recollection of this Disney movie may sound juvenile and somewhat comical, but it is important to note that the feelings of despair the characters endured resonated with me as a child. I was not raised by a gorilla, nor I am a man living in the wild. Instead, I am a biracial woman raised by my Caucasian mother. In the movie, I related to the gorilla, and I imagined my mother was Tarzan because there is a moment where the two characters touch one another's hand. Tarzan has a white hand and the gorilla has a black hand. I recall thinking to myself, 'That is like my mom and me'. The act of comparing my identity to a fictional character and identifying as an individual in distress because the world labelled me and the mother I love so dearly as different is difficult to digest. No child should have to observe the relationship of a wild man and gorilla to relate it to that of theirs and their parent's.

Fast forward to middle school me: my mother and I walk into a convenient store that we regularly frequent; the clerk asks my mother if I am her child, and my mother responds instantaneously, "Yes". The clerk takes a moment and responds, "But she is brown". Instead of responding with frustration and angst, my mother chuckled and simply responded, "She is". I cannot find fault in this convenient store clerk for vocally expressing the first thought that entered her mind. Whether I am showing someone a picture of my mother or introducing her as such, the look on that person's face often exemplifies the exact same thought. I am not adopted. I am brown. I am biracial. My mother and I look quite different, and the reality is that it is often hard for onlookers to see past the color of our skins. The response when introducing my father is the exact opposite. The similarity of our skin-color incites no question or confusion about our relation. There are few photos that I have with my mother and father together, and it is rare that the three of us are in the same social setting; but in the instances that we are, confused looks cease to exist. The combination of their two vastly different skin colors explicitly support the color of mine and our relation goes without question.

The older I get the more difficult it becomes to address my identity. The color of my skin is brown while the way that I speak and the mannerisms I carry are often regarded as "White". Researchers and linguists have spent decades dissecting the English language, and a language recognized as "American" as well as analyzing the variation of dialects and accents found around the United States. Researchers acknowledge that the English language grows increasingly informal and Black English is often exhibited throughout hip-hop and rap (McNeil & Lehrer, 2005). Walking through a suburban, White community and walking through a Black community may be two different experiences solely based on the vocabulary and slang that is used. Observations such as these are not so say that one is correct and one is incorrect; they are only to acknowledge that there are differences in dialect. Additionally, similar observations are made when visiting the East Coast of the United States as well as the South. Certain parts of the East Coast hold true to a very distinct accent and various parts of the South support a highly distinguishable Southern accent. I am a native of the West Coast, therefore I do not hold an East Coast or Southern accent. I have always been on the lower end of the middle-class spectrum in reference to the neighborhoods I have lived in and the schools that I have attended. These demographics and the household that I was raised in are contributing factors to the dialect in which I speak. Rather than inadvertently deeming my dialect "White", members of society continue to call me less overtly offensive terms such as *well-spoken* and *polite*, saying so, as if it comes as a surprise to them. Friends joke that I am barely Black, implying that I do not exemplify Black culture or embrace it. On the contrary, there are other peers that often regard me as Black, completely dismissing the fact that my mother is White. Each of these groups is incorrect in their categorization. I am both, Black *and* White. Identity continues to be a topic that is widely disagreed upon. Some people like pizza and others like salad, but how dare a person enjoy both. Proudly identifying as two of anything is absolutely bewildering to some people, but it is the only way that I can lead a life in an authentic state of self-awareness as well as self-discovery.

Adults often ask children what they want to be when they grow up, waiting with anticipation to hear the child's answer. In some instances, children respond with wide imaginations and choose occupations such as mermaids or superheroes. In other scenarios, children respond with two occupations versus just one. I have been in classrooms where teachers have asked children such questions, and I have heard teachers respond by telling students they cannot choose to have two aspirations, only one. From a young age many individuals are taught to choose one path, as if roads do not have wrong turns and exit signs, if the chosen road turns out to be the path that does not fit right, or the exploration of another journey is more alluring. Similarly, adolescent years are clouded by the pressure of finding identity (Brown & Leaman, 2007), choosing the crowd whose interests are most similar to yours, rather than finding community within groups that are deemed *different* or *outcasts*. Combating stereotypes and stepping outside of comfort zones often leads to self-discovery. In the instances that I have chosen to pursue friendships and hold valuable conversations with individuals whose views, appearances, or beliefs differ from my own have proven to be the ones that broaden my perspective the most. Recognizing the assumptions that I make about others and the boxes I constrict myself to can be broken and expanded continues to alter the way that I see the world and the way that I perceive myself.

As a biracial woman, my appearance often elicits conversations in regard to my race. People often ask, "What are you?" and I have grown to celebrate that I am Black and White amongst many other wonderful characteristics. I am biracial and equally proud of each race that comprises my identity, but that is not all. I am a woman, a student, an advocate for matters that I find important, an admirer of arts, a movie enthusiast, and so much more. Furthermore, every single day I am discovering different facets of my identity, things that I like and dislike, issues that I find more important than others, topics that I have placed less importance on and embracing the fact that each day I am alive I have the privilege of unearthing who I am. There are traits of my identity that will never change, such as being a biracial woman, but the person I am today is different than the person I was ten years ago and the individual I am in five years will vary from the person I identify as today. Each day brings forth experiences that shape and shift identities. Embracing the grand experiences, learning from the unfortunate ones and soaking up all of the experiences in between is imperative to my accepting my identity in its entirety.

The color of my skin has no relation to my character. Instead, my race has been a gracious reminder that character matters. Beginning each day with the intention of being kind, compassionate, empathetic, and hardworking is not synonymous with my race; it is instead a reflection of my life long pursuit; happiness and a regard for all of humanity, despite skin-color, race, culture, gender, sexuality, or religious affiliation. This is not to say that my race has no effect on my identity; instead, it is to assert that my race is simply one facet of my identity, an important one but not one that is responsible for its entirety. My identity is comprised of many different factors. Race has played its role in allowing me to recognize that outward appearances afford privileges as well as incite discrimination. Race elicits uncomfortable conversations, uneducated assumptions, unfathomable actions. Race also creates pathways for change, opportunities to grow, and renewed accountability for ourselves and those around us. In the moments that have shaped my character, personality, belief system, and general disposition there is one common denominator: adapting. Growing up biracial, in a single-parent household, with a White mother playing both the role of matriarch and patriarch, manicured dialects, cultural traditions, and mannerisms within me that society continues to deem "White". Exploring and tending to a relationship with my semi aloof African American father supports the absent "Black" dad narrative (Bell, 2006) that I have struggled so desperately to disassociate with. When I look in the mirror, I see the harmony of my mixed identity, although, when I see the way people look at me, I feel two worlds collide. Society often attempts to make me choose a racialized and binary side; Black or White.

In an effort to avoid succumbing to the racial stereotypes that the world works diligently to maintain, I walk the line. Friends, family members, peers, and colleagues place a quiet expectation for me to identify as one or the other, as if beyond physical traits I am not allowed to be both. I refuse to choose a side! In an act of opposition, I will continue to revel in the gift of endurance, advocacy, and self-discovery whilst embracing the privilege of not having to incorrectly identify as one race but fully relish in the beauty of being both. There is no playbook that exists to guide humanity through accepting your identity and the identities of others. The road to fully uncovering the intricate aspects of my individuality is a winding one with no end in sight. The beauty of being biracial allows for the exploration of two histories, two sets of customs and traditions to commemorate and one entire identity to embrace. An identity such as this is not incomplete because it shares itself with another, instead it is an identity that has an even greater complexity to contribute to the world.

Navigating through life as a biracial woman is an endless endeavor. Each and every day, I must actively choose to embrace my identity in its entirety. I am committed to a life that supports congruence. I refuse to lead a life that is plagued by the internal conflict of feeling like an imposter in my own skin. I am an entire individual that does not need to partake in the balancing act of two separate identities struggling to outshine and convince the other of its worth. The acceptance and exaltation of identity is a beautiful endeavor that serves as an invitation to us all. Accepting the invitation to welcome the attributes that my identity is comprised of has altered my perspective of viewing characteristics of my individuality as differences, hindrances or of lesser value. Growing up biracial and fully growing into who I am has afforded me the opportunity to discover that differences make the world diverse, a hindrance is actually a stepping stone in disguise, and if I am ever perceived as less than because of the color of my skin I will know it is because the onlooker has a misguided perspective and they too are still wrestling with their own identity. Choosing to travel against the current and be multifaceted in my likes, dislikes, dreams and aspirations would not be possible if I did not first learn to love all the parts that make me *me*, beginning with my mixed identity.

NOTES

1   White: being a member of a group or race characterized by light pigmentation of the skin.
2   Black: of or relating to any of various population groups having dark pigmentation of the skin.
3   Undergraduate: a student at a college or university who has not received a first and especially a bachelor's degree.

REFERENCES

Bell, J. (2006). Introductory essay on covenant III: Correcting the system of unequal justice. In T. Smiley (Ed.), *The covenant with Black America* (pp. 47–69). Chicago, IL: Third World Press.

Black. (2018). In *Merriam-Webster.com*. Retrieved April 8, 2018, from https://www.merriam-webster.com/dictionary/black

Brown, D. F., & Leaman, H. L. (2007). Recognizing and responding to young adolescents' ethnic identity development. In S. B. Mertens, V. Anfara, & M. M. Caskey (Eds.), *The young adolescent and the middle school* (pp. 219–236). Charlotte, NC: Information Age Publishing.

Cannady, W. (2005). Examining skin color perception on the effects of attractiveness and trust. *UW-L Journal of Undergraduate Research, 8*. Retrieved May 27, 2018, from https://www.uwlax.edu/urc/jur-online/pdf/2005/cannady.pdf

Collins, P. (1999). You'll be in my heart Tarzan [Recorded by P. Collins]. On *Tarzan: An original Walt Disney Records soundtrack* [CD single]. Burbank, CA: Walt Disney Records.

MacNeil/Lehrer Productions. (2005). In *Public Broadcasting System (PBS.org)*. Retrieved May 27, 2018, from http://www.pbs.org/speak/transcripts/1.html

Undergraduate. (2018). In *Merriam-Webster.com*. Retrieved April 8, 2018, from https://www.merriam-webster.com/dictionary/undergraduate

White. (2018). In *Merriam-Webster.com*. Retrieved April 8, 2018, from https://www.merriam-webster.com/dictionary/white

PART 6

CONCLUSION

ELLIS HURD

18. THE UNTOLD FUTURE OF BEING MIXED

Moving Forward While Remembering What Is Behind

LOOKING BACK

I recently travelled to Philadelphia, Pennsylvania, the city of brotherly love. Much like the transcontinental travels and locations discussed in the Introduction, I used this trip to further investigate one metropolitan area and the treatment of people of mixed identity. While there I walked the halls of the famed Philadelphia Museum of Art. As part of their European Art 1500 – 1850 exhibit, on the second floor, I witnessed the display of peoples with mixed identity. This section of the museum dedicated only two works of art to people of mixed identity, namely *Albinos* and *Coyotes* (see the Introduction table for a listing of Critical Mestizo variations). The paintings are attributed to artist José de Alcíbar, a well-known Mexican born painter who lived from 1725 until 1803 (Philadelphia Museum of Art, 2017). Apparently, *casta* paintings were "a popular genre that showed the intermingling of races in colonial Mexico, often documented the wealth of the country's resources, and most prominently its food" (Philadelphia Museum of Art, 2017). The two paintings were once part of a larger collection of 16 canvases, for which curators have identified 10 so far. The depictions of those with mixed identity in these paintings were exotic, even fantastical, meant to conjure feelings of those who were perhaps born from two people who committed forbidden love and pleasure. The left-placed oil on canvas painting (c. 1760), titled, *De Español, y Morisca. Albino. (From Spaniard and Morisca, Albino)*, portrays the child of a Spaniard father and Morisca[1] mother, thus resulting in an albino (or white skin-colored) child. Interestingly, the painting shows the child reaching toward the wealthy and nicely dressed Spaniard father, as if in want of the father's ancestry and wealth, as depicted in Figure 18.1.

The child's mother is in the background working at the table, pouring a drink mixture into a glass bowl. The images show the wealth of the family, the adornment of clothes and riches, and the possession of a well-bred horse outside. The other painting (c. 1760), titled, *De Indio, y Mestisa. Coyote (From Indian and Mestiza, Coyote)*, is of an Indian father and Mestiza mother with a darker skin-tone coyote child in her arms, as seen in Figure 18.2.

In this case, the source of wealth depicted in the painting is of food. There is an abundance of food displayed on the table, each basket or sack overflowing with rich morsels to consume. All the while, the father is clearly dressed as a field worker

© KONINKLIJKE BRILL NV, LEIDEN, 2019 | DOI:10.1163/9789004393813_018

Figure 18.1. From Spaniard and Morisca, Albino. *Gift of the nieces and nephews of Wright S. Ludington in his honor (1980-139-2). Courtesy: Philadelphia museum of art*

Figure 18.2. From Indian and Mestiza, Coyote. *Gift of the nieces and nephews of Wright S. Ludington in his honor (1980-139-1). Courtesy: Philadelphia museum of art*

258

with a hat to protect his skin and face while working in the hot sun, and the Mestiza mother still somehow benefitting from the wealth of her upbringing or ancestry. The child is accordingly dressed in fine colorful linens, juxtaposed against the mother's lighter toned-skin.

Several criticisms surface of José de Alcíbar's paintings and his perspectives of those who were of mixed identity. First, neither child in the paintings bore the ancestry of the parents, at least not by their names. In this case, José de Alcíbar presented them in their most derogatory view, as albino and coyote. As mentioned in the Introduction (see table), Coyote was a pejorative term attributed to those of mixed Spaniard and Indian blood. In the case of First peoples having been conquered by the Spaniards just some 200 years prior during the artist's time period, Indians were treated with contempt and were worse off than Mexicans and other mixed Spaniard and Spanish minorities (Burns, 1994; Foley, 2004). For Alcíbar to refer to the child as Coyote essentially means to relegate the child to an inferior societal position (Hurd, 2012b). Likewise, his use of the term albino for the child in painting two was inequitable. Sadly, many ill-placed feelings and superstitions surround people who identify as albino, leading some to be rejected at birth or even later murdered for their skin or body-parts as charms of good luck (Page, 2017). While the Merriam-Webster dictionary defines albino as one "who is congenitally deficient in pigment and usually has a milky or translucent skin, white or colorless hair" (Albino, 2018), the artist would have only recently heard of the term (c. 1708) and its use from mixed Latin and Portuguese languages, resulting in the term albino, or literally "white" (Albino, 2018). Furthermore, Alcíbar failed to highlight the fact that those of mixed identity were (and still are) heavily discriminated. They were considered outcasts of society for their intermarrying and for bringing into the world a child who could then neither fully identify with the father or mother (Hurd, 2012b). Lest we not forget that these works are only two paintings of more than 240,000 artistic artifacts in collection at Philadelphia's Museum of Art. Again, as discussed in the Introduction, the amount of asset-based and constructive research available on people of mixed identity pales in comparison to the number of negative or deficit ones. It is neither commensurate with the number of people who identify as of mixed identity. Hence, there is a great need for this volume.

This volume elucidates the historically silenced-voices of those who identify as of mixed heritage, of those who have a story to tell about their past, present, and futures, of those who negotiate between the pains and privileges of not belonging and yet of belonging to each identity. Its five parts contain works spanning Africa, Asia, Europe, the Middle East, and North, Central, and South America. The reflexivity of pain and privilege and these auto-ethnographic collections of mixed identity serve as a spring-board for the untold stories and homilies of millions of marginalized and mixed people and youth who may find solace here, in the stories of others.

Therefore, engaging in the slow, painstaking, and liberatory work and cause of giving voice to those of mixed identity may come at times in alternative forms, too, such as in social justice work which requires the acknowledgement of equity frameworks such as: the homily of pain and privilege (Hurd, 2008, 2012a, 2012b); culturally relevant pedagogy (Ladson-Billings, 1995, 2014); cultural responsiveness (Gay, 2000); culturally sustaining pedagogy (Paris, 2012; Paris & Alim, 2017); equity literacy (Gorski, 2017); critical teacher education pedagogy (Conklin & Hughes, 2016); critical race theory (Solórzano & Yosso, 2001); racial and cultural identity development (Sue & Sue, 2016); critical multiracial theory (MultiCrit) (Delgado & Stefancic, 2017); disability studies in education (Artiles, Dorn, & Bal, 2016; Artiles, King-Thorius, Bal, Waitoller, Neal, & Hernández-Saca, 2011; Hernández-Saca, Kahn, & Cannon, 2018); the theory of intersectionality (Collins, 2015); and third space/culture (Pollock, Van Reken, & Pollock, 2017). Authors in this volume referenced these and other justice venues. Constituents need to use this short list of comprehensive frameworks, such as middle school students themselves, by educators and researchers who want to learn more about or further investigate the stories of mixed identity, and by anyone else who wishes to engage with the dialectical discourse of mixed identity.

In the first part, we explored the reflexivity of pain and privilege through the ambiguity of Dian Mitrayani's mixed Chinese-Indonesian identity. Her story and work as a scholar in the US with roots from Indonesia remind us that mixed identities form resulting from family, communal, or even governmental choices in race and nationality. She also shared how one's mixed identity forms from socio-economic and educational factors. She encourages us with the duty of negotiating our identities in their fluidity. Likewise, Cristina Santamaría Graff shared about her bi-racial Mexicana White mixed identity. Despite the beautiful brownness we may see looking forward, the mirrors of our past oft remind us of our liminal phenotype, biological, and illness-bound spaces. Her vivid tightrope of irony challenges everyone to consider the binary opposites we tend to force on others (even ourselves) when thinking about race, language, class, and other areas. Our concepts of mixed identity must evolve, as she strongly argued. Thus, many face an "unbearable" pain and privilege in their simultaneous minority-majority stati. Even those who may identify with two historically minority stati (e.g., Indian and Black) may still also identify with other people of minority status in being familiar with the pain of being marginalized. Finally, Lisa A. Boskovich and David I. Hernández-Saca drew a clear path for those who have stepped towards healing in their intersectionality. Theirs were dual autoethnographies of learning disability pain and privilege structured through their entire schooling experiences, exploring their own multi-ethnicity, Spanish-English languages, and mixed class and gender identities. They point to the need for a systemic and pedagogical approach through praxis where the "system" itself is critiqued for improvement.

In Part 2, Hwa Pyung Yoo opened with his story of being a third culture kid with an unidentified nationality. His story helped us remember what it was like being a middle schooler while living in a space that others do not, cannot occupy. He navigated middle school as a third culture kid while also facing ethnicity, gender, and socioeconomic challenges. He drew on the notion of blended bilingualism where he could develop his intersecting identities (like blending languages) rather than as separate ones.

We were equally moved by Paloma E. Villegas' poem on her transnational roots between Mexico, the United States, and Canada. Susan Y. Leonard followed with her persuasion of what it was like to identify as a White person trapped in an Asian body. Her explanation of macro cultural psychological theory of identity helped us both understand and identify with her transracial personhood. Her strong case for framing the mixed identities of youth and adults as funds of identity will indeed inform and enrich interactions between and among adults and youth and the people with whom they work and interact daily. To augment this valuable work, Hannah R. Stohry provided comprehensive transformative consciousness raising questions which others can use to support youth and adults with whom students, educators, researchers, and other activist professionals work daily. The questions help to evaluate self, raise consciousness for self and others, and impact actions toward critical examination and change.

Part 3 offered two powerful stories. Raymond Adams explored the convergences of identity and cultural responsiveness by looking back at his African Louisiana Creole roots via a narrative on race, language, ethnicity, and belonging. Focused on a sociolinguistic and cultural identity, Raymond explained how Louisiana Creoles, specifically those of African descent, have been an intricate part of Louisiana culture for years but still struggle by others' non-acceptance of them. Current racialized structures once again point out that others deny us access because we are different and not like them and their categories. In similar fashion, Jessica Samuels, also known by her Indian name, Sika, relived her personal experiences regarding her mixed racial and ethnic identity. The push-pull dichotomy of being and not being mixed Nez Perce, U.S., Afro, and Latina revealed to her the deep hatred and non-acceptance that still exist, and not just from one racial group. She highlights the need to be one community, to examine ourselves for bias and discriminatory behaviour, to stand together against such ideologies that sustain racism, exploitation, and oppression.

The interrelated homilies of mixed identity from international lenses were part of Part 4. Lynnette Mawhinney discussed being ambiguously brown in Africa, and how her biracial identity was complicated around various areas of Africa (Kenya, Egypt, and South Africa). Through autoethnographic memoir, she reconstructs her identity experiences in these various African locations, and yet in none of these places is she Black enough or fully accepted. She concludes by acknowledging the lack of knowledge on this issue among young adolescent students and their teachers and offers several key principles and practices to circumvent it. Panamanian scholars Mariana León and Guillermina-Itzel de Gracia gave us the identity perceptions of youth in middle and high school in Panama City, Panama. Although an international hub of mixed identities and transnational peoples, Panama has some curricular opportunities on the horizon for further investigating and teaching their citizenry, namely middle and high school youth, about mixed identities. The authors poignantly shared how celebrations in schools and communities without critical discussions about ethnicity and mixed identities only reinforce phenotype differences among diverse youth, and these do not give the appropriate education to students required for them to understand their own and others' mixed identities. Likewise, the United States must consider how to better support its lack of information (for being an imperialist nation) and lack of sensitivity and acceptance of those who live on the borders. Siblings Francisco J. Villegas and Paloma E. Villegas made this clear in their autoethnographies of transnational precarity. Their stories explored their experiences of living with precarious immigration stati in two countries, Canada and the U.S. Their discussion of the resilience of borders and the ways class transitions can help others give hope for all who navigate their own precarity. Anne Ryen from Norway talked about her pervasive rank and the complexity of identity work in modern life. She explored the concepts of positions, boundary work, being and becoming, and the "self" and Otherness in her chapter. She reminded us that disrupting the social order allows the peeling back of layers woven into rank and ethnicity in order to question and move beyond normative experiences for ourselves and others.

Finally, Part 5 began where the others concluded: on being mixed and moving forward. Hannah R. Stohry wrote about her experiences being raised as a multi-racial "third culture kid". Her chapter explored the Westernization, racialization, and gendering of multi-racial TCKs and the impact on their lives. She highlights how multi-racial TCK journeys are complex, how elite monoracial people reduce the identities of TCKs to binary constructs. Yet her chapter attempts the possibilities of a world where realities are recognized and celebrated on individual terms. Following this narrative are the powerfully poems of David I. Hernández-Saca which explore learning disability oppression and healing. Similarly, rich poems on being mixed and moving forward are authored by Lisa A. Boskovich who explores privilege and identity. These collections of poems by both authors speak for themselves and need no further summary. Part 5 is concluded by undergraduate Iman Fagan who discussed what it is like to walk the line of a mixed identity. Growing up biracial, in a single-parent household, with a Caucasian mother playing both the role of matriarch and patriarch, Iman shared on her mixed White Black identity. Her chapter highlighted the necessity of endurance, advocacy, and self-discovery to embrace the gift of not having to incorrectly identify as one but fully revel in the beauty of being both Black and White.

The authors within these same five parts also offered information, principles, and practices for middle and high school adolescents, other students, educators, and researchers as they work in educational settings. The backdrop of the volume was set in the middle grades, namely Grades 6, 7, and 8 in the American educational system. However, the lessons and applications easily transfer to other grade configurations and other educational contexts in other territories (e.g., elementary and high school; international or transnational settings; etc.). The implications and insights provided uncover the philosophical and educational contexts of schooling and its structures. The authors also made connections to the work of the Association for Middle Grades Education (AMLE) and its current standards for young adolescents and middle grades schools. According to *This We Believe*

THE UNTOLD FUTURE OF BEING MIXED

(NMSA, 2010), an education for young adolescents should be empowering, equitable, and challenging. Researchers can respond and contribute to this effort (and others like it in their own territories) by examining youth of mixed identity using the frameworks mentioned at the beginning of this chapter. Efforts such as these become especially imperative as they concern marginalized and minoritized youth and youth of mixed identity. The systems of oppression and power that negatively affect them run rapid. Developing counter-hegemonic discourses that fit in a middle grades context, critically rethinking our positions for ecologically-based spaces, and integrating the middle school concept as a means to support equitable practices, even disrupt marginalized and oppressive practices, are all efforts that lay the essential foundation for this important work. As researchers, we must recognize that poorly defined teaching methods and a lack of curricular and instructional practices disconnected from the middle school concept may indeed perpetuate not only the status quo but also racist, discriminatory, and insensitive practices that further oppress those of different backgrounds from our own. Unfortunately, the AMLE is not immune or exempt from such mistakes. There is a growing critique that middle level education does not consider the needs of young adolescents from diverse backgrounds due to the over emphasis of developmentalism in the field (Hurd, Harrison, Brinegar, & Kennedy, 2018; Kennedy, Brinegar, Hurd, & Harrison, 2016; Vagle, 2012). I advocate that educators, schools, parents and communities, and other constituents – even youth of mixed identity – collectively work to end such deficit and oppressive practices, by considering the homily of pain and privilege for those of mixed identity.

MOVING FORWARD

Faith-Based Identities

Another significant aspect of mixed identity not fully developed in this volume as a whole is that of religious or faith-based identity (henceforth referred to as faith). Only two authors in this volume discuss or reference their faith and its influence on their mixed identities. In fairness, the call for this volume was specific to racial, linguistic, socio-economic, and ethnocultural identities. I did not highlight mixed faith identity; nor did I seek it in this volume, per se. But just as authors Hernández-Saca and Boskovich enlightened us with their duo autoethnographies of intersectionality on pain and privilege of dis/ability and mixed identities, we have two other authors who have written on their faith and mixed identities. Accordingly, faith is a significant aspect or central part of most people's lives and identities. Authors Mitrayani and Stohry mentioned several key things to which I wish to draw attention in terms of their resulting mixed identity. Mitrayani discussed Christianity at least 12 times, and Catholicism another eight. She discussed these in reference to the following: (1) her grandparents' (on her father's side and one from her mother's) and father's decision to abandon their Chinese religion and happily embrace Christianity to avoid communist perceptions; (2) her parents' educational backgrounds at the private Christian university due to enrollment caps and lack of finances for other schools; and (3) her own Christian background, schooling, and later university experiences. She described some of these conversions as forced. Nevertheless, her faith experiences and factors influenced her own identity formations. Similarly, Stohry explained how she was raised on military bases while attending local Christian schools (intentionally), directly impacting her own faith and identity. She described herself as a person of practicing faith with a belief in God and a high power and still is part of the missionary subculture. She even ended her chapter with a Proverb from the Holy Bible about knowing the direction where one is headed to find solid or certain ground (Proverbs 4:26; KJV).

My own faith story and identity runs counter-hegemonic to the pain and privilege contained in stories such as these and in my own. That is, it adds yet another layer to the homily of pain and privilege and how I navigated my way through rather difficult times growing up and surviving. In this way, my faith story serves as a master narrative to the idea of being mixed. It acts as a guiding heuristic or anchor to my other identity experiences. My mixed faith story began many years back.

I was born in Chicago in Grant Hospital which was at one time in Lincoln Park (now relocated). But I grew up in rural suburbs (in the 70s) when my family moved to Streamwood which is closer to Chicago than Elgin, what used to be 30–40 minutes outside of downtown. The village of Streamwood, as it once was called, was mainly an immigrant population town with many Italian, German, and Polish families residing to begin a new life. Over time, the populations changed to include Irish, Hispanic, and African American families beginning in the 70s and 80s. Ironically, I was always in a church, namely Grace Bible Church (once First Baptist of Streamwood) where my family attended when I was very young. I do not believe I was "saved" or converted to Christianity when I repeated the prayer of salvation[2] at seven years of age, based on the Biblical truth of repentance and grace I later learned about in another church. In fact, I had been exposed to a great deal of churches and doctrines over the years (mixed faith identity) that eventually helped me to more deeply study and understand the Bible later in life. At the same time, these experiences and differences left me with a disenchantment for modern Christian churches. I attended: Grace Bible Church in Streamwood; Christ Church of Oakbrook (an orthodox-liturgical church); Willow Creek Community Church in South Barrington, IL; First Baptist of Elgin; Harvest Bible Chapel in Rolling Meadows; First Baptist Church of Marshalltown, Iowa; Lexington Community Church in central IL; and eventually Grace Church in Normal, IL. I have been exposed to Armenian, Catholic, Covenant, Calvinist Reformed, Dispensational, Dutch Reformed, and Pentecostal theologies over the years. I daresay, I have also been exposed to some heretical teachings in some of those churches, too. But that is a story for another time.

The reason why the church history stands out to me in my mixed faith identity story is that regardless of the traumas and abuses I faced, God was always there to protect me, to draw me near to His side, and to eventually bend my will towards His will and purpose. I knew even at a young age that what I saw on Sunday mornings and what I witnessed at home were two very different things. I could not reconcile the differences. In summary, my home life was tumultuous. My mother was physically abusive to me and my siblings, hitting me with kitchen utensils, leaving welts on my legs with belts, and punching me with her fists when angry. But my one sister and I bore the brunt of that abuse more than my other two sisters. For some reason, this may have caused us even more pain in later actions. My dad sustained an autoimmune disorder and related back injury resulting from a chemical agent he may have been exposed to during the Korean War. Unfortunately, he struggled to cope which in turn affected me in my upbringing. He turned to prescription drugs, abused them, and also became addicted to pornography which I found and used to fuel my own sinful passions. These things in turn led me down a slippery slope of academic failures, physical violence, and wrong doing that stayed with me until college. I stole from stores, ran with wicked crowds, and engaged in sexual sins that nearly destroyed me. I was always just a few steps away from being caught, arrested, or expelled from school. But the truth was, I was already in darkness, depraved, and in need of a Savior like I never knew.

While at a local church during my junior year in high school, I heard the Gospel,[3] as I had heard numerous times before at some other churches. But this time, it was different. I was singing during a worship service and knew that I desperately needed Jesus, to turn and run from my sin, to abstain from it. I committed my life to Him in those moments and ever since, I have believed in Him. I was able to then begin rejecting sinful and sexual offers and advances from so-called friends, pornography and lying, stealing, and even hanging out with wicked company. I lost some of those older friends but gained a whole lot more.

Upon finishing high school, I felt convicted to become a pastor. But due to flunking out my first semester in college, and with poor grades from high school, Moody Bible Institute in Chicago rejected my admission. I was unsure about what to do. I had some serious educational gaps in my experience and was faced with nowhere to go. Then, someone at another local church told me about Judson College (now university) in Elgin, IL. They said it was a Baptist College where they had heard some good things were happening academically and spiritually. Little did I know at the time that God was orchestrating my steps for the rest of my life. I was accepted on academic probation for one-year, with required tutoring and life-skill classes. I was majoring in youth ministry, again a pastoral role in the local church due to my new faith in God and desire to serve Him and youth for the rest of my life. I eventually changed my major to education because I was not impressed with how my degree was progressing and because my former elementary school principal told me that God could still have me in ministry one day, even if I became a teacher. I switched. After an extra semester, more tutoring, and filling every summer, winter, and alternative break with classes, I graduated with a 3.2 GPA in 1998.

Eventually, I started graduate school (again, on academic probation) to study for my master's degree in education. Shortly thereafter, my mom died of cancer in 2002 which brought the family closer. But I finished with a 4.0 GPA (by God's grace), and we decided to move to Iowa. While there, God saw us through some struggles with finances, family, and with our infants. We were active in my wife's childhood church, serving in small groups and leadership. I eventually started graduate school again, this time for my doctorate and *not* on academic probation. God blessed me with a 3.98 GPA and position at Illinois State University before I even finished my defense. All the while, I continued to be involved in local churches but secretly struggled with the doctrines and practices of the faith. However, one thing that did not change was how the Bible spoke about those of alien or immigrant status, much like me and those around me with mixed identity.

One verse which comes from the Bible and speaks to those of mixed or various nationalities, ethnicities, and religions is found in the book of Galatians 3:23–28:

> But before faith came, we were kept in custody under the law, being shut up to the faith which was later to be revealed. Therefore the Law has become our tutor *to lead us* to Christ, so that we may be justified by faith. But now that faith has come, we are no longer under a tutor. For you are all sons of God through faith in Christ Jesus. For all of you who were baptized into Christ have clothed yourselves with Christ. There is neither Jew nor Greek, there is neither slave nor free man, there is neither male nor female; for you are all one in Christ Jesus. And if you belong to Christ, then you are Abraham's descendants, heirs according to promise. (NASB)

Similarly, the book of Ephesians 4:1–6 states the following about belonging:

> Therefore I, the prisoner of the Lord, implore you to walk in a manner worthy of the calling with which you have been called, with all humility and gentleness, with patience, showing tolerance for one another in love, being diligent to preserve the unity of the Spirit in the bond of peace. *There is* one body and one Spirit, just as also you were called in one hope of your calling; one Lord, one faith, one baptism, one God and Father of all who is over all and through all and in all. (NASB)

Besides having tolerance for others in love, this section speaks to a third space, a spiritual place to which others can belong regardless of upbringing, background, or group, if they believe and have been called forward into faith. Unlike one's blood of ancestry, this spiritual place is made on the blood of one: Jesus Christ.

In a broader sense, there are other verses from the Bible which speak directly about the treatment of foreigners, immigrants, and aliens. These have always brought comfort to me in being of mixed identity, as I am also a type of nomadic immigrant with being both minority and minority living in the majority; yet being and not belonging to either one. The first of these verses comes from one of the historical books of the Bible, Exodus. In chapter 23, verse 9, it states, "You shall not oppress a stranger, since you yourselves know the feelings of a stranger, for you *also* were strangers in the land of Egypt" (NASB). Later in the book of Deuteronomy, it says,

"You shall not oppress a hired servant who is poor and needy, whether he is one of your countrymen or one of your aliens [immigrant] who is in your land in your towns...You shall not pervert the justice due an alien [immigrant] or an orphan, nor take a widow's garment in pledge...When you gather the grapes of your vineyard, you shall not go over it again; it shall be for the alien [immigrant], for the orphan, and for the widow" (Deuteronomy 24:14, 17, 21, NASB). Finally, in one of the prophetic books there is a passage, speaking for those who were of mixed national Canaanite identity, as they sought to ethnoculturally identify with the historical people of Jerusalem, known at the time as Israelites (historical Hebrews or modern-day Israel and Palestine). Jeremiah 7:5–7 reads:

For if you truly amend your ways and your deeds, if you truly practice justice between a man and his neighbor, if you do not oppress the alien [immigrant], the orphan, or the widow, and do not shed innocent blood in this place, nor walk after other gods to your own ruin, then I will let you dwell in this place, in the land that I gave to your fathers forever and ever. (NASB)

The overarching point in these Biblical passages is that we are all called to love and have tolerance for our neighbor, regardless of their background, identities, and immigrant status. This is a far cry from many of the currently policies and practices of the Trump administration (and its treatment of aliens to/in the United States), and of other countries as well. Our faith should guide us beyond division, into a higher and greater acceptance of those who are different than us.

Oppositionally Open Identities

That our identities remain continually *open* is long-established by Du Bois (1982) who discussed *double consciousness*, and by Gregg (1991) who further developed the ideal of *dual identity*. These concepts, like the discourse of pain and privilege, illustrate how we of mixed identity live and negotiate between worlds from within a dichotomous framework. Furthermore, as with Anzaldúa's (2007) work on the *Mestiza consciousness*, we are caught between "spaces" or "borders", in what she believed were the crossfires of partial racial, cultural, and social transfusions. Thus, the *openness* or fluid and flexible nature of the mixed identity construct helps us to adjust and navigate these oppositional collective identities of pain and privilege.

In this way, those of mixed identity are pioneers or frontiersmen in the effort to clear a path for those that will follow. Some have fought for the betterment of others of mixed identity and will continue to offer more perspectives to society by further mingling, merging, intermarrying, and infiltrating the dominant cultures and discourses. Others have things of resistance to share to those who are willing to listen. There is the hope that we will soon transcend completely, not as token individuals or half-breeds, but as human beings and partners in the course of humanity. Such redemptive moves have been explained by Ellis (2009) as "meta-autoethnographic". As such, people of mixed identity are able "to connect the past to now", by reexamining themselves and their roles within their identity groups (p. 12). We reach better understandings of our work and ourselves, and we can began moving toward resolve, perhaps even forward as a society in the acknowledgment, understanding, and support of those of mixed identity. But this future is both unknown and untold.

OTHER UNTOLD FUTURES

Although this volume is international in scope, it has some boundaries. First, not everyone who identifies as being mixed will fit into these stories, its lessons, and the liminal space of its contributors or its editor. We must acknowledge that each person has their own story to tell, and those stories continue to advance the work and cause of those who indeed face daily oppressions resulting from being mixed. Second, some people of mixed identity choose to identify with only one racial, socioeconomic, lingual, and/or ethnocultural identity. They consciously choose *not* to identify with their other identity(ies) for specific reasons, some of which are only known to them. For example, those who have suffered from the traumas of familial or communal abuse, violence, neglect, abandonment, etc., may wish to identify (or not) with their biological parent(s); with foster or adoptive parent or guardian identity(ies); with national, cultural, or faith identities instead of racial or ethnic ones; or with none of those and create a new and unique identity of their own. Either way, some choose one identity instead of more than one. Finally, this volume and its scope is specific to those who are of mixed identity. These identities were focused on racial, socio-economic, linguistic, and ethnocultural identities. However, as discussed earlier, there are other identities by which people identify. These dualities include identities related but not limited to: gender and sexuality, faith, transnational displacement or amnesty, socio-economic advancement, etc. One single volume could not reasonably address – let alone adequately capture – the manifold identities that people hold to or use in reference to themselves.

But this is where the work of this volume continues, and that of others to follow. The openness of being of mixed identity remains just that: open. It is not finished! It goes on, as we all "walk the line" (see Fagan, Part 5) in our identity with race, linguistics, economics, ethnoculturalism, faith, work, education, joy, and love.

NOTES

[1]   Feminine conjugation of Morisco or Moor, a derogatory term for a former Muslim person from Southern Spain who may have accepted Christian baptism (faith conversion) and who was distinctly different from others in terms of religion, skin-tone, and geographical location.

[2]   The prayer of salvation, as it is commonly referred to, is when one repeats or prays the confession of acknowledgment that: (1) they have sin and need to be saved from hell and God's wrath; (2) that Jesus Christ is Lord of one's life, and that He was crucified for their sins; and (3) that Jesus was buried, and rose from the grave by the power of God, to bring those who believe in Him eternal life. In this sense, salvation is a gift of God by His grace; whereupon one is saved by God through faith and not of personal goodness or works (the books of John 3:16; Romans 3:23, 6:23; and Ephesians 2:8, 9, NASB).

[3] The Gospel is a term used to refer to the *Good News* (literally good tidings) of Jesus Christ which was previously explained as the confession of salvation (Romans 10:9–13, NASB).

REFERENCES

Albino. (2018). In *Merriam-Webster's dictionary*. Retrieved from http://www.merriam-webster.com/dictionary/albino

Anzaldúa, G. (2007). *Borderlands/La Frontera: The new Mestiza* (3rd ed.). San Francisco, CA: Aunt Lute Books.

Artiles, A. J., Dorn, S., & Bal, A. (2016). Objects of protection, enduring nodes of difference: Disability intersections with "other" differences, 1916–2016. *Review of Research in Education, 40*, 777–820.

Artiles, A. J., King-Thorius, K., Bal, A., Waitoller, F., Neal, R., & Hernández-Saca, D. I. (2011). Beyond culture as group traits: Future learning disabilities ontology, epistemology, and research knowledge use. *Learning Disability Quarterly, 34*, 167–179.

Burns, E. B. (1994). *Latin America: A concise interpretive history* (6th ed.). Englewood Cliffs, NJ: Prentice Hall.

Collins, P. H. (2015). Intersectionality's definitional dilemmas. *Annual Review of Sociology, 41*, 1–20.

Conklin, H. G., & Hughes, H. E. (2016). Practices of compassionate, critical, justice-oriented teacher education. *Journal of Teacher Education, 67*(1), 47–60.

Delgado, R., & Stefanic, J. (2017). *Critical race theory: An introduction* (3rd ed.). New York, NY: New York University Press.

Du Bois, W. B. (1982). *The souls of Black folks* (Rev. ed.). New York, NY: The New American Library.

Ellis, C. (2009). *Revision: Autoethnographic reflections on life and work*. Walnut Creek, CA: Left Coast Press.

Foley, N. (2005). Becoming Hispanic: Mexican Americans and Whiteness. In P. S. Rothenberg (Ed.), *White privilege: Essential readings on the other side of racism* (2nd ed., pp. 55–65). New York, NY: Worth Publishers.

Gay, G. (2000). *Culturally responsive teaching: Theory, research, and practice*. New York, NY: Teachers College Press.

Gorski, P. C. (2017). *Reaching and teaching students in poverty: Strategies for erasing the opportunity gap*. New York, NY: Teachers College Press.

Gregg, G. S. (1991). *Self representation: Life narrative studies in identity and ideology*. New York, NY: Greenwood Press.

Hernández-Saca, D. I., Kahn, L. G., & Cannon, M. A. (2018). Intersectionality dis/ability research: How dis/ability research in education engages intersectionality to uncover the multidimensional construction of dis/abled experiences. *Review of Research in Education, 42*, 286–311.

Hurd. E. (2008). *The reflexivity of pain and privilege: An autoethnography of (Mestizo) identity and other Mestizo voices* (Doctoral dissertation). Retrieved August 13, 2009, from ProQuest Dissertations and Theses database. (UMI No. 3343925)

Hurd, E. (2010). Confessions of belonging: My emotional journey as a medical translator. *Qualitative Inquiry, 16*(10), 783–791. doi:10.1177/1077800410383117

Hurd, E. (2012a). A framework for understanding multicultural identities: An investigation of a middle level student's French-Canadian Honduran-American (Mestizo) identity. *Middle Grades Research Journal, 7*(2), 111–127.

Hurd, E. (2012b). The reflexivity of pain and privilege. *International Journal of Critical Pedagogy, 4*(1), 36–46. Retrieved from http://libjournal.uncg.edu/ojs/index. php/ijcp/article/view/151

Hurd, E., Harrison, L., Brinegar, K., & Kennedy, B. L. (2018). Cultural responsiveness in the middle grades: A literature review. In S. B. Mertens & M. M. Caskey (Eds.), *Literature reviews in support of the middle level education research agenda* (pp. 25–51). Charlotte, NC: Information Age.

Kennedy, B. L., Brinegar, K., Hurd, E., & Harrison, L. (2016). Synthesizing middle grades research on cultural responsiveness: The importance of a shared conceptual framework. *Middle Grades Review, 2*(3), 1–20. Retrieved from http://scholarworks.uvm.edu/mgreview/vol2/iss3/2

Ladson-Billings, G. (2014). Culturally relevant pedagogy 2.0: A.K.A. the remix. *Harvard Educational Review, 84*(1), 74–84.

Ladson-Billings, G. (1995). Toward a theory of culturally relevant pedagogy. *American Educational Research Journal, 32*(3), 465–491.

National Middle School Association. (2010). *This we believe: Keys to educating young adolescents.* Westerville, OH: Author.

Page, T. (2017). *Inside Africa: Songs from Tanzania's island of Albinos.* Retrieved from https://www.cnn.com/2017/06/13/africa/ukerewe-tanzania-albinism-white-african-power/index.html

Paris, D. (2012). Culturally sustaining pedagogy: A needed change in stance, terminology, and practice. *Educational Researcher, 41*(3), 93–97.

Paris, D., & Alim, H. S. (Eds.). (2017). *Culturally sustaining pedagogies: Teaching and learning for justice in a changing world.* New York, NY: Teachers College Press.

Philadelphia Museum of Art. (2017). *European art 1500–1850: From Spaniard and Morisca, Albino; From Indian and Mestiza, Coyote* [Placard]. Philadelphia, PA: Philadelphia Museum of Art.

Pollock, D. C., & Van Reken, R. E. (2017). *Third culture kids: Growing up among worlds* (3rd ed.). Boston, MA: Nicholas Brealey Publishing.

Solórzano, D. G., & Yosso, T. J. (2001). Critical race and LatCrit theory and method: Counter-storytelling. *International Journal of Qualitative Studies in Education, 14*(4), 471–495.

Sue, D. W., & Sue, D. (2016). Racial/cultural identity development in people of color: Therapeutic implications. In D. W. Sue & D. Sue (Eds.), *Counseling the culturally diverse: Theory and practice* (7th ed., pp. 355–388). Hoboken, NJ: Wiley & Sons.

Vagle, M. D. (2012). Introduction: Being a bit disruptive. In M. D. Vagle (Ed.), *Not a stage! A critical re-conception of young adolescent education* (pp. 1–9). New York, NY: Peter Lang.

Printed in the United States
By Bookmasters